Certificate Paper C2

FUNDAMENTALS OF FINANCIAL ACCOUNTING

For assessments under the 2006 syllabus in 2008

Study Text

CIMA

In this January 2008 new edition

- A **user-friendly format** for easy navigation

- Regular **fast forward** summaries emphasising the key points in each chapter

- **Assessment focus points** showing you what the assessor will want you to do

- **Questions** and **quick quizzes** to test your understanding

- **Question bank** containing objective test questions with answers

- A full index

BPP Learning Media's **i-Pass** product also supports this paper.

FOR ASSESSMENTS UNDER THE 2006 SYLLABUS IN 2008

BPP

LEARNING MEDIA

First edition June 2006
Second edition January 2008

ISBN 9780 7517 5280 9 (previous edition 0 7517 2648 6)

British Library Cataloguing-in-Publication Data
A catalogue record for this book
is available from the British Library

Published by

BPP Learning Media
BPP House, Aldine Place
London W12 8AA

www.bpp.com/learningmedia

Printed in Great Britain by
W M Print
45-47 Frederick Street
Walsall, West Midlands
WS2 9NE

Your learning materials, published by BPP Learning
Media Ltd, are printed on paper sourced from
sustainable, managed forests.

We are grateful to the Chartered Institute of
Management Accountants for permission to reproduce
past examination questions. The suggested solutions
in the Answer bank have been prepared by BPP
Learning Media Ltd.

Contents

iii

Distance Learning from BPP Professional Education

You can access our exam-focussed interactive e-learning materials over the **Internet**, via BPP Learn Online, hosted by BPP Professional Education.

BPP Learn Online offers **comprehensive tutor support**, **revision guidance** and **exam tips**.

Visit www.bpp.com/cima/learnonline for further details.

Learning to Learn Accountancy

BPP Learning Media's ground-breaking **Learning to Learn Accountancy** book is designed to be used both at the outset of your CIMA studies and throughout the process of learning accountancy. It challenges you to consider how you study and gives you helpful hints about how to approach the various types of paper which you will encounter. It can help you **focus your studies on the subject and exam**, enabling you to **acquire knowledge**, **practise and revise efficiently and effectively**.

The BPP Learning Media Study Text

Aims of this Study Text

To provide you with the knowledge and understanding, skills and application techniques that you need if you are to be successful in your exams

This Study Text has been written around the **Fundamentals of Financial Accounting** syllabus.

- It is **comprehensive**. It covers the syllabus content. No more, no less.

- It is written at the **right level**. Each chapter is written with CIMA's precise learning outcomes in mind.

- It is targeted to the **exam**. We have taken account of the pilot paper, guidance the examiner has given and the assessment methodology.

To allow you to study in the way that best suits your learning style and the time you have available, by following your personal Study Plan (see page (viii))

You may be studying at home on your own until the date of the exam, or you may be attending a full-time course. You may like to (and have time to) read every word, or you may prefer to (or only have time to) skim-read and devote the remainder of your time to question practice. Wherever you fall in the spectrum, you will find the BPP Learning Media Study Text meets your needs in designing and following your personal Study Plan.

To tie in with the other components of the BPP Learning Media Effective Study Package to ensure you have the best possible chance of passing the exam (see page (vi))

The BPP Learning Media Effective Study Package

Recommended period of use	The BPP Learning Media Effective Study Package
From the outset and throughout	**Learning to Learn Accountancy** Read this invaluable book as you begin your studies and refer to it as you work through the various elements of the BPP Learning Media Effective Study Package. It will help you to acquire knowledge, practise and revise, efficiently and effectively.
Three to twelve months before the exam	**Study Text and i-Learn** Use the Study Text to acquire knowledge, understanding, skills and the ability to apply techniques. Use BPP Learning Media's **i-Learn** product to reinforce your learning.
Throughout	**Learn Online** Study, practise, revise and take advantage of other useful resources with BPP's fully interactive e-learning site with comprehensive tutor support.
Throughout	**i-Pass** **i-Pass**, our computer-based testing package, provides objective test questions in a variety of formats and is ideal for self-assessment.
One to six months before the exam	**Practice & Revision Kit** Try the numerous examination-format questions, for which there are realistic suggested solutions prepared by BPP Learning Media's own authors. Then attempt the two mock exams.
From three months before the exam until the last minute	**Passcards** Work through these short, memorable notes which are focused on what is most likely to come up in the exam you will be sitting.
One to six months before the exam	**Success CDs** The CDs cover the vital elements of your syllabus in less than 90 minutes per subject. They also contain exam hints to help you fine tune your strategy.

Help yourself study for your CIMA assessment

Exams for professional bodies such as CIMA are very different from those you have taken at college or university. You will be under **greater time pressure before** the assessment – as you may be combining your study with work. There are many different ways of learning and so the BPP Study Text offers you a number of different tools to help you through. Here are some hints and tips: they are not plucked out of the air, but **based on research and experience**. (You don't need to know that long-term memory is in the same part of the brain as emotions and feelings - but it's a fact anyway.)

The right approach

1   The right attitude

Believe in yourself	Yes, there is a lot to learn. Yes, it is a challenge. But thousands have succeeded before and you can too.
Remember why you're doing it	Studying might seem a grind at times, but you are doing it for a reason: to advance your career.

2   The right focus

Read through the Syllabus and learning outcomes	These tell you what you are expected to know and are supplemented by Assessment focus points in the text.

3   The right method

The whole picture	You need to grasp the detail - but keeping in mind how everything fits into the whole picture will help you understand better. • The **Introduction** of each chapter puts the material in context. • The **Syllabus content, Learning outcomes** and **Assessment focus points** show you what you need to **grasp**.
In your own words	To absorb the information (and to practise your written communication skills), it helps to **put it into your own words**. • **Take notes.** • Answer the **questions** in each chapter. You will practise your written communication skills, which become increasingly important as you progress through your CIMA exams. • Draw **mindmaps**. • Try **'teaching' a subject** to a colleague or friend.
Give yourself cues to jog your memory	The BPP Learning Media Study Text uses **bold** to **highlight key points**. • Try **colour coding** with a highlighter pen. • Write **key points** on cards.

4   The right review

Review, review, review	It is a **fact** that regularly reviewing a topic in summary form can **fix it in your memory**. Because **review** is so important, the BPP Learning Media Study Text helps you to do so in many ways.
	• **Chapter roundups** summarise the 'fast forward' key points in each chapter. Use them to recap each study session.
	• The **Quick quiz** is another review technique you can use to ensure that you have grasped the essentials.
	• Go through the **Examples** in each chapter a second or third time.

Developing your personal Study Plan

BPP Learning Media's **Learning to Learn Accountancy** book emphasises the need to prepare (and use) a study plan. Planning and sticking to the plan are key elements of learning success.

There are four steps you should work through.

Step 1   How do you learn?

First you need to be aware of your style of learning. The BPP Learning Media **Learning to Learn Accountancy** book commits a chapter to this **self-discovery**. What types of intelligence do you display when learning? You might be advised to brush up on certain study skills before launching into this Study Text.

BPP Learning Media's **Learning to Learn Accountancy** book helps you to identify what intelligences you show more strongly and then details how you can tailor your study process to your preferences. It also includes handy hints on how to develop intelligences you exhibit less strongly, but which might be needed as you study accountancy.

Are you a **theorist** or are you more **practical**? If you would rather get to grips with a theory before trying to apply it in practice, you should follow the study sequence on page (ix). If the reverse is true (you like to know why you are learning theory before you do so), you might be advised to flick through Study Text chapters and look at examples, case studies and questions (Steps 8, 9 and 10 in the **suggested study sequence**) before reading through the detailed theory.

Step 2   How much time do you have?

Work out the time you have available per week, given the following.

- The standard you have set yourself
- The time you need to set aside later for work on the Practice & Revision Kit and Passcards
- The other exam(s) you are sitting
- Very importantly, practical matters such as work, travel, exercise, sleep and social life

Hours

Note your time available in box A.   A [   ]

BPP LEARNING MEDIA

Step 3 **Allocate your time**

- Take the time you have available per week for this Study Text shown in box A, multiply it by the number of weeks available and insert the result in box B. B [   ]

- Divide the figure in box B by the number of chapters in this text and insert the result in box C. C [   ]

Remember that this is only a rough guide. Some of the chapters in this book are longer and more complicated than others, and you will find some subjects easier to understand than others.

Step 4 **Implement**

Set about studying each chapter in the time shown in box C, following the key study steps in the order suggested by your particular learning style.

This is your personal **Study Plan**. You should try and combine it with the study sequence outlined below. You may want to modify the sequence a little (as has been suggested above) to adapt it to your **personal style**.

BPP Learning Media's **Learning to Learn Accountancy** gives further guidance on developing a study plan, and deciding where and when to study.

Suggested study sequence

It is likely that the best way to approach this Study Text is to tackle the chapters in the order in which you find them. Taking into account your individual learning style, you could follow this sequence.

Key study steps	Activity
Step 1 **Topic list**	Each numbered topic is a numbered section in the chapter.
Step 2 **Introduction**	This gives you the big picture in terms of the context of the chapter, the learning outcomes the chapter covers, and the content you will read. In other words, it sets your objectives for study.
Step 3 **Knowledge brought forward boxes**	In these we highlight information and techniques that it is assumed you have 'brought forward' with you from your earlier studies. If there are topics which have changed recently due to legislation for example, these topics are explained in more detail.
Step 4 **Fast forward**	Fast forward boxes give you a quick summary of the content of each of the main chapter sections. They are listed together in the roundup at the end of each chapter to provide you with an overview of the contents of the whole chapter.
Step 5 **Explanations**	Proceed methodically through the chapter, reading each section thoroughly and making sure you understand.
Step 6 **Key terms and Assessment focus points**	• Key terms can often earn you *easy marks* if you state them clearly and correctly in an appropriate exam answer (and they are highlighted in the index at the back of the text). • Assessment focus points state how we think the examiner intends to examine certain topics.
Step 7 **Note taking**	Take brief notes, if you wish. Avoid the temptation to copy out too much. Remember that being able to put something into your own words is a sign of being able to understand it. If you find you cannot explain something you have read, read it again before you make the notes.

Key study steps	Activity
Step 8 **Examples**	Follow each through to its solution very carefully.
Step 9 **Case studies**	Study each one, and try to add flesh to them from your own experience. They are designed to show how the topics you are studying come alive (and often come unstuck) in the real world.
Step 10 **Questions**	Make a very good attempt at each one.
Step 11 **Answers**	Check yours against ours, and make sure you understand any discrepancies.
Step 12 **Chapter roundup**	Work through it carefully, to make sure you have grasped the significance of all the fast forward points.
Step 13 **Quick quiz**	When you are happy that you have covered the chapter, use the Quick quiz to check how much you have remembered of the topics covered and to practise questions in a variety of formats.
Step 14 **Question(s) in the question bank**	Either at this point, or later when you are thinking about revising, make a full attempt at the Question(s) suggested at the very end of the chapter. You can find these at the end of the Study Text, along with the Answers so you can see how you did.

Short of time: Skim study technique?

You may find you simply do not have the time available to follow all the key study steps for each chapter, however you adapt them for your particular learning style. If this is the case, follow the **skim study** technique below.

- Study the chapters in the order you find them in the Study Text.

- For each chapter:

    - Follow the key study steps 1-3

    - Skim-read through step 5, looking out for the points highlighted in the fast forward boxes (step 4)

    - Jump to step 12

    - Go back to step 6

    - Follow through steps 8 and 9

    - Prepare outline answers to questions (steps 10/11)

    - Try the Quick quiz (step 13), following up any items you can't answer

    - Do a plan for the Question (step 14), comparing it against our answers

    - You should probably still follow step 7 (note-taking), although you may decide simply to rely on the BPP Leaning Media Passcards for this.

Moving on...

However you study, when you are ready to embark on the practice and revision phase of the BPP Learning Media Effective Study Package, you should still refer back to this Study Text, both as a source of **reference** (you should find the index particularly helpful for this) and as a way to **review** (the Fast forwards, Assessment focus points, Chapter roundups and Quick quizzes help you here).

And remember to keep careful hold of this Study Text – you will find it invaluable in your work.

More advice on Study Skills can be found in BPP Learning Media's **Learning to Learn Accountancy** book.

Learning outcomes and Syllabus

Paper C2 Fundamentals of Financial Accounting

This is an introduction to financial accounting and assumes no prior knowledge of the subject. It deals with the recording of accounting transactions and the preparation of accounting statements for single entities. The basic concepts of accounting are dealt with and the student will be expected to understand the limitations of financial accounts in attempting to meet the needs of all users. An understanding of the different approaches to asset valuation and the resulting influence on profit management is required.

There is an introduction to the regulatory framework that determines published accounts requirements and a basic introduction to the role of accounting standards. An awareness of published accounts is required but students will not be asked to prepare accounts in a published accounts format. No knowledge of any specific accounting standard is required. There will be an introduction to accounting systems and their control.

Although the emphasis is on the basic methods and techniques of the subject, students will be expected to develop a critical approach by asking why the methods and techniques are used and in what circumstances they are appropriate.

This syllabus addresses the fundamentals of the subject and recognises that some terms and definitions vary from one area of the world to another. As a result students can use accepted alternative names to those that appear in this syllabus and be aware of alternative accounting formats. For example International Accounting Standard 1 (IAS 1) uses Income Statement instead of Profit and Loss Account and Non-current assets instead of Fixed Assets. Others include inventories, receivables and payables. All of these are acceptable for use in answers in this paper but it will be expected that they are applied consistently. Similarly, IAS 1 provides illustrations of accounting formats that are used widely in published accounts and are acceptable in this paper.

Learning aims

This syllabus aims to test the student's ability to:

- Explain the conceptual and regulatory framework of accounting
- Explain the nature of accounting systems and understand the control of such systems
- Prepare and interpret accounts for a single entity
- Interpret simple ratios

Assessment

The assessment is computer-based lasting 120 minutes and comprises 50 compulsory questions, each with one or more parts.

Learning outcomes and syllabus content

C2A Conceptual and regulatory framework – 20%

Learning outcomes

On completion of their studies students should be able to:

(i)   Identify the various user groups which need accounting information and the qualitative characteristics of financial statements

(ii)   Explain the function of, and difference between, financial and management accounting systems

(iii)   Identify the underlying assumptions, policies and changes in accounting estimates

(iv)   Explain and distinguish capital and revenue, cash and profit, income and expenditure, assets and liabilities

(v)   Identify the difference between tangible and intangible assets

(vi)   Explain the historical cost convention

(vii)   Identify the basic methods of valuing assets on current cost, fair value and value in use bases and their impact on profit measures and balance sheet values

(viii) Explain the influence of legislation (eg Companies Acts, EC directives) and accounting standards on the production of published accounting information for organisations

Syllabus content	Covered in chapter
1 Users of accounts and the objectives and the quantitative characteristics of financial statements; functions of financial and management accounts; purpose of accounting statements; stewardship; the accounting equation	1, 2, 22, 23
2 Underlying assumptions; policies; changes in accounting estimates; capital and revenue; cash and profit; income, expenditure, assets and liabilities	2, 3, 7
3 Tangible and intangible assets	2
4 Historical cost convention	7
5 Methods of asset valuation and their implications for profit measurement and the balance sheet	7
6 The regulatory influence of company law and accounting standards; items in formats for published accounts	3, 18, 22

C2B Accounting systems – 20%

Learning outcomes

On completion of their studies students should be able to:

(i)   Explain the purpose of accounting records and their role in the accounting system

(ii)   Prepare cash and bank accounts and bank reconciliation statements

(iii)   Prepare petty cash statements under an imprest system

(iv)   Prepare accounts for sales and purchases including personal accounts and control accounts

(v)   Identify the necessity for financial accounting codes and construct a simple coding system

(vi)   Prepare nominal ledger accounts, prepare journal entries and a trial balance

(vii)   Prepare accounts for indirect taxes

(viii)   Prepare accounts for payroll

Syllabus content	**Covered in chapter**
1 The accounting system and accounting records	4
2 Ledger accounts; double entry bookkeeping	5
3 Preparation of accounts for cash and bank; bank reconciliations; imprest system for petty cash	4, 5, 12
4 Accounting for sales and purchases including personal accounts and control accounts	4, 5, 13
5 Financial accounting codes and their uses	4
6 Nominal ledger accounting; journal entries	5
7 Trial balance	6
8 Accounting for indirect taxes (eg VAT)	14
9 Accounting for payroll	15

C2C Control of accounting systems – 15%

Learning outcomes

On completion of their studies students should be able to:

(i)   Identify the requirements for external audit and the basic processes undertaken

(ii)   Explain the purpose and basic procedures of internal audit

(iii)   Explain the meaning of fair presentation

(iv)   Explain the need for financial controls

(v)   Explain the purpose of audit checks and audit trails

(vi)   Explain the nature of errors and to be able to make accounting entries for them

(vii)   Explain the nature of fraud and basic ideas of fraud prevention

Syllabus content	**Covered in chapter**
1 External audit and the meaning of fair presentation	23
2 Internal audit	23
3 Financial controls; audit checks on financial controls; audit trails	23
4 Errors and fraud	16, 23

C2D Preparation of accounts for single entitites – 45%

Learning outcomes

On completion of their studies students should be able to:

(i)   Prepare accounts using accruals and prepayments

(ii)   Explain the difference between bad debts and allowances for receivables

(iii)   Prepare accounts for bad debts and allowances for receivables

(iv)   Calculate the methods of depreciation

(v)   Prepare accounts using each method of depreciation and for impairment values

(vi)   Prepare a non-current asset register

(vii)   Prepare accounts for inventories

(viii) Prepare income statements, statements of changes in equity and balance sheets from trial balance

(ix)   Prepare manufacturing accounts

(x)   Prepare income and expenditure accounts

(xi)   Prepare accounts from incomplete records

(xii)   Interpret basic ratios

(xiii) Prepare cash flow statements

Syllabus content		Covered in chapter
1	Adjustments to the trial balance: accruals and prepayments	8, 17
2	Bad debts and allowances for receivables	10
3	Accounting treatment for depreciation (straight line, reducing balance and revaluation methods) and impairment	9
4	Non-current asset register	9
5	Accounting for inventories (excluding construction contracts); methods of inventory measurement (FIFO, LIFO and average cost)	11
6	Income statements and balance sheets from trial balance: statement of changes in equity	6, 18
7	Manufacturing accounts	21
8	Income and expenditure accounts	20
9	Production of accounting statements from incomplete data	19
10	Ratios: return on capital employed; gross and net profit margins; asset turnover; trade receivables collection period and trade payables payment period; current and quick ratios; inventory turnover; gearing	25
11	Cash flow statements	24

The assessment

Format of computer-based assessment (CBA)

The CBA will not be divided into sections. There will be a total of fifty objective test questions and you will need to answer **ALL** of them in the time allowed, 2 hours.

Frequently asked questions about CBA

Q   What are the main advantages of CBA?

A   • Assessments can be offered on a continuing basis rather than at six-monthly intervals

    • Instant feedback is provided for candidates by displaying their results on the computer screen

Q   Where can I take CBA?

A   • CBA must be taken at a 'CIMA Accredited CBA Centre'. For further information on CBA, you can email CIMA at cba@cimaglobal.com.

Q   How does CBA work?

A   • Questions are displayed on a monitor

    • Candidates enter their answers directly onto a computer

    • Candidates have 2 hours to complete the Fundamentals of Financial Accounting examination

    • The computer automatically marks the candidate's answers when the candidate has completed the examination

    • Candidates are provided with some indicative feedback on areas of weakness if the candidate is unsuccessful

Q   What sort of questions can I expect to find in CBA?

Your assessment will consist entirely of a number of different types of **objective test question**. Here are some possible examples.

• **MCQs.** Read through the information on page (xviii) about MCQs and how to tackle them.

• **Data entry.** This type of OT requires you to provide figures such as the correct figure for payables in a balance sheet.

• **Multiple response.** These questions provide you with a number of options and you have to identify those which fulfil certain criteria.

This text provides you with **plenty of opportunities to practise** these various question types. You will find OTs **within each chapter** in the text and the **Quick quizzes** at the end of each chapter are full of them. The Question Bank contains more than one hundred and twenty objective test questions similar to the ones that you are likely to meet in your CBA.

Further information relating to OTs is given on page (xix).

The **Practice and Revision Kit** for this paper was published in **December 2007** and is **full of OTs**, providing you with vital revision opportunities for the fundamental techniques and skills you will require in the assessment.

BPP Learning Media's MCQ Cards were also published in **December 2007** and provide you with 100 MCQs to practice on, covering the whole syllabus.

Tackling multiple choice questions

In a multiple choice question on your paper, you are given how many **incorrect** options?

A   Two
B   Three
C   Four
D   Five

The correct answer is B.

The MCQs in your assessment contain four possible answers. You have to **choose the option that best answers the question**. The three incorrect options are called distracters. There is a skill in answering MCQs quickly and correctly. By practising MCQs you can develop this skill, giving you a better chance of passing the exam.

You may wish to follow the approach outlined below, or you may prefer to adapt it.

Step 1   **Skim read** all the MCQs and **identify** what appear to be the easier questions.

Step 2   Attempt each question – **starting with the easier questions** identified in Step 1. Read the question thoroughly. You may prefer to work out the answer before looking at the options, or you may prefer to look at the options at the beginning. Adopt the method that works best for you.

Step 3   Read the four options and see if one matches your own answer. **Be careful with numerical questions**, as the distracters are designed to match answers that incorporate common errors. Check that your calculation is correct. Have you followed the requirement exactly? Have you included every stage of the calculation?

Step 4   You may **find that none of the options matches your answer**.

- Re-read the question to ensure that you understand it and are answering the requirement.

- Eliminate any obviously wrong answers.

- Consider which of the remaining answers is the most likely to be correct and select the option.

Step 5   If you are still **unsure** make a note **and continue to the next question**.

Step 6   **Revisit unanswered** questions. When you come back to a question after a break you often find you are able to answer it correctly straight away. If you are still unsure have a guess. You are not penalised for incorrect answers, so **never leave a question unanswered!**

Assessment focus. After extensive practice and revision of MCQs, you may find that you recognise a question when you sit the exam. Be aware that the detail and/or requirement may be different. If the question seems familiar read the requirement and options carefully – do not assume that it is identical.

BPP Learning Media's i-Pass for this paper provides you with plenty of opportunity for further practice of MCQs.

BPP
LEARNING MEDIA

Tackling objective test questions

Of the total marks available for the paper, objective test questions (OTs) comprise 20/50 per cent. Questions will be worth between 2 to 4 marks.

What is an objective test question?

An **OT** is made up of some form of **stimulus**, usually a question, and a **requirement** to do something.

(a)   Multiple choice questions

(b)   Filling in blanks or completing a sentence

(c)   Listing items, in any order or a specified order such as rank order

(d)   Stating a definition

(e)   Identifying a key issue, term, figure or item

(f)   Calculating a specific figure

(g)   Completing gaps in a set of data where the relevant numbers can be calculated from the information given

(h)   Identifying points/zones/ranges/areas on graphs or diagrams, labelling graphs or filling in lines on a graph

(i)   Matching items or statements

(j)   Stating whether statements are true or false

(k)   Writing brief (in a specified number of words) explanations

(l)   Deleting incorrect items

(m)   Choosing right words from a number of options

(n)   Complete an equation, or define what the symbols used in an equation mean

OT questions in CIMA assessment

CIMA has offered the following **guidance** about OT questions in the assessment.

- Credit may be given for **workings** where you are asked to calculate a specific figure.

- If you **exceed a specified limit on the number of words** you can use in an answer, you will **not be awarded any marks**.

Examples of OTs are included within each chapter, in the **quick quizzes** at the end of each chapter and in the **objective test question bank**.

BPP Learning Media's i-Pass for this paper provides you with plenty of opportunity for further practice of OTs.

International terminology

Your Fundamentals of Financial Accounting assessment will use international accounting terms and this text is written in international accounting terms.

It is a good idea to start now getting used to these new terms. Below is a list of UK terms with their international equivalents.

UK term	International term
Profit and loss account	Income statement
Profit and loss reserve (in balance sheet)	Accumulated profits
Turnover	Revenue
Debtor account	Account receivable
Debtors (eg debtors have increased)	Receivables
Debtor	Customer
Creditor account	Account payable
Creditors (eg creditors have increased)	Payables
Creditor	Supplier
Debtors control account	Receivables control account
Creditors control account	Payables control account
Stock	Inventory
Fixed asset	Non-current asset (generally). Tangible fixed assets are also referred to as 'property, plant and equipment'.
Long term liability	Non-current liability
Provision (eg for depreciation)	Allowance (you will sometimes see 'provision' used too).
Nominal ledger	General ledger
VAT	Sales tax
Debentures	Loan notes
Preference shares/dividends	Preferred shares/dividends

Part A

Conceptual and regulatory framework

1

The nature and objectives of accounting

Introduction

The syllabus for the *Fundamentals of Financial Accounting* paper begins with the section 'conceptual and regulatory framework'. Before you learn how to prepare financial statements, it is important that you understand **why** accounting information is necessary and the assumptions on which it is based.

In Sections 1 to 2 of this chapter, you will discover the purposes and uses of accounting information.

As you have chosen to train for the CIMA qualification, you may be aware that there is a difference between a **management** accountant and a **financial** accountant. This topic is covered in Section 3.

Section 4 introduces you to the main financial statements - the income statement and the balance sheet.

Topic list	Syllabus references
1 What is accounting?	A (1)
2 Users of accounting information	A (1)
3 Management accounting and financial accounting	A (1)
4 The main financial statements	A (1)

1 What is accounting?

Accounting is the process of collecting, recording, summarising and communicating financial information.

Question

Accounting

(a) You will often meet with the terms 'an accounting statement' or 'a set of accounts'. Do you know what is meant by these terms?

(b) Who do you think has the task of preparing accounting statements? In an organisation of a reasonable size, would it be one person? One department? Several different departments?

(c) Who are the users of accounting information?

(d) What is the purpose of accounting?

Answer

(a) An accounting statement is, for example, an income statement or a balance sheet. A set of accounts is a number of accounting statements presented together with the intention of showing an overall view of an organisation's income, expenditure, assets and liabilities.

(b) Most organisations of reasonable size will have at least one accounts department, staffed by people with detailed knowledge of accounting systems and theory. In large organisations there may be several departments, or groups, responsible for preparing accounting information to meet the different needs of accounts users.

(c) The users of accounts include a variety of people and organisations, both internal and external, as explained in Section 2 of this chapter, such as current and potential workers, investors, customers and suppliers. Government bodies and the general public may also be interested. The extent of their information needs varies widely.

(d) There are many purposes of accounting. You may have considered the following.

- Control over the use of resources
- Knowledge of what the business owes and owns
- Calculation of profits and losses
- Cash budgeting
- Effective financial planning

1.1 Why keep accounts?

Accounting information is essential to the efficient running of a business. It helps managers to control the use of resources, keep track of the assets and liabilities of the business and plan effectively for the future.

Accounts show where money came from and how it has been spent, this

- **aids** the efficient running of a business
- **indicates** how successfully managers are performing
- **provides information** about the resources and activities of a business

Accounting information **aids** the efficient running of a business in many ways.

(a)   A business needs to pay bills for the goods and services it purchases, and collect money from its customers. It must, therefore, keep a record of such bills and invoices so that the correct amounts can be paid or collected at the correct times.

(b)   Keeping records of a business's assets (eg its motor vehicles or computers) helps to keep them secure.

Accounts **indicate how successfully** the managers are performing.

Modern businesses are often complicated, they seldom have a single owner (some very large enterprises, such as J Sainsbury, may be owned by millions of shareholders). Frequently the owners are not involved in the day-to-day running of the business but appoint managers to act on their behalf. In addition, there are too many activities and assets for the managers to keep track of simply from personal knowledge and an occasional glance at the bank statement, so accounts which summarise transactions are very useful.

A business should **provide information** about its resources and activities because there are many groups of people who want or need that information. We will look more closely at the classes of people who might need information about a business in Section 2.

Question   **Why keep accounts?**

Why should a business keep accounts?

A   To discover how well the business is doing
B   To record assets and liabilties
C   To help run the business efficiently
D   All of the above

Answer

D   All of the above statements are true.

2 Users of accounting information

Accounting information is required for a wide range of users both within and outside the business.

The following people might be interested in financial information about a large public company.

User group	Comment
Managers of the company	People appointed by the company's owners to supervise the daily activities of the company need information about the company's current and expected future financial situation, to make **planning decisions**.
Shareholders of the company, ie the company's owners	Want to assess how effectively management is performing and how much profit they can withdraw from the business for their own use.
Trade contacts, ie suppliers of goods to the company on credit and customers	Suppliers want to know about the company's **ability** to **pay its debts**; customers need to know that the company is a secure source of supply and is in no danger of closing down.
Providers of finance to the company, ie lenders both short and long term	Lenders will want to ensure that the company is able to meet **interest payments**, and eventually to repay the amounts advanced.
The tax authorities	Want to know about business profits in order to **assess** the tax payable by the company.
Employees	Need to know about the company's financial situation because their **future** careers and the level of their wages and salaries depend on it.
Financial analysts and advisers	Need information for their clients. For example, stockbrokers need information to advise investors, credit agencies want information to advise potential suppliers of goods to the company, journalists need information for their reading public.
Government and their agencies	Interested in the allocation of resources and in the activities of enterprises. Also require information in order to provide a basis for national statistics.
The public	Want information because enterprises affect them in many ways, eg by providing jobs and using local suppliers, or by affecting the environment (eg pollution).

Question

Accounting information

It is easy to see how 'internal' people get hold of accounting information. A manager, for example, can ask the accounts department to prepare whatever accounting statements he needs. But external users of accounts cannot do this. How, in practice, can a business contact or a financial analyst access accounting information about a company?

Answer

Limited liability companies (though not other forms of business such as partnerships) are required to make certain accounting information public. They send copies of the required information to the Registrar of Companies at Companies House. The information filed at Companies House is available, at a fee, to any member of the public who asks for it. Other sources include financial comment in the press and company brochures.

Mark the following statements as true or false.

(a) Shareholders receive annual accounts, prepared in accordance with legal and professional requirements.

(b) The accounts of limited liability companies are sometimes filed with the Registrar of Companies.

(c) Employees always receive the company's accounts and an employee report.

(d) The tax authorities will receive the published accounts and as much supplementary detail as they need to assess the tax payable on profits.

(e) Banks frequently require more information than is supplied in the published accounts when considering applications for loans and overdraft facilities.

Answer

True

(a) Yes, and, in addition, companies listed on the Stock Exchange have to comply with the regulations in the Stock Exchange's Listing Rules (Yellow Book).

(d) Yes.

(e) Yes, banks may require cash flow and profit forecasts and budgets prepared to show management's estimates of future activity in the business.

False

(b) The accounts of limited liability companies **must always** be filed with the Registrar of Companies and be available for public inspection. In addition, the company itself will often distribute these accounts on request to potential shareholders, the bank and financial analysts. These accounts are all that is usually available to suppliers and customers.

(c) Employees will not necessarily receive company accounts (unless they are shareholders for example), but many companies do distribute the accounts to employees as a matter of policy. Some companies produce employee reports which summarise and expand on matters which are covered in the annual accounts and are of particular interest to them.

Assessment focus point | Many different people use financial statements to acquire information about a business.

3 Management accounting and financial accounting

FAST FORWARD | Management accounts are produced for internal purposes – they provide information to assist managers in running the business. Financial accounts are produced to satisfy the information requirements of external users.

Key terms | **Financial accounting** is the preparation of accounting reports for external use.
Management accounting is the preparation of accounting reports for internal use.

3.1 Management accounting

Management accounting systems produce detailed information often split between different departments within an organisation (sales, production, finance etc). Although much of the information deals with past events and decisions, management accountants produce information which is forward-looking, and used to prepare budgets and make decisions about the **future activities** of a business. They also compare actual performance with budget and try to take corrective action where necessary.

3.2 Financial accounting

Financial accountants, however, are usually solely concerned with summarising historical data, often from the same basic records as management accountants but in a different way. This difference arises partly because external users have different interests from management and do not need very detailed information. In addition, financial statements are prepared under constraints (such as International Financial Reporting Standards and company law) which do not apply to management accounts.

Question
The Financial Accountant

Which of the following is a function of the financial accountant in a business which employs several accounting staff?

A   Preparing budgets
B   Costing products
C   Setting selling prices
D   Summarising historical accounting data

Answer

D   Correct; this is a function of financial accounting.
A   This is usually a job for the management accountant.
B   This is usually a job for the management accountant.
C   This is usually a job for the management accountant.

Assessment focus point

Management accounts are for **internal** use and the financial accounts for **external** use. Management accounts provide information for decisions affecting the future; financial accounts provide information about what has happened in the past.

4 The main financial statements

 The two most important financial statements are the balance sheet and the income statement.

4.1 The balance sheet

 The **balance sheet** is a list of all the assets owned by a business and all the liabilities owed by a business at a particular date.

Assets are the business's resources eg buildings to operate from, plant and machinery, inventory to sell and cars for its employees. These are all resources which it uses in its operations. Also, it may have bank balances, cash and amounts of money owed to it. These provide the funds it needs to carry out its operations and are also assets. It may owe money to the bank or to suppliers: these are liabilities.

4.2 The income statement

The **income statement** is a record of income generated and expenditure incurred over a given period.

The income statement which forms part of the financial accounts of a limited liability company will be made up for the period of a year, commencing from the date of the previous year's accounts.

Management accountants might need quarterly or monthly income statement. The incomes statement shows whether the business has more income than expenditure (a profit) or vice versa (a loss) during a period.

Organisations which are not run for profit (charities etc) produce a similar statement called an **income and expenditure account** which shows the surplus of income over expenditure (or a deficit where expenditure exceeds income).

4.3 Accruals concept

The **accruals concept** means that income and expenses are included in the income statement of the period in which they are earned or incurred, not received or paid.

The accruals concept is very important as it underlies the preparation of the income statement.

It is very important to grasp that, in nearly all businesses, accounts are not prepared on a cash basis but on an accruals basis. This is because cash accounting does not present a true picture of the business's activities in any given period.

4.4 Example: accruals concept

Emma has a business printing and selling T-shirts. In May 20X7 she makes the following purchases and sales.

Invoice date	Numbers bought/sold	Amount $	Date paid
Purchases			
7.5.X7	20	100	1.6.X7
Sales			
8.5.X7	4	40	1.6.X7
12.5.X7	6	60	1.6.X7
23.5.X7	10	100	1.7.X7

What is Emma's profit for May?

Solution

	$
Cash basis	
Sales	0
Purchases	0
Profit/loss	0
Accruals basis	
Sales ($40 + $60 + $100)	200
Purchases	(100)
Profit	100

The accruals basis gives a truer picture than the cash basis. Emma has no cash to show for her efforts until June, but her customers are legally bound to pay her and she is legally bound to pay for her purchases.

Her balance sheet as at 31 May 20X7 would therefore show her assets and liabilities as follows.

	$
Assets	
Receivables ($40 + $60 + $100)	200
Proprietor's capital	100
Liabilities	
Payables	100
	200

4.5 Capital

Key term

> **Capital** is a special form of liability, representing the amount owed by the business to its proprietor(s).

In Emma's case it represents the profit earned in May, which she, as owner of the business, is entitled to in full. Capital will also include the proprietor's initial capital, introduced as cash and perhaps equipment or other assets.

For example, if Emma had begun her business on 30 April 20X7 by opening a business bank account and paying in $100, her balance sheet immediately after this transaction would look like this.

	$
Assets	
Bank	100
Proprietor's capital	100

On 31 May 20X7 the balance sheet would look like this.

	$
Assets	
Receivables (customers who owe Emma money)	200
Bank	100
	300
Proprietor's capital	
Brought forward	100
Profit for the period	100
Carried forward	200
Liabilities	
Payables (suppliers to whom Emma owes money)	100
	300

sessment
cus point This example shows that both the balance sheet and the income statement are summaries of many transactions.

Question

Capital

By looking at the example of Emma, you may be able to see that there is a simple arithmetical relationship linking capital at the beginning of a period, capital at the end of the period, and profit earned during the period. Can you formulate the relationship?

Answer

The relationship is: opening capital + profit = closing capital. In more complicated examples it would be necessary to make adjustments for new capital introduced during the period, and for any capital withdrawn during the period.

Chapter roundup

- Accounting is the process of collecting, recording, summarising and communicating financial information.

- Accounting information is essential to the efficient running of a business. It helps managers to control the use of resources, keep track of the assets and liabilities of the business and plan effectively for the future.

- Accounting information is required for a wide range of users both within and outside the business.

- Management accounts are produced for internal purposes – they provide information to assist managers in running the business. Financial accounts are produced to satisfy the information requirements of external users.

- The two most important financial statements are the balance sheet and the income statement.

- The balance sheet is a list of all the assets owned by a business and all the liabilities owed by a business at a particular date.

- The income statement is a record of income generated and expenditure incurred over a given period.

- The accruals concept means that income and expenses are included in the income statement of the period in which they are earned or incurred, not received or paid.

Quick quiz

1   How has the increasing complexity of modern business contributed to the development of accounting?

    A   Lenders need more information

    B   Government needs more information

    C   Too many transactions, so managers need a means of summarising them

    D   Too many transactions, so investors need a means of summarising them

2   Five categories of people who might use accounting information about a business are:

    (1)   _____

    (2)   _____

    (3)   _____

    (4)   _____

    (5)   _____

3   Fill in the blanks.

The main distinction between financial accounting and management accounting is that financial accounting provides - _____ information to people _____ the organisation, whereas management accounting provides _____ information to _____ on which they can base _____.

4   Accounting information is limited to items having a monetary value. True or false?

5   Explain briefly:

    (a)   What is a balance sheet?

    (b)   What is an income statement?

6   Fill in the blanks.

The accruals concept means that _____ and _____ are included in the income statement of the period in which they are _____ or _____ not _____ or _____.

7   Which of the following user groups are **most** interested in the cash position of a business?

    A   Investors

    B   Government

    C   Suppliers

    D   Customers

Answers to quick quiz

1   C   There are too many activities for a manager to keep track of by himself and so he needs accounts which summarise transactions to monitor the business' performance.

2   Any five from the following list:

- Managers
- Owners (shareholders)
- Trade contacts
- Providers of finance
- Tax authority

- Employees
- Financial analysts and advisers
- Government and its agencies
- The public

3   The main distinction between financial accounting and management accounting is that financial accounting provides **historical** information to people **outside** the organisation, whereas management accounting provides **forward-looking** information to **management** on which they can base **decisions**.

4   True. Accounting information is limited to items having a monetary value.

5   (a)   A balance sheet shows all the assets and liabilities of a business at a certain date.
     (b)   An income statement shows the income and expenditure for a period.

6   The accruals concept means that **income** and **expenditure** are included in the income statement of the period in which they are **earned** or **incurred** not **received** or **paid**.

7   C   Suppliers are concerned whether the business has enough cash to pay them what they are owed.

Now try the questions below from the Question Bank

Question numbers	Page
1–4	395

Assets and liabilities

Introduction

We have used the terms 'business', 'assets' and 'liabilities' without looking too closely at their meaning. It is important to have a thorough understanding of how these terms are used in an accounting context.

Section 3 of the chapter introduces a concept which it is important for you to grasp: the **accounting equation**. You may already realise that a balance sheet has to balance. You are about to learn why!

Topic list	Syllabus references
1 The nature of a business	A (1)
2 The balance sheet: assets and liabilities	A (2), A (3)
3 The accounting equation	A (1)

1 The nature of a business

Question

You may already be familiar with certain terms. Can you distinguish, for example, between the terms 'an enterprise', 'a business', 'a company' and 'a firm'?

Answer

An 'enterprise' is the most general term, referring to just about any organisation in which people join together to achieve a common end. In the context of accounting it can refer to a multinational conglomerate, a small club, a local authority and so on *ad infinitum.*

A 'business' is also a very general term, but it does not extend as widely as the term 'enterprise' as it would not include a charity or a local authority. Any organisation existing to trade and make a **profit** could be called a business.

A 'company' is an enterprise constituted in a particular legal form, usually involving limited liability for its members. Companies need not be businesses eg many charities are constituted as companies.

A 'firm' is a much vaguer term. It is sometimes used loosely in the sense of a business or a company. Some writers, more usefully, try to restrict its meaning to that of an unincorporated business (ie a business **not** constituted as a company eg a partnership).

Key term

> A **business** is an organisation which sells something or provides a service with the objective of profit.

Businesses range in size from very small (the local shopkeeper or plumber) to very large (ICI), but the objective of earning profit is common to all of them.

FAST FORWARD

Profit is the excess of income over expenditure. When expenditure exceeds income, the business is running at a **loss**.

One of the jobs of an accountant is to measure income, expenditure and profit. It is not a straightforward exercise and in later chapters we will look at some of the theoretical and practical problems.

1.1 Non-profit-making enterprises

Organisations	Comment
Charities – exist to provide help to the needy.	Must keep expenditure within the level of income or cannot continue in operation.
Public sector organisations – exist to serve the community rather than to make profits.	Include government departments and services (eg the fire service, police force, national health service etc). Can only spend the money allowed to them by the government. Must be cost– conscious.
Certain **clubs and associations** – exist to provide services to their members.	To maintain and improve the services they offer, must ensure that income is at least equal to expenditure.

FAST FORWARD

All enterprises, profit-making or not, will produce financial statements to provide information to interested parties. For a business, the most important statements are the **balance sheet** and the **income statement**.

1.2 The business as a separate entity

Financial statements always treat the business as a separate entity.

It is crucial that you understand that the convention adopted in preparing accounts (the *entity concept*) is **always** to treat a business as a separate entity from its owner(s). This applies whether or not the business is recognised in law as a separate entity.

Suppose that Fiona Middleton sets up a business as a hairdresser ('Fiona's Salon'). The law sees no distinction between Fiona Middleton, the individual, and the business known as 'Fiona's Salon'. Any debts of the business which cannot be met from business assets must be met from Fiona's private resources.

However the law recognises a company as a legal entity, quite separate from its owners (the shareholders). A company may acquire assets, incur debts and enter into contracts. If a company's assets become insufficient to meet its liabilities, the company might become 'bankrupt'. The shareholders are not usually required to pay the deficit from their own private resources. The debts belong to the company alone, and the shareholders have limited liability.

Key term

> **Limited liability**: the liability of a shareholder to the company is **limited** to any unpaid amounts for shares issued by the company to the shareholder.

Question
The entity concpet

Fill in the missing words to make sure you understand the entity concept and how the law differs from accounting practice.

The entity concept regards a business as a ___ entity, distinct from its_____ . The concept applies to _____ businesses. However, the law only recognises a _____ as a legal entity separate from its _____. The liability of shareholders to the company is _____ to the amount they have not yet paid for their shares.

Answer

The missing words are:

separate; owners; all; company; owners; limited.

2 The balance sheet: assets and liabilities

The balance sheet is a list of all the assets owned by a business and all the liabilities owed by it at a particular date.

The income statement is a record of income generated and expenditure incurred over a given period.

2.1 Assets

Key term

> An **asset** is something valuable which a business owns. This in effect represents a right of the business to future economic benefits.

Non-current assets are held and used in operations to generate profit, such as an office building, or a machine. Current assets are held for only a short time with the intention of turning them into cash in the ordinary course of business.

2.2 Examples of assets

Non-current assets	
• Factories	• Plant and machinery
• Office building	• Computer equipment
• Warehouse	• Office furniture
• Delivery vans	
• Lorries	

Current assets	
• Cash	• Money owed by customers
• Raw materials	• Cash and bank accounts
• Finished goods held for sale to customers	

2.3 Liabilities

Key term

A **liability** is something which is owed to somebody else. 'Liabilities' is the accounting term for the amounts a business owes (the debts of the business).

2.4 Examples of liabilities

• A bank loan or bank overdraft
• Amounts owed to suppliers for goods purchased but not yet paid for
• Taxation owed to the government

Assessment focus point

It is essential that you can distinguish between assets and liabilities.

 Question   **Questions and liabilities**

Classify the following items as non-current assets, current assets or liabilities.

(a)   A personal computer used in the accounts department of a retail store
(b)   A personal computer on sale in an office equipment shop
(c)   Wages due to be paid to staff at the end of the week
(d)   A van for sale in a motor dealer's showroom
(e)   A delivery van used in a grocer's business
(f)   An amount owing to a leasing company for the acquisition of a van

Answer

(a)   Non-current asset
(b)   Current asset
(c)   Liability
(d)   Current asset
(e)   Non-current asset
(f)   Liability

2.5 Tangible and intangible assets

Non-current assets can be sub-divided into **tangible** and **intangible** assets.

Key term

Tangible assets (literally assets which can be touched) have a physical presence. Examples include factory buildings, machinery used to make goods for sale and office computers. As you will see, in later chapters, tangible assets are also called **property, plant and equipment**.

Key term

Intangible assets have no physical presence. Examples include royalties, trademarks and patents. They are also called **intellectual property** because they arise from discoveries or know-how.

2.6 The balance sheet

As you may remember from the examples in Chapter 1, the balance sheet is a list of the assets and liabilities (including capital) of the business.

Key term

Capital is the amount owed to the owner of the business by the business.

Owners put in money to start a business, and are owed any profits which are generated by the business.

3 The accounting equation

Formula to learn

The accounting equation is that in a balance sheet:

Assets = Capital + Liabilities

 ST FORWARD

The accounting equation demonstrates that the assets of a business are always equal to the liabilities + capital.

3.1 Example: the accounting equation

On 1 July 20X6, Courtney Spice opened a stall in the market, to sell herbs and spices. She had $2,500 to put into her business.

When the business is set up, it owns the cash that Courtney has put into it, $2,500. But does it owe anything?

The answer is yes. The business is a separate entity in accounting terms. It has obtained its assets (in this example cash) from its owner, Courtney Spice. It therefore owes this amount of money to its owner. If Courtney changed her mind and decided not to go into business after all, the business would have to repay the cash to Courtney.

The money put into a business by its owners is **capital**. A business proprietor invests capital with the intention of earning profit.

Good Example

 19

When Courtney Spice sets up her business:

Capital invested	=	$2,500
Cash	=	$2,500

Capital is a form of liability, because it is an amount owed by the business to its owner(s). As liabilities and assets are always equal amounts, we can state the accounting equation as follows.

Assets   **=**   **Capital**   **+**   **Liabilities**

For Courtney Spice, as at 1 July 20X6:

$2,500 (cash)   = $2,500   + $0

3.2 Example continued

Courtney Spice uses some of the money invested to buy a market stall for $1,800. She also purchases some herbs and spices at a cost of $650.

This leaves $50 in cash ($2,500 – $1,800 – $650). Courtney puts $30 in the bank and keeps $20 in small change. She is now ready for her first day of market trading on 3 July 20X6.

The assets and liabilities of the business have altered. At 3 July, before trading begins, the state of her business is as follows.

Assets		**=**	**Capital**	**+**	**Liabilities**
	$				
Stall	1,800	=	$2,500	+	$0
Herbs and spices	650				
Cash at bank	30				
Cash in hand	20				
	2,500				

3.3 Example continued: profit introduced into the accounting equation

On 3 July Courtney has a very successful day. She is able to sell all of her herbs and spices for $900 cash. Courtney has sold goods costing $650 to earn revenue of $900, we can say that she has earned a profit of $250 on the day's trading.

Profits belong to the owners of a business. So the $250 belongs to Courtney and are treated as an addition to the proprietor's capital.

Assets		**=**	**Capital**		**+**	**Liabilities**
	$			$		
Stall	1,800		Original investment	2,500		
Goods – herbs and spices	0					
Cash at bank	30					
Cash in hand (20 + 900)	920		Retained profit	250		
	2,750			2,750	+	$0

3.4 Drawings

Key term

> **Drawings** are amounts taken out of a business by its owner.

Courtney Spice has made a profit of $250 from her first day's work, she may decide to draw some of the profits out of the business for living expenses. Courtney decides to take $180 from the till for herself. This $180 is not an expense to be deducted in arriving at net profit. In other words, it would be **incorrect** to calculate the net profit earned by the business as follows.

	$
Profit on sale of herbs and spices	250
Less 'wages' paid to Courtney	180
Profit earned by business (incorrect)	70

(handwritten: IMPORTANT)

Any amounts paid by a business to its proprietor are treated by accountants as withdrawals of profit (drawings) and not as expenses incurred by the business.

In Courtney's case, the true position is that the net profit earned is the $250 surplus on sale of herbs and spices.

	$
Profit earned by business	250
Less profit withdrawn by Courtney	180
Profit retained in the business	70

(handwritten: WITHDRAWL OF PROFIT.)

The drawings are taken in cash, reducing the cash assets by $180. After the withdrawals, the accounting equation would be restated.

Assets		$	= Capital	$	+ Liabilities
Stall		1,800	Original investment	2,500	
Goods – herbs and spices		0	Retained profit (250 – 180)	70	
Cash at bank		30			
Cash in hand (920-180)		740			
		2,570		2,570	+ $0

ssessment
cus points

A balance sheet balances, ie Assets = Capital + liabilities.

Liabilities are what the business owes to third parties.

Capital is what the business owes to its owner.

Capital = Original investment *plus* profit *less* drawings.

Profit = Income – expenditure.

Drawings = Amounts taken out of a business by its owner.

3.5 Example continued

The next market is on 10 July and Courtney purchases more herbs and spices for $740 cash. She is not feeling well, however, and so she accepts help for the day from her cousin Bianca, for a wage of $40. On 10 July, they sell all the goods for $1,100 cash. Courtney pays Bianca her wage of $40 and draws out $200 for herself.

Required

(a) State the accounting equation before trading began on 10 July.

(b) State the accounting equation at the end of 10 July, after paying Bianca

(i) but before drawings are taken out.

(ii) after drawings have been made.

(handwritten: ↑ Debit / Expenses / Assets / Drawings   Credit / Liability / Income / capital)

The accounting equation for the business at the end of transactions for 3 July is given in section 3.4.

Solution

(a)   After the purchase of the goods for $740.

Assets		=		Capital	+	Liabilities
	$					
Stall	1,800					
Goods	740					
Cash at bank	30					
Cash in hand						
(740 – 740)	0					
	2,570	=		$ 2,570	+	$0

(b)   (i)   On 10 July after Bianca is paid $40.

Assets		=	Capital		+	Liabilities
	$			$		
Stall	1,800		At beginning of 10 July	2,570		
Goods	0		Profit earned (working)	320		
Cash at bank	30					
Cash in hand						
(0 + 1,100 – 40)	1,060					
	2,890			2,890	+	$0

Working

		$	$
Sales			1,100
Less: Cost of goods sold		740	
Bianca's wage		40	
			780
Profit earned			320

(ii)   After Courtney has taken drawings of $200.

Assets		=	Capital		+	Liabilities
	$			$		
Stall	1,800		At beginning of 10 July	2,570		
			Retained profits			
Cash at bank	30		(320 – 200)	120		
Cash in hand						
(1,060 – 200)	860					
	2,690			2,690	+	$0

Tutorial note. It is very important you should understand the principles described so far. Do not read on until you are confident that you understand the solution to this example.

Question

What is Courtney's profit on 10 July?

A $200
B $120
C $320
D $2,690

Answer

C   Her profit is $320 (see 3.5 (b) (i) above).

3.6 Receivables and payables

Key terms

> A **payable** is a person to whom a business owes money and is therefore a liability of a business.
>
> A **receivable** is a person who owes money to the business and is therefore an asset of the business.

It is common business practice to make purchases on credit, with a promise to pay within 30 days or two months or three months from the date of the bill (or 'invoice') for the goods. For example, A buys goods costing $2,000 on credit from B. B sends A an invoice for $2,000, dated 4 March, with credit terms that payment must be made within 30 days. If A pays on 31 March, B will be a **payable of A** between 4 and 31 March for $2,000.

Just as a business might buy goods on credit, so might it sell goods to customers on credit. A customer who buys goods on credit is a **receivable**. Taking the example above, **A is a receivable of B** for $2,000 between 4 and 31 March.

3.7 Example continued

Courtney Spice's market stall continues to trade during the following week to 17 July 20X6. (See Paragraph 3.5 (b)(ii) for the situation as at the end of 10 July.)

(a)   Courtney needs more money in the business and so she makes the following arrangements.

       (i)   She invests a further $250 of her own savings.

       (ii)   She persuades her Uncle Phil to lend her $500 immediately. Uncle Phil tells her that she can repay the loan whenever she likes but, in the meantime, she must pay him interest of $5 each week at the end of the market day. They agree that it will probably be quite a long time before the loan is eventually repaid.

(b)   She decides that she can afford to buy a second hand van to pick up herbs and spices from her supplier and bring them to her stall in the market. She buys a van on credit for $700. Courtney agrees to pay for the van after 30 days' trial use.

(c)   During the week before the next market day (17 July), Courtney's Uncle Grant asks her if she could sell him some spice racks and herb chopping boards as presents for his friends. Courtney agrees and she buys what Uncle Grant wants, paying $300 in cash. Uncle Grant accepts delivery of the goods and agrees to pay $350 to Courtney for them, but he asks if she can wait until the end of the month for payment. Courtney agrees.

(d) Courtney buys herbs and spices costing $800. Of these purchases $750 are paid for in cash, with the remaining $50 on seven days' credit. Courtney decides to use Bianca's services again as an assistant on market day, at an agreed wage of $40.

(e) On 17 July, Courtney once again sells all her goods, earning revenue of $1,250 cash. She takes out drawings of $240 for her week's work and pays Bianca $40 in cash. She will make the interest payment to her Uncle Phil the next time she sees him.

(f) Ignore any van expenses for the week, for the sake of relative simplicity.

Required

(a) State the accounting equation

(i) After Courtney and Uncle Phil have put more money into the business and after the purchase of the van.
(ii) After the sale of goods to Uncle Grant.
(iii) After the purchase of goods for the weekly market.
(iv) At the end of the day's trading on 17 July, after drawings have been 'appropriated' out of profit.

Solution

This solution deals with each transaction one at a time in chronological order.

(a) (i) The addition of Courtney's extra capital and Uncle Phil's loan

To the business, Uncle Phil is a long-term liability and, therefore, the amount owed to him is a liability of the business and not business capital.

Assets		=	Capital		+	Liabilities	
	$			$			$
Stall	1,800		As at end of 10 July	2,690		Loan	500
Cash at bank			Additional capital put in	250			
and in hand							
(30+860+							
250+500)	1,640						
	3,440	=		2,940	+		500

(ii) *The purchase of the van (cost $700) on credit.*

Assets		=	Capital		+	Liabilities	
	$			$			$
Stall	1,800		As at end of 10 July	2,690		Loan	500
Van	700		Additional capital	250		Payable	700
Cash at bank							
and in hand							
(30+860+							
250+500)	1,640						
	4,140	=		2,940	+		1,200

(iii)   *The sale of goods to Uncle Grant on credit ($350) at a cost of $300 (cash)*

Assets		=	Capital		+	Liabilities	
	$			$			$
Stall	1,800		As at end of 10 July	2,690		Loan	500
Van	700		Additional capital	250		Payable	700
Receivable	350		Profit on sale to Uncle				
			Grant (350 – 300)	50			
Cash at bank							
and in hand							
(1,640 – 300)	1,340						
	4,190	=		2,990	+		1,200

(iv)   *After the purchase of goods ($750 paid in cash and $50 on credit)*

Assets		=	Capital		+	Liabilities	
	$			$			$
Stall	1,800		As at end of 10 July	2,690		Loan	500
Van	700					Payable	
						for van	700
Goods	800		Additional capital	250		Payable	
						for goods	50
Receivable	350		Profit on sale to				
			Uncle Grant	50			
Cash at bank							
and in hand							
(1,340 – 750)	590						
	4,240	=		2,990	+		1,250

(v)   *After market trading on 17 July*

Assets		=	Capital		+	Liabilities	
	$			$			$
Stall	1,800		As at end of 10 July	2,690		Loan	500
Van	700		Additional capital	250		Payable for	
Receivable	350					van	700
Cash at bank						Payable for	
and in hand						goods	50
(590 + 1,250			Profits retained	215		Payable for	
–40 – 240)	1,560		(working)			interest	
						payment	5
	4,410			3,155			1,255

Working

	$	$
Sales		1,250
Cost of goods sold	800	
Wages	40	
Interest payable	5	
		845
Profit earned on 17 July		405
Profit on sale of goods to Uncle Grant		50
Profit for the week		455
Drawings appropriated out of profits		240
Retained profit		215

Question

The accounting equation

How would each of these transactions affect the accounting equation?

(a) Purchasing $800 worth of inventory on credit
(b) Paying the telephone bill $25
(c) Selling $450 worth of inventory for $650
(d) Paying $800 to the supplier

Answer

(a)	Increase in liabilities (payables)	$800
	Increase in assets (inventory)	$800
(b)	Decrease in assets (cash)	$25
	Decrease in capital (profit)	$25
(c)	Decrease in assets (inventory)	$450
	Increase in assets (cash)	$650
	Increase in capital (profit)	$200
(d)	Decrease in liabilities (payables)	$800
	Decrease in assets (cash)	$800

Chapter roundup

- Profit is the excess of income over expenditure. When expenditure exceeds income, the business is running at a loss.

- All enterprises, profit-making or not, will produce financial statements to provide information to interested parties. For a business, the most important statements are the balance sheet and the income statement.

- Financial statements always treat the business as a separate entity.

- The balance sheet is a list of all the assets owned by a business and all the liabilities owed by it at a particular date.

- The income statement is a record of income generated and expenditure incurred over a given period.

- The accounting equation demonstrates that the assets of a business are always equal to the liabilities + capital.

Quick quiz

1   Fill in the blanks.

If income exceeds expenditure, the business makes a _____.

If expenditure exceeds income, the business makes a _____.

2   Limited liability means what?

A   Members of a company need only pay part of the debts if the company becomes insolvent

B   Shareholders will receive only partial return of their investment if the company becomes insolvent

C   Upon liquidation, the maximum amount which a member can be called upon to pay is any outstanding monies on shares purchased

D   Losses of an insolvent company are shared between payables and members

3   State whether the following are non-current assets, current assets, liabilities, capital or drawings.

(a)   A delivery van
(b)   Money owed to a supplier
(c)   A mortgage owed to a bank
(d)   Money put into the business bank by the owner of the business
(e)   Profit made by a business
(f)   Money owed by a customer
(g)   Unsold goods
(h)   Money taken from the business bank account by the owner of a business.

4   Which of the following is a correct version of the 'fundamental accounting equation'?

A   Assets = liabilities
B   Assets = capital less liabilities
C   Assets plus liabilities = capital
D   Assets = capital + liabilities

5   Capital is?

A   The amount borrowed to set up a business
B   The amount owed by a business to its proprietor(s)
C   The value of the assets in a business
D   The total amount invested in a business by all the providers of capital

6   What is the definition of profit earned in a period?

A   Income less expenditure
B   Income less expenditure less drawings
C   The balance on the capital account
D   The total of assets less liabilities

Answers to quick quiz

1   If income exceeds expenditure, the business makes a **profit**.

     If expenditure exceeds income, the business makes a **loss**.

2   C   This is correct, obviously the members lose their investments.

     A   Incorrect; members cannot be called upon to meet any of the debts unless they have personally guaranteed them.

     B   Ordinary shareholders and preference shareholders will only receive a return of investment if funds exist to pay them in a liquidation (which is usually unlikely).

     D   Company law is designed to protect payables.

3   (a)   Non-current asset   (e)   Capital
     (b)   Liability   (f)   Current asset
     (c)   Liability   (g)   Current asset
     (d)   Capital   (h)   Drawings

4   D   Correct.
     A   This is correct, but it is usual to subdivide liabilities between 'capital' and other liabilities.
     B   Incorrect.
     C   Incorrect, assets less liabilities = net assets = capital.

5   B   Correct.
     A   Borrowings are liabilities of a business, not capital.
     C   Capital will equal net assets employed at a point in time.
     D   Loan capital could be provided – so this definition is not precise.

6   A   Correct.
     B   This is retained profit rather than the profit **earned**.
     C   Capital includes the original investment plus retained profit
     D   This is another way of arriving at capital

Now try the questions below from the Question Bank

Question numbers	Page
5–7	395

An introduction to
final accounts

Introduction

In Chapter 2 you met the accounting equation and the balance sheet. You also have some idea of what is meant by the income statement.

A **balance sheet** shows the liabilities, capital and assets of a business at a given moment in time. It is like a 'snapshot', since it captures a still image of something which is continually changing. Typically, a balance sheet is prepared to show the position at the end of the accounting period.

Only the basic details of a balance sheet are described in this chapter. We will add more detail in later chapters, as we look at other ideas and accounting methods.

The **income statement** matches the revenue earned in a period with the costs incurred in earning it. It is usual to distinguish between a **gross profit** (sales revenue less the cost of goods sold) and a **net profit** (the gross profit less the expenses of selling, distribution, administration etc).

There is a fair amount to learn before you will be able to prepare these statements yourself. It is important to introduce the financial statements now so you can see the final result. Keep them in mind as you tackle the basics of ledger accounting in the next few chapters.

If you buy an asset which you can use in the business over the next twenty years, it would be misleading to charge all the expenses in the first year. This is the principle behind the important distinction between **capital and revenue expenditure** which is explored in Section 3 of the chapter.

Topic list	Syllabus references
1 The balance sheet	A (2), (6)
2 The income statement	A (2), (6)
3 Capital and revenue expenditure	A (2)

1 The balance sheet

A balance sheet is a statement of the assets and liabilities of a business at a point in time.

1.1 Presentation of assets and liabilities

A balance sheet can be presented in two ways.

- Assets in one half and capital and liabilities in the other
- Net assets in one half and capital in the other

An illustrated balance sheet

(a)   NAME OF BUSINESS
      BALANCE SHEET AS AT (DATE)

	$
Assets (item by item)	X
	X
	X

	$
Capital	X
Liabilities (item by item)	X
	X

(b)   NAME OF BUSINESS
      BALANCE SHEET AS AT (DATE)

	$
Assets	X
Less liabilities	X
Net assets	X
Capital	X

Method (a) is the format preferred under International Financial Reporting Standards, while method (b) is the usual format under UK Standards. This Study Text generally uses method (a).

In either format, the total value in one half of the balance sheet will equal the total value in the other half. You should understand this from the accounting equation.

Capital, liabilities and assets are usually shown in more detail in a balance sheet. The following paragraphs give examples of this.

1.2 Capital (sole trader)

Capital is what the business owes to the owner.

The proprietor's capital can be analysed into difference sources.

	$	$
Capital as at the beginning of the accounting period (ie capital 'brought forward')		X
Add additional capital introduced during the period		X
		X
Add profit earned during the period	X	
Less drawings	(X)	
Retained profit for the period		X
Capital as at the end of the accounting period (ie capital 'carried forward')		X

'**Brought forward**' means 'brought forward from the previous period', and '**carried forward**' means 'carried forward to the next period'. The carried forward amount at the end of one period is also the brought forward amount of the next period. The word 'down' is sometimes used instead of 'forward'.

The figure for retained profit is sometimes referred to as a **return on the owner's investment**, in the sense that a return is a reward for investment in a business.

1.3 Liabilities

Liabilities are what the business owes to third parties. They represent the business's obligation to transfer economic benefits to a third party.

The various liabilities are detailed separately. A distinction is made between current liabilities and long-term liabilities.

1.4 Current liabilities

Key term

Current liabilities are debts of the business that must be paid within a fairly short period of time. By convention, a 'fairly short period of time' is taken as one year.

In the accounts of UK limited liability companies, the CA 2006 requires the use of the term 'creditors: amounts falling due within one year' rather than 'current liabilities'. However, International Financial Reporting Standards (IFRSs) use the term 'current liabilities'.

Examples of current liabilities

- Loans repayable within one year
- Bank overdraft (repayable on demand, in theory)
- Trade payables (suppliers to whom the business owes money)
- Taxation payable
- Accrued expenses (eg gas used between the date of the last bill and the end of the accounting period for which a bill has not yet been received)

Accrued expenses will be described more fully in a later chapter.

1.5 Non-current liabilities

Key term

A **non-current liability** is a debt which is not payable within the 'short term' and so any liability which is not current must be long-term.

By convention 'non-current' means more than one year. In UK limited liability company accounts, the CA 2006 requires use of the term: 'Creditors: amounts falling due after more than one year', but IFRSs use 'non-current liabilities'.

Examples of non-current liabilities

(a) **Loans** which are not repayable for more than one year, such as a bank loan or a loan from an individual.

(b) A **mortgage loan**, which is secured against a property. The lender then has 'first claim' on the property and can force its sale if the business fails to repay the loan.

(c) **Loan notes**, which are securities issued by a limited liability company at a fixed rate of interest. They are repayable on agreed terms by a specified date in the future. The holders' interests, including security for the loan, are protected by the terms of a trust deed.

1.6 Assets

> **FAST FORWARD**
>
> Assets are what the business owns. They can be non-current assets or current assets.

Assets in the balance sheet are divided into two groups.

(a) Non-current assets

- Tangible non-current assets (usually known as 'property, plant and equipment')
- Intangible non-current assets
- Investments (long term)

(b) Current assets

1.7 Non-current assets

> **FAST FORWARD**
>
> A **non-current asset** is an asset acquired for continuing use within the business, with a view to earning income or making profits from its use, either directly or indirectly.

A non-current asset is not acquired for sale to a customer.

(a) In manufacturing, a production machine is a non-current asset as it makes goods for sale.

(b) In a service industry, equipment used by employees giving service to customers is a non-current asset (eg the equipment used in a garage, furniture in a hotel).

(c) Factory premises, office furniture, computer equipment, company cars, delivery vans or pallets in a warehouse are all non-current assets.

In addition the asset must have a 'life' in use of more than one year (strictly, more than one 'accounting period' which might be less than one year).

> **Key term**
>
> A **tangible non-current asset** is a physical asset, ie one that can be touched. It has a real, 'solid' existence.

All the examples mentioned above are tangible non-current assets.

> **Key term**
>
> An **intangible non-current asset** is an asset which does not have a physical existence. It cannot be 'touched'.

Examples of 'intangible non-current assets' are goodwill and research and development costs. Goodwill arises when a business a business is sold. It represents the excess of the purchase price paid over the fair value of the net assets. Research and development costs (R&D) are incurred in developing new products, for example. If R&D costs meet certain conditions, they can be capitalised until the product goes into production. You do not need to know anything more about intangible non-current assets at this stage of your studies.

An **investment** can be a non-current asset. Investments are commonly found in the published accounts of large limited liability companies. Company A might invest in another company B, by purchasing some of its shares. These shares would earn income for A in the form of dividends paid out by B. If the investments are purchased by A with a view of holding them for more than one year, they would be non-current assets of A.

1.8 Non-current assets and depreciation

ST FORWARD

Depreciation is a means of spreading the cost of a non-current asset over its useful life. Non-current assets are normally valued at cost less depreciation.

Non-current assets can be held and used by a business for a number of years, but they wear out or lose their usefulness over time. Every tangible non-current asset has a limited life. (The only exception is land held freehold or on a very long leasehold.)

The accounts of a business try to recognise that the cost of a non-current asset is gradually used up with time. This is done by writing off the asset's cost in the income statement over several accounting periods. For example, a machine costs $1,000 and is expected to wear out after ten years. Therefore, we can write off the cost by $100 each year. This process is known as **depreciation**. We will look at depreciation in detail later in this text.

1.9 Current assets

Key term

Current assets are either:

(a)   items owned by the business with the intention of turning them into cash within one year; or

(b)   cash, including money in the bank, owned by the business.

These assets are 'current' because they are continually flowing through the business. For example, a trader, David Wickes, runs a business selling motor cars and purchases a showroom, which he stocks with cars for sale.

(a)   If he sells a car in a cash sale, the goods are immediately converted into cash.

(b)   If he sells a car in a credit sale, the car will be given to the customer who becomes a receivable of the business. Eventually, the receivable will pay what he owes in cash.

The transactions described above could be shown as a cash cycle.

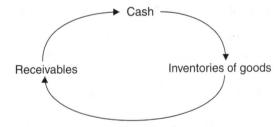

Cash is used to buy goods which are sold. Sales on credit create receivables, but eventually cash is received. Some, perhaps most, of the cash is then used to replenish inventories.

1.10 Main items of current assets

- Inventory
- Receivables
- Cash

ssessment focus point

It is important to realise that cars are current assets of David Wickes because he is a car trader. If he also has a car which he keeps and uses on business, this particular car would be a non-current asset. The difference between a non-current and a current asset is the purpose for which it is used in the business.

Question

A motor trader has a van for sale. How will this be shown in the accounts?

A   Non-current asset
B   Current asset
C   Non-current liability
D   Current liability

Answer

B   Current asset as it is part of the inventory for sale.

1.11 Some other categories of current assets

(a)   **Short-term investments**. These are stocks and shares of other businesses held with the intention of selling them in the near future, eg shares in Marks and Spencer, ICI or GEC. The shares will be sold when the business needs the cash again. If share prices rise in the meantime, the business will make a profit.

(b)   **Prepayments**. These are amounts already paid by the business for benefits which will be enjoyed within the next accounting period. A business pays an annual insurance premium of $240 to insure its premises against fire and theft. The premium is payable annually in advance on 1 December. If the business has an accounting year end of 31 December, it will only enjoy one month's insurance cover by the end of the year. The remaining 11 months' cover ($220) will be enjoyed in the next year. The prepayment of $220 is shown in the balance sheet at 31 December as a current asset.

A prepayment can be thought of as a form of receivable. At 31 December, the insurance company still owes the business 11 months' worth of insurance cover.

1.12 Trade receivables and other receivables

Although it is convenient to think of receivables as customers who buy goods on credit, it is more accurate to say that a receivable is anyone who owes the business money.

A distinction can be made between two groups of receivables.

(a)   Trade receivables, ie customers who still owe money for goods or services bought on credit in the course of the trading activities of the business.

(b)   Other receivables, ie anyone else owing money to the business (including prepayments).

Question

Categorise the following as tangible non-current assets, intangible non-current assets, investments, current assets, current liabilities or non-current liabilities.

(a)   Shares in BP, intended to be held long term
(b)   Machinery used in production
(c)   Goods for resale
(d)   An overdraft
(e)   A mortgage
(f)   Trade payables
(g)   Trade receivables
(h)   Goodwill
(i)   Prepayments
(j)   Accrued expenses

Answer

(a)   Investments
(b)   Tangible non-current assets
(c)   Current assets
(d)   Current liabilities
(e)   Non-current liabilities
(f)   Current liabilities
(g)   Current assets
(h)   Intangible non-current assets
(i)   Current assets
(j)   Current liabilities

1.13 Example: balance sheet preparation

You might like to attempt to prepare a balance sheet yourself before reading the solution.

Prepare a balance sheet for the Ted Hills Hardware Store as at 31 December 20X6, given the information below.

	$
Capital as at 1 January 20X6	47,600
Profit for the year to 31 December 20X6	8,000
Freehold premises, net book value at 31 December 20X6	50,000
Motor vehicles, net book value at 31 December 20X6	9,000
Fixtures and fittings, net book value at 31 December 20X6	8,000
Long-term loan (mortgage)	25,000
Bank overdraft*	2,000
Goods held in inventory for resale	16,000
Receivables	500
Cash in hand*	100
Payables	1,200
Taxation payable	3,500
Drawings	4,000
Accrued costs of rent	600
Prepayment of insurance	300

* A shop might have cash in its cash registers, but an overdraft at the bank.

Solution

TED HILLS
BALANCE SHEET
AS AT 31 DECEMBER 20X6

	$	$
Non-current assets at net book value		
Freehold premises		50,000
Fixtures and fittings		8,000
Motor vehicles		9,000
		67,000
Current assets		
Inventory	16,000	
Receivables	500	
Prepayment	300	
Cash	100	
		16,900
		83,900
Capital		
Capital as at 1 January 20X6		47,600
Profit for the year		8,000
		55,600
Less drawings		(4,000)
Capital as at 31 December 20X6		51,600
Non-current liabilities		
Loan		25,000
Current liabilities		
Bank overdraft	2,000	
Payables	1,200	
Taxation payable	3,500	
Accrued costs	600	
		7,300
		83,900

Question

Prepare the balance sheet for Abbax as at 31 December 20X4 from the information below.

	$
Freehold premises	80,000
Inventory	2,500
Payables	4,000
Profit for the year to 31.12.X4	6,600
Capital introduced in the year to 31.12.X4	5,000
Receivables	3,000
Furniture	27,000
Accruals	500
Drawings in the year to 31.12.X4	3,000
Prepayments	1,000
Delivery vans	15,000
Cash at bank	4,600
Mortgage	70,000
Capital brought forward at 1.1.X4	50,000

Answer

	$	$
Non-current assets at net book value		
Freehold premises		80,000
Furniture		27,000
Delivery vans		15,000
		122,000
Current assets		
Inventory	2,500	
Receivables	3,000	
Prepayments	1,000	
Cash	4,600	
		11,100
		133,100
Capital		
Capital brought forward at 1.1.X4		50,000
Capital introduced in the year		5,000
		55,000
Profit for the year		6,600
		61,600
Less: drawings		3,000
Capital carried forward at 31.12.X4		58,600
Non-current liabilities		
Mortgage		70,000
Current liabilities		
Payables	4,000	
Accruals	500	
		4,500
		133,100

1.14 The order of items in the balance sheet

The balance sheet format most commonly used is the vertical format. The following versions exist.

- (a)   Net assets above and capital below
- (b)   Non-current assets and net current assets above, with capital and non-current liabilities below
- (c)   Assets above with capital and liabilities below (as in the example above)
- (d)   Capital and liabilities above, with assets below

There is no general rule about which version of a vertical balance sheet should be used. However CA 2006 requires (a) to be used for the published accounts of most limited liability companies in the UK and IFRSs use format (c). We will be using format (c) in this Study Text.

1.15 Order of items within categories

By convention, a balance sheet lists assets and liabilities in a particular order.

- (a)   **Non-current assets** are listed in a descending order of '**length of useful life'**. Property has a longer life than fixtures and fittings, which usually have a longer life than motor vehicles. This is why the non-current assets in the example above are listed in that order.

- (b)   **Current assets** are listed in descending order of **the length of time it might be before the asset will be converted into cash**. Broadly speaking, inventory will convert into receivables, and receivables will convert into cash. So inventory, receivables and cash will be listed in that order. Prepayments, because they are similar to receivables, should be listed after receivables and before cash.

- (c)   **Current liabilities** are listed in the descending order in which payment is due. Since bank overdrafts are strictly repayable on demand, they are listed first. Then come payables and accruals. In the above example 'Taxation payable' is separately listed after payables, as it is a specific type of payable.

1.16 Working capital, or net current assets

FAST FORWARD

The **working capital** of a business is the difference between its current assets and current liabilities, ie net current assets.

In the balance sheet above, the Ted Hills Hardware Store has net current assets of $(16,900 − 7,300) = $9,600.

2 The income statement

Key term

The **income statement** is a statement showing in detail how the profit (or loss) of a period has been made.

The owners and managers of a business want to know how much profit or loss has been made, but there is only limited information value in the figure for profit shown in a balance sheet.

In order to exercise financial control effectively, managers need to know how much income has been earned, what costs have been incurred and whether the performance of sales or the control of costs appears to be satisfactory. This is the basic reason for preparing the income statement.

2.1 The gross profit

Key term

> **Gross profit** is the difference between the value of sales (excluding value added tax) and the cost of the goods sold

In a retail business, the cost of the goods sold is their purchase cost from the suppliers. In a manufacturing business, the cost of goods sold is the cost of raw materials plus the cost of the labour required to make the goods, and often plus an amount of production 'overhead' costs.

2.2 Net profit

Key term

> **Net profit** can be illustrated by the formula below.
>
> | Net profit | = | Gross profit | + | Income from other sources | − | Other business expenses |

2.3 Detail in the income statement

Examples of income from other sources

- Dividends or interest received from investments
- Profits on the sale of non-current assets
- Rental income
- Discounts received from suppliers

Examples of other business expenses

(a) **Selling and distribution expenses**. These are expenses associated with the process of selling and delivering goods to customers.

- Salaries of the sales director and sales management
- Salaries and commissions of salesmen
- Travelling and entertainment expenses of salesmen
- Marketing costs (eg advertising and sales promotion expenses)
- Costs of running and maintaining delivery vans
- Discounts allowed to customers (eg 5% discount for cash)
- Bad debts written off (ie when a customer does not pay all they owe)

Discounts and bad debts are described in more detail in later chapters.

(b) **Administration expenses**. These are the expenses of providing management and administration for the business.

- Salaries of directors, management and office staff
- Rent
- Insurance
- Telephone and postage
- Printing and stationery
- Heating and lighting

(c) **Finance expenses**.

- Interest on a loan
- Bank overdraft interest

You should try to group items of expenses (as shown above), but this will be dealt with in more detail in later chapters.

2.4 Example: income statement

On 1 June 20X5, Beppe de Marco commenced trading as an ice cream salesman.

(a)   He rented a van at a cost of $1,000 for three months. Running expenses for the van averaged $300 per month.

(b)   He hired a part time helper at a cost of $100 per month.

(c)   He borrowed $2,000 from his bank and the interest cost of the loan was $25 per month.

(d)   His main business was selling ice cream from the van, but he also did some special catering supplying ice creams for office parties. Sales to these customers were usually on credit.

(e)   For the three months to 31 August 20X5, his total sales were $10,000 (cash $8,900, credit $1,100).

(f)   He purchased his ice cream from a local manufacturer, Palmer Co. The cost of purchases in the three months to 31 August 20X5 was $6,200 and at 31 August he had sold every item of stock. He still owed $700 to Palmer Co for purchases on credit.

(g)   One of his credit sale customers has gone bankrupt, owing Beppe $250. Beppe has decided to write off the debt in full.

(h)   He used his own home for his office work. Telephone and postage expenses for the three months to 31 August were $150.

(i)   During the period he paid himself $300 per month.

Required

Prepare an income statement for the three months 1 June to 31 August 20X5.

Solution

BEPPE DE MARCO
INCOME STATEMENT
FOR THE THREE MONTHS ENDED 31 AUGUST 20X5

	$	$
Sales		10,000
Less cost of sales		6,200
Gross profit		3,800
Wages (3 × $100)	300	
Van rental	1,000	
Van expenses (3 × $300)	900	
Bad debt written off	250	
Telephone and postage	150	
Interest charges (3 × $25)	75	
		2,675
Net profit (transferred to the balance sheet)		1,125

Note: The cost of sales is $6,200 even though $700 of the costs have not yet been paid. This will be reflected in the balance sheet as a payable. The amount of $300 per month that Beppe paid to himself are drawings and so will be taken to the capital section of the balance sheet.

Question

On 1 January 20X2, Fred started a dress shop.

(a)   He rented a shop at $200 per month and spent $10,000 on fixtures and fittings.
(b)   He employed a shop assistant at $1,000 a month.
(c)   He bought dresses on credit for $38,000.
(d)   He sold three quarters of his inventory for $50,000.
(e)   He estimates he has used $2,000 worth of electricity (he has so far received bills for January–September for $1,400).
(f)   Fred estimates that his fixtures and fittings will last 10 years.

Required

Prepare an income statement for the year to 31 December 20X2.

Answer

FRED
INCOME STATEMENT
FOR THE YEAR TO 31 DECEMBER 20X2

	$	$
Sales		50,000
Less cost of sales (¾ × $38,000)		(28,500)
Gross profit		21,500
Rent ($200 × 12)	2,400	
Depreciation ($10,000 ÷ 10)	1,000	
Wages	12,000	
Electricity	2,000	
		17,400
Net profit		4,100

3 Capital and revenue expenditure

ST FORWARD

Capital expenditure is expenditure which results in the acquisition of non-current assets, or an improvement in their earning capacity.

Revenue expenditure is expenditure which is incurred for the purpose of the **trade** of the business or to maintain the existing earning capacity of non-current assets.

3.1 Revenue expenditure

Revenue expenditure is charged to the income statement. For example, a business buys ten widgets for $200 ($20 each) and sells eight of them during an accounting period. It will have two widgets left in inventory at the end of the period. The full $200 is revenue expenditure, but only $160 is a cost of goods sold during the period. The remaining $40 will be included in the balance sheet in inventory – ie as a **current asset** valued at $40.

3.2 Capital expenditure

A business purchases a building for $30,000. It then adds an extension to the building at a cost of $10,000. The building needs to have a few broken windows mended, its floors polished and some missing roof tiles replaced. These cleaning and maintenance jobs cost $900.

The original purchase ($30,000) and the cost of the extension ($10,000) are capital expenditure, because they are incurred to acquire and then improve a non-current asset. The other costs of $900 are revenue expenditure, because these merely maintain the building and so its 'earning capacity'. The $40,000 will appear as non-current assets in the balance sheet, while the $900 will be shown as an expense in the income statement.

3.3 Capital income and revenue income

Capital income is the proceeds from the sale of non-current assets, including non-current asset investments. The profits (or losses) from the sale of non-current assets are included in the income statement for the accounting period in which the sale takes place.

Revenue income comes from the following sources.

- Sale of trading assets
- Interest and dividends received from investments held by the business

3.4 Capital transactions

The above items do not include raising additional capital from the owner(s) of the business, or raising and repaying loans. These transactions add to the cash assets of the business, thereby creating a corresponding increase in capital or loan. When a loan is repaid, it reduces the liabilities (loan) and the assets (cash) of the business.

None of these transactions would be reported through the income statement.

3.5 Why is the distinction between capital and revenue items important?

Assessment focus point

Since revenue items and capital items are accounted for in different ways, the correct calculation of profit for any accounting period depends on the correct classification of items as revenue or capital.

Question | Capital and revenue items

Classify each of the following items as 'capital' or 'revenue' expenditure or income.

(a) The purchase of leasehold premises.

(b) The annual depreciation of leasehold premises.

(c) Solicitors' fees in connection with the purchase of leasehold premises.

(d) The costs of adding extra storage capacity to a mainframe computer used by the business.

(e) Computer repairs and maintenance costs.

(f) Profit on the sale of an office building.

(g) Revenue from sales by credit card.

(h) The cost of new machinery.

(i) Customs duty charged on the machinery when imported into the country.

(j)   The 'carriage' costs of transporting the new machinery from the supplier's factory to the premises of the business purchasing the machinery.

(k)   The cost of installing the new machinery in the premises of the business.

(l)   The wages of the machine operators.

Answer

(a)   Capital expenditure.

(b)   Depreciation of a non-current asset is revenue expenditure.

(c)   The legal fees associated with the purchase of a property may be added to the purchase price and classified as capital expenditure.

(d)   Capital expenditure (enhancing an existing non-current asset).

(e)   Revenue expenditure.

(f)   Capital income.

(g)   Revenue income (trading income).

(h)   Capital expenditure.

(i)   If customs duties are borne by the purchaser of the non-current asset, they may be added to the cost of the machinery and classified as capital expenditure.

(j)   Similarly, if carriage costs are paid for by the purchaser of the non-current asset, they may be included in the cost of the non-current asset and classified as capital expenditure.

(k)   Installation costs of a non-current asset are also added to the cost and classified as capital expenditure.

(l)   Revenue expenditure.

Chapter roundup

- A balance sheet shows the financial position of a business at a given moment in time.

- Capital is what the business owes to the owner.

- Liabilities are what the business owes to third parties. They represent the business's obligation to transfer economic benefits to a third party

- Assets are what the business owns. They can be non-current assets or current assets.

- Non-current assets are those acquired for continuing use within the business, with a view to earning income or making profits from its use, either directly or indirectly.

- Depreciation is a means of spreading the cost of a non-current asset over its useful life. Non-current assets are normally valued at cost less depreciation.

- The working capital of a business is the difference between its current assets and current liabilities, ie net current assets.

- Capital expenditure is expenditure which results in the acquisition of non-current assets or an improvement in their earning capacity.

- Revenue expenditure is incurred for the purpose of the trade of the business or to maintain the existing earning capacity of non-current assets.

Quick quiz

1   What is a balance sheet?

   A   A list of all the assets and liabilities of a business.
   B   A statement of the net worth of a business.
   C   A statement which shows how the net assets of a business have changed over time.
   D   A statement of the assets and liabilities of a business at a point in time in financial terms.

2   Fill in the blanks.

   _____ and _____ are examples of non-current liabilities.

3   Which of the following is *not* a current asset?

   A   Machinery
   B   Inventory
   C   Prepayments
   D   Receivables

4   Working capital is another term for net assets. True or false?

5   Gross profit is best described as?

   A   Sales less expenses
   B   Invoiced sales less purchases of inventory
   C   Net profit less business overheads
   D   Sales less cost of goods sold

6   Three sources of income other than the sale of goods which could appear in an income statement are:

   (i)   _____

   (ii)   _____

   (iii) _____

7   Four items which might be included in selling and distribution expenses are:

   (i)   _____

   (ii)   _____

   (iii) _____

   (iv)   _____

8   Which of the following explains the distinction between capital and revenue expenditure?

   A   Revenue expenditure is an expense in the income statement, capital expenditure is an asset in the balance sheet.

   B   Revenue expenditure is an expense in the income statement, capital expenditure is a liability in the balance sheet.

   C   Capital expenditure results in the acquisition or improvement of non-current assets, revenue expenditure is incurred for the purpose of trade or to maintain the earning capacity of non-current assets.

   D   Revenue expenditure results in the acquisition or improvement of non-current assets, capital expenditure is incurred for the purpose of trade or to maintain the earning capacity of non-current assets.

Answers to quick quiz

1   D   Correct, the balance sheet is only correct at a point in time.

     A   Incorrect; businesses have assets (and liabilities) which do not appear on the balance sheet (eg the skills of the employees).

     B   Incorrect because the balance sheet is not intended to represent the true values of the net assets.

     C   Incorrect, the income statement will reveal the extent to which profits (or losses) have increased (or decreased) net assets in the period.

2   Choose from: loans, mortgages, loan stock.

3   A   Correct. Machinery is an asset which will be consumed over its useful life in excess of one year.

     B, C and D are all current assets.

4   False. Working capital is another term for net **current** assets.

5   D   Correct; cost of goods sold will include certain overheads such as carriage costs of purchases.

6   Choose from:

     (i)   Profit on sale of non-current assets
     (ii)   Interest or dividends from investments
     (iii) Discounts received
     (iv)   Rental income

7   Choose from:

     (i)   Salaries, commission or expenses paid to sales personnel
     (ii)   Marketing costs
     (iii) Delivery van costs
     (iv)   Discounts allowed to customers
     (v)   Bad debts written off.

8   C   Correct. Capital expenditure buys or improves a non-current asset. Revenue expenditure maintains non-current assets or is incurred for the purpose of the trade.

     A   Incorrect. This does not *explain* the difference, merely describes their different treatment.

     B and D are incorrect as they are the reverse of the other statements

Now try the questions below from the Question Bank

Question numbers	Page
8–11	396

Part B

Accounting systems and accounts preparation

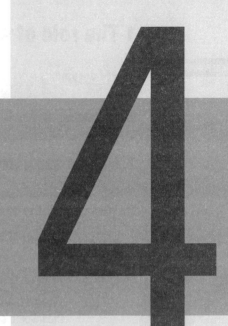

Sources, records and the books of prime entry

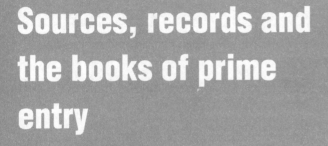

Introduction

From your studies of Part A you have grasped important points about the nature and purpose of accounting. You will realise that most organisations exist to make a profit for their owners, which they do by receiving money for goods and services provided. The role of the accounting system is to record these transactions and create information about them. You also understand the basic principles underlying the balance sheet and income statement and have an idea of what they look like.

We now turn our attention to how a business transaction works its way through to the financial statements.

It is usual to record a business transaction on a **document**. Such documents include invoices, orders, credit notes and goods received notes, all of which will be discussed in Section 1 of this chapter. In terms of the accounting system these are known as **source documents**. The information on them is processed by the system by, for example, aggregating (adding together) or classifying.

Records of source documents are kept in **'books of prime entry'**, which, as the name suggests, are the first stage at which a business transaction enters into the accounting system. The various types of books of prime entry are discussed in Sections 2 to 5.

To help enter documents in the records, it is useful to have a coding system. Section 6 deals with this.

In the next chapter we consider what happens to transactions after the books of prime entry stage.

Topic list	Syllabus references
1 The role of source documents	B (1)
2 Books of prime entry	B (1)
3 Sales and purchase day books	B (1), (4)
4 Sales and purchase return day books	B (1), (4)
5 Cash books	B (1), (3)
6 Coding systems	B (5)

1 The role of source documents

Source documents record business transactions. Examples are invoices, sales and purchase orders, wage slips, credit notes, goods received notes, till rolls etc. They are the source of all information for the financial statements.

Business transactions are sales or purchases, the paying or receiving of money or recognising that money is owed or owing.

1.1 Sales and purchase orders

A business will record its customer's requests for goods or services on a sales order. Purchase orders record a business's requests to its suppliers for goods or services.

1.2 Invoices

An **invoice** relates to a sales order or a purchase order.

(a) When a business sells goods or services on credit to a customer, it sends out an invoice. The details on the invoice should match up with the details on the sales order. The invoice is a request for the customer to pay what he owes.

(b) When a business buys goods or services on credit it receives an invoice from the supplier. The details on the invoice should match up with those on the purchase order.

The invoice is primarily a demand for payment, but it is used for other purposes as well. Since it has several uses, an invoice is often produced on multi-part stationery, or photocopied, or carbon-copied. The top copy will go to the customer and other copies will be used by various people within the business. The following information is usually shown on an invoice.

- Invoice number
- Name and address of the seller and the purchaser
- Date of the sale
- Reference number of the sales order (if applicable)
- Description of what is being sold
- Quantity and unit price of what has been sold (eg 20 pairs of shoes at $25 a pair)
- Details of trade discount, if any (eg 10% reduction in cost if buying over 100 items)
- Total amount of the invoice including (in the UK) any details of VAT
- Sometimes, the date by which payment is due and other terms of sale

1.3 Credit notes

A credit note reduces or cancels an invoice because the goods or services were not received or were rejected as substandard, or there was an error on the invoice. A credit note is sometimes printed in red to distinguish it from an invoice. Otherwise, it will be made out in much the same way as an invoice.

A **debit note** is issued to a supplier to formally request a credit note.

1.4 Goods received notes

Goods received notes (GRNs) record a receipt of goods, most commonly in a warehouse. Often, the accounts department will want to see the relevant GRN before paying a supplier's invoice. Even where GRNs are not routinely used, the details of a consignment from a supplier which arrives without an advice note must always be recorded.

Make sure you understand what a source document is as you may get a question listing a number of items and asking you to select the source document.

2 Books of prime entry

 ST FORWARD

Books of prime entry are used to list and summarise the information on source documents.

The books of prime entry are where all the documents received and issued are initially recorded. Each book of prime entry lists a different type of document. At the end of a period of time: a day, a week or a month, the list is totalled and the totals are then recorded in the **nominal ledger.** It is the nominal ledger which is summarised at the end of the accounting period in the balance sheet and the income statement.

ST FORWARD

The following are the main books of prime entry.

- Sales day book
- Purchase day book
- Sales returns day book
- Purchase returns day book
- Cash book
- Petty cash book
- Journal (described in the next chapter)

ssessment ocus point

For convenience, this chapter describes books of prime entry as if they are actual books. Books of prime entry are often not books at all, but rather files in the memory of a computer. However, the principles remain the same whether they are manual or computerised.

3 Sales and purchase day books

3.1 The sales day book

Key term

The **sales day book** lists all invoices sent out to customers.

An extract from a sales day book might look like this.

SALES DAY BOOK

Date 20X0	Invoice	Customer	Sales ledger ref	Total amount invoiced $
Jan 10	247	Jones & Co	SL14	105.00
	248	Smith Ltd	SL 8	86.40
	249	Alex & Co	SL 6	31.80
	250	Enor College	SL 9	1,264.60
				1,487.80

The column called 'sales ledger ref' is a reference to the sales ledger which is a record of what each customer owes the business. It means, for example, that the sale to Jones & Co for $105 is also recorded on page 14 of the sales ledger.

Most businesses 'analyse' their sales as it gives the managers of the business useful information which helps them to decide how best to run the business. For example, a business sells boots and shoes. The sale to Smith was entirely boots, the sale to Alex was entirely shoes and the other two sales were a mixture of both. Then the sales day book might look like this.

SALES DAY BOOK

Date 20X0	Invoice	Customer	Sales ledger ref	Total amount invoiced $	Boot sales $	Shoe sales $
Jan 10	247	Jones & Co	SL 14	105.00	60.00	45.00
	248	Smith Ltd	SL 8	86.40	86.40	
	249	Alex & Co	SL 6	31.80		31.80
	250	Enor College	SL 9	1,264.60	800.30	464.30
				1,487.80	946.70	541.10

3.2 The purchase day book

Key term

> The **purchase day book** lists all invoices received from suppliers.

An extract from a purchase day book might look like this.

PURCHASE DAY BOOK

Date 20X8	Supplier	Purchase ledger ref	Total amount invoiced $	Purchases $	Electricity etc $
Mar 15	Cook & Co	PL 31	315.00	315.00	
	W Butler	PL 46	29.40	29.40	
	EEB	PL 42	116.80		116.80
	Show Fair Ltd	PL 12	100.00	100.00	
			561.20	444.40	116.80

The 'purchase ledger reference' is a reference to the purchase ledger which is a record of what each supplier is owed.

There is no 'invoice number' column in this example, because the purchase day book records other people's invoices, which have all sorts of different numbers. However, some businesses might allocate their own sequential reference number to purchase invoices received.

The purchase day book analyses the invoices which have been received. In this example, three of the invoices related to goods which the business intends to re-sell (called simply 'purchases') and the other invoice was an electricity bill.

4 Sales and purchase returns day books

4.1 The sales returns day book

Key term

> The **sales returns day book** lists goods (or services) returned (or rejected) by customers for which credit notes are issued.

An extract from the sales returns day book might look like this.

SALES RETURNS DAY BOOK

Date 20X8	Customer and goods	Sales ledger ref	Amount $
30 April	Owen Plenty		
	3 pairs 'Texas' boots	SL 82	135.00

Some sales returns day books analyse what goods were returned; it makes sense to keep as complete a record as possible.

4.2 The purchase returns day book

Key term

The **purchase returns day book** lists goods (or services) returned to suppliers (or rejected) for which credit notes have been received or are expected.

An extract from the purchase returns day book might look like this.

PURCHASE RETURNS DAY BOOK

Date	Supplier and goods	Purchase ledger ref	Amount
20X8			$
29 April	Boxes Ltd		
	300 cardboard boxes	PL 123	46.60

Question
Invoice received

An invoice received from supplier is recorded in:

A   The sales day book
B   The purchase day book
C   The sales returns day book
D   The purchases returns day book

Answer

B is correct.

Question
Invoice sent out

An invoice sent to a customer is recorded in:

A   The sales day book
B   The purchases day book
C   The sales returns day book
D   The purchases returns day book

Answer

A is correct.

5 Cash books

> The **cash book** lists all money received into and paid out of the business **bank** account.

5.1 The cash book

The cash book records transactions involving the bank account, such as cheque payments, lodgements of cash and cheques into the bank account, standing orders, direct debits and bank charges.

Some cash, in notes and coins, is usually kept on the premises in order to make occasional payments for small items of expense. This cash is accounted for separately in a **petty cash book** (which we will look at shortly).

5.2 Example: cash book

At the beginning of 1 September, Robin Plenty had $900 in the bank.

During 1 September 20X7, Robin Plenty had the following receipts and payments.

(a)   Cash sale – receipt of $80
(b)   Payment from credit customer Hay $400 less discount allowed $20
(c)   Payment from credit customer Been $720
(d)   Payment from credit customer Seed $150 less discount allowed $10
(e)   Cheque received for cash to provide a short-term loan from Len Dinger $1,800
(f)   Second cash sale – receipts of $150
(g)   Cash received for sale of machine $200
(h)   Payment to supplier Kew $120
(i)   Payment to supplier Hare $310
(j)   Payment of telephone bill $400
(k)   Payment of gas bill $280
(l) $100 in cash withdrawn from bank for petty cash
(m)   Payment of $1,500 to Hess for new plant and machinery

Solution

The receipts part of the cash book for 1 September would look like this.

CASH BOOK (RECEIPTS)

Date	Narrative	Total
20X7		$
1 Sept	Balance b/d*	900
	Cash sale	80
	Receivable: Hay	380
	Receivable: Been	720
	Receivable: Seed	140
	Loan: Len Dinger	1,800
	Cash sale	150
	Sale of non-current asset	200
		4,370
2 Sept	Balance b/d*	1,660

* 'b/d' = brought down (ie brought forward)

The cash received in the day amounted to $3,470. Added to the $900 at the start of the day, this comes to $4,370. However this is not the amount to be carried forward to the next day. First we have to subtract all the payments made during 1 September.

The payments part of the cash book for 1 September would look like this.

CASH BOOK (PAYMENTS)

Date	Narrative	Total
20X7		$
1 Sept	Payable: Kew	120
	Payable: Hare	310
	Telephone	400
	Gas bill	280
	Petty cash	100
	Machinery purchase	1,500
	Balance c/d	1,660
		4,370

Payments during 1 September totalled $2,710. We know that the total of receipts was $4,370. That means that there is a balance of $4,370 – $2,710 = $1,660 to be 'carried down' to the start of the next day. As you can see this 'balance carried down' is noted at the end of the payments column, so that the receipts and payments totals show the same figure of $4,370 at the end of 1 September. And if you look to the receipts part of this example, you can see that $1,660 has been brought down ready for the next day.

It is usual to analyse the receipts and payments. With analysis columns completed, the cash book given in the examples above might look as follows.

CASH BOOK (RECEIPTS)

Date	Narrative	Total $	Receivables $	Cash sales $	Other $
20X7					
1 Sept	Balance b/d	900			
	Cash sale	80		80	
	Receivable – Hay	380	380		
	Receivable – Been	720	720		
	Receivable – Seed	140	140		
	Loan – Len Dinger	1,800			1,800
	Cash sale	150		150	
	Sale of fixed asset	200			200
		4,370	1,240	230	2,000

CASH BOOK (PAYMENTS)

Date	Narrative	Total $	Payables $	Petty cash $	Wages $	Other $
20X7						
1 Sept	Payable – Kew	120	120			
	Payable – Hare	310	310			
	Telephone	400				400
	Gas bill	280				280
	Petty cash	100		100		
	Machinery purchase	1,500				1,500
	Balance c/d	1,660				
		4,370	430	100	–	2,180

5.3 Bank statements

Weekly or monthly, a business will receive a **bank statement**. Bank statements are used to check that the balance shown in the cash book agrees with the amount on the bank statement. This agreement or **'reconciliation'** is the subject of a later chapter.

5.4 Petty cash book

Key term

The **petty cash book** lists all cash payments for small items, and occasional small receipts.

Most businesses keep a small amount of cash on the premises to make occasional small payments in cash – eg to pay the milkman, to buy a few postage stamps etc. This is often called the cash float or petty cash account. Petty cash can also be used for occasional small receipts, such as cash paid by a visitor to make a phone call or to take some photocopies.

There are usually more payments than receipts and petty cash must be 'topped up' with cash from the business bank account.

FAST FORWARD

Under what is called the **imprest system**, the amount of money in petty cash is kept at an agreed sum or 'float' (say $100). Expense items are recorded on vouchers as they occur.

	$
Cash still held in petty cash	X
Plus voucher payments	X
Must equal the agreed sum or float	X

The total float is made up regularly (to $100, or whatever the agreed sum is) by means of a cash payment from the bank account into petty cash. The amount paid into petty cash will be the total of the voucher payments since the previous top-up.

The format of a petty cash book is the same as for the cash book, with analysis columns for items of expenditure.

5.5 Summary of books of prime entry

FAST FORWARD

Business transactions are recorded on source documents which are listed and summarised in books of prime entry.

Question   Books of prime entry

State in which books of prime entry the following transactions would be entered.

(a)   Your business pays A Brown (a supplier) $450.00.
(b)   You send D Smith (a customer) an invoice for $650.
(c)   Your accounts manager asks you for $12 urgently in order to buy some envelopes.
(d)   You receive an invoice from A Brown for $300.
(e)   You pay D Smith $500.
(f)   F Jones (a customer) returns goods to the value of $250.
(g)   You return goods to J Green to the value of $504.
(h)   F Jones pays you $500.

Answer

(a)   Cash book
(b)   Sales day book
(c)   Petty cash book
(d)   Purchase day book
(e)   Cash book
(f)   Sales returns day book
(g)   Purchase returns day book
(h)   Cash book

6 Coding systems

T FORWARD

The coding system is the means by which data is entered into the accounting system.

Each account in an accounting system has a **unique code** used to identify the correct account for a posting (to be keyed into the computer if the system is computerised). If there are two suppliers called Jim Jones, you can only tell their accounts apart by a different code.

Coding also saves time in copying out data because **codes are shorter** than 'longhand' descriptions. For the same reason, and also to save storage space, computer systems make use of coded data.

6.1 Coding purchase invoices

In purchase accounting systems, the most obvious examples of codes are as follows.

- Supplier account numbers (to identify each individual supplier)

- Nominal ledger account numbers (which identify the accounts which record each category of purchases, such as goods, electricity etc)

- Inventory item codes (to identify each individual inventory line)

These are all codes a business sets up and applies internally. External codes which affect the business include **bank account numbers** and **bank sort codes**.

Various coding systems (or combinations of them) may be used when designing codes. The systems are described below.

6.2 Sequence codes

Sequence codes make no attempt to classify the item to be coded. It is simply given the next available number in a rising sequence. New items can only be inserted at the end of the list and therefore the codes for similar items may be very different. For example:

1 =   saucepans
2 =   kettles
3 =   pianos
4 =   dusters

Sequence codes are rarely used when a large number of items are involved, except for document numbering (eg invoice numbers).

6.3 Block codes

Block codes provide a different sequence for each different group of items. For example , suppliers may be divided up according to area.

North East	code numbers 10,000-19,999
North West	code numbers 20,000-29,999
Scotland	code numbers 30,000-39,999

The coding of supplier accounts is then sequential within each block.

6.4 Significant digit codes

Significant digit codes use some digits which are part of the description of the item being coded. An example is:

5000	Electric light bulbs
5025	25 watt
5040	40 watt
5060	60 watt
5100	100 watt

etc

6.5 Hierarchical codes

Hierarchical codes are allocated on the basis of a tree structure, where the relationship between items is of utmost importance. A well known example is the Universal Decimal Code used by most libraries. For example:

5	Business
5 2	Finance
5 2 1	Cost accounting
5 2 1.4	Standard costing
5 2 1.4 7	Variance analysis
5 2 1.4 7 3	Fixed overhead variances

6.6 Faceted codes

Faceted codes consist of a number of sections, each section of the code representing a different feature of the item. For example in a clothing store there might be a code based on the following facets.

Garment type	Customer type	Colour	Size	Style

If SU stood for suit, M for man and B for blue, a garment could be given the code SU M B 40 17. Similarly ND F W 14 23 could stand for a woman's white nightdress size 14, style 23. One of the great advantages of this system is that the type of item can be recognised from the code.

Faceted codes may be entirely numeric. For example, a large international company allocates code numbers for each suppliers' representative.

Digit 1	Continent (eg America – 1, Europe – 2)
Digits 2/3	Country (eg England – 06)
Digit 4	Area (eg North – 3)
Digits 5/6	Representative's name (eg Mr J Walker – 14)

The code number is then expressed as 2/06/3/14.

6.7 Coding in the nominal ledger

A nominal ledger will consist of a **large number of coded accounts**. For example, part of a nominal ledger might be as follows.

Account code	Account name
100200	Plant and machinery (cost)
100300	Motor vehicles (cost)
300000	Total receivables
400000	Total payables
500130	Wages and salaries
500140	Rent
500150	Advertising expenses
500160	Bank charges
500170	Motor expenses
500180	Telephone expenses
600000	Sales
700000	Cash

A business will, of course, choose its own codes for its nominal ledger accounts. The codes given in the above table are purely imaginary.

Question

Coding

State what type of code is being used in paragraph 6.7 above. Explain your answer.

Answer

This is a significant digit code. The digits are part of the description of the item being coded. So 100000 represents non-current assets and the '200' in 100200 represents plant and machinery, '300' motor vehicles, etc.

Question

Coding systems

An item is given the code 472.615. This is an example of what type of code?

A   Sequence code
B   Significant digit code
C   Block code
D   Hierarchical code

Answer

D   This is an example of a hierarchical code.

Chapter roundup

- **Source documents** record business transactions. Examples are invoices, sales and purchase orders, wage slips, credit notes, goods received notes, till rolls etc. They are the source of all information for the financial statements.

- **Business transactions** are sales or purchases, the paying or receiving of money or recognising that money is owed or owing.

- **Books of prime entry** are used to list and summarise the information on source documents.

  The following are the main books of prime entry.

  - Sales day book
  - Purchase day book
  - Sales returns day book
  - Purchase returns day book
  - Cash book
  - Petty cash book
  - Journal (described in the next chapter)

- The **cash book** lists all money received into and paid out of the business **bank** account.

- Under what is called the **imprest system**, the amount of money in petty cash is kept at an agreed sum or 'float' (say $100). Expense items are recorded on vouchers as they occur.

- Business transactions are recorded on source documents which are listed and summarised in books of prime entry.

- The coding system is the means by which data is entered into the accounting system.

Quick quiz

1   Five pieces of information normally shown on an invoice are:

(1) _____

(2) _____

(3) _____

(4) _____

(5) _____

2   A business issues a credit note. Where is this first recorded?

A   In the sales ledger
B   In the sales returns day book
C   In the sales day book
D   In the journal

3   The sales day book is:

A   A record of cash received from customers
B   A record of the balances on customers accounts
C   A record of invoices received
D   A record of credit sales made

4   The purchase day book is:

A   A record of cash paid to suppliers
B   A record of the balances on suppliers accounts
C   A record of invoices received from suppliers
D   A record of invoices sent to customers

5   Fill in the blanks.

The cash book records _____
_____ .

The petty cash book records _____
_____ .

6   On June there was $90 in the petty cash tin. By the end of June there were vouchers for $35 of expenses and $5 had been paid in (by a member of staff for some private phone calls). A cheque for $30 was cashed to 'top up' the petty cash. What is the imprest total?

A $30
B $40
C $60
D $90

Answers to quick quiz

1   Choose five from:

(1) Name and address of supplier and customer
(2) Details of goods purchased
(3) Details of any discount
(4) Date of the sale
(5) Total amount due

(6) Invoice number
(7) Reference number of sales order
(8) VAT details
(9) Sometimes, the payment terms

2   B   Correct

A   Incorrect, the ledgers are posted from day books

C   Incorrect, an invoice would be recorded in the sales day book.

D   Incorrect, the journal is used to make transfers or correct errors or to record transactions which do not go through another prime entry record

3   D   Correct
A   This would be recorded in the cash book
B   This would be referred to as the sales ledger
C   This would be the purchase day book

4   C   Correct
A   This would be recorded in the cash book
B   This would be referred to as the purchase ledger
D   This would be the sales day book

5   The cash book records money received into and paid out of the business bank account.

The petty cash book records minor items of expenditure (eg postage stamps) paid or received in cash.

6   D is correct (90 − 35 + 5 + 30 = 90). The imprest total is the balance to which the petty cash is restored at the end of each month.

Now try the question below from the Question Bank

Question number	Page
12	396

BPP
LEARNING MEDIA

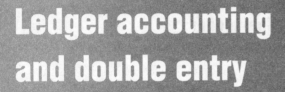

Ledger accounting
and double entry

Introduction

We have studied the theory of preparing accounts for a business. We have seen, by means of the accounting equation, that it is possible to prepare an income statement and a balance sheet on any date, relating to any period of time. A business is continually making transactions and we do not want to prepare accounts after every transaction. To do so is too time-consuming.

A business should keep a record of its transactions and, when the time comes to prepare the accounts, the relevant information can be taken from those records. The records of transactions, assets and liabilities should be in chronological order and dated so that transactions can be related to a particular period of time (eg daily, weekly, monthly, yearly).

We have already seen the first step in this process, which is to list all the transactions in various books of prime entry. Now we study the method used to summarise these records.

This chapter introduces **double entry bookkeeping**, the cornerstone of accounts preparation.

This is a very important topic and you must understand it before proceeding further in your studies.

Topic list	Syllabus references
1 The nominal ledger	B (6)
2 Double entry bookkeeping	B (2)
3 The journal	B (6)
4 Posting from day books to nominal ledger accounts	B (2)
5 The imprest system	B (3)
6 The sales and purchase ledger	B (4)

1 The nominal ledger

Key term

> The **nominal ledger** is an accounting record which summarises the financial affairs of a business. It contains accounts for each asset, liability, capital, income, expenditure and profit and loss.

The nominal ledger is sometimes called the **'general ledger'**. It consists of a large number of different accounts, each account having its own purpose or 'name' and an identity code.

FAST FORWARD

> The nominal ledger contains a separate account for each item which appears in a balance sheet or income statement.

1.1 Examples of accounts included in the nominal ledger

- Plant and machinery at cost (non-current asset)
- Motor vehicles at cost (non-current asset)
- Plant and machinery, provision for depreciation (liability)
- Motor vehicles, provision for depreciation (liability)
- Proprietor's capital (liability)
- Inventory – raw materials (current asset)
- Inventory – finished goods (current asset)
- Total receivables (current asset) often called sales ledger control account
- Total payables (current liability) often called purchase ledger control account
- Wages and salaries (expense item)
- Rent (expense item)
- Advertising expenses (expense item)
- Bank charges (expense item)
- Motor expenses (expense item)
- Telephone expenses (expense item)
- Sales (income)
- Total cash or bank overdraft (current asset or liability) often called cash control account
- Petty cash (current asset)

1.2 The format of a ledger account

If a ledger account is kept in an actual book, its format is as follows.

ADVERTISING EXPENSES

Date	Narrative	Ref	$	Date	Narrative	Ref	$
20X6							
15 April	JFK Agency for quarter to 31 March	PL 348	2,500				

Only one entry is shown here, as an example simply to illustrate the general format.

There are two sides to the account and a heading on top, so it is usually called a **'T' account.**

NAME OF ACCOUNT

DEBIT SIDE	$	CREDIT SIDE	$

2 Double entry bookkeeping

T FORWARD

The **double entry system of bookkeeping** means that for every debit there is an equal credit. This is sometimes referred to as the concept of **duality.**

Remember the **accounting equation** said that the total of liabilities plus capital is always equal to total assets, so any transaction which changes the amount of total assets must also change the total liabilities plus capital, and vice versa. Alternatively, a transaction may use up assets of a certain value to obtain other assets of the same value. For example, a business pays $50 for some goods. Its total assets will be unchanged, but the amount of cash falls by $50 and the value of inventory rises by $50.

2.1 Debits and credits

Ledger accounts, with their **debit** and **credit** sides, allow the two-sided nature of business transactions to be recorded. This system of accounting was first used in Venice in 1494 AD.

2.1.1 The rules of double entry bookkeeping

The basic rule is that every financial transaction gives rise to two accounting entries, one a debit and one a credit. The total value of debit entries in the nominal ledger is therefore always equal to the total value of credit entries. The meaning of the terms 'debit' and 'credit' are given below. It will be worth spending some time, at this point, committing them to memory.

Debit	**Credit**
• Increase in an expense (eg purchase of stationery)	• Increase in income (eg a sale)
• Increase in an asset (eg a purchase of office furniture	• Increase in a liability (eg obtaining a bank loan)
• Decrease in a liability (eg clearing a payable)	• Decrease in an asset (eg making a cash payment)

A good starting point is the cash account where receipts and payments of cash are recorded. The rule to remember about the cash account is as follows.

(a) A cash **payment** is a **credit** entry, because the cash **asset is decreasing**. Cash may be used to pay an expense (eg rent) or to purchase an asset (eg a machine). The matching debit entry is made in the appropriate expense or asset account.

(b) A cash **receipt** is a **debit** entry, because the cash **asset is increasing**. Cash is received by a retailer who makes a cash sale. The credit entry is then made in the sales account.

2.2 Example: double entry for cash transactions

A business has the following transactions.

(a) A cash sale (ie a receipt) of $200
(b) Payment of a rent bill totalling $150
(c) Buying some goods for cash at $100
(d) Buying some shelves for cash at $200

How would these four transactions be posted to the ledger accounts?

Solution

(a)   The two sides of the transaction are: cash is received (debit entry in the cash account) because the asset cash is increasing) and sales increase by $200 (credit entry in the sales account because sales income is increasing).

CASH ACCOUNT

	$		$
Sales a/c	200		

SALES ACCOUNT

	$		$
		Cash a/c	200

Note how the entry in the cash account is cross-referenced to the sales account and vice-versa. This enables a person looking at one of the accounts to trace where the other half of the double entry can be found.

(b)   The two sides of the transaction are: cash is paid (credit entry in the cash account because the asset cash is reduced) and rent expense increases by $150 (debit entry in the rent account because the expense is increasing).

CASH ACCOUNT

	$		$
		Rent a/c	150

RENT ACCOUNT

	$		$
Cash a/c	150		

(c)   The two sides of the transaction are: cash is paid (credit entry in the cash account because the asset cash is reduced) and purchases increase by $100 (debit entry in the purchases account because purchase expense is increasing).

CASH ACCOUNT

	$		$
		Purchases a/c	100

PURCHASES ACCOUNT

	$		$
Cash a/c	100		

(d)   The two sides of the transaction are: cash is paid (credit entry in the cash account because the asset cash is reduced) and assets increase by $200 (debit entry in shelves account because the non-current asset is increasing).

CASH ACCOUNT

	$		$
		Shelves a/c	200

SHELVES (ASSET) ACCOUNT

	$		$
Cash a/c	200		

The cash account of the business would end up looking as follows.

CASH ACCOUNT

	$		$
Sales a/c	200	Rent a/c	150
		Purchases a/c	100
		Shelves a/c	200

Question   **Posting transactions**

Show how these transactions would be recorded in the accounts in the nominal ledger.

The bank has a balance of $1,000.

(a) Buy goods for resale costing $100
(b) Sell goods for $150
(c) Pay electricity bill for $120
(d) Buy a delivery van for $600
(e) Buy petrol costing $10

Answer

CASH ACCOUNT

	$		$
Balance b/d	1,000	Purchases a/c (a)	100
Sales a/c (b)	150	Electricity expense a/c (c)	120
		Non-current asset van a/c (d)	600
		Motor expense a/c (e)	10

PURCHASES ACCOUNT

	$		$
Cash a/c (a)	100		

SALES ACCOUNT

	$		$
		Cash a/c (b)	150

ELECTRICITY EXPENSE ACCOUNT

	$		$
Cash a/c (c)	120		

NON-CURRENT ASSET VAN ACCOUNT

	$		$
Cash a/c (d)	600		

MOTOR EXPENSES ACCOUNT

	$		$
Cash a/c (e)	10		

2.3 Credit transactions

Cash transactions are settled immediately. Credit transactions give rise to receivables and payables.

Transactions that are settled immediately are known as cash transactions, even if paid by means of a cheque, as they usually are. However, not all transactions are settled immediately in cash. A business can purchase goods or non-current assets from its suppliers on credit terms. Equally, the business can grant credit terms to its customers. Clearly no entries can be made in the cash book when a credit transaction occurs, because no cash has been received or paid. The solution is to use receivables and payables accounts instead. A receivable is someone who owes money to the business. A payable is someone to whom the business owes money.

2.4 Example: credit transactions

Recorded in the sales day book and the purchase day book are the following transactions.

(a)   The business sells goods on credit to a customer Mr A for $2,000.
(b)   The business buys goods on credit from a supplier B Co for $100.

How and where are these transactions posted in the ledger accounts?

Solution

(a)

RECEIVABLES ACCOUNT

	$		$
Sales a/c	2,000		

SALES ACCOUNT

	$			$
			Receivables account	2,000

(b)

PAYABLES ACCOUNT

	$			$
			Purchases a/c	100

PURCHASES ACCOUNT

	$		$
Payables a/c	100		

2.5 When cash is paid to payables or by receivables

What happens when a credit transaction is eventually settled in cash?

Example continued

Suppose that, in the example above, the business paid $100 to B Co one month after the goods were acquired. The two sides of this new transaction are: cash is paid (credit entry in the cash account) and the amount owing to payables is reduced (debit entry in the payables account).

CASH ACCOUNT

	$		$
		Payables a/c (B Co)	100

PAYABLES ACCOUNT

	$		$
Cash a/c	100		

Bringing together the two parts of this example.

CASH ACCOUNT

	$		$
		Payables a/c	100

PURCHASES ACCOUNT

	$		$
Payables a/c	100		

PAYABLES ACCOUNT

	$		$
Cash a/c	100	Purchases a/c	100

The two entries in the payables account cancel each other out, indicating that no money is owing to payables any more. We are left with a credit entry of $100 in the cash account and a debit entry of $100 in the purchases account. These are exactly the entries which would have been made to record a **cash** purchase of $100 (compare example above). After the business has paid off its payables, it is in exactly the same position as if it had made cash purchases of $100.

Similar reasoning applies when a customer settles his debt. In the example above when Mr A pays his debt of $2,000 the two sides of the transaction are: cash is received (debit entry in the cash account) and the amount owed by receivables is reduced (credit entry in the receivables account).

CASH ACCOUNT

	$		$
Receivables a/c	2,000		

RECEIVABLES ACCOUNT

	$		$
		Cash a/c	2,000

The accounts recording this sale to, and payment by, Mr A now appear as follows.

CASH ACCOUNT

	$		$
Receivables a/c	2,000		

SALES ACCOUNT

	$		$
		Receivables a/c	2,000

RECEIVABLES ACCOUNT

	$		$
Sales a/c	2,000	Cash a/c	2,000

The two entries in the receivables account cancel each other out, while the entries in the cash account and sales account reflect the same position as if the sale had been made for cash.

Question

Debits and credits

List the debit and credit entries for the following transactions.

(a) Bought a machine on credit from A, cost $8,000.
(b) Bought goods on credit from B, cost $500.
(c) Sold goods on credit to C, value $1,200.
(d) Paid D (a payable) $300.
(e) Collected $180 from E, a receivable.
(f) Paid wages $4,000.
(g) Received rent bill of $700 from landlord G.
(h) Paid rent of $700 to landlord G.
(i) Paid insurance premium $90.

Answer

			$	$
(a)	DEBIT	Machine account (non-current asset)	8,000	
	CREDIT	Payables account (A)		8,000
(b)	DEBIT	Purchases account	500	
	CREDIT	Payables account (B)		500
(c)	DEBIT	Receivables account (C)	1,200	
	CREDIT	Sales account		1,200
(d)	DEBIT	Payables account (D)	300	
	CREDIT	Cash account		300
(e)	DEBIT	Cash account	180	
	CREDIT	Receivables account (E)		180
(f)	DEBIT	Wages account	4,000	
	CREDIT	Cash account		4,000
(g)	DEBIT	Rent account	700	
	CREDIT	Payables account (G)		700
(h)	DEBIT	Payables account (G)	700	
	CREDIT	Cash account		700
(i)	DEBIT	Insurance account	90	
	CREDIT	Cash account		90

Question

Record the ledger entries for the following transactions in appropriate ledger accounts. Ron Knuckle set up a business selling keep fit equipment. He put $7,000 of his own money into a business bank account (transaction A) and in his first period of trading, the following transactions occurred.

		$
Transaction		
B	Paid rent of shop for the period	3,500
C	Purchased equipment for resale on credit	5,000
D	Raised loan from bank	1,000
E	Purchased shop fittings (for cash)	2,000
F	Sales of equipment: cash	10,000
G	Sales of equipment: on credit	2,500
H	Payments to trade payables	5,000
I	Payments from receivables	2,500
J	Interest on loan (paid)	100
K	Administration expenses (all paid in cash)	1,900
L	Drawings	1,500

All keep fit equipment purchased during the period were sold and so there were no closing inventories.

Try to do as much of this exercise as possible yourself before reading the solution.

Answer

CASH ACCOUNT

	$		$
Capital – Ron Knuckle (A)	7,000	Rent (B)	3,500
Bank loan (D)	1,000	Shop fittings (E)	2,000
Sales (F)	10,000	Trade payables (H)	5,000
Receivables (I)	2,500	Bank loan interest (J)	100
		Other expenses (K)	1,900
		Drawings (L)	1,500
			14,000
		Balancing figure – the amount of cash left over after payments have been made	
			6,500
	20,500		20,500

CAPITAL (RON KNUCKLE) ACCOUNT

	$		$
		Cash (A)	7,000

BANK LOAN ACCOUNT

	$		$
		Cash (D)	1,000

PURCHASES ACCOUNT

	$		$
Trade payables (C)	5,000		

TRADE PAYABLES ACCOUNT

	$		$
Cash (H)	5,000	Purchases (C)	5,000

RENT EXPENSE ACCOUNT

	$		$
Cash (B)	3,500		

NON-CURRENT ASSETS (SHOP FITTINGS) ACCOUNT

	$		$
Cash (E)	2,000		

SALES ACCOUNT

	$		$
		Cash (F)	10,000
		Receivables (G)	2,500
			12,500

RECEIVABLES ACCOUNT

	$		$
Sales (G)	2,500	Cash (I)	2,500

BANK LOAN INTEREST ACCOUNT

	$		$
Cash (J)	100		

OTHER EXPENSES ACCOUNT

	$		$
Cash (K)	1,900		

DRAWINGS ACCOUNT

	$		$
Cash (L)	1,500		

If you want to make sure that this solution is complete, you should go through all the transactions ticking each off in the ledger accounts, once as a debit and once as a credit. When you have finished, all transactions in the 'T' account should be ticked, with only totals left over.

There is an easier way to check that the solution does 'balance' properly, which we will meet in the next chapter. It is called a trial balance.

**ssessment
ocus point**

Remember for every debit, there must be an equal and opposite credit.

3 The journal

As mentioned in the last chapter, one of the books of prime entry is the journal.

Key term

The **journal** is a record of unusual transactions. It is used to record any double entries made which do not arise from the other books of prime entry.

Whatever type of transaction is being recorded, the format of a journal entry is as follows.

Date	Debit $	Credit $
Account to be debited	X	
Account to be credited		X
(Narrative to explain the transaction)		

A narrative explanation must accompany each journal entry. It is required for audit and control, to indicate the purpose and authority of every transaction which is not first recorded in a book of prime entry.

3.1 Example: journal entries

The following is a summary of the transactions of 'Hair by Fiona Middleton'.

1 January	Put in cash of $2,000 as capital
	Purchased brushes and combs for cash $50
	Purchased hair driers from Gilroy Ltd on credit $150
30 January	Paid three months rent to 31 March $300
	Collected and paid-in takings $600
31 January	Gave Mrs Sullivan a perm, highlights etc on credit $80

Although these entries would normally go through the other books of prime entry (eg the cash book), it is good practice for you to show these transactions as journal entries.

Solution

JOURNAL

			$	$
1 January	DEBIT	Cash account	2,000	
	CREDIT	Fiona Middleton – capital account		2,000
	Initial capital introduced			
1 January	DEBIT	Brushes and combs (asset) account	50	
	CREDIT	Cash account		50
	The purchase for cash of brushes and combs as non-current assets			
1 January	DEBIT	Hair dryer asset account	150	
	CREDIT	Sundry payables account *		150
	The purchase on credit of hair driers as non-current assets			

				$	$
30 January	DEBIT	Rent expense account		300	
	CREDIT	Cash account			300
	The payment of rent to 31 March				
30 January	DEBIT	Cash account		600	
	CREDIT	Sales account			600
	Cash takings				
31 January	DEBIT	Receivables account		80	
	CREDIT	Sales account			80
	The provision of a hair-do on credit				

* *Note*. Payables who have supplied **non-current assets** are included amongst sundry payables. Payables who have supplied raw materials or goods for resale are **trade payables**. It is quite common to have separate payables accounts for trade and sundry payables.

> **Assessment focus point**
>
> As journal entries are a good test of your double entry skills, be prepared for assessment questions that ask how you would post a transaction and then give a selection of journal entries to choose from.

3.2 The correction of errors

FAST FORWARD

> The journal is commonly used to record **corrections** of **errors** that have been made in writing up the nominal ledger accounts.

There are several types of error which can occur. They are looked at in detail in a later chapter along with the way of using journal entries to correct them.

4 Posting from day books to nominal ledger accounts

FAST FORWARD

> Individual transactions are recorded in day books. Day book totals are recorded in double entry in the nominal ledger.

So far in this session we have made entries in nominal ledger accounts for each individual transaction, ie each source document has been recorded by a separate debit and credit. This means that every accounts department would need a lot of people who understand the double entry system, and that nominal ledger accounts would contain a huge number of entries. These two problems are avoided by using the books of prime entry or day books (remember these are lists of similar transactions). In practice, source documents are recorded in books of prime entry, and totals are posted from them to the nominal ledger accounts.

In the previous chapter, we used the following example of four transactions entered into the sales day book.

SALES DAY BOOK

Date 20X0	Invoice	Customer	Sales ledger refs	Total amount invoiced $	Boot sales $	Shoe sales $
Jan 10	247	Jones & Co	SL 14	105.00	60.00	45.00
	248	Smith Ltd	SL 8	86.40	86.40	
	249	Alex & Co	SL 6	31.80		31.80
	250	Enor College	SL 9	1,264.60	800.30	464.30
				1,487.80	946.70	541.10

This day book could be posted to the ledger accounts as follows.

DEBIT	Receivables account	$1,487.80	
CREDIT	Total sales account		$1,487.80

However a total sales account is not very informative. In our example, it is better to have a 'sale of shoes' account and a 'sale of boots' account.

		$	$
DEBIT	Receivables account	1,487.80	
CREDIT	Sale of shoes account		541.10
	Sale of boots account		946.70

This is why the sales are analysed in the day book. Exactly the same reasoning lies behind the analyses kept in other books of prime entry, so that we can record it in the nominal ledger.

Question   **Purchase day book**

The correct posting for the total column of the purchase day book is:

A   Debit payables account
     Credit purchases account

B   Debit purchases account
     Credit payables account

C   Debit receivables account
     Credit sales account

D   Debit sales account
     Credit receivables account

Answer

B is correct.

5 The imprest system

In the last chapter, we saw how the petty cash book was used to operate the **imprest** system for petty cash. It is now time to see how the double entry works in the imprest system.

5.1 Example: the imprest system

A business starts off a cash float on 1.3.20X7 with $250. This will be a payment from cash at bank to petty cash.

DEBIT	Petty cash	$250	
CREDIT	Cash at bank		$250

Five payments were made out of petty cash during March 20X7.

Receipts $	Date	Narrative	Total $	Payments Postage $	Travel $
250.00	1.3.X7	Cash			
	2.3.X7	Stamps	12.00	12.00	
	8.3.X7	Stamps	10.00	10.00	
	19.3.X7	Travel	16.00		16.00
	23.3.X7	Travel	5.00		5.00
	28.3.X7	Stamps	11.50	11.50	
250.00			54.50	33.50	21.00

At the end of each month (or at any other suitable interval) the total credits in the petty cash book are posted to ledger accounts. For March 20X7, $33.50 would be debited to postage account and $21.00 to travel account. The credit of $54.50 would be to the petty cash account. The cash float would need to be topped up by a payment of $54.50 from the main cash book.

			$	$
DEBIT	Petty cash		54.50	
CREDIT	Cash			54.50

The petty cash book for the month of March 20X7 will look like this.

Receipts $	Date	Narrative	Total $	Payments Postage $	Travel $
250.00	1.3.X7	Cash			
	2.3.X7	Stamps	12.00	12.00	
	8.3.X7	Stamps	10.00	10.00	
	19.3.X7	Travel	16.00		16.00
	23.3.X7	Travel	5.00		5.00
	28.3.X7	Stamps	11.50	11.50	
	31.3.X7	Balance c/d	195.50		
250.00			250.00	33.50	21.00
195.50	1.4.X7	Balance b/d			
54.50	1.4.X7	Cash			

The cash float is back up to $250 on 1.4.X7, ready for more payments to be made.

Question

A business has a petty cash imprest of $150. During a period, expenses are paid out totalling $86. What amount is needed to top up the imprest?

A $150

B $86

C $64

D $250

Answer

B $86 – the amount of the expenses for the period.

Question

The following is a summary of the petty cash transactions of Jockfield for May 20X2.

May	1	Received from cashier $300 as petty cash float	$
	2	Postage	18
	3	Travelling	12
	4	Cleaning	15
	7	Petrol for delivery van	22
	8	Travelling	25
	9	Stationery	17
	11	Cleaning	18
	14	Postage	5
	15	Travelling	8
	18	Stationery	9
		Cleaning	23
	20	Postage	13
	24	Delivery van 5,000 miles service	43
	26	Petrol	18
	27	Cleaning	21
	29	Postage	5
	30	Petrol	14

Required

(a)   Rule up a suitable petty cash book with analysis columns for expenditure on cleaning, motor expenses, postage, stationery and travelling.

(b)   Enter the month's transactions.

(c)   Enter the receipt of the amount necessary to restore the imprest and carry down the balance for the commencement of the following month.

(d)   State how the double entry for the expenditure is completed.

Answer

(a),(b),(c)   PETTY CASH BOOK

Receipts $	Date	Narrative	Total $	Postage $	Travelling $	Cleaning $	Stationery $	Motor $
300	May 1	Cash						
	May 2	Postage	18	18				
	May 3	Travelling	12		12			
	May 4	Cleaning	15			15		
	May 7	Petrol	22					22
	May 8	Travelling	25		25			
	May 9	Stationery	17				17	
	May 11	Cleaning	18			18		
	May 14	Postage	5	5				
	May 15	Travelling	8		8			
	May 18	Stationery	9				9	
	May 18	Cleaning	23			23		
	May 20	Postage	13	13				
	May 24	Van service	43					43
	May 26	Petrol	18					18
	May 27	Cleaning	21			21		
	May 29	Postage	5	5				
	May 30	Petrol	14					14
			286	41	45	77	26	97
286	May 31	Cash						
		Balance c/d	300					
586			586					
300	June 1	Balance b/d						

(d)   The analysis totals are posted to the relevant ledger accounts by double entry:

		$	$
DEBIT	Postage expense account	41	
DEBIT	Travelling expense account	45	
DEBIT	Cleaning expense account	77	
DEBIT	Stationery expense account	26	
DEBIT	Motor expense account	97	
CREDIT	Petty cash account		286

and

		$	$
* DEBIT	Petty cash account	286	
* CREDIT	Cash account		286

*Note that this final double entry to top up the imprest would normally be posted from the cash book payments rather than from the petty cash book.

6 The sales and purchase ledgers

FORWARD

Personal accounts are not part of the double entry system. They record how much is owed by a customer or to a supplier. They are **memorandum** accounts only.

6.1 Impersonal accounts and personal accounts

The accounts in the nominal ledger (ledger accounts) give figures for the balance sheet and income statement. They are called **impersonal** accounts. However, there is also a need for **personal** accounts (most commonly for receivables and payables) and these are contained in the sales ledger and purchase ledger.

6.2 The sales ledger (receivables ledger)

FORWARD

The **sales ledger** contains separate accounts for each credit customer so that, at any time, a business knows how much it is owed by each customer.

The **sales day book** provides a chronological record of invoices sent out by a business to credit customers. For many businesses, this can involve very large numbers of invoices per day or per week. The same customer can appear in several different places in the sales day book. So at any point in time, a customer may owe money on several unpaid invoices.

A business needs to keep a record of how much money each individual credit customer owes because:

(a) A customer might telephone and ask how much he currently owes.

(b) It provides the information needed for statements sent to credit customers at the end of each month.

(c) It assists the business in keeping a check on the credit position of each customer to ensure that he is not exceeding his credit limit.

(d) Most important is the need to match payments received against invoices. If a customer makes a payment, the business must set it off against the correct invoice.

Sales ledger accounts are written up in the following way.

(a) When entries are made in the sales day book (invoices sent out), they are recorded on the **debit side** of the relevant customer account in the sales ledger.

(b) Similarly, when entries are made in the cash book (payments received) or in the sales returns day book, they recorded on **credit side** of the customer account.

Each customer account is given a reference or code number, the 'sales ledger reference' in the **sales day book**.

6.3 Example: a sales ledger account

ENOR COLLEGE

A/c no: SL 9

	$		$
Balance b/f	250.00		
10.1.X0 Sales – SDB 48			
(invoice no 250)	1,264.60	Balance c/d	1,514.60
	1,514.60		1,514.60
11.1.X0 Balance b/d	1,514.60		

The debit side of this personal account shows amounts owed by Enor College. When Enor pays some of the money it owes it will be entered into the cash book (receipts) and subsequently entered in the credit side of the personal account. For example, if the college paid $250 on 10.1.20X0.

ENOR COLLEGE

A/c no: SL 9

		$				$
Balance b/f		250.00	10.1.X0	Cash		250.00
10.1.X0	Sales – SDB 48					
	(invoice no 250)	1,264.60	Balance c/d			1,264.60
		1,514.60				1,514.60
11.1.X0	Balance b/d	1,264.60				

6.4 The purchase ledger (payables ledger)

> The **purchase ledger** contains separate accounts for each credit supplier, so that, at any time a business knows how much it owes to each supplier.

The purchase ledger, like the sales ledger, consists of a number of personal accounts. These are separate accounts for each individual supplier and they enable a business to keep a check on how much it owes each supplier.

The purchase invoice is recorded in the purchases day book. Then the purchases day book is used to update accounts in the purchase ledger.

6.5 Example: purchase ledger account

COOK & CO

A/c no: PL 31

	$			$
Balance c/d	515.00	Balance b/f		200.00
		15 Mar 20X8		
		Invoice received		
		PDB 37		315.00
	515.00			515.00
		16 March 20X8		
		Balance b/d		515.00

The credit side of this personal account shows amounts owing to Cook & Co. If the business paid Cook & Co some money, it would be entered into the cash book (payments) and subsequently be posted to the debit side of the personal account. For example, if the business paid Cook & Co $100 on 15 March 20X8.

COOK & CO

A/c no: PL 31

		$			$
15.3.X8	Cash	100.00	15.3.X8	Balance b/f	200.00
			15.3.X8	Invoice received	
	Balance c/d	415.00		PDB 37	315.00
		515.00			515.00
			16.3.X8	Balance b/d	415.00

The roles of the sales day book and purchases day book are very similar, with one book dealing with invoices sent out and the other with invoices received. The sales ledger and purchase ledger also serve similar purposes, with one consisting of personal accounts for credit customers and the other consisting of personal accounts for credit suppliers.

Question	Sales and purchase ledger postings

At 1 May 20X3 amounts owing to Omega by his customers in respect of their April purchases were:

	$
Alpha	210
Beta	1,040
Gamma	1,286
Delta	279
Epsilon	823

The amounts owing by Omega to his suppliers at 1 May were:

	$
Zeta	2,173
Eta	187
Theta	318

Transactions made by Omega during May were listed in the day books as follows.

Sales day book

	$
Gamma	432
Epsilon	129
Beta	314
Epsilon	269
Alpha	88
Delta	417
Epsilon	228
	1,877

Purchase day book

	$
Eta	423
Zeta	268
Eta	741
	1,432

Sales returns day book

	$
Epsilon	88

Cash book payments

	$
Eta	187
Theta	318
Zeta	1,000
	1,505

Cash book receipts

	$
Beta	1,040
Delta	279
Gamma	826
Epsilon	823
	2,968

Required

(a) Open accounts for Omega's customers and suppliers and record therein the 1 May balances.

(b) Record the transactions in the appropriate personal account and nominal ledger accounts.

(c) Balance the personal accounts where necessary.

(d) Extract a list of receivables at 31 May.

Answer

SALES LEDGER

(a),(b),(c)   ALPHA

	$		$
Opening balance	210		
May sales	88	Balance c/d	298
	298		298

BETA

	$		$
Opening balance	1,040	Cash	1,040
May sales	314	Balance c/d	314
	1,354		1,354

GAMMA

	$		$
Opening balance	1,286	Cash	826
May sales	432	Balance c/d	892
	1,718		1,718

DELTA

	$		$
Opening balance	279	Cash	279
May sales	417	Balance c/d	417
	696		696

EPSILON

	$		$
Opening balance	823	Cash	823
May sales	129	Returns	88
May sales	269	Balance c/d	538
May sales	228		
	1,449		1,449

PURCHASES LEDGER

ZETA

	$		$
Cash	1,000	Opening balance	2,173
Balance c/d	1,441	May purchases	268
	2,441		2,441

ETA

	$		$
Cash	187	Opening balance	187
Balance c/d	1,164	May purchases	423
		May purchases	741
	1,351		1,351

THETA

	$		$
Cash	318	Opening balance	318

NOMINAL LEDGER

SALES ACCOUNT

	$		$
		May sales	1,877

PURCHASES ACCOUNT

	$		$
May purchases	1,432		

SALES RETURNS ACCOUNT

	$		$
May returns	88		

RECEIVABLES ACCOUNT

	$		$
Opening balance	3,638	May returns	88
May sales	1,877	May receipts	2,968
		Balance c/d	2,459
	5,515		5,515

PAYABLES ACCOUNT

	$		$
May payments	1,505	Opening balance	2,678
		May purchases	1,432

CASH ACCOUNT

	$		$
May receipts	2,968	May payments	1,505

(d)   RECEIVABLES AS AT 31 MAY

	May
	$
Alpha	298
Beta	314
Gamma	892
Delta	417
Epsilon	538
	2,459

Note. Compare the above total to the balance on the receivables account! We will return to this in Chapter 13 on control accounts. However you should not be surprised that the total of the individual customer accounts in the sales ledger agrees to the balance on the receivables account.

6.6 Summary

(a)   Business transactions are recorded on source documents.
(b)   Source documents are recorded in day books.
(c)   Totals of day books are recorded by double entry in nominal ledger accounts.
(d)   Single transactions are recorded from day books to individual customer and supplier accounts by single entry.
(e)   Customer accounts are in the sales ledger
(f)   Supplier accounts are in the purchase ledger
(g)   The sales and purchase ledger are not part of the double entry system
(h)   The nominal ledger contains one account for each item in the balance sheet and income statement.

Chapter roundup

- The nominal ledger contains a separate account for each item which appears in a balance sheet or income statement.

- The double entry system of bookkeeping means that for every debit there is an equal credit. This is sometimes referred to as the concept of duality.

- Cash transactions are settled immediately. Credit transactions give rise to receivables and payables.

- The journal is commonly used to record corrections of errors that have been made in writing up the nominal ledger accounts.

- Individual transactions are recorded in day books. Day book totals are recorded in double entry in the nominal ledger.

- Personal accounts are not part of the double entry system. They record how much is owed by a customer or to a supplier. They are memorandum accounts only.

- The sales ledger contains separate accounts for each credit customer so that, at any time, a business knows how much it is owed by each customer.

- The purchase ledger contains separate accounts for each credit supplier, so that, at any time a business knows how much it owes to each supplier.

Quick quiz

1   The suppliers personal accounts will appear in which of the following business records?

   A   The nominal ledger
   B   The sales ledger
   C   The purchase day book
   D   The purchase ledger

2   The double entry to record a cash sale of $50 is:

   DEBIT   _____ $50

   CREDIT   _____ $50

3   The double entry to record a purchase of office chairs for $1,000 is:

   DEBIT   _____ $1,000

   CREDIT   _____ $1,000

4   The double entry to record a credit sale is:

   DEBIT   _____

   CREDIT   _____

5   Which of these statements are correct?

   (i)   The purchase day book is part of a double entry system.
   (ii)   The purchase ledger is part of a double entry system.

   A   (i) only
   B   (i) and (ii)
   C   (ii) only
   D   Both are false

6   Personal accounts contain records of

   A   Receivables and payables
   B   Assets and liabilities
   C   Income and expenditure
   D   Transactions with the proprietor of the business

7   A credit sale of $2,000 would be recorded using which of the following journals?

   A   DEBIT sales $2,000
       CREDIT receivables $2,000

   B   DEBIT receivables $2,000
       CREDIT sales $2,000

   C   DEBIT sales ledger $2,000
       CREDIT sales $2,000

   D   DEBIT sales $2,000
       CREDIT sales ledger $2,000

Answers to quick quiz

1 D This is correct
   A This ledgers is used to record impersonal accounts.
   B Customers accounts are kept in the sales ledger.
   C This is simply a record of purchase invoices received.

2 DEBIT: CASH $50; CREDIT: SALES $50

3 DEBIT: NON-CURRENT ASSETS $1,000; CREDIT: CASH $1,000

4 DEBIT: RECEIVABLES; CREDIT: SALES

5 D is correct. The purchase day book is a book of prime entry, and the purchase ledger shows balances on suppliers accounts. Neither are part of the double entry in the nominal ledger.

6 A Correct.
   B These would be in the nominal ledger.
   C These would be in the nominal ledger.
   D These would be in either the nominal ledger or a 'private ledger' not accessible by accounting staff.

7 B Correct.
   A This is a reversal of the correct entries.
   C&D Remember that the sales ledger is not usually part of the double entry system.

Now try the questions below from the Question Bank

Question numbers	Page
13–19	396

BPP
LEARNING MEDIA

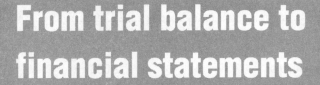

From trial balance to financial statements

Introduction

In the previous chapters you learned the principles of double entry and how to post to the ledger accounts. The next step in our progress towards the financial statements is the trial balance.

Before transferring the relevant balances at the year end to the income statement and putting closing balances carried forward into the balance sheet, it is usual to test the accuracy of the double entry bookkeeping records by preparing a trial balance. This is done by taking all the balances on every account. Due to the nature of double entry, the total of the debit balances will be exactly equal to the total of the credit balances.

In very straightforward circumstances, it is possible to prepare accounts directly from a trial balance. This is covered in Section 4.

Topic list	Syllabus references
1 The trial balance	B (7)
2 The income statement	D (6)
3 The balance sheet	D (6)
4 Balancing accounts and preparing financial statements	D (6)

BPP
LEARNING MEDIA

1 The trial balance

FAST FORWARD

A **trial balance** is a list of nominal ledger account balances. It is prepared to check that the total of debit balances is the same as the total of credit balances and offer reassurance that the double entry recording from day books has been done correctly.

1.1 Example: trial balance

Here are the accounts of Ron Knuckle from the last chapter.

CASH

	$		$
Capital – Ron Knuckle	7,000	Rent	3,500
Bank loan	1,000	Shop fittings	2,000
Sales	10,000	Trade payables	5,000
Receivables	2,500	Bank loan interest	100
		Incidental expenses	1,900
		Drawings	1,500
			14,000
		(Balancing figure – the amount of cash left over after payments have been made) Balance c/d	6,500
	20,500		20,500
Balance b/d	6,500		

CAPITAL (RON KNUCKLE)

	$		$
		Cash	7,000

BANK LOAN

	$		$
		Cash	1,000

PURCHASES

	$		$
Trade payables	5,000		

TRADE PAYABLES

	$		$
Cash	5,000	Purchases	5,000

RENT

	$		$
Cash	3,500		

SHOP FITTINGS

	$		$
Cash	2,000		

SALES

	$		$
		Cash	10,000
		Receivables	2,500
			12,500

RECEIVABLES

	$		$
Sales	2,500	Cash	2,500

BANK LOAN INTEREST

	$		$
Cash	100		

OTHER EXPENSES

	$		$
Cash	1,900		

DRAWINGS ACCOUNT

	$		$
Cash	1,500		

At the end of an accounting period, a balance is struck on each account in turn. This means that all the debits on the account are totalled and so are all the credits. If the total debits exceed the total credits there is said to be a debit balance on the account. If the credits exceed the debits, then the account has a credit balance.

In our example, there is very little balancing to do. Both the trade payables account and the receivables account balance off to zero. The cash account has a debit balance of $6,500 and the total on the sales account is $12,500, which is a credit balance. Otherwise, the accounts have only one entry each, so there is no totalling to do to arrive at the balance on each account.

If the basic principle of double entry has been correctly applied throughout the period, the credit balances equal the debit balances in total.

	Debit	Credit
	$	$
Cash	6,500	
Capital		7,000
Bank loan		1,000
Purchases	5,000	
Trade payables		–
Rent	3,500	
Shop fittings	2,000	
Sales		12,500
Receivables	–	–
Bank loan interest	100	
Other expenses	1,900	
Drawings	1,500	
	20,500	20,500

It does not matter in what order the various accounts are listed, because the trial balance is not a document that a business **has** to prepare. It is just a method used to test the accuracy of the double entry bookkeeping.

1.2 What if the trial balance shows unequal debit and credit balances?

If the two columns of the trial balance are not equal, there must be an error in recording the transaction. However, a trial balance will not disclose the following types of errors.

- Complete **omission** of a transaction, because neither a debit nor a credit is made. This is called an **error of omission**.

- Posting of a transaction to the wrong **account,** although the right type of account, is called an error of **commission** (eg a petrol purchase debited to heat and light expense account rather than motor expenses: both are revenue expense accounts).

- **Compensating** errors (eg an error of $100 is exactly cancelled by another $100 error elsewhere).

- Errors of **principle** occur when the wrong type of account has been used (eg the purchase of a motor van is debited to a revenue expense account, such as motor expenses, rather than a non-current asset account).

- Errors of **original entry**, when the wrong amount is debited and credited to the correct accounts.

We will look at errors in detail at a later date.

Question		Trial balance

As at 30.3.20X7, your business has the following balances on its ledger accounts.

Accounts	Balance
	$
Bank loan	12,000
Cash	11,700
Capital	13,000
Rent	1,880
Trade payables	11,200
Purchases	12,400
Sales	14,600
Sundry payables	1,620
Receivables	12,000
Bank loan interest	1,400
Other expenses	11,020
Vehicles	2,020

On 31.3.X7 the business made the following transactions.

(a) Bought materials for $1,000, half for cash and half on credit.
(b) Made $1,040 sales, $800 of which was for credit.
(c) Paid wages to shop assistants of $260 in cash.

Required

Draw up a trial balance showing the balances as at the end of 31.3.X7.

Answer

First you must put the original balances into a trial balance – ie decide which are debit and which are credit balances.

Account	Dr $	Cr $
Bank loan		12,000
Cash	11,700	
Capital		13,000
Rent	1,880	
Trade payables		11,200
Purchases	12,400	
Sales		14,600
Sundry payables		1,620
Receivables	12,000	
Bank loan interest	1,400	
Other expenses	11,020	
Vehicles	2,020	
	52,420	52,420

Now we must take account of the effects of the three transactions which took place on 31.3.X7.

			$	$
(a)	DEBIT	Purchases	1,000	
	CREDIT	Cash		500
		Trade payables		500
(b)	DEBIT	Cash	240	
		Receivables	800	
	CREDIT	Sales		1,040
(c)	DEBIT	Other expenses	260	
	CREDIT	Cash		260

When these figures are included in the trial balance, it becomes:

Account	Dr $	Cr $
Bank loan		12,000
Cash (11,700 – 500 + 240 – 260)	11,180	
Capital		13,000
Rent	1,880	
Trade payables (11,200 + 500)		11,700
Purchases (12,400 + 1,000)	13,400	
Sales (14,600 + 1,040)		15,640
Sundry payables		1,620
Receivables (12,000 + 800)	12,800	
Bank loan interest	1,400	
Other expenses (11,020 + 260)	11,280	
Vehicles	2,020	
	53,960	53,960

And it balances!

Assessment focus point	A trial balance is done prior to producing the financial statements. It provides reassurance that the double entry bookkeeping has been done correctly, but it does not reveal all possible errors.

2 The income statement

FAST FORWARD

An income statement ledger account is opened up to gather all items relating to income and expenses. When rearranged, the items make up the income statement for the financial statements.

2.1 The ledger account

The first step in preparing the financial statements is to open up another ledger account in the nominal ledger called the income statement. In it a business summarises its results for the period by gathering together all the ledger account balances relating to income and expenses. This account is still part of the double entry system, so the basic rule of double entry still applies: every debit must have an equal and opposite credit entry.

This income statement is not the financial statement we are aiming for, even though it has the same name. The difference between the two is not very great, because they contain the same information. However, the financial statement lays it out differently and may be much less detailed.

The first step is to look through the ledger accounts and identify which ones relate to income and expenses. In the case of Ron Knuckle, the income and expense accounts consist of purchases, rent, sales, bank loan interest, and other expenses.

The balances on these accounts are then transferred to the new income statement account. For example:

		$	$
Debit	Income statement account	5,000	
Credit	Purchases account		5,000

PURCHASES

	$		$
Trade payables	5,000	I/S a/c	5,000

RENT

	$		$
Cash	3,500	I/S a/c	3,500

SALES

	$		$
I/S a/c	12,500	Cash	10,000
		Receivables	2,500
	12,500		12,500

BANK LOAN INTEREST

	$		$
Cash	100	I/S a/c	100

BPP
LEARNING MEDIA

OTHER EXPENSES

	$			$
Cash	1,900	I/S a/c		1,900

INCOME STATEMENT ACCOUNT

	$		$
Purchases	5,000	Sales	12,500
Rent	3,500		
Bank loan interest	100		
Other expenses	1,900		

(Note that the income statement account is not yet balanced-off.)

2.2 The financial statement

The items we have gathered together in the income statement are the same items needed to draw up the income statement in the form of a financial statement. With a little rearrangement they could be presented as follows.

RON KNUCKLE
INCOME STATEMENT

	$	$
Sales		12,500
Cost of sales (= purchases in this case)		(5,000)
Gross profit		7,500
Expenses		
Rent	3,500	
Bank loan interest	100	
Other expenses	1,900	
		(5,500)
Net profit		2,000

3 The balance sheet

ST FORWARD

> The balances on all remaining ledger accounts (including the income statement account) can be listed and rearranged to form the balance sheet.

Look back at the ledger accounts of Ron Knuckle to see which ones are left. We still have cash, capital, bank loan, trade payables, shop fittings, receivables and the drawings account.

Are these the only ledger accounts left? No: there is still the last one we opened up, the income statement account. The balance on this account represents the profit earned by the business. It has a credit balance – a profit – of $2,000. (This is the figure shown in the income statement financial statement.)

These remaining accounts must also be balanced-off, but since they represent assets and liabilities of the business (not income and expenses) their balances are **carried down** in the books of the business. This means that they become opening balances for the next accounting period.

3.1 Balancing off accounts

The usual method of balancing-off a ledger account at the end of an accounting period is illustrated by the bank loan account in Ron Knuckle's books.

BANK LOAN ACCOUNT

	$		$
Balance carried down (c/d)	1,000	Cash	1,000
		Balance brought down (b/d)	1,000

A credit balance brought down denotes a liability. An asset is represented by a debit balance brought down.

3.2 The capital account

A proprietor's capital comprises any cash introduced by him, plus any profits less any drawings. These three elements are contained in different ledger accounts: cash introduced of $7,000 appears in the capital account, drawings of $1,500 in the drawings account and the profit is the $2,000 credit balance on the income statement account. It is convenient to gather together all these amounts into one capital account, in the same way as we earlier gathered together income and expense accounts into one income statement account.

DRAWINGS

	$		$
Cash	1,500	Capital a/c	1,500

INCOME STATEMENT ACCOUNT

	$		$
Purchases	5,000	Sales	12,500
Rent	3,500		
Bank loan interest	100		
Other expenses	1,900		
Capital a/c	2,000		
	12,500		12,500

CAPITAL

	$		$
Drawings	1,500	Cash	7,000
Balance c/d	7,500	I/S a/c	2,000
	9,000		9,000
		Balance b/d	7,500

3.3 The balance sheet

A re-arrangement of the outstanding balances completes Ron Knuckle's balance sheet.

RON KNUCKLE
BALANCE SHEET AT END OF FIRST TRADING PERIOD

	$
Non-current assets	
Shop fittings	2,000
Current assets	
Cash	6,500
Total assets	8,500
Proprietor's capital	7,500
Liabilities	
Bank loan	1,000
	8,500

When a balance sheet is drawn up for an accounting period which is not the first one, then it ought to show the capital at the start of the accounting period and the capital at the end of the accounting period. This will be illustrated in the next example.

3.4 Summary

At the end of an accounting period, in preparation for producing the balance sheet and income statement:

(a)   Ledger accounts are balanced

(b)   A trial balance is prepared to check that the total of debit balances equals the total of credit balances

(c)   A new ledger account called income statement account is opened

(d)   Using double entry, accounts relating to income and expenses are transferred to the new income statement ledger account

(e)   Accounts relating to balance sheet items are left as balances in the nominal ledger

Finally, the profit or loss on the income statement account, and the balance on the drawings account are transferred to the capital account.

ssessment ocus point

The trial balance is a useful starting point for the preparation of financial statements. Be prepared for an extract from a trial balance, from which you then need to calculate a figure for inclusion in the income statement or balance sheet.

4 Balancing accounts and preparing financial statements

The exercise which follows is the most important so far. It uses all the accounting steps from entering up ledger accounts to preparing the financial statements. It is very important that you try the question by yourself: if you do not, you will be missing out a vital part of this text.

✎ Question

A business is established with capital of $2,000, and this amount is paid into a business bank account by the proprietor. During the first year's trading, the following transactions (in summary) occurred:

	$
Purchases of goods for resale, on credit	4,300
Payments to trade payables	3,600
Sales, all on credit	5,800
Payments from receivables	3,200
Non-current assets purchased for cash	1,500
Other expenses, all paid in cash	900

The bank has provided an overdraft facility of up to $3,000.

Prepare the ledger accounts, an income statement for the year and a balance sheet as at the end of the year.

Answer

Open the ledger accounts so that the transactions can be posted. The next step is to work out the double entry bookkeeping for each transaction. Normally you would write them straight into the accounts, but to make this example easier to follow, they are first listed below.

(a)	Establishing business ($2,000)	DR	Cash	CR	Capital
(b)	Purchases ($4,300)	DR	Purchases	CR	Payables
(c)	Payments to creditors ($3,600)	DR	Payables	CR	Cash
(d)	Sales ($5,800)	DR	Receivables	CR	Sales
(e)	Payments by debtors ($3,200)	DR	Cash	CR	Receivables
(f)	Fixed assets ($1,500)	DR	Non-current assets	CR	Cash
(g)	Other (cash) expenses ($900)	DR	Other expenses	CR	Cash

CASH

	$		$
Capital	2,000	Payables	3,600
		Non-current assets	1,500
Receivables	3,200	Other expenses	900

CAPITAL

	$		$
		Cash	2,000

TRADE PAYABLES

	$		$
Cash	3,600	Purchases	4,300

PURCHASES

	$		$
Payables	4,300		

NON-CURRENT ASSETS

	$		$
Cash	1,500		

BPP
LEARNING MEDIA

SALES

	$		$
		Receivables	5,800

RECEIVABLES

	$		$
Sales	5,800	Cash	3,200

OTHER EXPENSES

	$		$
Cash	900		

The next thing to do is to balance all these accounts. It is at this stage that you could draw up a trial balance to make sure the double entries are accurate. There is not very much point in this simple example, but if you did draw up a trial balance, it would look like this.

	Dr	Cr
	$	$
Cash		800
Capital		2,000
Payables		700
Purchases	4,300	
Non-current assets	1,500	
Sales		5,800
Receivables	2,600	
Other expenses	900	
	9,300	9,300

After balancing the accounts, the income statement account is opened and all the balances relating to income and expenses are transferred. The balance on the income statement account is finally transferred to the capital account.

CASH

	$		$
Capital	2,000	Trade payables	3,600
Receivables	3,200	Non-current assets	1,500
Balance c/d	800	Other expenses	900
	6,000		6,000
		Balance b/d (overdraft)	800

CAPITAL

	$		$
Balance c/d	2,600	Cash	2,000
		I/S a/c	600
	2,600		2,600

TRADE PAYABLES

	$		$
Cash	3,600	Purchases	4,300
Balance c/d	700		
	4,300		4,300
		Balance b/d	700

PURCHASES ACCOUNT

	$		$
Trade payables	4,300	I/S a/c	4,300

NON-CURRENT ASSETS

	$		$
Cash	1,500	Balance c/d	1,500
Balance b/d	1,500		

SALES

	$		$
I/S a/c	5,800	Receivables	5,800

RECEIVABLES

	$		$
Sales	5,800	Cash	3,200
		Balance c/d	2,600
	5,800		5,800
Balance b/d	2,600		

OTHER EXPENSES

	$		$
Cash	900	I/S a/c	900

I/S ACCOUNT

	$		$
Purchases	4,300	Sales	5,800
Gross profit c/d	1,500		
	5,800		5,800
Other expenses	900	Gross profit b/d	1,500
Net profit (transferred to capital account)	600		
	1,500		1,500

So the financial statements will be as follows.

INCOME STATEMENT
FOR THE ACCOUNTING PERIOD

	$
Sales	5,800
Cost of sales (purchases)	(4,300)
Gross profit	1,500
Expenses	900
Net profit	600

BALANCE SHEET AS AT THE END OF THE PERIOD

	$	$
Non-current assets		1,500
Receivables		2,600
		4,100
Capital		
At start of period		2,000
Net profit for period		600
At end of period		2,600
Current liabilities		
Bank overdraft	800	
Trade payables	700	
		1,500
		4,100

Chapter roundup

- A **trial balance** is a list of nominal ledger account balances. It is prepared to check that the total of debit balances is the same as the total of credit balances and offer reassurance that the double entry recording from day books has been done correctly.

- An income statement ledger account is opened up to gather all items relating to income and expenses. When rearranged, the items make up the income statement for the financial statements.

- The balances on all remaining ledger accounts (including the income statement account) can be listed and rearranged to form the balance sheet.

Quick quiz

1   Fill in the blanks.

A trial balance is a list of _____

_____.

2   Five circumstances in which a trial balance might balance although some of the balances are wrong are:

(1)   _____

(2)   _____

(3)   _____

(4)   _____

(5)   _____

3   Which of the following errors would result in a trial balance failing to agree?

A   Failing to record an invoice from a supplier in the accounting system
B   Recording a non-current asset purchase as an item of revenue expenditure
C   Recording an expense payment as:
     Dr bank a/c Cr expense a/c
D   Recording an expense payment as:
     Dr expense a/c Dr bank a/c

4   When preparing a trial balance, the clerk omits the balance of $2,000 on the receivables account. This error means that the total of debit balances will exceed the total of credit balances by $2,000. True or false?

5   A business has the following extract from its trial balance

	$
Trade receivables	5,000
Bank overdraft	2,000
Trade payables	7,000
Inventory	4,500

What is the figure for current assets?

A $9,500
B $7,000
C $11,500
D $9,000

Answers to quick quiz

1   A trial balance is a list of nominal ledger account balances.

2   (1) Omission of a transaction completely
     (2) Posting to the wrong ledger account
     (3) Compensating errors
     (4) Errors of principle
     (5) Errors of original entry

3   D   This is an example of a failure of the basic rules of double entry, so the trial balance will not agree.
     A   This is an error of omission, the financial records will be incomplete but the integrity of the double entry process is not impaired.

     B   This is an error of principle, confusion between capital and revenue expenditure has occurred.
     C   This is a reversal error, the trial balance will agree because debits = credits, however the accounts are incorrect.

4   False. The omitted balance is an asset account and thus a debit. So in the trial balance the total of **credit** balances will exceed the total of debit balances by $2,000.

5   A   Current assets are inventory ($4,500) and trade receivables ($5,000)

Now try the questions below from the Question Bank

Question numbers	Page
20–22	398

Preparing accounts: concepts and conventions

Introduction

IAS 1 *Presentation of financial statements* identifies a number of accounting concepts which it describes as **fundamental assumptions** of accounting. These are explained in Section 1.

Section 2 covers how values are determined.

Topic list	Syllabus references
1 Accounting concepts and principles	A (2)
2 Costs and values	A (4), (5)

1 Accounting concepts and principles

Assessment focus point

Eight accounting concepts and principles

1   Going concern
2   Accruals
3   Prudence
4   Consistency
5   Materiality
6   Substance over form
7   Business entity (the entity concept)
8   Money measurement

FAST FORWARD

IAS 1 describes **going concern, accruals and consistency** as **fundamental assumptions** of accounting.

1.1 Going concern

Key term

Going concern implies that the business will continue in operation for the foreseeable future, and that there is no intention to put the company into liquidation or to make drastic cutbacks to the scale of operations.

The main significance of the going concern concept is that the assets of the business should not be valued at their 'break-up' value, which is the amount that they would fetch if they were sold piecemeal and the business were thus broken up. Rather, they are included in the balance sheet at a value which reflects their value to the business.

1.2 Accruals

Key term

The **accruals concept** states that, in computing profit, amounts are included in the accounts in the **period** when they are **earned** or **incurred**, not received or paid.

This is illustrated in the example of Emma (5.6 in Chapter 1). Profit of $100 was computed by in effect matching the revenue ($200) earned from the sale of 20 T-shirts against the cost ($100) of acquiring them.

However, if had Emma sold 18 T-shirts, it would be incorrect to charge her income statement with the cost of 20 T-shirts, as she would still have two T-shirts in inventory. Therefore, only the purchase cost of 18 T-shirts ($90) would be matched with her sales revenue ($180), leaving her with a profit of $90.

Her balance sheet would therefore look like this.

	$
Assets	
Inventory (at cost, ie 2 × $5)	10
Receivables (18 × $10)	180
	190
Proprietor's capital (profit for the period)	90
Liabilities	
Payables	100
	190

In this example, the concepts of going concern and accruals are linked. As the business is assumed to be a going concern, it is possible to carry forward the cost of the unsold T-shirts as a charge against profits of the next period.

Question

Going concern

If Emma decided to give up selling T-shirts, how would the two T-shirts in the balance sheet be valued?

Answer

The going concern concept no longer applies and the value of the two T-shirts in the balance sheet will be a break-up valuation rather than cost. Similarly, if the two unsold T-shirts are unlikely to be sold at more than their cost of $5 each (perhaps because of damage or a fall in demand) then they will be shown on the balance sheet at their net realisable value (ie the likely eventual sales price less any expenses to make them saleable, eg repairs) rather than cost. This shows the application of the prudence concept.

UK company legislation gives legal recognition to the accruals concept, stating that: 'all income and charges relating to the financial year to which the accounts relate shall be taken into account, without regard to the date of receipt or payment.' This requires businesses to take account of sales and purchases when made (rather than when paid for) and to carry unsold inventory forward in the balance sheet rather than to deduct its cost from profit for the period.

1.3 Prudence

Key term

> **Prudence** is the concept that specifies, in situations where there is uncertainty, appropriate caution is exercised in recognising transactions in financial records.

For example, inventory should be stated in the balance sheet at cost rather than their selling price so as to take into account the **uncertainty** of disposal.

Prudence guards against the understatement of assets and overstatement of liabilities. It encourages a **even handed** approach to the recognition of liabilities, in particular.

Question

Prudence 1

A retailer commences business on 1 January and buys inventory of 20 washing machines, each costing $100. During the year he sells 17 machines at $150 each. How should the remaining machines be valued at 31 December if:

(a)   He is forced to close down his business at the end of the year and the remaining machines will realise only $60 each in a forced sale?

(b)   He intends to continue his business into the next year?

Answer

(a)   If the business is to be closed down, the remaining three machines must be valued at the amount they will realise in a forced sale, ie 3 × $60 = $180.

(b)   If the business is regarded as a going concern, the inventory unsold at 31 December will be carried forward into the following year. The three machines will therefore appear in the balance sheet at 31 December at cost, 3 × $100 = $300. The prudence concept dictates that they be valued at cost, not expected sales value.

Question

Prudence 2

Samson Feeble trades as a carpenter. He has undertaken to make a range of kitchen furniture for a customer at an agreed price of $1,000. At the end of Samson's accounting year the job is unfinished (being two thirds complete) and the following data has been assembled.

	$
Costs incurred in making the furniture to date	800
Further estimated cost to completion of the job	400
Total cost	1,200

The incomplete job represents **work in progress** at the end of the year which is an asset, like inventory. Its cost to date is $800, but by the time the job is completed Samson will have made a loss of $200. What is the effect of this on Samson's balance sheet and income statement?

Answer

The full $200 loss should be charged against profits of the current year. The value of work in progress at the year end should be its **net realisable value**, which is lower than its cost. The net realisable value is $600, comprising costs incurred to date of $800, less the loss foreseen of $200.

Sales revenue will be 'realised' and so 'recognised' in the income statement in the following cases.

(a)   The sale transaction is for a specific quantity of goods at a known price, so that the sales value of the transaction is known for certain.

(b)   The sale transaction has been completed, or else it is certain that it will be completed (eg in the case of long-term contract work, when the job is well under way but not yet completed by the end of an accounting period).

(c)   The **critical event** in the sale transaction has occurred ie when it becomes virtually certain that cash will eventually be received from the customer or cash is actually received.

Usually, revenue is 'recognised' either when a cash sale is made, or when the customer promises to pay on or before a specified future date, and the debt is legally enforceable.

The prudence concept is applied here in the sense that revenue should not be anticipated, before it is reasonably certain to 'happen'.

Assessment focus point | The application of the prudence concept to revenue is also known as the **realisation concept.**

Question

Realised profit

A realised profit arises when?

A   A customer's order is received

B   A receivable pays an invoice

C   A property is revalued upwards

D   Goods are sent to a customer, who will purchase on credit, the invoice will be sent later

Answer

B   Correct.

A   The sale has not yet occurred, it is far too early to recognise profit.

C   This is an unrealised surplus, it will only become realised if the property is sold.

D   This is too early in the sales cycle to recognise a profit. The sale is not for cash and the customer has not yet accepted the goods.

1.4 Consistency

Accounting is not an exact science. There are many areas where judgement must be used in determining money values for items appearing in accounts. Certain procedures and principles are recognised as good accounting practice, but there are often various acceptable methods of accounting for similar items.

Key term

The **consistency concept** states that in preparing accounts consistency should be observed in two respects.

(a)   **Similar** items within a single set of accounts should be given **similar** accounting treatment.

(b)   The **same** treatment should be applied from one period to **another** in accounting for similar items. This enables valid comparisons to be made from one period to the next.

1.5 Materiality

Apart from error, there will be many areas where two different accountants will come up with different figures for the same item. The materiality concept is relevant in this context.

Key term

A matter is **material** if its omission or misstatement would reasonably influence the decisions of a user of the accounts.

In preparing accounts it is important to decide what is material and what is not, so that time and money are not wasted in the pursuit of excessive detail.

Question
Materiality

You have recently paid $4.95 for a waste paper bin which should have a useful life of about five years. Should you treat it as a non-current asset?

Answer

No, because of the materiality concept. The cost of the bin is very small. Treat the $4.95 as an expense in this year's income statement.

1.6 Substance over form

Key term

> **Substance over form** is the principle that transactions and other events are accounted for and presented in accordance with their substance and economic reality and not merely their legal from.

Substance over form usually applies to fairly complicated transactions. It is very important because it stops businesses distorting their results by using the letter of the law instead of commercial reality.

1.7 The entity concept

Key term

> **Entity concept**: accountants regard a business as a separate entity, distinct from its owners or managers.

This concept applies whether the business is a limited liability company (and so recognised in law as a separate entity) or a sole trader or partnership (in which case the business is not legally separate). So, in the example of Emma in chapter 1, the money she transferred to her business bank account becomes, in accounting terms, a **business** asset (but legally remains a **personal** asset).

Acceptance of this concept has important practical consequences. In the case of a small business run by a single individual, the owner's personal affairs and business affairs may appear to be inextricably linked eg Emma may conduct her business from home. In preparing the business accounts, it is essential to separate out her private transactions.

Question   **Entity concept**

Suppose that Emma withdraws a number of T-shirts from her stock to give to friends, how would this be reflected in her accounts?

Answer

The correct accounting treatment is to regard her as having purchased the goods from the business, which is a completely separate entity. The subsequent gift to her friends is then a private transaction and is not recorded in the books of the business. Emma should pay for the T-shirts by taking money from her own purse and putting it into the till, or she should regard the withdrawal as a repayment of capital. Otherwise, the business accounts will give a misleading picture.

1.8 The money measurement concept

Key term

> **Money measurement concept**: accounts deal only with items to which a monetary value can be attributed.

In Chapter 1, we distinguished between an asset such as a machine (which might be valued at its original purchase cost, its replacement cost etc) and an asset such as the flair of a manager or the dedication of the workforce. The machine is valued and included in the balance sheet, flair and dedication are not included, yet they can be of enormous importance to the success of a business. Recognising this, accountants in recent years have tried to suggest ways of 'bringing them on to the balance sheet' by attributing values to them. 'Human resource accounting' is beyond the scope of this book, but you should be aware of the problems it attempts to address.

Question
Money measurement

Perhaps it is too glib to say that monetary values can never be attributed to the skill of the workforce. There is at least one high-profile industry where such valuations are commonplace. Can you think of it? And do you know what the accounting consequences are in that industry?

Answer

The industry referred to is of course the world of sport, particularly football, where transfer fees appear to provide an objective valuation of a player's worth. Many football clubs are run as substantial businesses, some of them with shares quoted on the UK Stock Exchange. As such, their accounting practices are widely publicised and discussed. In almost all cases, however, they make no attempt to include the value of players on their balance sheet, presumably because such values fluctuate wildly with the form and fitness of the players concerned. Transfer fees are usually shown simply as a cost in the income statement.

1.9 Accounting policies and accounting estimates

> **T FORWARD**
>
> IAS 1 also considers three other concepts extremely important. **Prudence**, **substance over form** and **materiality** should govern the selection and application of accounting policies.

Accounting policies should be chosen in order **to comply with International Accounting Standards.** Where there is **no specific requirement** in an IAS or IFRS, policies should be developed so that information provided by the financial statements is:

    (a)   **Relevant** to the decision-making needs of users.

    (b)   **Reliable** in that they:

        (i)   represent faithfully the **results and financial position** of the entity.

        (ii)   reflect the **economic substance** of events and transactions and not merely the legal form.

        (iii)   are **neutral**, that is free from bias.

        (iv)   are **prudent**.

        (v)   are **complete in all material respects**.

    (c)   **Comparable**

    (d)   **Understandable**

Accounting policies are different to **accounting estimates**. Estimates arise due to the uncertainties in business dealings eg bad debt allowances, depreciation. If there is a **change in an accounting estimate**, the difference should be written off to the same income statement expense item that the original provision was charged to.

2 Costs and values

2.1 Historical cost

> **T FORWARD**
>
> A basic principle of accounting is that resources are normally stated in accounts at **historical cost**, ie at the amount which the business paid to acquire them.

An important advantage of doing this is that the objectivity of accounts is maximised: there is usually documentary evidence to prove the amount paid to buy an asset or pay an expense. In general, accountants prefer to deal with costs, rather than 'values'. Valuations tend to be subjective and to vary according to what the valuation is for.

A company acquires a machine to manufacture its products, with an expected useful life of four years. At the end of two years the company is preparing a balance sheet and has to value the asset.

Possible costs and values

- **Original cost** (historical cost)
- **Half** of the historical cost (half of its useful life has expired)
- **Secondhand value**
- **Replacement cost** of an **identical** machine
- **Replacement cost** of a **more modern** (technologically advanced) machine
- **Economic value** (ie the amount of the profits it is expected to generate during its remaining life)

All of these valuations have something to commend them, but the great advantage of the first two is that they are based on the machine's historical cost, which is verifiable. The subjective judgement involved in the other valuations, particularly the last, is so great as to lessen the reliability of any accounts based on them. The second method, or a variation of it, is the one which will normally be used (see Chapter 9).

2.2 Example: costs and values

Brian sets up in business on 1 January 20X6 selling accountancy textbooks. He buys 100 books for $5 each and by 31 December 20X6 he manages to sell his entire inventory, all for cash, at a price of $8 each. On 1 January 20X7 he replaces his inventory by purchasing another 100 books. This time the cost of the books has risen to $6 each. Calculate the profit for 20X6.

Solution

In conventional historical cost accounting, Brian's profit would be computed as follows.

	$
Sale of 100 books (@ $8 each)	800
Cost of 100 books (@ $5 each)	500
Profit for the year	300

The purchase of the books is stated at their historical cost. Although this is accepted accounting practice, and is the method we will be using, it involves an anomaly which can be seen if we look at how well off the business is.

On 1 January 20X6 the assets of the business consist of the 100 books which Brian has purchased as inventory. On 1 January 20X7 the business has an identical inventory of 100 books, and also has cash of $200 (ie $800 received from customers, less the $600 cost of replacing inventory). So despite making a profit of $300, measured in the conventional way, the business appears to be only $200 better off.

This anomaly can be removed if an alternative accounting convention is used. Suppose that profit is the difference between the selling price of goods and the cost of replacing the goods sold. Brian's profit is as follows.

	$
Sale of 100 books	800
Cost of replacing 100 books sold @ $6 each	600
Profit for the year	200

Now the profit for the year is exactly matched by the increase in the company's assets over the year.

2.3 Capital maintenance

> The **capital** of a business (also called its net worth) is the excess of its **assets** over its **liabilities**, and represents the proprietor's interest in the business.

One way of calculating profit measures how well off a business is at the beginning of a period compared to the end of the period. The difference (after allowing for drawings and injections of new capital) is the profit or loss for the period. On this basis, profit depends on the valuation of the assets and liabilities

Returning to the example of Brian and using historical cost, the value of his business at 1 January 20X6 and 1 January 20X7 is as follows.

	20X6	20X7
	$	$
Inventory (at historical cost)	500	600
Cash	0	200
	500	800

The value of the business has risen by $300 over the year and this is the amount of profit we calculated on the historical cost basis. We can say that the original capital of the business, $500, has been maintained and an additional $300 created. This is the financial capital maintenance concept.

However, in times of high inflation, if we keep capital at its historic cost the value in real terms will be diminished. So, in order to maintain capital, it is necessary to adjust for inflation.

Question   Capital maintenance

At 31.12.X1, the capital of a business was $100,000. During the year ended 31.12.X2 the business made a profit of $20,000. If inflation was running at 10%, what amount should be needed to maintain the capital?

A $100,000
B $120,000
C $110,000
D $90,000

Answer

C. At the beginning of the year, the capital was $100,000. With inflation running at 10%, the capital needs to increase by 10% to maintain capital ($100,000 + 10% × $100,000 = $110,000).

Instead of using historical costs, it is theoretically possible to measure capital in physical terms. Brian's physical capital was originally 100 books; on 1 January 20X7, it consists of an identical 100 books plus $200 cash. We can say that Brian's original physical capital has been maintained and an addition to capital of $200 has been created. This is equivalent to the profit we computed on a replacement cost basis.

A system of accounting based principally on replacement costs, and measuring profit as the increase in physical capital, was used in the UK for some years (called **current cost accounting**).

The main accounting system has always been, and will continue to be, historical cost accounting. However, current cost accounting was developed as a possible solution to certain problems which arise in periods of rising prices. Theoretical and practical problems in the current cost accounting system led to its withdrawal in the UK.

Attempts to solve the problems of inflation have a long history in the UK and abroad. One step common in practice is to prepare **modified** historical cost accounts. This means that up-to-date valuations are included in the historical cost balance sheet for some or all of a company's non-current assets, without any other adjustments being made. No attempt is made to tackle the difficulties of profit measurement.

For the foreseeable future, historical cost accounting is likely to be the most important system in the UK, despite its inability to reflect the effects of inflation.

There are a number of reasons why this is so.

(a) It is **easy and cheap**. Other methods tend to be far more complicated and onerous to use, particularly for small businesses. Also, there is no agreement on an alternative.

(b) The fact that **non-current asset revaluation** is permitted or encouraged means that there is less likelihood of a serious understatement of actual value distorting the balance sheet valuation of the business.

(c) It is easy to understand and users are **aware of its limitations**, so make appropriate allowances. Alternative methods generally involve much more complex concepts.

(d) The figures are easy to obtain and are **objective** and **readily verifiable**, being tied to actual transactions. Other methods depend more on subjective valuations.

It is important to note that, legally, a business does not have to account for inflation.

Question
Inflation

In a period when prices are rising, the profit shown under the historical cost convention will differ from that shown under the current cost convention. In the case of a retail trading company, which of the two profit figures will be higher?

Answer

The profit shown under the historical cost convention will be higher. This is because the value of the resources used is their cost at the time they were purchased. Under the current cost convention, the value of these resources is their cost at the (later) time when they were replaced. Given that prices are rising, this cost will be higher and so reported profits will be less.

Chapter roundup

- IAS 1 describes **going concern, accruals and consistency** as **fundamental assumptions** of accounting.

- IAS 1 also considers three other concepts extremely important. **Prudence, substance over form** and **materiality** should govern the selection and application of accounting policies.

- A basic principle of accounting is that resources are normally stated in accounts at **historical cost**, ie at the amount which the business paid to acquire them.

Quick quiz

1   The eight accounting concepts or principles are:

(1)   _____   (5)   _____

(2)   _____   (6)   _____

(3)   _____   (7)   _____

(4)   _____   (8)   _____

2   Fill in the blanks.

(a)   The entity concept means that a business is treated as a _____ _____ , distinct from its _____ or _____ .

(b)   The money measurement concept means that accounts deal only with items _____ _____ .

(c)   The going concern concept implies that a business _____ _____ .

(d)   The prudence concept means that in situations of uncertainty, _____ _____ .

(e)   The accruals concept means that in computing profit, _____ _____ .

(f)   The consistency concept means that similar items in a set of accounts _____ _____ and that the same treatment should be applied _____ _____ .

(g)   Substance over form means that transactions are disclosed in accordance with _____ .

(h)   The materiality concept states that a matter is material if its _____ _____ _____ .

3   At what stage is it normal to recognise the revenue arising from a credit sale?

A   When the goods are dispatched
B   When the goods are delivered and accepted
C   When the invoice is raised
D   When payment is received

4   Are these statements true or false?

(a)   If the accruals concept and the prudence concept conflict, prudence prevails.
(b)   If the consistency concept and the prudence concept conflict, prudence prevails.

5   Six possible values that might be attributed to a piece of machinery in a balance sheet are:

(1)   _____   (4)   _____

(2)   _____   (5)   _____

(3)   _____   (6)   _____

6   Financial capital maintenance means?

A   The business has the same quantity of assets at the end of the year as it had at the start

B   The business has made a profit in the year

C   The business proprietor has withdrawn only sufficient profits so that the business is able to replace its stock

D   The original financial capital of the business is the same at the end of the year as it was at the start allowing for profit and drawings

Answers to quick quiz

1   (1)   Entity
      (2)   Money measurement
      (3)   Going concern
      (4)   Prudence
      (5)   Accruals
      (6)   Consistency
      (7)   Substance over form
      (8)   Materiality

2   (a)   The entity concept means that a business is treated as a **separate entity**, distinct from its **owners** or **managers**.

      (b)   The money measurement concept means that accounts deal only with items **to which a monetary value can be attributed**.

      (c)   The going concern concept implies that a business **will continue in operation for the foreseeable future.**

      (d)   The prudence concept means that **where there is uncertainty, appropriate caution is exercised when recognising transactions.**

      (e)   The accruals concept means that in computing profits **amounts are included in accounts in the period they are earned or incurred, not received or paid.**

      (f)   The consistency concept means that similar items in a set of accounts **should be given similar accounting treatment** and that the same treatment should be applied **from one period to another in accounting for similar items**.

      (g)   Substance over form means that transactions are disclosed in with **the commercial reality, not the letter of the law**.

      (h)   The materiality concept states that a matter is material if its **omission or misstatement would reasonably influence the decision of a user of accounts**.

3   B   When the sale has been completed and the customer has accepted the goods. At this point the debt is legally enforceable.

4   Both (a) and (b) are false. A balanced or 'neutral' approach should be adopted, the objective being to produce a 'true presentation'.

5   (1)   Original cost
        (2)   Original cost, written down across its useful life
        (3)   Secondhand value
        (4)   Replacement cost of an identical machine
        (5)   Replacement cost of a more modern machine
        (6)   Economic value

6   D   Correct. This is the characteristic of a financial capital system.

        A   This describes one of the key elements of a system of current cost accounting.

        B   Under historic accounting, net profit equals the increase in net assets for the period. If no drawings are made, financial capital will increase.

        C   This reflects a system of capital maintenance in real terms.

Now try the questions below from the Question Bank

Question numbers	Page
23–29	398

Accruals and prepayments

Introduction

Profit is the excess of income over expenses. But it is not always immediately clear how much income and expenses are. A variety of difficulties can arise in measuring them. The purpose of this chapter is to describe some of these problems and their solutions.

We shall consider the accounting treatment of accruals and prepayments. Their common feature is that they are applications of the accruals concept or matching concept described in Chapter 7.

Topic list	Syllabus references
1 Accruals	D (1)
2 Prepayments	D (1)
3 Accounting for accruals and prepayments	D (1)

1 Accruals

1.1 introduction

The accruals concept says that income and expenses should be included in the income statement of the period in which they are earned or incurred, not paid or received.

Expenses might not be paid for during the period to which they relate. For example, a business rents a shop for $20,000 per annum, paid in full on 1 July each year. If we calculate the profit of the business for the first six months of the year 20X7, the correct charge for rent in the income statement will be $10,000 even though nothing has been paid in that period. Similarly, the rent charge in the second six months of the year is $10,000, even though $20,000 is paid in that period.

Accruals and prepayments can seem difficult at first, but the following examples will clarify the principle involved: that expenses are matched against the period to which they relate.

Accruals and prepayments are the means by which we move charges into the correct accounting period. If we pay in this period for something which relates to the next accounting period, we use a prepayment to transfer that charge forward to the next period. If we have incurred an expense in this period which will not be paid for until the next period, we use an accrual to bring the charge back into this period.

1.2 Accruals

Key term

Accruals or **accrued expenses** are expenses which are charged against the profit for a particular period, even though they have not yet been paid for.

Accruals are current liabilities.

1.3 Example: accruals

Horace Goodrunning, trading as Goodrunning Motor Spares, ends his financial year on 28 February each year. His telephone was installed on 1 April 20X6 and he receives his telephone account quarterly at the end of each quarter. He pays it promptly as soon as it is received. On the basis of the following data, calculate the telephone expense to be charged to the profit and loss account for the year ended 28 February 20X7.

Goodrunning Motor Spares – telephone expenses paid.

	$
30.6.20X6	23.50
30.9.20X6	27.20
31.12.20X6	33.40
31.3.20X7	36.00

Solution

The telephone expenses for the year ended 28 February 20X7.

	$
1 March – 31 March 20X6 (no telephone)	0.00
1 April – 30 June 20X6	23.50
1 July – 30 September 20X6	27.20
1 October – 31 December 20X6	33.40
1 January – 28 February 20X7 (two months)	24.00
	108.10

The charge for the period 1 January – 28 February 20X7 is two-thirds of the quarterly bill received on 31 March. As at 28 February 20X7, no telephone bill has been received because it is not due for another month. However, it is inappropriate to ignore the telephone expenses for January and February, and so an accrual is charged of $24.

The accrued charge will also appear in the balance sheet of the business as at 28 February 20X7, as a current liability.

1.4 Example: accruals

Cleverley started in business as a paper plate and cup manufacturer on 1 January 20X2, making up accounts to 31 December 20X2. Electricity bills received were as follows.

	20X2	20X3	20X4
	$	$	$
31 January	–	6,491.52	6,753.24
30 April	5,279.47	5,400.93	6,192.82
31 July	4,663.80	4,700.94	5,007.62
31 October	4,117.28	4,620.00	5,156.40

What should the electricity charge be for the year ended 31 December 20X2?

Solution

The three invoices received during 20X2 totalled $14,060.55, but this is not the full charge for the year: the November and December electricity charge was not invoiced until the end of January. To show the correct charge for the year, it is necessary to **accrue** the charge for November and December based on January's bill. The charge for 20X2 is:

	$
Paid in year	14,060.55
Accrual ($^2/_3 \times$ $6,491.52)	4,327.68
	18,388.23

The double entry for the accrual (using the **journal**) will be:

DEBIT	Electricity account	$4,327.68	
CREDIT	Accruals (liability)		$4,327.68

2 Prepayments

Key term

> **Prepayments** are payments which have been made in one accounting period, but should not be charged against profit until a later period, because they relate to that later period.

ssessment cus point

> Accruals are current liabilities and prepayments are current assets in the balance sheet.

2.1 Example: prepayments

A business opens on 1 January 20X4 in a shop which is on a 20 year lease. The rent is $20,000 per year and is payable quarterly in advance. Payments were made on what are known as the 'quarter-days' (except the first payment) as follows.

	$
1 January 20X4	5,000.00
25 March 20X4	5,000.00
24 June 20X4	5,000.00
29 September 20X4	5,000.00
25 December 20X4	5,000.00

What will the rental charge be for the year ended 31 December 20X4?

Solution

The total amount paid in the year is $25,000. The yearly rental, however, is only $20,000. The last payment was almost entirely a prepayment (give or take a few days) as it is payment in advance for the first three months of 20X5. The charge for 20X4 is therefore:

	$
Paid in year	25,000.00
Prepayment	(5,000.00)
	20,000.00

The double entry for this prepayment is:

DEBIT	Prepayments (asset)	$5,000.00	
CREDIT	Rent account		$5,000.00

3 Accounting for accruals and prepayments

3.1 Double entry for accruals and prepayments

You can see from the double entry shown for both the above examples that the other side of the entry is taken to an asset or a liability account.

- **Prepayments** are included in **receivables** in current assets in the balance sheet. They are **assets** as they represent money that has been paid out in advance of the expense being incurred.

- **Accruals** are included in **payables** in **current liabilities** as they represent liabilities which have been incurred but for which no invoice has yet been received.

Transaction	DR	CR	Description
Accrual	Expense	Liability	Expense incurred in period, not recorded
Prepayment	Asset	(Reduction in) expense	Expense recorded in period, not incurred until next period

3.2 Reversing accruals and prepayments in subsequent periods

FAST FORWARD

Accruals and prepayments are **reversed** at the beginning of the next accounting period.

The double entry will be **reversed** in the following period, otherwise the organisation will charge itself twice for the same expense (accruals) *or* will never charge itself (prepayments). It may help to see the accounts in question. These are the postings for the example in 1.4.

ELECTRICITY ACCOUNT

20X2		$	20X2		$
30.4	Cash	5,279.47	31.12	I/S	18,388.23
31.7	Cash	4,663.80			
31.10	Cash	4,117.28			
31.12	Balance c/d (accrual)	4,327.68			
		18,388.23			18,388.23

BPP LEARNING MEDIA

20X3			20X3		
31.1	Cash	6,491.52	1.1	Balance b/d	
30.4	Cash	5,400.93		(accrual reversed)	4,327.68
31.7	Cash	4,700.94	31.12	I/S	21,387.87
31.10	Cash	4,620.00			
31.12	Balance c/d (accrual)	4,502.16			
		25,715.55			25,715.55

The income statement charge and accrual for 20X3 can be checked as follows.

Invoice paid		Proportion charged in 20X3	$
31.1.X3	6,491.52	1/3	2,163.84
30.4.X3	5,400.94	all	5,400.93
31.7.X3	4,700.94	all	4,700.94
31.10.X3	4,620.00	all	4,620.00
31.1.X4	6,753.24	2/3	4,502.16
Charge to I/S in 20X3			21,387.87

In the example in paragraph 2.1 it should be clear to you that the $5,000 rent prepaid in 20X2 will be added to by the payments in 20X3, and the balance will then be reduced at the end of 20X3 in the same way.

Question   Accruals

Ratsnuffer deals in pest control. Its owner, Roy Dent, employs a team of eight who were paid $12,000 per annum each in the year to 31 December 20X5. At the start of 20X6 he raised salaries by 10% to $13,200 per annum each.

On 1 July 20X6, he hired a trainee at a salary of $8,400 per annum.

He pays his work force on the first working day of every month, one month in arrears, so that his employees receive their salary for January on the first working day in February, etc.

Required

(a)   Calculate the cost of salaries charged in the income statement for the year ended 31 December 20X6.

(b)   Calculate the amount actually paid in salaries during the year.

(c)   State the amount of accrued salaries in the balance sheet as at 31 December 20X6.

Answer

(a)   Salaries cost in the income statement

	$
Cost of 8 employees for a full year at $13,200 each	105,600
Cost of trainee for a half year	4,200
	109,800

(b)   Salaries actually paid in 20X6

	$
December 20X5 salaries paid in January (8 employees × $1,000 per month)	8,000
Salaries of 8 employees for January – November 20X6 paid in February – December (8 employees × $1,100 per month × 11 months)	96,800
Salary of trainee (for July – November paid in August – December 20X6: 5 months × $700 per month)	3,500
Salaries actually paid	108,300

(c)   Accrued salaries costs as at 31 December 20X6
       (ie costs charged in the I/S, but not yet paid)

	$
8 employees x 1 month x $1,100 per month	8,800
1 trainee x 1 month x $700 per month	700
	9,500

(d)   Summary

	$
Accrued wages costs as at 31 December 20X5	8,000
Add salaries cost for 20X6 (I/S)	109,800
	117,800
Less salaries paid	108,300
Equals accrued wages costs as at 31 December 20X6	9,500

3.3 Example: prepayments

The Square Wheels Garage pays fire insurance annually in advance on 1 June each year. From the following record of insurance payments, calculate the charge to profit and loss for the financial year to 28 February 20X8.

	Insurance paid
	$
1.6.20X6	600
1.6.20X7	700

Solution

Insurance cost for:

		$
(a)	the 3 months, 1 March – 31 May 20X7 (3/12 × $600)	150
(b)	the 9 months, 1 June 20X7 – 28 February 20X8 (9/12 × $700)	525
	Insurance cost for the year, charged to the I/S	675

At 28 February 20X8 there is a prepayment for fire insurance, covering the period 1 March – 31 May 20X8. This insurance premium was paid on 1 June 20X7, but only nine months worth of the full annual cost is charged in the accounting period ended 28 February 20X8. The prepayment of (3/12 × $700) $175 appears as a current asset in the balance sheet of the Square Wheels Garage.

In the same way, there was a prepayment of (3/12 × $600) $150 in the balance sheet one year earlier as at 28 February 20X7.

Summary

	$
Prepaid insurance premiums as at 28 February 20X7	150
Add insurance premiums paid 1 June 20X7	700
	850
Less insurance costs charged to the I/S for the year ended 28 February 20X8	675
Equals prepaid insurance premiums as at 28 February 20X8	175

Question   **Accruals and prepayments**

The Batley Print Shop rents a photocopying machine for which it makes a quarterly payment as follows.

- Three months rental in advance
- A further charge of 2 pence per copy made during the quarter just ended

The rental agreement began on 1 August 20X4 and the first six quarterly bills were as follows.

Bills dated and received	Rental	Costs of copies taken	Total
	$	$	$
1 August 20X4	2,100	0	2,100
1 November 20X4	2,100	1,500	3,600
1 February 20X5	2,100	1,400	3,500
1 May 20X5	2,100	1,800	3,900
1 August 20X5	2,700	1,650	4,350
1 November 20X5	2,700	1,950	4,650

The bills are paid promptly, as soon as they are received.

(a) Calculate the charge for photocopying expenses for the year to 31 August 20X4 and the amount of prepayments and/or accrued charges as at that date.

(b) Calculate the charge for photocopying expenses for the following year to 31 August 20X5, and the amount of prepayments and/or accrued charges as at that date.

Answer

(a) Year to 31 August 20X4

	$
One months' rental (1/3 × $2,100) *	700
Accrued copying charges (1/3 × $1,500) **	500
Photocopying expense (I/S)	1,200

* From the quarterly bill dated 1 August 20X4
** From the quarterly bill dated 1 November 20X4

There is a prepayment for 2 months' rental ($1,400) and an accrual ($500) for copying charges as at 31 August 20X4.

(b)   Year to 31 August 20X5

	$	$
Rental from 1 September 20X4 – 31 July 20X5 (11 months at $2,100 per quarter or $700 per month)		7,700
Rental from 1 August – 31 August 20X5 (1/3 × $2,700)		900
Rental charge for the year		8,600
Copying charges		
1 September – 31 October 20X4 (2/3 × $1,500)	1,000	
1 November 20X4 – 31 January 20X5	1,400	
1 February – 30 April 20X5	1,800	
1 May – 31 July 20X5	1,650	
Accrued charges for August 20X5 (1/3 × $1,950)	650	
		6,500
Total photocopying expenses (I/S)		15,100

There is a prepayment for 2 months' rental ($1,800) and an accrual for copying charges ($650) as at 31 August 20X5.

Summary of year 1 September 20X4 – 31 August 20X5

	Rental charges $	Copying costs $
Prepayments as at 31.8.20X4	1,400	
Accrued charges as at 31.8.20X4		(500)
Bills received during the year		
1 November 20X4	2,100	1,500
1 February 20X5	2,100	1,400
1 May 20X5	2,100	1,800
1 August 20X5	2,700	1,650
Prepayment as at 31.8.20X5	(1,800)	
Accrued charges as at 31.8.20X5		650
Charge to the I/S for the year	8,600	6,500
Balance sheet items as at 31 August 20X5		
Prepaid rental (current asset)	1,800	
Accrued copying charges (current liability)		650

3.4 Further example: accruals

Willie Woggle opens a shop on 1 May 20X6. The rent of the shop is $12,000 per annum, payable quarterly in arrears (with the first payment on 31 July 20X6). Willie decides that his accounting period should end on 31 December each year.

The rent account as at 31 December 20X6 will record only two rental payments (on 31 July and 31 October) and there will be two months' accrued rental expenses for November and December 20X6 ($2,000). The charge to the I/S for the period to 31 December 20X6 will be for 8 months' rent (May–December inclusive) ie $8,000.

The rent account appears as follows.

RENT EXPENSE ACCOUNT

20X6		$	20X6		$
31 July	Cash	3,000			
31 Oct	Cash	3,000	31 Dec	I/S	8,000

The accrual of $2,000 has to be put in to bring the balance in the account up to the full charge for the year. At the beginning of the next year the accrual is reversed.

RENT EXPENSE ACCOUNT

			$				$
20X6				*20X6*			
31 July	Cash		3,000				
31 Oct	Cash		3,000				
31 Dec	Balance c/d (accruals)		2,000	31 Dec	I/S		8,000
			8,000				8,000
				19X7			
				1 Jan	Balance b/d (accrual reversed)		2,000

The rent account for the **next** year to 31 December 20X7, assuming no increase in rent in that year, would be as follows.

RENT EXPENSE ACCOUNT

			$				$
20X7				*20X7*			
31 Jan	Cash		3,000	1 Jan	Balance b/d		
30 Apr	Cash		3,000		(accrual reversed)		2,000
31 Jul	Cash		3,000				
31 Oct	Cash		3,000				
31 Dec	Balance c/d (accruals)		2,000	31 Dec	I/S		12,000
			14,000				14,000
				20X8			
				1 Jan	Balance b/d (accrual reversed)		2,000

Here you will see that, for a full year, a full twelve months' rental charges are taken as an expense to the income statement. The accrual appears as a credit balance on the account and is, therefore, shown on the balance sheet as a liability.

3.5 Further example: prepayments

Terry Trunk commences business as a landscape gardener on 1 September 20X5. He joins his local trade association, the Confederation of Luton Gardeners, at an annual membership subscription of $180, payable annually in advance. He paid this amount on 1 September. Terry decides that his account period should end on 30 June each year.

In the first period to 30 June 20X6 (10 months), a full year's membership will have been paid, but only ten twelfths of the subscription is charged to the period (ie 10/12 × $180 = $150). There is a prepayment of two months of membership subscription (ie 2/12 × $180 = $30).

The prepayment is recognised in the ledger account for subscriptions by using the balance carried down/brought down technique.

SUBSCRIPTIONS EXPENSE ACCOUNT

		$			$
20X5			*20X6*		
1 Sept	Cash	180	30 Jun	I/S	150
			30 Jun	Balance c/d (prepayment)	30
		180			180
20X6					
1 Jul	Balance b/d (prepayment reversed)	30			

The subscription account for the next year, assuming no increase in the annual charge and that Terry Trunk remains a member of the association, will be as follows.

SUBSCRIPTIONS EXPENSE ACCOUNT

		$			$
20X6			*20X7*		
1 Jul	Balance b/d (prepayment reversed)	30	30 Jun	I/S	180
1 Sep	Cash	180	30 Jun	Balance c/d (prepayment)	30
		210			210
20X7					
1 Jul	Balance b/d (prepayment reversed)	30			

Again, we see the charge to the I/S is for a full year's subscription. The credit balance represents the prepayment which will be debited to prepayments and will appear as an asset on the balance sheet.

Chapter roundup

- The accruals concept says that income and expenses should be included in the income statement of the period in which they are earned or incurred, not paid or received.

- Accruals and prepayments are the means by which we move charges into the correct accounting period. If we pay in this period for something which relates to the next accounting period, we use a prepayment to transfer that charge forward to the next period. If we have incurred an expense in this period which will not be paid for until the next period, we use an accrual to bring the charge back into this period.

- Accruals and prepayments are **reversed** at the beginning of the next accounting period.

Quick quiz

1   If a business has paid rent of $1,000 for the year to 31 March 20X9, the prepayment in the accounts for the year to 31 December 20X8 is $ _____.

2   _____ in the balance sheet are amounts incurred but not yet paid.

   _____ in the balance sheet are amounts paid but not yet incurred. (Fill in the blanks.)

3   A draft income statement shows a gross profit of $2,000 and net profit of $1,000. It is then realised that $400 of rent that should be treated as a prepayment has been incorrectly treated as an accrual. When this mistake is corrected what happens to gross and net profit?

	Gross profit	Net profit
A	No change	No change
B	Falls $400	Falls $400
C	Falls $400	Rises $400
D	No change	Rises $800

4   A business pays $2,400 for a year's insurance on 1 December 20X1. The year end is 31 March 20X2. At that date, what is the balance carried forward on the insurance account?

   A $800 debit
   B $800 credit
   C $1,600 debit
   D $1,600 credit

5   A business prepares its accounts to 31 December 20X7. The trial balance includes $9,000 for electricity used from 1 January to 30 September 20X7. How much needs to be accrued at the year end?

   A $9,000
   B $3,000
   C $6,000
   D $12,000

Answers to quick quiz

1      $250 (3/12 × $1,000)

2   **Accruals** are amounts incurred but not yet paid. **Prepayments** are amounts paid but not yet incurred.

3   D   There is no change in gross profit. Net profit has been charged with $400 accrual instead of a prepayment, so we need to reduce costs by $400 to reverse the accrual and a further $400 to reinstate the prepayment. Therefore net profit will rise by $800.

4   D   The prepayment is 8 months ie $1,600 (8/12 × $2,400). This will be c/f as a credit (reducing the amount charged to the income statement by $1,600).

5   B   The accrual is 3/9 × $9,000 ($3,000).

Now try the questions below from the Question Bank

Question numbers	Page
30–32	399

Non-current assets – depreciation, revaluation and disposal

Introduction

You are familiar with the distinction between non-current and current assets, a non-current asset being one bought for ongoing use in the business. (If you are unsure look back to Chapter 2.)

Non-current assets are held and used by a business for a number of years, but they wear out or lose their usefulness over time. Every tangible non-current asset has a limited life. The only exception is land held freehold or on a very long leasehold.

The accounts of a business recognise that the cost of a non-current asset is consumed as the asset wears out, by writing off the asset's cost in the income statement over several accounting periods. For example, a machine costs $1,000 and is expected to wear out after ten years. We can reduce the balance sheet value by $100 each year. This process is known as depreciation. Depreciation is the subject of a *reporting standard* (IAS 16). Although you do not need to know IAS 16 specifically as such, the key principles are relevant. This is discussed in Section 1.

Generally the market value of a non-current asset, particularly land or buildings, will rise with time. The asset may then be **revalued**. The accounting treatment of revaluations and the effect on depreciation are considered in Section 2. Section 3 deals with disposals of non-current assets. A profit or loss may arise on the sale of a non-current asset.

Section 4 deals with a more practical issue: the non-current assets register. You are sure to encounter this in real life, nearly all organisations have one.

Topic list	Syllabus references
1 Depreciation	D (3)
2 Revaluation of non-current assets	D (3)
3 Non-current asset disposals	D (3)
4 The non-current assets register	D (4)

1 Depreciation

The cost of a non-current asset, less its estimated residual value, is allocated fairly between accounting periods by means of depreciation. The provision for depreciation is charged against profit and deducted from the value of the non-current asset in the balance sheet.

Key term

Since a non-current asset has a cost, a limited useful life and a declining value, a charge is made in the income statement to reflect the use. This charge is called **depreciation**. Depreciation is a means of spreading the cost of a non-current asset over its useful life. This matches the cost against the period over which it earns profits for the business (the accruals concept).

1.1 Non-current assets and depreciation

A **non-current asset** is acquired with a view to earning profits. Its life extends **over more** than one accounting period, and so it earns profits over more than one period. With the exception of land held on freehold or very long leasehold, every non-current asset eventually wears out over time. Machines, cars and other vehicles, fixtures and fittings, and even buildings do not last for ever. When a business acquires a non-current asset, it will have some idea about how long its useful life will be. Its policy may be one of the following.

- Use the non-current asset until it is worn out, useless, and worthless
- Sell off the non-current asset at the end of its useful life as second-hand or as scrap

1.2 Example: depreciation

A business buys a machine for $40,000. Its expected life is four years, and at the end of that time it is expected to be worthless. Calculate the annual depreciation charge.

10,000

Solution

Since the non-current asset will earn profits for four years, it seems reasonable to charge the cost of the asset over those four years at $10,000 per annum. (By the end of the four years, the total cost will have been written off against profits.)

1.3 IAS 16 Property, plant and equipment

 The CA 2006 requires that all non-current assets having a limited useful life should be depreciated. IAS 16 *Property, plant and equipment* gives a useful discussion of the purpose of depreciation and supplements the statutory requirements in important respects.

Key terms

Depreciation can be defined as 'the measure of the cost or revalued amount of the economic benefits of the tangible non-current asset that have been consumed during the period. Consumption includes the wearing out, using up or other reduction in the useful life of a tangible non-current asset whether arising from use, effluxion (passing) of time or obsolescence through either changes in technology or demand for the goods and services produced by the asset'.

Net book value is cost (or revalued amount) less depreciation to date.

NBV

Question

Depreciation

A business buys a machine on 1 January 20X2 for $10,000. It expects to use it for 4 years and then sell it for $2,000.

Calculate the annual depreciation charge and the net book value at 31 December 20X2, 20X3, 20X4 and 20X5 (the expected sale date).

Answer

The annual depreciation charge is $\dfrac{\$10,000-2,000}{4}$ = $2,000

	Cost	Depreciation to date	Net book value
	$	$	$
31 December 20X2	10,000	2,000	8,000
31 December 20X3	10,000	4,000	6,000
31 December 20X4	10,000	6,000	4,000
31 December 20X5	10,000	8,000	2,000

The net book value (NBV) of an asset is not equal to its net realisable value and so the object of depreciation is not to reflect the fall in value of an asset over its life.

Another misconception is that depreciation provides funds to replace the asset at the end of its useful life. This is not the case, there is no movement of cash when depreciation is calculated and charged in the income statement.

Key term

The **depreciable amount** is the total amount to be charged over the life of a non-current asset, usually its cost less any expected 'residual' sales or disposal value at the end of its life.

1.4 Calculating depreciation

IAS 16 states factors that need to be considered in determining the useful life, residual value and depreciation method of an asset.

- **Expected usage** with reference to the asset's expected capacity or physical output
- **Expected physical deterioration** through use or passing of time
- **Economic or technological obsolescence** (eg typesetters replaced by word processors)
- **Legal or similar limits** on the use of the asset (eg the expiry date of a lease)

The cost at which non-current assets are to be stated in the accounts is defined by the CA1985 and is, broadly speaking, purchase price or manufacturing cost, plus incidental expenses.

The estimated residual value of an asset is a matter of judgement. If it is expected to be a relatively small amount in relation to the asset's cost, it is usually taken to be nil.

The expected life of an asset is again a matter of judgement. IAS 16 comments that an asset's useful life may be affected by the following points.

- Pre-determined (eg leaseholds)
- Directly governed by extraction or consumption (eg a mine or quarry)
- Dependent on the extent of use (eg a motor car)
- Reduced by economic or technological obsolescence (eg last year's fashions)

If the original estimate of an asset's useful life is incorrect, it should be revised. Normally, no adjustment is made in respect of the depreciation charged in previous years; but the remaining NBV of the asset should be depreciated over the new estimate of its remaining useful life. However, if future results could be **materially** distorted, the adjustment to accumulated depreciation should be recognised in the accounts.

1.5 Examples: depreciation

(a) A non-current asset costing $20,000, with an expected life of five years and an expected residual value of nil, will be depreciated by $20,000 in total over the five year period.

(b) A non-current asset costing $20,000, with an expected life of five years and an expected residual value of $3,000, will be depreciated by $17,000 in total over the five years.

Assessment focus points	(a) A depreciation charge (provision) is made in the income statement in each accounting period for every depreciable non-current asset. Nearly all non-current assets are depreciable, the most important exceptions being freehold land and long-term investments.
	(b) The total accumulated depreciation builds up as the asset gets older. Therefore, for an asset with no residual value, the total provision for depreciation increases until the non-current asset is fully depreciated (NBV is nil).

1.6 The ledger accounting entries for depreciation

(a) There is a provision for depreciation account for each separate category of non-current assets, eg plant and machinery, land and buildings, fixtures and fittings.

(b) The depreciation charge for an accounting period is a charge against profit and is recorded as:

DEBIT   Depreciation expense account
CREDIT   Provision for depreciation account

(c) The balance on the provision for depreciation account is the total accumulated depreciation. This is always a credit balance.

(d) The non-current asset accounts are unaffected by depreciation. Non-current assets are recorded in these accounts at cost (or, if they are revalued, at their revalued amount).

(e) In the balance sheet of the business, the accumulated depreciation is deducted from the cost of non-current assets (or revalued amount) to arrive at the net book value of the non-current assets.

1.7 Example: accounting for depreciation

Using the information in Question 1 (Depreciation), write up the depreciation expense and provision for depreciation accounts for 20X2, 20X3, 20X4 and 20X5.

Solution

DEPRECIATION EXPENSE ACCOUNT

		$			$
31.12.X2	Provision	2,000	31.12.X2	I/S	2,000
31.12.X3	Provision	2,000	31.12.X3	I/S	2,000
31.12.X4	Provision	2,000	31.12.X4	I/S	2,000
31.12.X5	Provision	2,000	31.12.X5	I/S	2,000

DEPRECIATION PROVISION ACCOUNT

		$			$
31.12.X2	Balance c/d	2,000	31.12.X2	Depreciation expense a/c	2,000
		2,000			2,000
			1.1.X3	Balance b/d	2,000
31.12.X3	Balance c/d	4,000	31.12.X3	Depreciation expense a/c	2,000
		4,000			4,000
			1.1.X4	Balance b/d	4,000
31.12.X4	Balance c/d	6,000	31.12.X4	Depreciation expense a/c	2,000
		6,000			6,000
			1.1.X5	Balance b/d	6,000
31.12.X5	Balance c/d	8,000	31.12.X5	Depreciation expense a/c	2,000
		8,000			8,000

1.8 Methods of depreciation

There are several different methods of depreciation but the straight line method and the reducing balance method are most commonly used in practice.

There are several different methods of depreciation. The ones you need to know about are:

- Straight-line method
- Reducing balance method

Assessment focus point

Another method is the revaluation method, but we will look at this in Section 2.

1.8.1 Straight line method

Key term

The **straight line method** means that the total depreciable amount is charged in equal instalments to each accounting period over the expected useful life of the asset

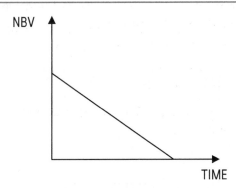

The straight line method is a fair allocation of the total depreciable amount, if it is reasonable to assume that the business enjoys equal benefits from the use of the asset throughout its life.

Formula to learn

The annual depreciation charge is calculated as:

$$\frac{\text{Cost of asset minus residual value}}{\text{Expected useful life of the asset}}$$

1.8.2 Example: straight line depreciation

(a) A non-current asset costs $20,000 with an estimated life of 10 years and no residual value.

$$\text{Depreciation} = \frac{\$20,000}{10 \text{ years}} = \$2,000 \text{ per annum}$$

(b) A fixed asset costs $60,000 with an estimated life of 5 years and a residual value of $7,000.

$$\text{Depreciation} = \frac{\$(60,000 - 7,000)}{5 \text{ years}} = \$10,600 \text{ per annum}$$

The net book value of the fixed asset is calculated as follows.

	After 1 year $	After 2 years $	After 3 years $	After 4 years $	After 5 years $
Cost of the asset	60,000	60,000	60,000	60,000	60,000
Accumulated depreciation	10,600	21,200	31,800	42,400	53,000
Net book value	49,400	38,800	28,200	17,600	7,000 *

* ie its estimated residual value.

Since the depreciation charge per annum is the same amount every year, it is often stated that depreciation is charged at the rate of x per cent per annum on the cost of the asset. In the example above, the depreciation charge per annum is 10% of cost (ie 10% of $20,000 = $2,000). **Assessment questions** often describe straight line depreciation in this way.

1.8.3 Reducing balance method

Key term

The **reducing balance method** of depreciation calculates the annual charge as a fixed percentage of the **net book value** of the asset, as at the end of the previous accounting period.

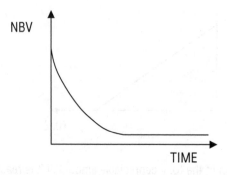

Formula to learn

Reducing balance method = Net book value × X%.

1.8.4 Example: reducing balance depreciation

A business purchases a non-current asset at a cost of $10,000. Its expected useful life is 3 years and its estimated residual value is $2,160. The business uses the reducing balance method and calculates that the rate of depreciation should be 40% of the reducing (net book) value of the asset. (The method of deciding that 40% is a suitable annual percentage is outside of the scope of your syllabus.)

Calculate the depreciation charge per annum and the net book value of the asset as at the end of each year.

Solution

	$	Accumulated depreciation $	
Asset at cost	10,000		
Depreciation in year 1 (40%)	4,000	4,000	
Net book value at end of year 1	6,000		
Depreciation in year 2			
(40% of reducing balance)	2,400	6,400	(4,000 + 2,400)
Net book value at end of year 2	3,600		
Depreciation in year 3 (40%)	1,440	7,840	(6,400 + 1,440)
Net book value at end of year 3	2,160		

With the reducing balance method, the annual charge for depreciation is higher in the earlier years of the asset's life, and lower in the later years. Therefore, it is used when it is considered fair to allocate a greater proportion of the total depreciable amount to the earlier years. The assumption is that the benefits obtained by the business from using the asset decline over time.

Question

Straight line and reducing balance methods

A lorry bought for a business cost $17,000. It is expected to last for five years and then be sold for scrap for $2,000.

Required

Work out the depreciation to be charged each year under the following methods.

(a)   The straight line method
(b)   The reducing balance method (using a rate of 35%)

Answer

(a)   Under the straight line method, depreciation for each of the five years is:

$$\text{Annual depreciation} = \frac{\$17,000 - 2,000}{5} = \$3,000$$

(b)   Under the reducing balance method, depreciation for each of the five years is:

Year	Depreciation		
1	35% × $17,000	=	$5,950
2	35% × ($17,000 − $5,950) = 35% × $11,050	=	$3,868
3	35% × ($11,050 − $3,868) = 35% × $7,182	=	$2,514
4	35% × ($7,182 − $2,514) = 35% × $4,668	=	$1,634
5	Balance to bring book value down to $2,000 = $4,668 − $1,634 − $2,000	=	$1,034

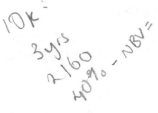

1.9 Choice of method

Neither the CA 2006 nor IAS 16 states which method should be used. Management must exercise its judgement and IAS 16 states that:

'The depreciable amount of a tangible non-current asset should be allocated on a **systematic** basis over its useful economic life. The depreciation method used should reflect as fairly as possible the pattern in which the asset's economic benefits are consumed by the entity. The depreciation charge for each period should be recognised as an expense in the profit and loss account unless it is permitted to be included in the carrying amount of another asset.'

'A variety of methods can be used to allocate the depreciable amount of a tangible non-current asset on a systematic basis over its useful life. The method chosen should result in a **depreciation charge throughout the asset's useful** economic life and not just towards the end of its useful life or when the asset is falling in value.'

IAS 16 also states that a change from one method of providing depreciation to another is allowed only if the new method will give a fairer presentation of the company's results and financial position. Such a change is not a change of accounting policy and so no disclosure of a prior year adjustment is needed. Instead, the asset's net book amount is written off over its remaining useful life. The change of method, the reason for the change, and its quantitative effect, is disclosed by note to the accounts.

Many companies carry non-current assets in their balance sheets at revalued amounts, particularly in the case of freehold buildings. When this is done, the depreciation charge is calculated on the basis of the revalued amount (not the original cost).

1.10 Disclosure requirements of IAS 16

The following information should be disclosed separately in the financial statements for each class of tangible non-current assets.

- Depreciation methods used

- Useful lives or the depreciation rates used

- Total depreciation charged for the period

- Where material, the financial effect of a change during the period in either the estimate of useful economic lives or the estimate of residual values

- The cost or revalued amount at the beginning and end of the financial period

- The cumulative amount of depreciation at the beginning of and end the financial period

- A reconciliation of the movements (separately disclosing additions, disposals, revaluations, transfers, depreciation, impairment losses, and reversals of past impairment losses written back in the financial period)

- The NBV at the beginning and end of the financial period

Question

Depreciation: ledger accounts

Brian Box set up his own computer software business on 1 March 20X6. He purchased a computer system, at a cost of $16,000. The system has an expected life of three years and a residual value of $2,500.

Using the straight line method of depreciation, produce the non-current asset account, provision for depreciation account, income statement (extract) and balance sheet (extract) for each of the three years, 28 February 20X7, 20X8 and 20X9.

Answer

NON-CURRENT ASSET – COMPUTER EQUIPMENT

	Date		$	Date		$
(a)	1.3.X6	Payable	16,000	28.2.X7	Balance c/d	16,000
(b)	1.3.X7	Balance b/d	16,000	28.2.X8	Balance c/d	16,000
(c)	1.3.X8	Balance b/d	16,000	28.2.X9	Balance c/d	16,000
(d)	1.3.X9	Balance b/d	16,000			

The non-current asset has now lasted its expected useful life. However, until it is sold or scrapped, the asset still appears in the balance sheet at cost (less accumulated depreciation) and it remains in the ledger account for computer equipment until disposal.

PROVISION FOR DEPRECIATION

	Date		$	Date		$
(a)	28.2.X7	Balance c/d	4,500	28.2.X7	I/S	4,500
(b)	28.2.X8	Balance c/d	9,000	1.3.X7	Balance b/d	4,500
				28.2.X8	I/S	4,500
			9,000			9,000
(c)	28.2.X9	Balance c/d	13,500	1.3.X8	Balance b/d	9,000
				28.2.X9	I/S	4,500
			13,500			13,500
				1 Mar 20X9	Balance b/d	13,500

The annual depreciation charge is $\dfrac{(\$16,000 - 2,500)}{3 \text{ years}} = \$4,500 \text{ pa}$

The asset is depreciated to its residual value. If it continues to be used, it will not be depreciated any further (unless its residual value is reduced).

INCOME STATEMENT (EXTRACT)

	Date		$
(a)	28 Feb 20X7	Provision for depreciation	4,500
(b)	28 Feb 20X8	Provision for depreciation	4,500
(c)	28 Feb 20X9	Provision for depreciation	4,500

BALANCE SHEET (EXTRACT) AS AT 28 FEBRUARY

	20X7	20X8	20X9
	$	$	$
Computer equipment at cost	16,000	16,000	16,000
Less accumulated depreciation	4,500	9,000	13,500
Net book value	11,500	7,000	2,500

1.11 Assets acquired in the middle of an accounting period

A business can purchase new non-current assets at any time during the course of an accounting period. So it may seem fair to charge depreciation in the period of purchase which reflects the limited amount of use the business has had in that period.

1.12 Example: depreciation charge

A business, with an accounting year ending on 31 December, purchases a new non-current asset on 1 April 20X1, at a cost of $24,000. The expected life of the asset is 4 years, and its residual value is nil. What is the depreciation charge for 20X1?

Solution

The annual depreciation charge will be $\dfrac{24,000}{4 \text{ years}}$ = $6,000 per annum

However, since the asset was acquired on 1 April 20X1, the business has only benefited from the use of the asset for 9 months. Therefore it seems fair to charge depreciation in 20X1 for only 9 months.

$\dfrac{9}{12} \times \$6,000 = \$4,500$

In practice, however, many businesses ignore part-year depreciation, and charge a full year's depreciation in the year of purchase and none in the year of sale.

Assessment focus point

> If a question gives you the purchase date of a non-current asset, which is in the middle of an accounting period, unless told otherwise, you should assume that depreciation will be calculated on the basis of 'part year' use.
>
> However, be sure to read the question carefully. A question may clearly state that depreciation on office equipment is charged at 20% per annum on the net book value at the year end. This means that any equipment introduced during the year will have a **full year's** depreciation charge.

1.13 Example: provision for depreciation with assets acquired part-way through the year

Brian Box purchases a car for himself and later for his chief assistant Bill Ockhead. Relevant data is as follows.

	Date of purchase	Cost	Estimated life	Estimated residual value
Brian Box car	1 June 20X6	$20,000	3 years	$2,000
Bill Ockhead car	1 June 20X7	$8,000	3 years	$2,000

The straight line method of depreciation is to be used.

Prepare the motor vehicles account and provision for depreciation of motor vehicle account for the years to 28 February 20X7 and 20X8. (You should allow for the part-year's use of a car in computing the annual charge for depreciation.) Calculate the net book value of the motor vehicles as at 28 February 20X8.

Solution

(a) (i) Brian Box car   Annual depreciation $\dfrac{\$(20,000-2,000)}{3 \text{ years}}$ = $6,000 pa

Monthly depreciation $500

	Depreciation	1 June 20X6 – 28 February 20X7 (9 months)	$4,500
		1 March 20X7 – 28 February 20X8	$6,000

(ii) Bill Ockhead car   Annual depreciation $\dfrac{\$(8,000-2,000)}{3 \text{ years}}$ = $2,000 pa

Depreciation   1 June 20X7 – 28 February 20X8 (9 months) $1,500

(b)

MOTOR VEHICLES

Date		$	Date		$
1 Jun 20X6	Payables (or cash)	20,000	28 Feb 20X7	Balance c/d	20,000
1 Mar 20X7	Balance b/d	20,000			
1 Jun 20X7	Payables (or cash)	8,000	28 Feb 20X8	Balance c/d	28,000
		28,000			28,000
1 Mar 20X8	Balance b/d	28,000			

PROVISION FOR DEPRECIATION OF MOTOR VEHICLES

Date		$	Date		$
28 Feb 20X7	Balance c/d	4,500	28 Feb 20X7	I/S	4,500
			1 Mar 20X7	Balance b/d	4,500
28 Feb 20X8	Balance c/d	12,000	28 Feb 20X8	I/S	
				(6,000+1,500)	7,500
		12,000			12,000
			1 Mar 20X8	Balance b/d	12,000

BALANCE SHEET WORKINGS AS AT 28 FEBRUARY 20X8

	Brian Box car		Bill Ockhead car		Total
	$	$	$	$	$
Asset at cost		20,000		8,000	28,000
Accumulated					
depreciation: (4,500 + 6,000)		10,500		1,500	12,000
Net book value		9,500		6,500	16,000

1.14 Applying a depreciation method consistently

The business has to decide which method of depreciation to use. Once that decision is made, however, it should not be changed – the chosen method should be applied consistently from year to year. This is an example of the consistency concept.

Similarly, the business has to decide a sensible life span for a non-current asset. Once that life span is chosen, it should not be changed unless something unexpected happens to the non-current asset.

However a business can depreciate different categories of non-current assets in different ways. If a business owns three cars, then each car is depreciated in the same way (eg the straight line method) but another category of non-current asset (photocopiers) can be depreciated using a different method (eg by the reducing balance).

Assessment focus point

(a) Depreciation is a measure of the 'wearing out' of a non-current asset.

(b) The accruals concept requires that depreciation be charged over the useful life of an asset.

(c) Two common methods of calculating depreciation are straight line and reducing balance.

(d) To record depreciation:

DEBIT Depreciation expense account
CREDIT Depreciation provision

Then to get the charge into the income statement

DEBIT Income statement
CREDIT Depreciation expense account

2 Revaluation of non-current assets

FAST FORWARD

When a non-current asset is revalued, depreciation is charged on the revised amount.

2.1 Revaluations

Due to inflation, it is now quite common for the market value of certain non-current assets to go up. The most obvious example of rising market values is land and buildings.

A business is not obliged to revalue non-current assets in its balance sheet. However, in order to give a 'true and fair view' it may decide to revalue some non-current assets upwards. When non-current assets are revalued, depreciation is charged on the revalued amount.

2.2 Example: the revaluation of non-current assets

Ira Vann commenced trading on 1 January 20X1 and purchased freehold premises for $50,000.

For the purpose of accounting for depreciation, he decided that

(a) the freehold land part of the business premises was worth $20,000 and would not be depreciated.

(b) the building part of the business premises was worth the remaining $30,000. This would be depreciated by the straight-line method to a nil residual value over 30 years.

After five years, on 1 January 20X6, the business premise is now worth $150,000.

	$
Land	75,000
Building	75,000
	150,000

He estimates that the building still has a further 25 years of useful life remaining.

Calculate the annual charge for depreciation in each of the 30 years of its life, and the balance sheet value of the land and building as at the end of each year.

BPP
LEARNING MEDIA

Solution

Before the revaluation, the annual depreciation charge is $1,000 ($30,000/30) per annum on the building. This charge is made in each of the first five years of the asset's life.

The net book value of the total asset will decline by $1,000 per annum.

(a) $49,000 as at 31.12.X1
(b) $48,000 as at 31.12.X2
(c) $47,000 as at 31.12.X3
(d) $46,000 as at 31.12.X4
(e) $45,000 as at 31.12.X5

When the revaluation takes place, the amount of the revaluation is:

	$
New asset value	150,000
Net book value as at end of 20X5	45,000
Amount of revaluation	105,000

The asset will be revalued by $105,000 to $150,000. If you remember the accounting equation, you will realise that if assets go up in value by $105,000, capital or liabilities must increase by the same amount. Since the increased value benefits the owner of the business, the amount of the revaluation is added to capital, usually as a separate **revaluation reserve**.

After the revaluation, depreciation will be charged on the building at a new rate.

$$\frac{\$75,000}{25 \text{ years}} = \$3,000 \text{ per annum}$$

The net book value of the property will then fall by $3,000 per annum over 25 years, from $150,000 as at 1 January 20X6 to only $75,000 at the end of the 25 years – ie the building part of the property value will be fully depreciated.

The consequence of an upwards revaluation is therefore a higher annual depreciation charge.

2.3 Revaluation method of depreciation

Under the revaluation method of depreciation, an asset is revalued at the end of every year. The difference between the two amounts is then taken as depreciation.

Question   Revaluation method of depreciation

A machine is revalued at the end of the financial year at $240,000. At the end of the previous financial year, it had been valued at $250,000. Historical cost was $280,000. What is the charge for deprecation of this asset under the revaluation method in the income statement?

A $40,000
B $30,000
C $10,000
D $20,000

Answer

C   Over the course of the year the machine's value has dropped from $250,000 to $240,000 ($10,000).

2.4 A fall in the value of a non-current asset (impairment)

When the 'market' value of a non-current asset falls to below its net book value, and the fall in value is expected to be permanent, the asset is written down to its new market value. The charge in the income statement for the impairment in the value of the asset during the accounting period is:

	$
Net book value at the beginning of the period	X
Less: new value	(X)
Equals: the charge for the impairment in the asset's value in the period.	X

However, if the asset has been previously revalued, then the impairment should be charged to the revaluation reserve.

Assessment focus point

> Impairment in this case is different to the revaluation method of depreciation. A review for impairment is usually only carried out every 2 or 3 years. It is not a method of depreciation.

2.5 Example: fall in asset value

A business purchased a leasehold property on 1 January 20X1 at a cost of $100,000. The lease has a 20 year life. After 5 years' use, on 1 January 20X6, the leasehold is now worth only $60,000 and the reduction is permanent.

Solution

Before the asset is reduced in value, the annual depreciation charge is:

$$\frac{\$100,000}{20 \text{ years}} = \$5,000 \text{ per annum} (= 5\% \text{ of } \$100,000)$$

After 5 years, the accumulated depreciation is $25,000 and the net book value $75,000, which is $15,000 more than the new asset value. This $15,000 is written off in year 5, so that the total charge in year 5 is

	$
Net book value of the leasehold after 4 years ($100,000 − 20,000)	80,000
Revised asset value at end of year 5	60,000
Charge against profit in year 5	20,000

An alternative method of calculation is

	$
Normal' depreciation charge per annum	5,000
Further fall in value, from net book value at end of year 5 to revised value	15,000
Charge against profit in year 5	20,000

The leasehold has a further 15 years to run and its value is now $60,000. From year 6 to year 20, the annual charge for depreciation will be

$$\frac{\$60,000}{15 \text{ years}} = \$4,000 \text{ per annum}$$

Question Land and buildings

PS acquired its premises on 1 January 20X4 at a cost of

Buildings	$140,000
Land	$60,000

The depreciation policy of the company is to write off assets having a finite life over their estimated useful life, using the straight-line method and assuming a nil residual value. Buildings are deemed to have a useful life of 25 years.

On 1 January 20X9 the buildings and land were revalued at:

Buildings	$200,000
Land	$100,000

Required

Calculate the following.

(i)   The net book value of land and buildings at 31 December 20X8
(ii) The net book value of land and buildings at 31 December 20X9
(iii) The capital reserve at 31 December 20X9

Answer

(i)   **Valuation of land and buildings at 31 December 20X8**

	$
Buildings (a finite life asset)	140,000
Depreciation	
$140,000 ÷ 25 years = $5,600 pa	
$5,600 × 5 years	28,000
	112,000
Land (an infinite asset)	60,000
	172,000

(ii) **Valuation of land and buildings at 31 December 20X9**

	$
Buildings at valuation	200,000
Depreciation	
$200,000 ÷ 20 years	(10,000)
	190,000
Land	100,000
	290,000

(iii) **Revaluation reserve**

	$
Buildings at valuation on 1 January 20X9	200,000
Land at valuation on 1 January 20X9	100,000
	300,000
Less book value at 31 December 20X8	(172,000)
Revaluation reserve	128,000

3 Non-current asset disposals

> When a non-current asset is sold, there is likely to be a profit or loss on disposal. This is the difference between the net sale price of the asset and its net book value at the time of disposal.

3.1 The disposal of non-current assets

Non-current assets are not purchased by a business with the intention of reselling them in the normal course of trade. However, they may be sold either when their useful life is over or before then. A non-current asset could be sold early if it is no longer needed for the trade.

When non-current assets are sold, there will be a **profit or loss on disposal**. These gains or losses are reported in the profit and loss account of the business (and not in the trading account). They are commonly referred to as 'profit on disposal of non-current assets' or 'loss on disposal'.

Key term

> **The profit or loss on the disposal of a non-current asset** is the difference between:
>
> - **Net book value** of the asset at the time of sale, and
> - Net **sale price** (the price minus any costs of making the sale)
>
> A profit is made when the sale price exceeds the NBV, and vice versa for a loss.

3.2 Example: disposal of a non-current asset

A business purchased a non-current asset on 1 January 20X1 for $25,000, with an estimated life of six years and an estimated residual value of $7,000. The asset was sold after three years on 1 January 20X4, for $17,500.

What was the profit or loss on disposal, assuming that the business uses the straight line method for depreciation?

Solution

$$\text{Annual depreciation} = \frac{\$(25,000 - 7,000)}{6 \text{ years}} = \$3,000 \text{ per annum}$$

	$
Cost of asset	25,000
Less accumulated depreciation (three years)	9,000
Net book value at date of disposal	16,000
Sale price	17,500
Profit on disposal	1,500

This profit will be shown in the income statement as other income added to the gross profit brought down from the trading account.

Question   **Profit/loss on disposal**

A business purchased a machine on 1 July 20X1 for $35,000. The machine had an estimated residual value of $3,000 and a life of eight years. The machine was sold for $18,600 on 31 December 20X4, the last day of the accounting year. The business incurred dismantling costs and transformation costs of $1,200.

The business uses the straight line method of depreciation. What was the profit or loss on disposal of the machine?

Answer

Annual depreciation $\dfrac{\$(35,000 - 3,000)}{8 \text{ years}}$ = $4,000 per annum

It is assumed that in 20X1 only one-half year's depreciation was charged, because the asset was purchased six months into the year.

	$	$
Non-current asset at cost		35,000
Depreciation in 20X1 (6 months)	2,000	
20X2, 20X3 and 20X4	12,000	
Accumulated depreciation		14,000
Net book value at date of disposal		21,000
Sale price	18,600	
Costs incurred in making the sale	(1,200)	
Net sale price		17,400
Loss on disposal		(3,600)

This capital loss will be shown as an expense in the income statement of the business.

3.3 The disposal of non-current assets: ledger accounting entries

The disposal of non-current assets is recorded in a **disposal of non-current assets** account.

(a)   The following items appear in the disposal of non-current assets account.

- Cost (or revalued amount of the asset)
- Accumulated depreciation up to the date of sale } ie net book value
- Sale price of the asset

(b)   The ledger accounting entries are as follows.

(i)   DEBIT   Disposal of non-current asset account
      CREDIT   Non-current asset account

with the cost of the asset disposed of.

(ii) DEBIT   Provision for depreciation account
      CREDIT   Disposal of non-current asset account

with the accumulated depreciation on the asset as at the date of sale.

(iii) DEBIT   Receivable account or cash book
      CREDIT   Disposal of non-current asset account

with the sale price of the asset.

(iv) The balance on the disposal account is the profit or loss on disposal and the corresponding double entry is recorded in the income statement.

3.4 Example: disposal of assets: ledger accounting entries

A business has machinery costing $110,000. Depreciation is provided at 20% per annum straight line. The total provision now stands at $70,000. The business sells for $19,000 a machine which it purchased exactly two years ago for $30,000.

Show the relevant ledger entries.

Solution

PLANT AND MACHINERY ACCOUNT

	$		$
Balance b/d	110,000	Plant disposals account	30,000
		Balance c/d	80,000
	110,000		110,000
Balance b/d	80,000		

PLANT AND MACHINERY DEPRECIATION PROVISION

	$		$
Plant disposals (20% of $30,000 for 2 years)	12,000	Balance b/d	70,000
Balance c/d	58,000		
	70,000		70,000
		Balance b/d	58,000

PLANT DISPOSALS

	$		$
Plant and machinery account	30,000	Depreciation provision	12,000
I/S (profit on sale)	1,000	Cash	19,000
	31,000		31,000

Check:

	$
Asset at cost	30,000
Accumulated depreciation at time of sale	12,000
Net book value at time of sale	18,000
Sale price	19,000
Profit on sale	1,000

3.5 Example continued: part exchange

Taking the example above, assume that the machine was exchanged for a new machine costing $60,000. $19,000 is the trade-in received for the old machine. Now what are the relevant ledger account entries?

Solution

PLANT AND MACHINERY ACCOUNT

	$		$
Balance b/d	110,000	Plant disposal	30,000
Cash (60,000 – 19,000)	41,000	Balance c/d	140,000
Plant disposals	19,000		
	170,000		170,000
Balance b/d	140,000		

The new asset is recorded in the non-current asset account at cost $(41,000 + 19,000) = $60,000.

PLANT AND MACHINERY DEPRECIATION PROVISION

	$		$
Plant disposals (20% of $30,000 for 2 years)	12,000	Balance b/d	70,000
Balance c/d	58,000		
	70,000		70,000
		Balance b/d	58,000

PLANT DISPOSALS

	$		$
Plant and machinery	30,000	Depreciation provision	12,000
Profit transferred to I/S	1,000	Plant and machinery	19,000
	31,000		31,000

On disposal of non-current assets

(a)   DEBIT   Disposal account   } original cost of the asset
         CREDIT   Non-current asset account

(b)   DEBIT   Provision for depreciation account   } depreciation charged to date
         CREDIT   Disposals account

(c)   DEBIT   Cash (if money)
                      Non-current asset (if part exchange)   } sales value
         CREDIT   Disposals account

The balance on the disposals account is transferred to the income statement.

Question

Ledger accounts for disposal

A business purchased two widget-making machines on 1 January 20X5 at a cost of $15,000 each. Each had an estimated life of five years and a nil residual value. The straight line method of depreciation is used.

Owing to an unforeseen slump in market demand for widgets, one widget-making machine was sold (on credit) for $8,000 on 31 March 20X7.

Later in the year, it was decided to abandon production of widgets altogether, and the second machine was sold on 1 December 20X7 for $2,500 cash.

Prepare the machinery account, provision for depreciation of machinery account and disposal of machinery account for the accounting year to 31 December 20X7.

Answer

MACHINERY ACCOUNT

20X7		$	20X7		$
1 Jan	Balance b/f	30,000	31 Mar	Disposal of machinery	15,000
			1 Dec	Disposal of machinery	15,000
		30,000			30,000

PROVISION FOR DEPRECIATION OF MACHINERY

20X7		$	20X7		$
31 Mar	Disposal of machinery*	6,750	1 Jan	Balance b/f (W1)	12,000
1 Dec	Disposal of machinery**	8,750	31 Dec	I/S***	3,500
		15,500			15,500

*   Depreciation at date of disposal ($3,000 × 2 + $750)
** Depreciation at date of disposal ($3,000 × 2 + $2,750)
*** Depreciation charge for the year ($750 + $2,750) (W2)

DISPOSAL OF MACHINERY

20X7		$	20X7		$
31 Mar	Machinery	15,000	31 Mar	Receivable account (sale price)	8,000
			31 Mar	Provision of depreciation	6,750
1 Dec	Machinery	15,000	1 Dec	Cash (sale price)	2,500
			1 Dec	Provision of depreciation	8,750
			31 Dec	I/S (loss on disposal)	4,000
		30,000			30,000

You should be able to calculate that there was a loss on the first disposal of $250, and on the second disposal of $3,750, giving a total loss of $4,000.

Workings

1   At 1 January 20X7, accumulated depreciation on the machines will be 2 machines × 2 years × $\dfrac{\$15,000}{5}$ per machine pa = $12,000, or $6,000 per machine

2   Monthly depreciation is $\dfrac{\$3,000}{12}$ = $250 per machine per month. Therefore the machine disposed of on 31 March has 3 months' depreciation ($750) and the 1 December disposal has 11 months' depreciation ($2,750).

4 The non-current assets register

FORWARD

Most organisations keep a non-current asset register. This is a listing of all non-current assets owned by the organisation. This must be kept up to date.

Key term

The **non-current assets register** is a listing of all non-current assets owned by the organisation, broken down perhaps by department, location or asset type.

A non-current assets register is maintained primarily for internal purposes. It shows an organisation's investment in capital equipment. A fixed asset register is also part of the **internal control system**.

4.1 Data kept in a non-current assets register

Details likely to be kept about each non-current asset are:

- The internal reference number (for physical identification purposes)
- Manufacturer's serial number (for maintenance purposes)
- Description of asset
- Location of asset
- Department which 'owns' asset
- Purchase date (for calculation of depreciation)
- Cost
- Depreciation method and estimated useful life (for calculation of depreciation)
- Net book value (or written down value)

The following events give rise to entries in a non-current asset register.

- Purchase of an asset
- Sale of an asset
- Loss or destruction of an asset
- Transfer of assets between departments
- Revision of estimated useful life of an asset
- Scrapping of an asset
- Revaluation of an asset

'Outputs' from a non-current assets register include the following.

- Reconciliations of NBV to the nominal ledger
- Depreciation charges posted to the nominal ledger
- Physical verification/audit purposes

4.2 Control

Discrepancies between the non-current assets register and the physical assets or the nominal ledger must be investigated.

It is important, for external reporting (ie the audit) and for internal purposes, that there are controls over non-current assets.

(a) **Purchase** of non-current assets must be authorised and must only be made by a responsible official. The purchaser should obtain several quotations. The person authorising the expenditure should not be the person using the asset.

(b) Procedures should exist and be enforced for **disposal** of non-current assets to ensure that the sales proceeds are not misappropriated.

(c) The non-current assets register must reconcile with the non-current asset and provision for depreciation accounts in the nominal ledger.

(d) The non-current assets register must reconcile with the physical presence of capital items.

4.2.1 The non-current assets register and the nominal ledger

The non-current assets register is not part of the double entry and is there for **memorandum** and **control** purposes. It must be reconciled to the nominal ledger to make sure that all additions, disposals and depreciation charges have been posted. For example, the total of all the 'cost' figures in the register for motor vehicles should equal the balance on the 'motor vehicles cost' account in the nominal ledger. The same goes for accumulated depreciation.

4.2.2 The non-current assets register and the physical assets

It is possible that the non-current assets register may not reconcile with the non-current assets actually present because:

- An asset has been stolen or damaged, which has not been noticed or recorded
- Excessive wear and tear or obsolescence has not been recorded
- New assets not yet recorded in the register because it has not been kept up to date
- Errors made in entering details in the register
- Improvement and modifications have not been recorded in the register

It is important that the company physically inspects all the items in the non-current assets register and keeps the non-current assets register up to date.

The nature of the inspection will vary between organisations. A large company could inspect 25% of assets by value each year, aiming to cover all categories every five years. A small company may inspect all its non-current assets very quickly, although this 'inspection' may not be formally recorded.

4.2.3 Dealing with discrepancies

As mentioned above, some assets may require an adjustment in their expected life due to excessive wear and tear or damage. The proper person must authorise any change to estimates of the life of an asset. The accounts department will need a copy of the authorised changes to make the right adjustments in the journal, the register and the ledger.

When discrepancies are discovered, it may be possible to resolve them by updating the non-current assets register and/or nominal ledger. It may not be possible for the person who discovers the discrepancy to resolve it himself. For example, if a non-current asset has to be revalued downwards due to wear and tear or obsolescence, it should be authorised by his superior.

Chapter roundup

- The cost of a non-current asset, less its estimated residual value, is allocated fairly between accounting periods by means of depreciation. The provision for depreciation is charged against profit and deducted from the value of the non-current asset in the balance sheet.

- There are several different methods of depreciation, but the straight line method and the reducing balance method are most commonly used in practice.

- When a non-current asset is revalued, depreciation is charged on the revised amount.

- When a non-current asset is sold, there is likely to be a profit or loss on disposal. This is the difference between the net sale price of the asset and its net book value at the time of disposal.

- Most organisations keep a non-current assets register. This is a listing of all non-current assets owned by the organisation. This must be kept up to date.

- Discrepancies between the non-current assets register and the physical assets or the nominal ledger must be investigated.

Quick quiz

1   Fill in the blanks. Net book value is _____ less _____,

2   Two common depreciation methods are:

    1)   _____

    2)   _____

3   A non-current asset (cost $10,000, depreciation $7,500) is given in part exchange for a new asset costing $20,500. The agreed trade-in value was $3,500. The income statement will include?

    A   A loss on disposal $1,000
    B   A profit on disposal $1,000
    C   A loss on purchase of a new asset $3,500
    D   A profit on disposal $3,500

4   The details about a non-current asset that would be included in a non-current assets register are:

    (1)   _____   (4)   _____

    (2)   _____   (5)   _____

    (3)   _____   (6)   _____

5   A non-current asset originally cost $120,000. At 31 December 20X5, its net book value is $90,000. The asset is revalued to $150,000 and its remaining useful life is 10 years. What is the annual depreciation for the year ended 31 December 20X5?

    A $30,000
    B $6,000
    C $15,000
    D $12,000

Answers to quick quiz

1   Net book value is **cost** less **accumulated depreciation**.

2   (1)   Straight-line
     (2)   Reducing balance

3   B   Correct.
		$
	Net book value at disposal	2,500
	Trade-in allowance	3,500
	Profit	1,000

4   (1)   Date of purchase
     (2)   Description and location
     (3)   Original cost
     (4)   Depreciation rate and method
     (5)   Accumulated depreciation to date
     (6)   Date and amount of any revaluation

5   C   The new rate of depreciation is $\dfrac{\$150,000}{10}$ ie $15,000 pa.

Now try the questions below from the Question Bank

Question numbers	Page
33–40	400

Bad debts and allowances for receivables

Introduction

The accounting problems discussed in this chapter are concerned with sales on credit. With credit transactions, the time when a sale is recognised in the accounts is not the same as the time when cash is eventually received or paid. There is a gap, during which something might happen which results in the amount of cash eventually paid (if any) being different from the original value of the sale on the invoice.

We shall consider two such events.

- Bad debts, which arise when a credit customer does not pay the money he owes
- Allowance for receivables, a provision for credit customers who may not pay

Topic list	Syllabus references
1 Bad debts	D (2)
2 Allowance for receivables	D (2)

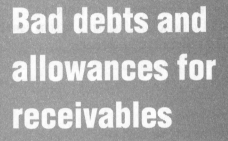

1 Bad debts

A **bad** debt is one that is no longer expected to be paid. For instance, the customer may have gone into liquidation. This debt will be written off.

1.1 Bad debts

Credit customers may fail to pay for goods, out of dishonesty or because they have gone bankrupt and cannot pay. Customers in another country may be prevented from paying by the unexpected introduction of foreign exchange control during the credit period. For whatever reason, a business may decide to write the debt off as uncollectable.

1.2 Writing off bad debts

Bad debts written off are accounted for as follows.

    (a)   Sales are shown at their invoice value in the income statement. The sale has been made, and gross profit earned. The failure to collect the debt is a separate matter.

    (b)   Bad debts written off are shown as an expense in the income statement.

If a sale of $300 became a bad debt:

	$
Sale	300
Cost of sales, say	200
Gross profit	100
Bad debt written off	300
Net loss on this transaction (= cost of sales)	(200)

When a debt is written off, the value of the receivable as a current asset falls to zero.

1.3 Bad debts written off: ledger accounting entries

Bad debts written off are posted to a bad debts account.

    (a)   When a particular debt will not be paid, the customer is no longer a receivable.

        DEBIT   Bad debts account (expense)
        CREDIT   Receivables account

    (b)   At the end of the accounting period, the balance on the bad debts account is transferred to the I/S ledger account (like all other expense accounts).

        DEBIT   I/S account
        CREDIT   Bad debts account

1.4 Example: bad debts written off

At 1 October 20X5 a business had total outstanding debts of $8,600. During the year to 30 September 20X6.

    (a)   Credit sales amounted to $44,000

    (b)   Payments from various receivables amounted to $49,000

    (c)   Two debts, for $180 and $420, are declared bad and these are to be written off

Required

Prepare the receivables account and the bad debts account for the year.

Solution

RECEIVABLES

	$		$
Opening balance b/f	8,600	Cash	49,000
Sales	44,000	Bad debts	180
		Bad debts	420
		Closing balance c/d	3,000
	52,600		52,600
Opening balance b/d	3,000		

BAD DEBTS

	$		$
Receivables	180	I/S a/c: bad debts written off	600
Receivables	420		
	600		600

In the sales ledger, balances on the personal accounts of the customers whose debts are bad will be written off. The business should ensure it does not sell goods on credit to those customers again.

1.5 Bad debts written off and subsequently paid

A bad debt which has been written off may be unexpectedly paid. The only accounting problem arising is when a debt written off as bad in one accounting period is subsequently paid in a later period. The amount paid is recorded as income in the income statement of the period in which payment is received. So the entry is:

DEBIT   Cash account
CREDIT   Debts paid previously written off as bad account

1.6 Example: bad debts recovered

An income statement for the Blacksmith's Forge for the year to 31 December 20X5 is prepared from the following information.

	$
Inventories of goods in hand, 1 January 20X5	6,000
Purchases of goods	122,000
Inventories of goods in hand, 31 December 20X5	8,000
Cash sales	100,000
Credit sales	70,000
Bad debts written off	9,000
Debts paid in 20X5 which were previously written off as bad in 20X4	2,000
Other expenses	31,000

Solution

BLACKSMITH'S FORGE
INCOME STATEMENT FOR THE YEAR ENDED 31.12.20X5

	$	$
Sales		170,000
Opening inventory	6,000	
Purchases	122,000	
	128,000	
Less closing inventory	8,000	
Cost of goods sold		120,000
Gross profit		50,000
Add: debts paid, previously written off as bad		2,000
		52,000
Expenses		
Bad debts written off	9,000	
Other expenses	31,000	
		40,000
Net profit		12,000

Assessment focus point

(a)   To write off a bad debt:

DEBIT	Bad debts expense account
CREDIT	Receivables account

(b)   To record a receipt from a debt previously written off:

DEBIT	Cash account
CREDIT	Debts paid, previously written off as bad account

2 Allowance for receivables

FAST FORWARD

An **allowance for receivables** occurs when there is uncertainty over whether a debt will be paid. The debt is not written off, but an allowance is made against non-payment.

When bad debts are written off, specific debts owed to the business are identified as unlikely ever to be collected.

However, because of the risks involved in selling goods on credit, a certain percentage of outstanding debts at any time are unlikely to be collected. Although it might be estimated that 5% of debts will be bad, the business will not know which specific debts are bad.

When a business expects bad debts, it can make an allowance for receivables. The business is more likely to avoid claiming profits which subsequently fail to materialise because of bad debts (the prudence concept).

2.1 Accounting for the allowance

FAST FORWARD

(a)   When an allowance is first made, the amount is charged as an expense in the income statement.

(b)   When an allowance already exists, but is subsequently increased in size, the amount of the **increase** is charged as an expense in the income statement.

(c)   When an allowance already exists, but is subsequently reduced in size, the amount of the **decrease** is recorded as an item of 'income' in the income statement.

The balance sheet must also be adjusted to show an allowance for receivables. **The value of receivables in the balance sheet must be shown after deducting the allowance.** This is because the net realisable value of all the receivables of the business is estimated to be less than their 'sales value'.

2.2 Example: allowance for receivables

A business has receivables of $50,000 and creates an allowance for receivables at 30 June 20X5 of 5% ($2,500). Although total receivables are $50,000, eventual payment of only $47,500 is expected. What will be shown in the income statement and balance sheet?

Solution

(a)　In the income statement, the increase in the allowance of $2,500 (from nil to $2,500) will be shown as an expense.

(b)　In the balance sheet, receivables will be shown as

	$
Total receivables at 30 June 20X5	50,000
Less allowance for receivables	2,500
	47,500

2.3 Allowance for receivables: ledger accounting entries

The procedure is to leave the total receivables account in the nominal ledger and the receivables' personal balances in the sales ledger completely untouched, and to open up an allowance account by the following entries.

DEBIT　　　　Allowance account (expense in I/S)
CREDIT　　　Allowance for receivables (balance sheet)

The expense in the income statement is sometimes debited to the increase or decrease in the allowance for receivables account or sometimes to bad debts. In the remainder of this section we will refer to the income statement posting as being to the 'I/S account'.

Assessment focus point

> Read questions carefully to decide where the increase or decrease in the allowance is posted. It is usually included in with bad debts.

When preparing a balance sheet, remember the credit balance on the allowance account is deducted from the debit balance on the receivables account.

In subsequent years, adjustments may be needed to the amount of the allowance. The procedure to be followed then is as follows.

(a)　Calculate the new allowance required.

(b)　Compare it with the existing balance on the allowance account (ie the balance b/f from the previous accounting period).

(c)　Calculate increase or decrease required.

　　(i)　If a higher provision is required, post the **increase** as follows.

　　　　DEBIT　　　　I/S account
　　　　CREDIT　　　Allowance for receivables

(ii)   If a lower provision is needed, post the **decrease** as follows.

DEBIT   Allowance for receivables
CREDIT   I/S account

2.4 Example: accounting entries for allowance for receivables

Alex Gullible has total receivables' balances outstanding at 31 December 20X2 of $28,000. He believes that about 1% of these balances will not be collected and wishes to make an appropriate allowance. Before now, he has not made any allowance for receivables.

On 31 December 20X3 his receivables balances amount to $40,000. His experience during the year has convinced him that an allowance of 5% should be made.

What accounting entries should Alex make on 31 December 20X2 and 31 December 20X3, and what figures for receivables will appear in his balance sheets as at those dates?

Solution

At 31 December 20X2

Provision required = 1% × $28,000 = $280

Alex will make the following entries.

DEBIT   I/S account (allowance for receivables) $280
CREDIT   Allowance for receivables $280

In the balance sheet receivables will appear as follows under current assets.

	$
Sales ledger balances (= total receivables account)	28,000
Less allowance for receivables	280
	27,720

At 31 December 20X3

Following the procedure described above, Alex will calculate as follows.

	$
Allowance required now (5% × $40,000)	2,000
Existing allowance	(280)
∴ Additional allowance required	1,720

He will make the following entries.

DEBIT   I/S account $1,720
CREDIT   Allowance for receivables $1,720

The allowance account will by now appear as follows.

ALLOWANCE FOR RECEIVABLES

		$			$
20X2			*20X2*		
31 Dec	Balance c/d	280	31 Dec	I/S account	280
20X3			*20X3*		
31 Dec	Balance c/d	2,000	1 Jan	Balance b/d	280
			31 Dec	I/S account	1,720
		2,000			2,000
			20X4		
			1 Jan	Balance b/d	2,000

For the balance sheet receivables will be valued as follows.

	$
Sales ledger balances	40,000
Less allowance for receivables	2,000
	38,000

In practice, it is unnecessary to show the total receivables balances and the allowance as separate items in the balance sheet. A balance sheet would normally show only the net figure ($27,720 in 20X2, $38,000 in 20X3).

Question   Bad debts and allowance for receivables

Corin Flakes owns and runs the Aerobic Health Foods Shop in Dundee. He commenced trading on 1 January 20X1. Customers are allowed to purchase up to $200 of goods on credit but must repay a certain proportion of their outstanding debt every month.

This credit system gives rise to a large number of bad debts, and Corin Flakes' results for his first three years of operations are as follows.

Year to 31 December 20X1	
Gross profit	$27,000
Bad debts written off	$8,000
Debts owed by customers as at 31 December 20X1	$40,000
Allowance for receivables	2½% of outstanding receivables
Other expenses	$20,000
Year to 31 December 20X2	
Gross profit	$45,000
Bad debts written off	$10,000
Debts owed by customers as at 31 December 20X2	$50,000
Allowance for receivables	2½% of outstanding receivables
Other expenses	$28,750
Year to 31 December 20X3	
Gross profit	$60,000
Bad debts written off	$11,000
Debts owed by customers as at 31 December 20X3	$30,000
Allowance for receivables	3% of outstanding receivables
Other expenses	$32,850

Required

For each of these three years, prepare the income statement of the business, and state the value of receivables appearing in the balance sheet as at 31 December.

Answer

AEROBIC HEALTH FOOD SHOP
INCOME STATEMENTS FOR THE YEARS ENDED 31 DECEMBER

	20X1		20X2		20X3	
	$	$	$	$	$	$
Gross profit		27,000		45,000		60,000
Reduction in allowance for receivables*						350
						60,350
Expenses:						
Bad debts written off	8,000		10,000		11,000	
Increase in allowance for receivables*	1,000		250			
Other expenses	20,000		28,750		32,850	
		29,000		39,000		43,850
Net(loss)/profit		(2,000)		6,000		16,500

*At 1 January 20X1 the allowance for receivables was nil. At 31 December 20X1 the allowance required was $2^1/2$% of $40,000 = $1,000. The increase in the allowance is therefore $1,000. At 31 December 20X2 the allowance required was 2½% of $50,000 = $1,250. The 20X1 allowance must therefore be increased by $250. At 31 December 20X3 the allowance required is 3% × $30,000 = $900. The 20X2 allowance is therefore reduced by $350.

Note: In practice the bad debts figure and the increase (or decrease) in the allowances for receivables are usually combined under the heading 'bad debts' in the income statement. You should be prepared for this in the assessment.

VALUE OF RECEIVABLES IN THE BALANCE SHEET

	As at 31.12.20X1	As at 31.12.20X2	As at 31.12.20X3
	$	$	$
Total value of receivables	40,000	50,000	30,000
Less allowance for receivables	1,000	1,250	900
Balance sheet value	39,000	48,750	29,100

Question

Receivables

Horace Goodrunning decides to make an allowance for receivables of 2% of outstanding receivables at the balance sheet date from 28 February 20X6. On 28 February 20X8, Horace decides that the allowance has been over-estimated and he reduces it to 1% of outstanding receivables. Outstanding receivables balances at the various balance sheet dates are as follows.

	$
28.2.20X6	15,200
28.2.20X7	17,100
28.2.20X8	21,400

You are required to show extracts from the following accounts for each of the three years above.

(a)   Receivables
(b)   Allowance for receivables
(c)   Income statement

Show how receivables would appear in the balance sheet at the end of each year.

Answer

The entries for the three years are denoted by (a), (b) and (c) in each account.

RECEIVABLES (EXTRACT)

			$		$
(a)	28.2.20X6	Balance	15,200		
(b)	28.2.20X7	Balance	17,100		
(c)	28.2.20X8	Balance	21,400		

ALLOWANCE FOR RECEIVABLES

			$			$
(a)	28.2.20X6	Balance c/d		28.2.20X6	I/S	304
		(2% of 15,200)	304			
			304			304
(b)	28.2.20X7	Balance c/d		1.3.20X6	Balance b/d	304
		(2% of 17,100)	342	28.2.20X7	I/S (note (i))	38
			342			342
(c)	28.2.20X8	I/S (note (ii))	128	1.3.20X7	Balance b/d	342
	28.2.20X8	Balance c/d				
		(1% of 21,400)	214			
			342			342
				1.3.20X8	Balance b/d	214

INCOME STATEMENT (EXTRACT)

		$
28.2.20X6	Allowance for receivables	304
28.2.20X7	Allowance for receivables	38
28.2.20X8	Allowance for receivables	(128)

Notes

(i)   The increase in the allowance is $(342 – 304) = $38
(ii)   The decrease in the allowance is $(342 – 214) = $128
(iii)   We calculate the net receivables figure for inclusion in the balance sheet as follows.

	20X6	20X7	20X8
	$	$	$
Current assets			
Receivables	15,200	17,100	21,400
Less allowance for receivables	304	342	214
	14,896	16,758	21,186

2.5 Specific allowance for receivables

So far we have dealt with a general allowance for receivables. Sometimes a business may want to make an allowance against a specific receivable. If this is the case, then the general allowance is calculated on the balance of receivables after deducting the specific receivable.

2.6 Example: Specific allowance

XY Co has a balance of receivables of $250,000. It wishes to provide a specific allowance of 60% on a debt of $20,000. It also wishes to set up a general allowance of 2% of receivables. What is the charge to the income statement?

Answer

Specific allowance

60% × $120,000 = $12,000

General allowance

	$
Total receivables	250,000
Specific provision against	(20,000)
Balance	230,000

General allowance = 2% × $230,000
= $4,600

Total allowance charged in income statement = $12,000 + $4,600
= $16,600

Chapter roundup

- A **bad** debt is one that is no longer expected to be paid. For instance, the customer may have gone into liquidation. This debt will be written off.

- An allowance for receivables occurs when there is uncertainty over whether a debt will be paid. The debt is not written off, but an allowance is made against non-payment.

- When an allowance is first made, the amount is charged as an expense in the income statement.

- When an allowance already exists, but is subsequently increased in size, the amount of the **increase** is charged as an expense in the income statement.

- When an allowance already exists, but is subsequently reduced in size, the amount of the **decrease** is recorded as an item of 'income' in the income statement.

Quick quiz

1   The entry to record a bad debt is:

DEBIT   _____ account

CREDIT   _____ account

2   The entry to record money received from a debt previously written off is:

DEBIT   _____ account

CREDIT   _____ account

3   The entry to record the creation of an allowance for receivables is:

DEBIT   _____ account

CREDIT   _____ account

4   The entry to record an increase in an allowance for receivables is:

DEBIT   _____ account

CREDIT   _____ account

5   Which of the fundamental accounting concepts are being applied when an allowance for receivables is set up?

A   Accruals and going concern
B   Accruals and consistency
C   Accruals and prudence
D   Going concern and prudence

6   Y has an allowance for receivables of $20,000, this is to be changed to 3% of the sales ledger balance of $500,000. Which of the following entries records the transaction?

A   Dr   I/S a/c   } $5,000
     Cr   Receivables a/c

B   Dr   Allowance for receivables a/c   } $5,000
     Cr   I/S a/c

C   Dr   I/S a/c   } $5,000
     Cr   Allowance for receivables

D   Dr   I/S a/c   } $15,000
     Cr   Allowance for receivables

Answers to quick quiz

1 DEBIT   Bad debts expense account
   CREDIT   Receivables account

2 DEBIT   Cash account
   CREDIT   Debts paid previously written off account

3 DEBIT   Allowance expense account
   CREDIT   Allowance for receivables account

4 DEBIT   Allowance expense account (with increase only!)
   CREDIT   Allowance for receivables account (with increase only)

5 C   This is correct because the accruals or matching concept requires bad debt expenses to be matched against related sales revenue on a prudent basis.

   A   Going concern is always presumed unless there are contrary indications.

   B   As the allowance has just been created, there are no prior year allowance against which consistency can be judged.

   D   Incorrect for reasons stated in above explanations.

6 B   Correct: the required allowance is 3% of the sales ledger balance $500,000 = $15,000. So the required reduction is $5,000, ($20,000 – $15,000).

   A   Incorrect; this entry will write off receivables balances not make an allowance.

   C   Incorrect; this entry will increase the allowance.

   D   Incorrect; this entry will increase the allowance a/c by the full amount of the allowance required.

Now try the questions below from the Question Bank

Question numbers	Page
41–42	401

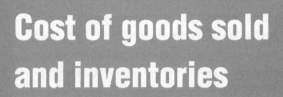

Cost of goods sold and inventories

Introduction

Inventory is one of the most important assets in a company's balance sheet. It also affects the income statement.

We shall see that in order to calculate gross profit it is necessary to work out the cost of goods sold, and in order to calculate the cost of goods sold it is necessary to have values for the opening inventory and closing inventory. We also need to deal with carriage costs

You should remember that the trading part of an income statement includes the following:

	$
Opening inventory	X
Plus purchases	X
Less closing inventory	(X)
Equals cost of goods sold	X

However this formula hides three basic problems.

(a)   How do you manage to get a precise **count of inventory** in hand at any one time?

(b)   Once it has been counted, how do you **value** the inventory?

(c)   Assuming the inventory is given a value, how does the **double entry** bookkeeping for inventory work?

Topic list	Syllabus references
1 The accounting treatment of inventories and carriage costs	D (5)
2 Accounting for opening and closing inventories	D (5)
3 Inventory count	D (5)
4 Valuing inventories	D (5)

1 The accounting treatment of inventories and carriage costs

> **FAST FORWARD**
>
> The accruals concept requires us to match income with the expenses incurred in earning that income. Goods can be unsold at the end of an accounting period and so still be held in inventory. The purchase cost of these goods should **not** be included in the cost of sales of the period.

1.1 Example: cost of sales

Perry P Louis ends his financial year on 30 September each year. On 1 October 20X4 he had no goods in inventory. During the year to 30 September 20X5, he purchased 30,000 umbrellas costing $60,000. He resold 20,000 of the umbrellas for $5 each, and sales for the year amounted to $100,000. At 30 September there were 10,000 unsold umbrellas left in inventory. What was Perry P Louis's gross profit for the year?

Solution

Perry P Louis purchased 30,000 umbrellas, but only sold 20,000. Purchase costs of $60,000 and sales of $100,000 do not represent the same quantity of goods. The gross profit for the year is calculated by 'matching' the sales value of the 20,000 umbrellas sold with the cost of those 20,000 umbrellas.

	$	$
Sales (20,000 units)		100,000
Purchases (30,000 units)	60,000	
Less closing inventory (10,000 units @ $2)	20,000	
Cost of sales (20,000 units)		40,000
Gross profit		60,000

1.2 Example continued

The next accounting year is 1 October 20X5 to 30 September 20X6. During the course of this year, Perry P Louis purchased 40,000 umbrellas at a total cost of $95,000. During the year he sold 45,000 umbrellas for $230,000. At 30 September 20X6 he had 5,000 umbrellas left in inventory, which had cost $12,000.

What was his gross profit for the year?

Solution

In this accounting year he purchased 40,000 umbrellas to add to the 10,000 he already had in inventory at the start of the year. He sold 45,000, leaving 5,000 umbrellas in inventory at the year end. Once again, gross profit should be calculated by matching the value of 45,000 units of sales with the cost of those 45,000 units.

The cost of sales is the value of the 10,000 umbrellas in inventory at the beginning of the year, plus the cost of the 40,000 umbrellas purchased, less the value of the 5,000 umbrellas in inventory at the year end.

	$	$
Sales (45,000 units)		230,000
Opening inventory (10,000 units) *	20,000	
Add purchases (40,000 units)	95,000	
	115,000	
Less closing inventory (5,000 units)	12,000	
Cost of sales (45,000 units)		103,000
Gross profit		127,000

*Taken from the closing inventory value of the previous accounting year, see example 1.1.

1.3 The cost of goods sold

 The cost of goods sold is calculated by adding the value of opening inventory to the cost of purchases and subtracting the value of closing inventory.

Formula to learn

	$
Opening inventory value	X
Add: purchases (or, in the case of a manufacturing company, the cost of production)	X
	X
Less: closing inventory value	(X)
Equals cost of goods sold	X

Assessment focus point

The above formula is very important. You **must** learn it for your assessment.

Question   **Gross profit**

On 1 January 20X6, the Grand Union Food Stores had goods in inventory valued at $6,000. During 20X6 it purchased supplies costing $50,000. Sales for the year to 31 December 20X6 amounted to $80,000. The cost of goods in inventory at 31 December 20X6 was $12,500.

Calculate the gross profit for the year.

Answer

GRAND UNION FOOD STORES
TRADING ACCOUNT FOR THE YEAR ENDED 31 DECEMBER 20X6

	$	$
Sales		80,000
Opening inventories	6,000	
Add: purchases	50,000	
	56,000	
Less: closing inventories	12,500	
Cost of goods sold		43,500
Gross profit		36,500

1.4 Carriage inwards and outwards

Key term

'**Carriage**' refers to the cost of transporting purchased goods from the supplier to the purchaser. Someone has to pay for these delivery costs: sometimes the supplier pays, and sometimes the purchaser pays. When the purchaser pays, the cost to the purchaser is recorded in his books as **carriage inwards**; when the supplier pays, the cost to the supplier is recorded in his books as **carriage outwards**.

FAST FORWARD

> Carriage inwards is part of 'purchases'. Carriage outwards is part of selling and distribution expenses.

The cost of carriage inwards is usually added to the cost of purchases, and is therefore included in the trading account. The cost of carriage outwards is a selling and distribution expense in the income statement.

1.5 Example: income statement

Gwyn Tring, trading as Clickety Clocks, imports and resells cuckoo clocks and grandfather clocks. He pays for the costs of delivering the clocks from his supplier in Switzerland to his shop in Wales. He resells the clocks to other traders throughout the country, paying the costs of carriage to his customers.

On 1 July 20X5, he had clocks in inventory valued at $17,000. During the year to 30 June 20X6 he purchased more clocks at a cost of $75,000. Carriage inwards amounted to $2,000. Sales for the year were $162,100. Other expenses of the business amounted to $56,000 excluding carriage outwards which cost $2,500. Gwyn Tring took drawings of $20,000 from the business during the course of the year. The value of the goods in inventory at the year end was $15,400.

Required

Prepare the income statement of Clickety Clocks for the year ended 30 June 20X6.

Solution

CLICKETY CLOCKS
INCOME STATEMENT FOR THE YEAR ENDED 30 JUNE 20X6

	$	$
Sales		162,100
Opening inventory	17,000	
Purchases	75,000	
Carriage inwards	2,000	
	94,000	
Less closing inventory	15,400	
Cost of goods sold		78,600
Gross profit		83,500
Carriage outwards	2,500	
Other expenses	56,000	
		58,500
Net profit (transferred to balance sheet)		25,000

Income statement

Sam's trial balance at 31.12.X6 was:

	Dr	Cr
	$	$
Inventory at 1.1.X6	500	
Sales		12,800
Purchases	6,000	
Carriage inwards	800	
Carriage outwards	500	
Selling expenses	1,200	
Administration expenses	1,000	
Fixtures and fittings	20,000	
Vans	10,000	
Receivables	900	
Payables		600
Capital at 1.1.X6		27,500
	40,900	40,900

Inventory at 31.12.X6 was valued at $1,500.

For the year ended 31.12.X6, calculate:

(a)   The gross profit
(b)   The cost of sales
(c)   The net profit

(a) $7,000
(b) $5,800
(c) $4,300

	$	$
Sales		12,800
Cost of sales		
Opening inventory	500	
Purchases	6,000	
Carriage inwards	800	
	7,300	
Closing inventory	(1,500)	
		5,800
Gross profit		7,000
Selling and delivery expenses (500 + 1,200)		(1,700)
Administration expenses		(1,000)
Net profit		4,300

1.6 Goods written off or written down

A trader might be unable to sell all the goods that he purchases if they are:

- Lost or stolen
- Damaged
- Obsolete or out of fashion, and so thrown away or possibly sold off in a clearance sale

When goods are lost, stolen or thrown away as worthless, the business will make a loss on those goods because their 'sales value' will be nil.

Similarly, when goods lose value because they are obsolete or out of fashion, the business will make a loss if their clearance sales value is less than their cost. For example, if goods which originally cost $500 are now obsolete and can only be sold for $150, the business will suffer a loss of $350.

Key term

> **Net realisable value** is the sales value less any costs that will be incurred in making the sale.

If, at the end of an accounting period, a business still has goods in inventory which are either worthless or worth less than their original cost, the value of the inventories should be written down to one of the following.

- Nothing, if they are worthless
- Their net realisable value, if this is less than their original cost

The loss will be reported as soon as it is foreseen, even if the goods have not yet been scrapped or sold off at a cheap price. This is an application of the prudence concept.

The costs of inventories written off or written down should not usually cause any problems in calculating the gross profit of a business, because the cost of goods sold will include the cost of stocks written off or written down, as the following example shows.

1.7 Example: inventories written off and written down

Lucas Wagg, trading as Fairlock Fashions, ends his financial year on 31 March. At 1 April 20X5 he had goods in inventory valued at $8,800. During the year to 31 March 20X6, he purchased goods costing $48,000. Fashion goods which cost $2,100, were still held in inventory at 31 March 20X6 that can only be sold at a sale price of $400. The goods still held in inventory at 31 March 20X6 (including the fashion goods) had an original purchase cost of $7,600. Sales for the year were $81,400.

Required

Calculate the gross profit of Fairlock Fashions for the year ended 31 March 20X6.

Solution

INVENTORY COUNT

	At cost	Realisable value (if lower than cost)	Value of closing inventory
	$	$	$
Fashion goods	2,100	400	400
Other goods (balancing figure)	5,500		5,500
	7,600		5,900

FAIRLOCK FASHIONS
INCOME STATEMENT FOR THE YEAR ENDED 31 MARCH 20X6

	$	$
Sales		81,400
Value of opening inventory	8,800	
Purchases	48,000	
	56,800	
Less closing inventory	5,900	
Cost of goods sold		50,900
Gross profit		30,500

ssessment cus points

(a) Cost of sales in the income statement is the cost of goods actually sold in the period (not bought), which is opening inventory add purchases less closing inventory.

(b) Carriage in is part of cost of sales, and this affects gross profit. Carriage out is an expense and affects net profit.

(c) Inventory is valued at the lower of cost and net realisable value.

Question   **Inventory**

A business has three items of inventory X, Y and Z.

	Cost	NRV
	$	$
X	15,000	20,000
Y	5,000	2,000
Z	17,000	13,000

What is the closing value of inventory?

A $37,000
B $35,000
C $30,000
D $42,000

Answer

C   Each item has to be valued at the lower of cost and NRV ($15,000 + $2,000 + $13,000).

2 Accounting for opening and closing inventories

FAST FORWARD Businesses must account accurately for inventory. **Inventory in hand** can be a substantial asset and **inventory used** must be known in order to compute **cost of sales**.

2.1 Ledger accounting for inventories

FAST FORWARD The value of closing inventories is accounted for in the nominal ledger by debiting a inventory account and crediting the trading account at the end of an accounting period. At the beginning of the next accounting period the opening inventory value b/f in the inventory account is transferred to the trading account.

A inventory account must be kept. This inventory account is only ever used at the end of an accounting period, when the business counts up and values the inventory in hand (an inventory count). To record this inventory value:

DEBIT   Inventory account (closing inventory value) $X
CREDIT   Trading account $X

The debit balance on inventory account represents an asset, which will be shown as part of current assets in the balance sheet, and the credit in the trading account is **closing inventory**, in cost of sales.

Closing inventory at the end of one period becomes opening inventory at the start of the next period. The inventory account remains unchanged until the end of the next period, when the value of opening inventory is taken to the trading account.

DEBIT   Trading account $X
CREDIT   Inventory account (value of opening inventory) $X

Question	Final accounts with inventory

A business is established with capital of $2,000 and this amount is paid into a business bank account by the proprietor. During the first year's trading, the following transactions occurred:

	$
Purchases of goods for resale, on credit	4,300
Payments to trade payables	3,600
Sales, all on credit	4,000
Payments from receivables	3,200
Non-current assets purchased for cash	1,500
Other expenses, all paid in cash	900

The bank has provided an overdraft facility of up to $3,000.

All 'other expenses' relate to the current year (ie no accruals or prepayments).

Closing inventories of goods are valued at $1,800. (This is the first year of the business, so there are no opening inventories.)

Ignore depreciation and drawings.

Required

Prepare the ledger accounts, an income statement for the year and a balance sheet as at the end of the year.

Answer

CASH

	$		$
Capital	2,000	Trade payable	3,600
Receivables	3,200	Non-current assets	1,500
Balance c/d	800	Other expenses	900
	6,000		6,000
		Balance b/d	800

CAPITAL

	$		$
Balance c/d	2,600	Cash	2,000
		I/S a/c	600
	2,600		2,600
		Balance b/d	2,600

TRADE PAYABLES

	$		$
Cash	3,600	Purchases	4,300
Balance c/d	700		
	4,300		4,300
		Balance b/d	700

PURCHASES ACCOUNT

	$		$
Trade payables	4,300	Trading a/c	4,300

NON-CURRENT ASSETS

	$		$
Cash	1,500	Balance c/d	1,500
Balance b/d	1,500		

SALES

	$		$
Trading a/c	4,000	Receivables	4,000

RECEIVABLES

	$		$
Sales	4,000	Cash	3,200
		Balance c/d	800
	4,000		4,000
Balance b/d	800		

OTHER EXPENSES

	$		$
Cash	900	I/S a/c	900

INCOME STATEMENT

	$		$
Purchases account	4,300	Sales	4,000
Gross profit c/d	1,500	Closing inventory (inventory account)	1,800
	5,800		5,800
Other expenses	900	Gross profit b/d	1,500
Net profit (transferred to capital account)	600		
	1,500		1,500

INVENTORY ACCOUNT

	$		$
Trading account (closing inventory)	1,800	Balance c/d	1,800
Balance b/d	1,800		

BALANCE SHEET AS AT THE END OF THE PERIOD

	$	$
Non-current assets		1,500
Current assets		
Inventory	1,800	
Receivables	800	
		2,600
		4,100
Capital		
At start of period		2,000
Profit for period		600
		2,600
Current liabilities		
Bank overdraft	800	
Trade payables	700	
		1,500
		4,100

Make sure you understand the entries. The balance on the inventory account was $1,800, which appears in the balance sheet as a current asset. The transfer from the inventory account to the trading account is the closing inventory in the calculation of cost of sales. The $1,800 closing inventory was the only entry in the inventory account – there was no figure for opening inventory.

If there had been, it would be eliminated by transferring it as a debit balance to the trading account.

DEBIT	Trading account (with value of opening inventory)
CREDIT	Inventory account (with value of opening inventory)

The debit in the trading account would then have increased the cost of sales, ie opening inventory is added to purchases in calculating cost of sales. Remember the formula: opening inventory + purchases – closing inventory = cost of sales.

2.2 Example: inventory account

A trader starts a business on 1 January 20X1.

On   31 December 20X1 inventory is $2,000
      31 December 20X2 inventory is $2,500
      31 December 20X3 inventory is $3,000

Draw up the inventory account for 20X1, 20X2 and 20X3.

Solution

INVENTORY ACCOUNT

		$			$
31.12.X1	Trading a/c (closing inventory)	2,000 2,000	31.12.X1	Balance c/d	2,000 2,000
1.1.X2	Balance b/d	2,000	31.12.X2	Trading a/c (opening inventory)	2,000
31.12.X2	Trading a/c (closing inventory)	2,500 4,500	31.12.X2	Balance c/d	2,500 4,500
1.1X3	Balance b/d	2,500	31.12.X3	Trading a/c (opening inventory)	2,500
31.12.X3	Trading a/c (closing inventory)	3,000 5,500	31.12.X3	Balance c/d	3,000 5,500
1.1.X4	Balance b/d	3,000			

Assessment focus point

The main points

(a)   Closing inventory is an asset (a debit) in the balance sheet and a credit in the trading account.

(b)   Opening inventory is a debit in the trading account.

(c)   At the year end

   (i)   Debit trading account
          Credit inventory account   } with opening inventory value

   (ii)   Debit inventory account
          Credit trading account   } with closing inventory valuation

(d)   The balance on the inventory account is the figure for the balance sheet.

3 Inventory count

The quantity of inventories held at the year end is established by means of a physical count of inventory in an annual inventory count exercise, or by a 'continuous' inventory count.

3.1 Carrying out the physical inventory count

The continuous nature of trading activity may cause a problem in that inventory movements may continue during the physical inventory count. Two possible solutions are as follows.

- Close down the business while the count takes place
- Keep detailed records of inventory movements during the course of the inventory count

Closing down the business for a short period for a inventory count (eg over a weekend or at Christmas) is considerably easier than trying to keep detailed records of inventory movements during a inventory count. So most businesses prefer that method unless they happen to keep detailed records of inventory movements anyway (for example, because they wish to keep strict control on inventory movements).

In more complicated cases, an alternative approach to establishing inventory quantities is to maintain continuous inventory records. This means that a card is kept for every item of inventory, showing receipts and issues from the stores, and a running total. A few inventory items are counted each day to make sure the record cards are correct. This is called a 'continuous' inventory count because it is spread out over the year.

4 Valuing inventories

Inventory is valued in accordance with the prudence concept at the lower of cost and net realisable value (NRV). Cost comprises purchase costs and costs of conversion.

Net realisable value is the selling price less all costs to completion and less selling costs.

4.1 Applying the basic valuation rule

If a business has many inventory items on hand, the comparison of cost and NRV should be carried out for each item separately. It is not sufficient to compare the total cost of all inventory items with their total NRV.

4.2 Example: closing inventory

A company has four items of inventory and their cost and NRVs are as follows.

Inventory item	Cost	NRV	Lower of cost/NRV
	$	$	$
1	27	32	27
2	14	8	8
3	43	55	43
4	29	40	29
	113	135	107

What is the value of closing inventory?

Solution

It would be incorrect to compare total costs ($113) with total NRV ($135) and to state inventories at $113 in the balance sheet. The company can foresee a loss of $6 on item 2 and this should be recognised. By performing the cost/NRV comparison for each item separately the prudent valuation of $107 can be derived. This is the value which should appear in the balance sheet.

However, for a company with large amounts of inventory this procedure may be impracticable. In this case it is acceptable to group similar items into categories and perform the comparison of cost and NRV category by category, rather than item by item.

4.3 Determining the purchase cost

Inventory may be raw materials or components bought from suppliers, finished goods which have been made by the business but not yet sold, or work in the process of production, but only part-completed (this is called work in progress or WIP). It will simplify matters, however, if we think about the cost of purchased raw materials and components.

A business may be continually purchasing a particular component. As each consignment is received from suppliers they are stored in the appropriate 'bin', where they will be mingled with previous consignments. When the storekeeper issues components to production, he will simply pull out the nearest components to hand, which may have arrived in the latest consignment or in an earlier consignment or in several different consignments.

There are several techniques to attribute cost to the components.

FORWARD The possible methods of valuing inventories include FIFO, LIFO, average cost, standard cost and replacement cost. **Financial** accounts will normally require the use of FIFO or average cost.

Key terms

(a) **FIFO (first in, first out).** We assume that components are used in the order in which they are received from suppliers, so that the issue is part of the oldest consignment still unused and is costed accordingly, inventories are themselves recent receipts.

(b) **Average cost.** Each component in the bin is assumed to have been purchased at the weighted average price of all components in the bin at that moment.

(c) **LIFO (last in, first out).** Components issued to production formed part of the most recent delivery, inventories are the oldest receipts.

(d) **Standard cost.** A pre-determined standard cost is applied to all inventory items. If this standard price differs from prices actually paid during the period, the difference is written off as a 'variance' in the profit and loss account.

(e) **Replacement cost.** It is assumed that the cost at which a inventory unit was purchased is the amount it would cost to replace it.

It is worth mentioning here that if you are preparing **financial** accounts you would normally expect to use FIFO or average costs for the balance sheet valuation of inventory. IAS 2 specifically bans the use of LIFO and replacement costs. (CA 2006 allows any method the directors think appropriate, so long as, under the historical cost accounting rules, inventory is stated at production cost or purchase price.)

4.4 Example: inventory valuation

To illustrate the two pricing methods, the following transactions will be used in each case.

TRANSACTIONS DURING MAY 20X3

	Quantity Units	Unit cost $	Total cost $
Opening balance 1 May	100	2.00	200
Receipts 3 May	400	2.10	840
Issues 4 May	200		
Receipts 9 May	300	2.12	636
Issues 11 May	400		
Receipts 18 May	100	2.40	240
Issues 20 May	100		
Closing balance 31 May	200		
			1,916

'Receipts' means goods received into store, and 'issues' means the issue of goods from store.

How would issues and closing inventory be valued using the following bases.

(a)   FIFO?
(b)   Average cost?

4.5 FIFO (first in, first out)

Key term

> **FIFO** assumes that materials are issued out of inventory in the order in which they were delivered into inventory, ie issues are priced at the cost of the earliest delivery remaining in inventory.

Solution

The cost of issues and closing inventory value in the example, using FIFO would be as follows.

Date of issue	Quantity Units	Value issued	Cost of issues $	$
4 May	200	100 at $2	200	
		100 at $2.10	210	
				410
11 May	400	300 at $2.10	630	
		100 at $2.12	212	
				842
20 May	100	100 at $2.12		212
				1,464
Closing inventory value	200	100 at $2.12	212	
		100 at $2.40	240	
				452
				1,916

Note that the cost of materials issued plus the value of closing inventory equals the cost of purchases plus the value of opening inventory ($1,916).

4.6 Average cost

Key term

> The **cumulative weighted average pricing method** calculates a weighted average price for all units in inventory. Issues are priced at this average cost, and the balance of inventory remaining would have the same unit valuation.

A new weighted average price is calculated whenever a new delivery of materials into store is received. This is the key feature of cumulative weighted average pricing.

Solution continued

In our example, issue costs and closing inventory values would be as follows.

Date	Received Units	Issued Units	Balance Units	Total inventory value $	Unit cost $	Price of issue $
Opening inventory			100	200	2.00	
3 May	400			840	2.10	
			500	1,040	2.08 *	
4 May		200		(416)	2.08 **	416
			300	624	2.08	
9 May	300			636	2.12	
			600	1,260	2.10 *	
11 May		400		(840)	2.10 **	840
			200	420	2.10	
18 May	100			240	2.40	
			300	660	2.20 *	
20 May		100		(220)	2.20 **	220
						1,476
Closing inventory value			200	440	2.20	440
						1,916

* A new unit cost of inventory is calculated whenever a new receipt of materials occurs.

** Whenever inventories are issued, the unit value of the items issued is the current weighted average cost per unit at the time of the issue.

For this method too, the cost of materials issued plus the value of closing inventory equals the cost of purchases plus the value of opening inventory ($1,916).

4.7 Example: inventory valuations and profit

On 1 November 20X2 a company held 300 units of finished goods item No 9639 in inventory. These were valued at $12 each. During November 20X2 three batches of finished goods were received into store from the production department as follows.

Date	Units received	Production cost per unit
10 November	400	$12.50
20 November	400	$14
25 November	400	$15

Goods sold out of inventory during November were as follows.

Date	Units sold	Sale price per unit
14 November	500	$20
21 November	500	$20
28 November	100	$20

What was the profit from selling inventory item 9639 in November 20X2, applying the following principles of inventory valuation.

(a)　FIFO
(b)　Cumulative weighted average costing
(c)　LIFO

Ignore administration, sales and distribution costs.

Solution

(a)　FIFO

Date	Issue costs	Issue cost Total $	Closing inventory $
14 November	300 units × $12 plus		
	200 units × $12.50	6,100	
21 November	200 units × $12.50 plus		
	300 units × $14	6,700	
28 November	100 units × $14	1,400	
Closing inventory	400 units × $15		6,000
		14,200	6,000

(b)   Cumulative weighted average costs

		Unit cost	Balance in inventory	Total cost of issues	Closing inventory
		$	$	$	$
1 November	Opening inventory	12	3,600		
	300				
10 November	400	12.50	5,000		
	700	12.286	8,600		
14 November	500	12.286	6,143	6,143	
	200	12.286	2,457		
20 November	400	14	5,600		
	600	13.428	8,057		
21 November	500	13.428	6,714	6,714	
	100	13.428	1,343		
25 November	400	15	6,000		
	500	14.686	7,343		
28 November	100	14.686	1,469	1,469	
30 November	Closing inventory	14.686	5,874	14,326	5,874
	400				

(c)   LIFO

		Balance in inventory	Total cost of issues	Closing inventory
		$	$	$
1 November	Opening inventory	3,600		
	300			
10 November	400	5,000		
	700	8,600		
14 November	(400: 10/11 + 100 o/s)	500	6,200	6,200
	200	2,400		
20 November	400	5,600		
	600	8,000		
21 November	(400: 20/11 + 100 o/s)	500	6,800	6,800
	100	1,200		
25 November	400	6,000		
	500	7,200		
28 November	(100: 25/11)	100	1,500	1,500
30 November	(300: 25/11 + 100 o/s)	400	5,700	14,500	5,700

Summary

	FIFO $	Weighted average $	LIFO $
Opening inventory	3,600	3,600	3,600
Cost of production	16,600	16,600	16,600
	20,200	20,200	20,200
Closing inventory	6,000	5,874	5,700
Cost of sales	14,200	14,326	14,500
Sales (1,100 × $20)	22,000	22,000	22,000
Profit	7,800	7,674	7,500

Different inventory valuations have produced different cost of sales figures, and therefore different profits.

The profit differences are only temporary. In our example, the opening inventory in December 20X2 will be $6,000, $5,874 or $5,700, depending on the inventory valuation used. Different opening inventory values will affect the cost of sales and profits in December, so that in the long run inequalities in costs of sales each month will even themselves out.

Question

Inventory valuation

In times of inflation, changing from a FIFO method of inventory valuation to a LIFO method is likely to:

A   Increase reported profit
B   Reduce reported profit
C   Have no effect on reported profit
D   Have an unpredictable effect on reported profit

Answer

B is correct. Under FIFO, inventory was the most recent purchases. Under LIFO, inventory is the oldest (and cheapest) purchases. Thus, changing to LIFO puts up the cost of sales and reduces reported profits.

Chapter roundup

- The accruals concept requires us to match income with the expenses incurred in earning that income. Goods can be unsold at the end of an accounting period and so still be held in inventory. The purchase cost of these goods should **not** be included in the cost of sales of the period.

- The cost of goods sold is calculated by adding the value of opening inventory to the cost of purchases and subtracting the value of closing inventory.

- Carriage inwards is part of 'purchases'. Carriage outwards is part of selling and distribution expenses.

- Businesses must account accurately for inventory. **Inventory in hand** can be a substantial asset and **inventory used** must be known in order to compute **cost of sales**.

- The value of closing inventories is accounted for in the nominal ledger by debiting a inventory account and crediting the trading account at the end of an accounting period. At the beginning of the next accounting period the opening inventory value b/f in the inventory account is transferred to the trading account.

- The quantity of inventories held at the year end is established by means of a physical count of inventory in an annual inventory count exercise, or by a 'continuous' inventory count.

- Inventory is valued in accordance with the prudence concept at the lower of cost and net realisable value (NRV). Cost comprises purchase costs and costs of conversion.

- Net realisable value is the selling price less all costs to completion and less selling costs.

- The possible methods of valuing inventories include FIFO, LIFO, average cost, standard cost and replacement cost. **Financial** accounts will normally require the use of FIFO or average cost.

Quick quiz

1   Cost of sales is calculated as _____ plus _____ less _____. (Fill in the blanks.)

2   Carriage inwards reduces gross profit and net profit. True or false?

3   Carriage outwards reduces gross profit and net profit. True or false?

4   Carriage inwards is added to cost of sales because

    A   It is an expense of the business
    B   It is an expense connected with purchasing stock for resale
    C   It is not a controllable expense of running the business
    D   If it appeared in the profit and loss account, net profit would be incorrect

5   Put debit or credit in the blanks.

Closing inventory is a _____ in the balance sheet and a _____ in the trading account.

6   Net realisable value is _____
_____.

7   IAS 2 requires inventory to be valued using a consistent approach. Which of the following valuation methods describes the correct approach?

    A   At the higher of cost or net realisable value
    B   At cost
    C   At net realisable value
    D   At the lower of cost or net realisable value

8   IAS 2 requires inventory to be valued using acceptable methods.

Which of the following is an unacceptable method of valuing inventory?

    A   'First in First out'
    B   'Average cost'
    C   'Last in First out'
    D   Standard cost

9   At the year end a business has inventories of bags and bells.

	Bags	Bells
	$	$
Original purchase price (per unit)	10	12
Number in shock	100	80
Estimated future sales price (per unit)	9	15
Estimated selling costs (per unit)	1	1

The value of closing inventory is $_____.

BPP LEARNING MEDIA

Answers to quick quiz

1   Opening inventory + purchases (or cost of production) – closing inventory

2   True

3   False. It affects net profit only.

4   B   Correct.
     A   This is not a precise answer.
     C   It is controllable as a result of buying decisions.
     D   Net profit would be unchanged regardless of how it is reported. Gross profit would be affected, however.

5   Closing inventory is a **debit** in the balance sheet and a **credit** in the trading account.

6   Net realisable value is the expected selling price less any costs to be incurred in getting the inventory ready for sale and any costs of sale.

7   D   Correct.
     A   Incorrect, inventory valuation must be prudent.
     B   Incorrect.
     C   Incorrect.

8   C   Not acceptable according to IAS 2, but it remains a permissible method under CA85.
     A   Acceptable.
     B   Acceptable.
     D   Acceptable provided that variances are appropriately treated.

9   Bags: Cost $10, NRV $8, value $8 × 100 = $800
     Bells: Cost $12, NRV $14, value $12 × 80 = 960

     ∴ The value of closing inventory is $(800 + 960) = $1,760

Now try the questions below from the Question Bank

Question numbers	Page
43–51	401

Bank reconciliations

Introduction

The cash book of a business is the record of how much cash the business believes that it has in the bank.

Why might the business' estimate of its bank balance be different from the amount shown on the bank statement? There are three common explanations.

(a)   **Error**. Errors in calculation or recording transactions are more likely to be made by themselves than by the bank.

(b)   **Bank charges or bank interest**. The bank usually only shows these on the bank statement.

(c)   **Timing differences.** These include amounts banked, but not yet 'cleared' and added to the account. Similarly, payments by cheque not yet recorded by the bank.

The comparison of the cash book balance with the bank statements is called a bank reconciliation.

Topic list	Syllabus references
1 The bank reconciliation	B (3)
2 Carrying out the reconciliation	B (3)

1 The bank reconciliation

FAST FORWARD

A **bank reconciliation** is a comparison of a bank statement (sent monthly, weekly or even daily by the bank) with the cash book. Differences between the balance on the bank statement and the balance in the cash book will be errors or timing differences, and they should be identified and satisfactorily explained.

1.1 The bank statement

It is a common practice for a business to issue a monthly statement to each credit customer. In the same way, a bank sends a statement to its short-term receivables and payables – ie customers with bank overdrafts and those with money in their account – itemising the balance on the account at the beginning of the period, receipts and payments during the period, and the balance at the end of the period.

Remember, however, that if a customer has money in his account, the bank owes him that money and so the customer is a payable of the bank (hence the phrase 'to be in credit' means to have money in your account). If a business has $8,000 cash in the bank, it will have a debit balance in its own cash book, but the bank statement will show a credit balance of $8,000. (The bank's records are a 'mirror image' of the customer's own records, with debits and credits reversed.)

If you are having difficulties, think of a bank statement as a supplier's statement.

1.2 Why is a bank reconciliation necessary?

FAST FORWARD

It is important to check the cash book against the bank statement regularly. There will almost always be differences – arising from errors, omissions and timing differences.

A bank reconciliation identifies differences between the cash book and bank statement.

These can be due to:

- **Errors** – errors in the cash book or errors made by the bank

- **Bank charges** or bank interest, shown on the bank statement but not in the cash book

- **Timing differences** – items appearing in the cash book in one period but not appearing on the bank statement until a later period

Assessment focus point

A bank reconciliation is an important **control** to ensure that no unauthorised transactions go through the bank account.

1.3 What to look for when doing a bank reconciliation

The cash book and bank statement will rarely agree at a given date. When doing a bank reconciliation, you need to look for the following items.

(a) **Correction of errors**

(b) **Adjustments to the cash book**
- Payments by standing order into or from the account, not yet entered into the cash book
- Dividends received direct into the bank account, not yet entered in the cash book
- Bank interest and bank charges, not yet entered in the cash book

(c) **Timing differences reconciling the corrected cash book balance to the bank statement**
- Cheque payments credited in the cash book, not yet on the bank statement

- Cheques received, paid into the bank and debited in the cash book, but not yet on the bank statement

Key terms

Unpresented cheques are cheques sent out which do not yet appear on the statement.

Uncleared lodgements are cheques received and paid into the bank which do not yet appear on the statement.

Unpresented cheques reduce the balance at the bank, uncleared lodgements increase it.

2 Carrying out the reconciliation

When the discrepancies due to errors, omissions and timing differences are noticed, appropriate adjustments must be made. Errors must be corrected and omissions from the cash book entered. Any remaining differences should then be identified as timing differences.

2.1 Example: bank reconciliation

At 30 September 20X6, the cash book balance is $805.15 (debit). A bank statement on 30 September 20X6 shows a balance of $1,112.30.

On investigation of the difference between the two sums, the following points arise.

(a) The cash book had been undercast by $90.00 on the debit side*.
(b) Cheques paid in, not yet credited by the bank amounted to $208.20.
(c) Cheques drawn, not yet presented to the bank amounted to $425.35.

* 'Casting' is an accountant's term for adding up.

Required

(a) Show the correction to the cash book.
(b) Prepare a statement reconciling the bank statement and cash book balance.

Solution

(a)

	$
Cash book balance brought forward	805.15
Add	
Correction of undercasting	90.00
Corrected balance	895.15

(b)

	$	$
Balance per bank statement		1,112.30
Add		
Uncleared lodgements	208.20	
Less		
Unpresented cheques	425.35	
		(217.15)
Balance per cash book		895.15

Differences

Which two of the following statements are true?

(i)   Unpresented cheques should be treated as a timing difference.
(ii)   Unpresented cheques should be written back into the cash book.
(iii)   Uncleared lodgements reduce the figure per the bank statement.
(iv)   Uncleared lodgements increase the figure per bank statement.

Answer

(i) and (iv) are true.

2.2 Example: more complicated bank reconciliation

On 30 June 20X0, Cook's cash book showed an overdraft of $300 on his current account. A bank statement as at the end of June 20X0 showed that Cook was in credit with the bank by $65.

On checking the cash book with the bank statement you find the following.

(a)   Cheques drawn of $500, entered in the cash book but not yet presented.

(b)   Cheques received of $400, entered in the cash book, but not yet credited by the bank.

(c)   The bank had transferred interest received on deposit account of $60 to current account, recording the transfer on 5 July 20X0. This amount had been credited in the cash book as on 30 June 20X0.

(d)   Bank charges of $35 in the bank statement had not been entered in the cash book.

(e)   The payments side of the cash book had been undercast by $10.

(f)   Dividends received amounting to $200 were paid direct to the bank and not entered in the cash book.

(g)   A cheque for $50 drawn on deposit account had been shown in the cash book as drawn on current account.

(h)   A cheque issued to Jones for $25 was replaced when out of date. It was credited again in the cash book, no other entry being made. Both cheques were included in the total of unpresented cheques shown above.

Required

(a)   Indicate the appropriate adjustments in the cash book.
(b)   Prepare a statement reconciling the amended balance with that shown in the bank statement.

BPP
LEARNING MEDIA

Solution

(a)   The errors to correct are given in notes (c) (e) (f) (g) and (h). Bank charges (note (d)) also need adjustment.

		Adjustments in cash book	
		Debit	*Credit*
		(ie add to	*(ie deduct from*
		cash balance)	*cash balance)*
Item		$	$
(c)	Cash book incorrectly credited with interest on 30 June, should have been debited with the receipt	60	
(c)	Debit cash book (current a/c) with transfer of interest from deposit a/c (note 1)	60	
(d)	Bank charges		35
(e)	Undercast on payments (credit) side of cash book		10
(f)	Dividends received should be debited in the cash book	200	
(g)	Cheque drawn on deposit account, not current account. Add cash back to current account	50	
(h)	Cheque paid to Jones is out of date and so cancelled. Cash book should now be debited, since previous credit entry is no longer valid (note 2)	25	
		395	45

	$	$
Cash book: balance on current account as at 30 June 20X0		(300)
Adjustments and corrections:		
Debit entries (adding to cash)	395	
Credit entries (reducing cash balance)	(45)	
Net adjustments		350
Corrected balance in the cash book		50

Notes

1   Item (c) is rather complicated. The transfer of interest from the deposit to the current account was presumably given as an instruction to the bank on or before 30 June 20X0. Since the correct entry is to debit the current account (and credit the deposit account) the correction in the cash book is to debit the current account with 2 × $60 = $120 – ie to cancel out the incorrect credit entry in the cash book and then to make the correct debit entry. However, the bank does not record the transfer until 5 July and so it will not appear in the bank statement.

2   Item (h). Two cheques have been paid to Jones, but one is now cancelled. Since the cash book is credited whenever a cheque is paid, it should be debited whenever a cheque is cancelled. The amount of unpresented cheques is reduced by the amount of the cancelled cheque.

(b)   BANK RECONCILIATION STATEMENT AT 30 JUNE 20X0

	$	$
Balance per bank statement		65
Add: outstanding lodgements		
(ie cheques paid in but not yet credited)	400	
deposit interest not yet credited (note 1)	60	
		460
		525
Less: unpresented cheques	500	
less cheque to Jones cancelled (note 2)	25	
		475
Balance per corrected cash book		50

Assessment focus point

Notice that in preparing a bank reconciliation it is good practice to begin with the balance shown by the bank statement and end with the balance shown by the cash book. It is this corrected cash book balance which will appear in the balance sheet as 'cash at bank'. Questions sometimes give the information in the reverse order: as always, read the question carefully.

Question

Bank reconciliations

From the information given below relating to PWW you are required:

(a)   To make such additional entries in the cash account of PWW as you consider necessary to show the correct balance at 31 October 20X2.

(b)   To prepare a statement reconciling the corrected cash account balance as shown in (a) above with the balance at 31 October 20X2 on the bank statement.

CASH AT BANK ACCOUNT IN THE LEDGER OF PWW

20X2 October		$	20X2 October		$
1	Balance b/f	274	1	Wages	3,146
8	Q Manufacturing	3,443	1	Petty Cash	55
8	R Cement	1,146	8	Wages	3,106
11	S Limited	638	8	Petty Cash	39
11	T & Sons	512	15	Wages	3,029
11	U & Co	4,174	15	Petty Cash	78
15	V	1,426	22	A & Sons	929
15	W Electrical	887	22	B	134
22	X and Associates	1,202	22	C & Company	77
26	Y	2,875	22	D & E	263
26	Z	982	22	F	1,782
29	ABC	1,003	22	G Associates	230
29	DEE Corporation	722	22	Wages	3,217
29	GHI	2,461	22	Petty Cash	91
31	Balance c/f	14	25	H & Partners	26
			26	J Sons & Co	868
			26	K & Co	107
			26	L, M & N	666
			28	O	112
			29	Wages	3,191
			29	Petty Cash	52
			29	P & Sons	561
		21,759			21,759

Z BANK – STATEMENT OF ACCOUNT WITH PWW

20X2 October		Payments $	Receipts $		Balance $
1					1,135
1	cheque	55			
1	cheque	3,146			
1	cheque	421		O/D	2,487
2	cheque	73			
2	cheque	155		O/D	2,715
6	cheque	212		O/D	2,927
8	sundry credit		4,589		
8	cheque	3,106			
8	cheque	39		O/D	1,483
11	sundry credit		5,324		3,841
15	sundry credit		2,313		
15	cheque	78			
15	cheque	3,029			3,047
22	sundry credit		1,202		
22	cheque	3,217			
22	cheque	91			941
25	cheque	1,782			
25	cheque	134		O/D	975
26	cheque	929			
26	sundry credit		3,857		

20X2 October		Payments $	Receipts $	Balance $
26	cheque	230		1,723
27	cheque	263		
27	cheque	77		1,383
29	sundry credit		4,186	
29	cheque	52		
29	cheque	3,191		
29	cheque	26		
29	dividends on investments		2,728	
29	cheque	666		4,362
31	bank charges	936		3,426

Answer

(a) CASH BOOK

		$			$
31 Oct	Dividends received (W5)	2,728	31 Oct	Unadjusted balance b/f (overdraft)	14
			31 Oct	Bank charges (W4)	936
			31 Oct	Adjusted balance c/f	1,778
		2,728			2,728

(b) BANK RECONCILIATION STATEMENT
AT 31 OCTOBER 20X2

	$	$
Corrected balance as per cash book		1,778
Cheques paid out but not yet presented (W3)	1,648	
Cheques paid in but not yet cleared by bank (W7)	0	
		1,648
Balance as per bank statement		3,426

Workings

1   Payments shown on bank statement but not in cash book $(421 + 73 + 155 + 212)* $861
    * Presumably recorded in cash book before 1 October 20X2
    but not yet presented for payment as at 30 September 20X2

2   Payments in the cash book and on the bank statement $20,111
    $(3,146 + 55 + 3,106 + 39 + 78 + 3,029 + 3,217 + 91 + 1,782 + 134 + 929 + 230 +
    263 + 77 + 52 + 3,191 + 26 + 666)

3   Payments in the cash book but not on the bank statement (Total payments in cash $1,648
    book $21,759 minus $20,111)

		$
Alternatively	J & Sons	868
	K & Co	107
	O	112
	P & Sons	561
		1,648

4	Bank charges, not in the cash book	$936
5	Receipts recorded by bank statement but not in cash book: dividends on investments	$2,728
6	Receipts in the cash book and also bank statement (8 Oct $4,589; 11 Oct $5,324; 15 Oct $2,313; 22 Oct $1,202; 26 Oct $3,857; 29 Oct $4,186)	$21,471
7	Receipts recorded in cash book but not bank statement	None

Chapter roundup

- A **bank reconciliation** is a comparison of a bank statement (sent monthly, weekly or even daily by the bank) with the cash book. Differences between the balance on the bank statement and the balance in the cash book will be errors or timing differences, and they should be identified and satisfactorily explained.

- It is important to check the cash book against the bank statement regularly. There will almost always be differences – arising from errors, omissions and timing differences.

- When the discrepancies due to errors, omissions and timing differences are noticed, appropriate adjustments must be made. Errors must be corrected and omissions from the cash book entered. Any remaining differences should then be identified as timing differences.

Quick quiz

1   The bank column of a cash book showed a closing balance of $550 (credit). Unpresented cheques amount to $1,500 and receipts undeposited at the bank were $500. The bank statement balance was? (Hint: prepare a bank reconciliation.)

A $1,550 (in hand)
B $450 (in hand)
C $1,450 (in hand)
D $2,550 (overdrawn)

2   The cash book balance was $1,500 (debit). The bank statement revealed an overdrawn balance of $500. Unpresented cheques were $1,200 and receipts undeposited were $3,000. The bank has incorrectly charged another customers cheque to the company account. How much was the incorrect cheque drawn for?

A $3,200
B $6,200
C $3,800
D $200

Answers to quick quiz

1   B   Cash book   (550)
        Add unpresented cheques   1,500
        Less undeposited receipts   (500)
        B/S balance   450 (in hand)

    A   Incorrect, you have treated the opening balance as a debit in the reconciliation.

    C   Incorrect, you have treated the undeposited receipts incorrectly.

    D   Incorrect, because you have treated the unpresented cheques incorrectly.

2   D   Correct. $
        Cash book   1,500 (debit)
        Add: unpresented cheques   1,200
                                               2,700
        Less: undeposited receipts (3,000)
                                                 (300)
        Bank error   (200)
        Bank balance   (500) o/d

    A   Incorrect, you have omitted the undeposited receipts from the reconciliation.

    B   Incorrect, you have added back the undeposited receipts instead of deducting them from the cash book balance.

    C   Incorrect, you have reversed the treatments of the unpresented cheques and the undeposited receipts.

Now try the questions below from the Question Bank

Question numbers	Page
52–55	404

Control accounts

Introduction

In this chapter (and in Chapter 16) we explain how accounting errors can be detected, what kinds of error might exist, and how to post corrections and adjustments to produce final accounts.

The main control accounts we look at are those for receivables and payables.

Sometimes the amount received, or paid, will not be the same as the invoice total due to **discounts**.

Topic list	Syllabus references
1 Discounts	B (4)
2 What are control accounts?	B (4)
3 The purpose of control accounts	B (4)
4 The operation of control accounts	B (4)
5 Balancing and reconciling control accounts with sales and purchases ledgers	B (4)

1 Discounts

1.1 Types of discount

Key term

> A **discount** is a reduction in the price of goods.

There are two types of discount.

- Trade discount
- Cash discount, or settlement discount

Key term

> **Trade discount** is a reduction in the cost of goods resulting from the nature of the trading transaction. It usually results from buying goods in bulk.

For example, a customer is quoted $1 per unit for a particular item, but a lower price of 95 cents per unit for 100 units or more at a time. An important or regular customer can be offered a discount on all goods, regardless of the order size, because the total volume of his purchases over time is so large.

Key term

> **Cash discount** is a reduction in the amount payable to the supplier in return for immediate payment rather than credit.

For example, a supplier charges $1,000 for goods, but offers a discount of 5% if the goods are paid for immediately in cash.

Key term

> **Settlement discount** is similar to cash discount. It is a discount on the price of the goods purchased for credit customers who pay their debts promptly.

For example, a discount of 5% for payment within 30 days of the invoice date.

1.2 Accounting for trade discount

FAST FORWARD

> Trade discount is a reduction in the amount of money demanded from a customer at the time of the sale. If trade discount is **received** by a business, the amount of money payable will be net of discount (ie it will be the normal sales value less the discount). Similarly, if a trade discount is given by a business to a customer, the amount of money due will be after deduction of the discount.

Trade discount is accounted for as follows.

(a) Trade discount received is deducted from the gross cost of purchases. Purchases are recorded at the net invoiced amount which is after deducting the discount.

(b) Trade discount allowed is deducted from the gross sales price, so that sales are recorded at net invoiced value which is after deducting the discount.

1.3 Cash discounts and settlement discounts received

FAST FORWARD

> Unlike trade discounts, cash and settlement discounts are **not** deducted from the invoice price of the goods. The invoice is processed in the normal way and any discount received when payment is made is credited to a 'discounts received' account.

When a business is given the opportunity to take advantage of a cash discount or a settlement discount for prompt payment, the decision as to whether or not to take the discount is a matter of financing policy, not trading policy, and the benefit is at the time of payment.

1.4 Example: cash discount received

A buys goods from B, on the understanding that A will be allowed a period of credit before having to pay for the goods. The terms of the transaction are as follows.

- Date of sale: 1 July 20X6
- Credit period allowed: 30 days
- Invoice price of the goods: $2,000
- Discount offered: 4% for prompt payment

A has a choice between holding on to his money for 30 days and then paying the full $2,000, or paying $2,000 less 4% ($1,920) now. This is a financing decision whether it is worthwhile for A to save $80 by paying its debts sooner.

If A decides to take the cash discount, he will pay $1,920, instead of the invoiced amount $2,000. The cash discount received ($80) will be accounted for in the books of A as follows.

(a) In the trading account, the cost of purchases will be at the invoiced price of $2,000.
(b) In the income statement, the cash discount received is shown as though it were income received.

We would have:

	$
Cost of purchase from B by A (trading account)	2,000
Discount received (income in the I/S)	(80)
Net cost	1,920

Settlement discounts received are accounted for in exactly the same way as cash discounts received.

1.5 Cash discounts and settlement discounts allowed

The same principle is applied in accounting for cash discounts or settlement discounts allowed to customers. Goods are sold and the offer of a discount is a matter of financing policy for the business, and not trading policy.

1.6 Example: settlement discount received

X sells goods to Y at a price of $5,000. Y is allowed 60 days' credit before payment, but is also offered a settlement discount of 2% for payment within 10 days of the invoice date. X issues an invoice to Y for $5,000. X has no idea whether or not Y will take advantage of the discount. In trading terms Y is a debtor for $5,000.

If Y subsequently decides to take the discount, he will pay $5,000 less 2% ($4,900) ten days later. The discount allowed ($100) will be accounted for by X as follows.

(a) In the trading account, sales are valued at their full invoice price, $5,000.
(b) In the profit and loss account, the discount allowed will be shown as an expense.

We would have:

	$
Sales (trading account)	5,000
Discounts allowed (I/S)	(100)
Net sales	4,900

Cash discounts allowed are accounted for in exactly the same way as settlement discounts allowed.

Assessment focus point

(a)   Trade discounts are received at the time of sale. Sales and purchases are recorded net of trade discounts (ie after deducting the discount).

(b)   Cash and settlement discounts are received at the time of payment. Sales and purchases are recorded gross (ie before deducting the discount) when payment is made or received. Any discount received from suppliers is credited to a discounts received income account and any discount allowed to customers is debited to discounts allowed expense account.

Question

Income statement with discounts

You are required to prepare the income statement of Seesaw Timber Merchants for the year ended 31 March 20X6, given the following information.

	$
Inventory, 1 April 20X5	18,000
Purchases at gross cost	120,000
Trade discounts received	4,000
Cash and settlement discounts received	1,500
Goods in inventory, 31 March 20X6	25,000
Cash sales	34,000
Credit sales at invoice price	150,000
Cash and settlement discounts allowed	8,000
Selling expenses	32,000
Administrative expenses	40,000
Drawings by proprietor, Tim Burr	22,000

Answer

SEESAW TIMBER MERCHANTS
INCOME STATEMENT
FOR THE YEAR ENDED 31 MARCH 20X6

	$	$
Sales (note 1)		184,000
Opening inventory	18,000	
Purchases (note 2)	116,000	
	134,000	
Less closing inventory	25,000	
Cost of goods sold		109,000
Gross profit		75,000
Discounts received		1,500
		76,500
Expenses		
Selling expenses	32,000	
Administrative expenses	40,000	
Discounts allowed	8,000	
		80,000
Net loss transferred to balance sheet		(3,500)

Notes

1   $(34,000 + 150,000)
2   $(120,000 − 4,000)
3   Drawings are not an expense, but an appropriation of profit.

Question   **Discounts allowed**

Fill in the blanks.

(a)   Fred sells goods on special offer to Bert. The goods usually sell for $100 but Bert pays $90. The double entry to record this sale in Fred's books is:

DEBIT   _____ account $

CREDIT   _____ account $

(b)   Fred sells goods to Tom for $100, but agrees to accept $95 if payment is within 30 days. The double entry to record this sale in Fred's books is:

DEBIT   _____ account $

CREDIT   _____ account $

The double entry to record the receipt of $95 is:

DEBIT   _____ account $

DEBIT   _____ account $

CREDIT   _____ account $

Answer

(a)   DEBIT   Cash account $90
      CREDIT   Sales account $90

(b)   DEBIT   Receivables account $100
      CREDIT   Sales account $100

      Then:

      DEBIT   Cash account $95
      DEBIT   Discounts allowed account $5
      CREDIT   Receivables account $100

2 What are control accounts?

Key term

A **control account** is an account in the nominal ledger in which a record is kept of the total value of a number of similar but individual items.

T FORWARD

The two most important control accounts are those for receivables and payables. They are part of the double-entry system.

201
LEARNING MEDIA

2.1 Receivables and payables control accounts

A **receivables control account** is an account in which records are kept of transactions involving all receivables in total. The balance on the receivables control account at any time will be the total amount due to the business from its receivables. The receivables control account is also called the sales ledger control account, and is the account which we have referred to earlier in the text as the receivables account.

A **payables control account** is an account in which records are kept of transactions involving all payables in total, and the balance on this account at any time will be the total amount owed by the business at that time to its payables. Other names for this account include the purchase ledger control account and bought ledger control account. It is the payables account that we have used in earlier chapters.

Control accounts can also be kept for other items, such as stocks of goods, wages and salaries and VAT.

2.2 Control accounts and personal accounts

The personal accounts of individual receivables are kept in the sales ledger. The amount owed by all the receivables added together is the balance on the receivables control account. At any time the balance on the receivables control account should be equal to the sum of the individual balances on the personal accounts in the sales ledger.

2.3 Example: receivables control account

A business has three receivables, A Arnold who owes $80, B Bagshaw who owes $310 and C Cloning who owes $200, the debit balances on the various accounts would be

Sales ledger (personal accounts)

	$
A Arnold	80
B Bagshaw	310
C Cloning	200
Nominal ledger – receivables control account	590

 FAST FORWARD

> The individual entries in cash and day books will have been entered one by one in the appropriate personal accounts contained in the sales ledger and purchase ledger. These personal accounts are not part of the double entry system; they are memorandum only.

Assessment focus point

> The balance on the receivables control account should be the same as the sum of all customers accounts in the sales ledger because they have been posted from the same day books.

3 The purpose of control accounts

FAST FORWARD

> Receivables and payables control accounts serve the functions of internal check and location of errors and provide a figure for total receivables /payables without the need to total the individual balances.

3.1 Why control accounts are kept

(a) They provide a check on the accuracy of entries made in the personal accounts in the sales and purchase ledgers. It is very easy to make a mistake in posting entries. Figures can get transposed. Some entries can be omitted altogether, so that an invoice or a payment does not appear in a personal account. Comparison of the balance on the receivables control account with the total of individual personal account balances in the sales ledger will show if any errors have occurred. Similarly the payables control account provides a check on the purchase ledger.

(b) The control accounts also assist in the location of errors. If a clerk fails to record an invoice or a payment in a personal account, it would be difficult to locate the error or errors at the end of a year. By using the control account, a comparison with the individual balances in the sales or purchase ledger can be made daily or weekly and the error found much more quickly.

(c) Where there is separation of bookkeeping duties, the control account provides an **internal check**. The person posting entries to the control accounts will act as a check on a different person(s) posting entries to the sales and purchase ledger.

(d) Control accounts provide the total receivables and payables balances more quickly for producing a trial balance or balance sheet.

In computerised systems, it may be possible to use sales and purchase ledgers as part of the double entry without needing separate control accounts. The sales or purchase ledger printouts provide the list of individual balances, as well as a total (control account) balance.

4 The operation of control accounts

T FORWARD

Entries are posted **individually** from the books of prime entry to the individual receivable and payable accounts. These entries are also posted **in total** to the receivables and payables control account. Cash books and day books are totalled periodically and the totals are posted to the control accounts.

4.1 Example: accounting for receivables

The following example shows how transactions involving receivables are accounted for. Reference numbers are shown in the accounts to illustrate the cross-referencing that is needed.

(a) SDB refers to a page in the sales day book.
(b) SL refers to a particular account in the sales ledger.
(c) NL refers to a particular account in the nominal ledger.
(d) CB refers to a page in the cash book.

At 1 July 20X2, the Outer Business Company had no receivables at all. During July, the following credit sale transactions occurred.

(a) July 3 invoiced A Arnold for the sale on credit of hardware goods: $100.

(b) July 11 invoiced B Bagshaw for the sale on credit of electrical goods: $150.

(c) July 15 invoiced C Cloning for the sale on credit of hardware goods: $250.

(d) July 10 received payment from A Arnold of $90, in settlement of his debt in full, having taken a permitted discount of $10 for payment within seven days.

(e)   July 18   received a payment of $72 from B Bagshaw in part settlement of $80 of his debt. A discount of $8 was allowed for payment within seven days.

(f)   July 28   received a payment of $120 from C Cloning, who was unable to claim any discount.

Account numbers are:

SL 4   Personal account: A Arnold
SL 9   Personal account: B Bagshaw
SL 13   Personal account: C Cloning
NL 6   Receivables control account
NL 7   Discounts allowed
NL 21   Sales: hardware
NL 22   Sales: electrical
NL 1   Cash control account

Required

Write up the day books, nominal ledger postings and personal account postings to record these transactions.

Solution

The accounting entries are:

			SALES DAY BOOK		SDB 35
Date 20X2	*Name*	*Ref*	*Total* $	*Hardware* $	*Electrical* $
July 3	A Arnold	SL 4	100.00	100.00	
11	B Bagshaw	SL 9	150.00		150.00
15	C Cloning	SL13	250.00	250.00	
			500.00	350.00	150.00
			NL 6	NL 21	NL 22

Note. The personal accounts in the sales ledger are debited on the day the invoices are sent out. The double entry in the nominal ledger accounts is made when the day book is totalled. Here it is made at the end of the month, by posting as follows.

			$	$
DEBIT	NL 6	Receivables control account	500	
CREDIT	NL 21	Sales: hardware		350
	NL 22	Sales: electrical		150

CASH BOOK EXTRACT
RECEIPTS CASH BOOK – JULY 20X2   CB 23

Date 20X2	*Narrative*	*Ref*	*Total* $	*Discount* $	*Receivables* $
July 10	A Arnold	SL 4	90.00	10.00	100.00
18	B Bagshaw	SL 9	72.00	8.00	80.00
28	C Cloning	SL13	120.00	–	120.00
			282.00	18.00	300.00
			NL 1 Dr	NL 7 Dr	NL 6 Cr

MEMORANDUM SALES LEDGER
ARNOLD
A/c no: SL 4

Date 20X2	Narrative	Ref	$	Date 20X2	Narrative	Ref	$
July 3	Sales	SDB 35	100.00	July 10	Cash	CB 23	90.00
					Discount	CB 23	10.00
			100.00				100.00

B BAGSHAW
A/c no: SL 9

Date 20X2	Narrative	Ref	$	Date 20X2	Narrative	Ref	$
July 11	Sales	SDB 35	150.00	July 18	Cash	CB 23	72.00
					Discount	CB 23	8.00
				July 31	Balance	c/d	70.00
			150.00				150.00
Aug 1	Balance	b/d	70.00				

C CLONING
A/c no: SL 13

Date 20X2	Narrative	Ref	$	Date 20X2	Narrative	Ref	$
July 15	Sales	SDB 35	250.00	July 28	Cash	CB 23	120.00
				July 31	Balance	c/d	130.00
			250.00				250.00
Aug 1	Balance	b/d	130.00				

NOMINAL LEDGER (EXTRACT)
TOTAL RECEIVABLES (SALES LEDGER) CONTROL ACCOUNT
A/c no: NL 6

Date 20X2	Narrative	Ref	$	Date 20X2	Narrative	Ref	$
July 31	Sales	SDB 35	500.00	July 31	Cash and discount	CB 23	300.00
				July 31	Balance	c/d	200.00
			500.00				500.00
Aug 1	Balance	b/d	200.00				

Note. At 31 July the closing balance on the receivables control account ($200) is the same as the total of the individual balances on the personal accounts in the sales ledger ($0 + $70 + $130).

DISCOUNT ALLOWED
A/c no: NL 7

Date 20X2	Narrative	Ref	$	Date	Narrative	Ref	$
July 31	Receivables	CB 23	18.00				

CASH CONTROL ACCOUNT
A/c no: NL 1

Date 20X2	Narrative	Ref	$	Date	Narrative	Ref	$
July 31	Cash received	CB 23	282.00				

SALES – HARDWARE   A/c no: NL 21

Date	Narrative	Ref	$	Date 20X2	Narrative	Ref	$
				July 31	Receivables	SDB 35	350.00

SALES – ELECTRICAL   A/c no: NL 22

Date	Narrative	Ref	$	Date 20X2	Narrative	Ref	$
				July 31	Receivables	SDB 35	150.00

If we took the balance on the accounts as at 31 July 20X2, the trial balance would be as follows.

TRIAL BALANCE

	Debit $	Credit $
Cash (all receipts)	282	
Receivables	200	
Discount allowed	18	
Sales: hardware		350
Sales: electrical		150
	500	500

The trial balance emphasises the point that it includes the balances on control accounts, but excludes the personal account balances in the sales and purchase ledgers.

4.2 Accounting for payables

If you were able to follow the above example, you should have no difficulty in dealing with similar examples relating to purchases/payables. If necessary revise the entries in the purchase day book and purchase ledger personal accounts.

4.3 Entries in control accounts

Typical entries in the control accounts are shown below. Reference Jnl indicates that the transaction is first lodged in the journal before posting to the control account and other accounts indicated. References SRDB and PRDB are to sales returns and purchase returns day books.

RECEIVABLES CONTROL

	Ref	$		Ref	$
Opening debit balances	b/d	7,000	Opening credit balances		
Sales	SDB	52,390	(if any)	b/d	200
Dishonoured bills or	Jnl	1,030	Cash received	CB	52,250
cheques			Discounts allowed	CB	1,250
Cash paid to clear credit			Returns inwards from		
balances	CB	80	receivables	SRDB	800
Closing credit balances	c/d	120	Bad debts	Jnl	300
			Closing debit balances	c/d	5,820
		60,620			60,620
Debit balances b/d		5,820	Credit balances b/d		120

Note. Opening credit balances are unusual in the receivables control account. They represent receivables to whom the business owes money, probably as a result of the over payment of debts or for advance payments of debts for which no invoices have yet been sent.

PAYABLES CONTROL

	Ref	$		Ref	$
Opening debit balances			Opening credit balances	b/d	8,330
(if any)	b/d	70	Purchases	PDB	31,000
Cash paid	CB	29,840	Cash received clearing		
Discounts received	CB	30	debit balances	CB	30
Returns outwards to	PRDB		Closing debit balances		
suppliers		60	(if any)	c/d	40
Closing credit balances	c/d	9,400			
		39,400			39,400
Debit balances	b/d	40	Credit balances	b/d	9,400

Note. Opening debit balances in the payables control account represent suppliers who owe the business money, perhaps because debts have been overpaid or because debts have been prepaid before the supplier has sent an invoice.

Posting from the journal is shown in the following example, where C Cloning has returned goods with a sales value of $50.

Journal entry	Ref		Dr	Cr
			$	$
Sales	NL 21		50	
To receivables' control	NL 6			50
To C Cloning (memorandum)	SL 13		–	50

Return of electrical goods inwards.

4.4 Contras

It is sometimes the case that a customer is also a supplier. In this situation they may have a balance in both the sales and purchase ledgers.

For instance: A is a customer of B and A's account in B's sales ledger shows $2,500 due from A to B. A is also a supplier of B and A's account in B's purchase ledger shows $1,000 due from B to A. In this case A and B can agree that, rather than A paying $2,500 to B and B paying $1,000 to A, these amounts can be settled by **contra** and A will simply pay B $1,500.

In B's accounts the contra entry will be:

DEBIT	Payables control	$1,000	
CREDIT	Receivables control		$1,000

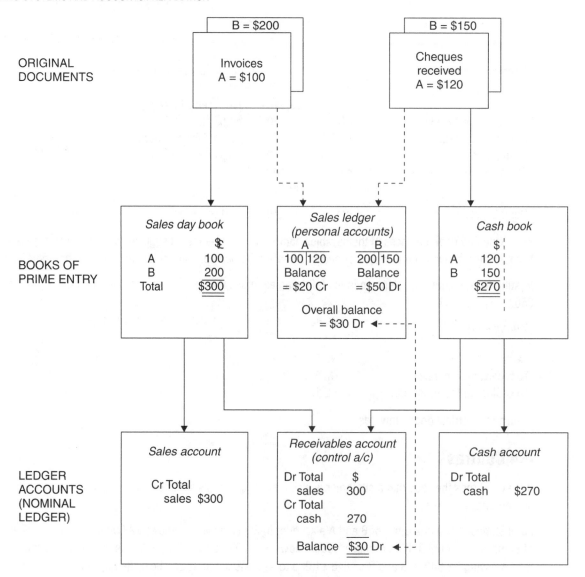

ORIGINAL
DOCUMENTS

BOOKS OF
PRIME ENTRY

LEDGER
ACCOUNTS
(NOMINAL
LEDGER)

**Assessment
focus point**

(a)   The sales ledger is **not** part of the double entry system.

(b)   The total balance on the sales ledger (ie all the personal account balances added up) should equal the balance on the receivables control account.

(c)   This diagram implies that the memorandum accounts (sales or purchase ledger) are written up from the original documents rather than from the sales day book. This is CIMA's official line, although the other treatment is possible in practice.

Question

Receivables and payables control accounts

On 1 October 20X8 the sales ledger balances were $8,024 debit and $57 credit, and the purchase ledger balances on the same date were $6,235 credit and $105 debit.

For the year ended 30 September 20X9 the following particulars are available.

	$
Sales	63,728
Purchases	39,974
Cash received from receivables	55,212
Cash paid to payables	37,307
Discount received	1,475
Discount allowed	2,328
Returns inwards	1,002
Returns outwards	535
Bad debts written off	326
Cash received in respect of debit balances in purchase ledger	105
Amount due from customer as shown by sales ledger, offset against amount due to the same firm as shown by purchase ledger (settlement by contra)	434
Cash received in respect of debt previously written off as bad	94
Allowances to customers on goods damaged in transit	212

On 30 September 20X9 there were no credit balances in the sales ledger except those outstanding on 1 October 20X8, and no debit balances in the purchase ledger.

You are required to write up the following accounts recording the above transactions and bringing down the balances as on 30 September 20X9.

(a) Receivables control account
(b) Payables control account

Answer

(a)

RECEIVABLES CONTROL ACCOUNT

20X8		$	20X8		$
Oct 1	Balances b/f	8,024	Oct 1	Balances b/f	57
20X9			20X9		
Sept 30	Sales	63,728	Sept 30	Cash received from receivables	55,212
	Balances c/f	57		Discount allowed	2,328
				Returns	1,002
				Bad debts written off	326
				Transfer payables control account (contra)	434
				Allowances on goods damaged	212
				Balances c/f	12,238
		71,809			71,809

(b)
PAYABLES CONTROL ACCOUNT

		$			$
20X8			**20X8**		
Oct 1	Balances b/f	105	Oct 1	Balances b/f	6,235
20X9			**20X9**		
Sept 30	Cash paid to payables	37,307	Sept 30	Purchases	39,974
	Discount received	1,475		Cash	105
	Returns outwards	535			
	Transfer receivables control account (contra)	434			
	Balances c/f	6,458			
		46,314			46,314

Note. The double entry in respect of cash received for the bad debt previously written off is:

DEBIT	Cash	$94
CREDIT	Debts paid, previously written off as bad account	$94

5 Balancing and reconciling control accounts with sales and purchase ledgers

FAST FORWARD

At suitable intervals the balances on the personal accounts are extracted from the ledgers, listed and totalled. The total of the outstanding balances can then be reconciled to the balance on the appropriate control account and any errors located and corrected.

5.1 Reconciling the control account

The control accounts should be balanced regularly (at least monthly) and the balance agreed with the sum of the individual receivables or payables balances in the sales or purchase ledgers respectively. The balance on the control account may not agree with the sum of balances extracted, for one or more of the following reasons.

(a) An **incorrect amount** may be posted to the control account because of a miscast of the book of prime entry (ie adding up incorrectly the total value of invoices or payments). The nominal ledger debit and credit postings will balance, but the control account balance will not agree with the sum of individual balances extracted from the sales ledger or purchase ledger. A journal entry must then be made in the nominal ledger to correct the control account and the corresponding sales or expense account.

(b) A **transposition error** may occur in posting an individual's balance eg the sale to C Cloning of $250 might be posted to his account as $520. This means that the sum of balances extracted from the memorandum ledger must be corrected. No accounting entry is required except to alter the figure in C Cloning's account.

(c) A transaction may be recorded in the control account and **not** in the memorandum ledger, or vice versa. This requires a double posting if the control account has to be corrected, or a single posting to the individual's balance in the memorandum ledger.

(d) The sum of balances extracted from the memorandum ledger may be incorrectly extracted or **miscast**. This would involve simply correcting the total of the balances.

5.2 Example: agreeing control account balances with the sales and purchase ledgers

The balance on the receivables control account is $15,091. The total of the list of balances taken from the sales ledger is $15,320. It is discovered that:

(a) $10 received from a receivables and put in the petty cash tin was correctly recorded in his personal account but excluded from the nominal ledger.

(b)   The sales day book for March was undercast by $100.

(c)   When posting an invoice for $95 to a customers account it was recorded as $59 by mistake.

(d)   A credit balance of $60 in the sales ledger was treated as a debit balance when adding up the list of balances.

(e)   The list of balances has been overcast by $90.

(f)   The returns inwards for June totalling $35 have been correctly recorded in the sales ledger, but no entries have been made in the nominal ledger.

Required

Show the adjustments necessary to the list of balances and to the receivables control account.

Solution

	$	$
Sales ledger total		
Original total extracted		15,320
Add difference arising from transposition error ($95 written as $59)		36
		15,356
Less		
Credit balance of $60 extracted as a debit balance ($60 × 2)	120	
Overcast of list of balances	90	
		210
		15,146

RECEIVABLES CONTROL

	$		$
Balance before adjustments	15,091	Petty cash – posting omitted	10
		Returns inwards – individual posting omitted from control account	35
Undercast of total invoices issued in sales day book	100	Balance c/d (now in agreement with the corrected total of individual balances in (a))	15,146
	15,191		15,191
Balance b/d	15,146		

Question

(i)   An invoice for $39 is recorded in the sales day book as $93.

(ii) The sales day book is overcast by $100.

To correct these errors we will need to adjust:

	Receivables control a/c	Sales ledger
A	For (i) and (ii)	For (i) and (ii)
B	No adjustment necessary	No adjustment necessary
C	For (i) and (ii)	For (i) only
D	For (i) only	For (i) and (ii)

Answer

C is correct. Both affect the control account and because totals are not posted to the sales ledger, (ii) does not affect the sales ledger.

Chapter roundup

- Trade discount is a reduction in the amount of money demanded from a customer at the time of the sale. If trade discount is **received** by a business, the amount of money payable will be net of discount (ie it will be the normal sales value less the discount). Similarly, if a trade discount is given by a business to a customer, the amount of money due will be after deduction of the discount.

- Unlike trade discounts, cash and settlement discounts are **not** deducted from the invoice price of the goods. The invoice is processed in the normal way and any discount received when payment is made is credited to a 'discounts received' account.

- The two most important control accounts are those for receivables and payables. They are part of the double-entry system.

- The individual entries in cash and day books will have been entered one by one in the appropriate personal accounts contained in the sales ledger and purchase ledger. These personal accounts are *not* part of the double entry system; they are memorandum only.

- Receivables and payables control accounts serve the functions of internal check and location of errors and provide a figure for total receivables /payables without the need to total the individual balances.

- Entries are posted **individually** from the books of prime entry to the individual receivable and payable accounts. These entries are also posted **in total** to the receivables and payables control account. Cash books and day books are totalled periodically and the totals are posted to the control accounts.

- At suitable intervals the balances on personal accounts are extracted from the ledgers, listed and totalled. The total of the outstanding balances can then be reconciled to the balance on the appropriate control account and any errors located and corrected.

Quick quiz

1   What is a trade discount received?

    A   An allowance given by a supplier to reduce the value of an invoice received.

    B   A reduction in invoice price as a result of (eg) buying in quantity.

    C   A suppliers response when a debit note is received.

    D   A discount for prompt payment.

2   Sam buys goods invoiced at $250 but is offered a 4% discount if she pays within 30 days which she does. What are the entries to record this payment in her books?

DEBIT   _____ account $_____

CREDIT   _____ account $_____

CREDIT   _____ account $_____

3   XYZ has a sales ledger control account containing the following. Balances b/f $12,200, credit sales $87,000, receipts from receivables $56,000, bad debts written off $1,800, refunds to credit customers $500, discounts allowed $1,500. The closing receivables balance is?

    A $42,700

    B $44,000

    C $38,400

    D $40,400

4   Which of the following items will not appear in a receivables control account?

    A   Discount allowed

    B   Bad debts written off

    C   Increases in the allowance for debtors

    D   Allowances to credit customers

5   Four reasons to maintain a control account as well as a sales ledger are:

    (1)   _____

    (2)   _____

    (3)   _____

    (4)   _____

Answers to quick quiz

1   B   Correct
    A   Incorrect. Trade discounts are deducted from invoice prices before a purchase invoice is finalised.
    C   The response should be to issue a credit note if the debit note is accepted.
    D   This is a cash discount.

2   DEBIT   Payable account $250
    CREDIT   Cash account $240
    CREDIT   Discounts received (income) account $10

3   D   Correct.

Receivables control

Balance b/d	12,200	Bank: receipts	56,000
Sales	87,000	Bad debts	1,800
Bank: refunds	500	Discount allowed	1,500
		Balance c/d	40,400
	99,700		99,700

A   Incorrect: you have transposed the figures for bad debts and refunds in the control account.

B   Incorrect: you have not recorded bad debts correctly – as a credit in the sales ledger control account.

C   Incorrect: you have recorded refunds as a credit entry in the sales ledger control account.

4   C   Correct. Will not appear, the debts are not actually written off
    A   Will appear – credit entry.
    B   Will appear – credit entry.
    D   Will appear – credit entry.

5   (1)   To provide a check on the accuracy of entries in the personal accounts
    (2)   To assist in the location of errors
    (3)   To provide separation of duties
    (4)   Control accounts provide the balance sheet receivables figure

Now try the questions below from the Question Bank

Question numbers	Page
56–59	404

Accounting for sales tax

Introduction

Many business transactions involve **sales tax (eg value added tax in the UK)**. Invoices and bills show any sales tax charged separately.

Sales tax is charged on the supply of goods and services. It is an **indirect tax**.

Section 1 explains how a sales tax works.

Section 2 deals with the accounting treatment of sales tax. If you understand the principle behind the tax and how it is collected, you will understand the accounting treatment.

Topic list	Syllabus references
1 The nature of a sales tax and how it is collected	B (8)
2 Accounting for sales tax	B (8)

1 The nature of a sales tax and how it is collected

FAST FORWARD

Sales tax is an indirect tax levied on the sale of goods and services. It is administered by the tax authorities.

1.1 How is sales tax levied?

Sales tax is a cumulative tax, collected at various stages of a product's life. In the illustrative example below, a manufacturer of a television buys materials and components and then sells the television to a wholesaler, who in turn sells it to a retailer, who then sells it to a customer. It is assumed that the rate for sales tax is 17.5% on all items. All the other figures are for illustration only.

1.2 Example

			Price net of sales tax $	Sales tax 17.5% $	Total price $
(a)	(i)	Manufacturer purchases raw materials and components	40	7	47
	(ii)	Manufacturer sells the completed television to a wholesaler	200	35	235
		The manufacturer hands over to tax authorities		28	
(b)	(i)	Wholesaler purchases television for	200	35	235
	(ii)	Wholesaler sells television to a retailer	320	56	376
		Wholesaler hands over to tax authorities		21	
(c)	(i)	Retailer purchases television for	320	56	376
	(ii)	Retailer sells television	480	84	564
		Retailer hands over to tax authorities		28	
(d)		Customer purchases television for	480	84	564

The total tax of $84 is borne by the ultimate consumer. However, the tax is handed over to the authorities in stages. If we assume that the sales tax of $7 on the initial supplies to the manufacturer is paid by the supplier, the tax authorities would collect the sales tax as follows.

	$
Supplier of materials and components	7
Manufacturer	28
Wholesaler	21
Retailer	28
Total sales tax paid	84

1.3 Input and output sales tax

Key term

Sales tax charged on goods and services sold by a business is referred to as **output sales tax**. Sales tax paid on goods and services 'bought in' by a business is referred to as **input sales tax**.

ST FORWARD

If output sales tax exceeds input sales tax, the business pays the difference in tax to the authorities. If output sales tax is less than input sales tax in a period, the tax authorities will refund the difference to the business.

The example above assumes that the supplier, manufacturer, wholesaler and retailer are all sales tax-registered traders.

A sales tax-registered trader must carry out the following tasks.

(a) Charge sales tax on the goods and services sold at the rate prescribed by the government. This is output sales tax.

(b) Pay sales tax on goods and services purchased from other businesses. This is input sales tax.

(c) Pay to the tax authorities the difference between the sales tax collected on sales and the sales tax paid to suppliers for purchases. Payments are made at quarterly intervals.

1.4 Irrecoverable sales tax

There are some circumstances in which traders are not allowed to reclaim sales tax paid on their inputs. In these cases the trader must bear the cost of sales tax and account for it accordingly. Three such cases need to be considered.

(a) Non-registered persons
(b) Registered persons carrying on exempted activities
(c) Non-deductible inputs

1.4.1 Non-registered persons

Traders whose sales (outputs) are below a certain minimum level need not register for sales tax. Non-registered persons will pay sales tax on their inputs and, because they are not registered, they cannot reclaim it. The sales tax paid will effectively increase the cost of their income statement expenses and the cost of any non-current assets they may purchase. Non-registered persons do not charge sales tax on their outputs.

1.4.2 Registered persons carrying on exempted activities

All outputs of registered traders are either taxable or exempt. Taxable outputs are charged to sales tax either at zero per cent (zero-rated items) or at 17.5% (standard-rated items).

Traders carrying on exempt activities (such as banks) cannot reclaim sales tax paid on their inputs, even though they may be sales tax-registered. Some traders and companies carry on a mixture of taxable and exempt activities. Such traders need to apportion the sales tax paid on inputs. Only sales tax relating to taxable outputs may be reclaimed.

1.4.3 Non-deductible inputs

There are a few special cases where the input tax is not deductible even for a taxable person with taxable outputs. These are as follows.

(a) Sales tax on motor cars is never reclaimable unless a car is acquired new for resale, ie by a car dealer. Sales tax on a car used wholly for business purposes is reclaimable. However, company cars usually have some private use, so you should assume that the sales tax is not reclaimable unless told otherwise. Sales tax on accessories such as car radios is deductible if ordered on a separate purchase order and fitted after delivery. The sales tax charged when a car is hired is reclaimable if all use is business use. If there is some non-business use and the leasing company reclaimed sales tax, the hirer can only reclaim 50% of the sales tax on the hire charge.

(b) Sales tax on business entertaining is not deductible other than sales tax on entertaining staff.

(c)   Sales tax on expenses incurred on domestic accommodation for directors.

(d)   Sales tax on non-business items passed through the business accounts with limited relief where the goods are used partly in the business.

(e)   Sales tax which does not relate to the making of supplies in the course of a business.

Where sales tax is not recoverable, for any of the reasons described above, it must be regarded as part of the cost of the items purchased and included in the I/S charge or in the balance sheet as appropriate.

1.5 Relief for bad debts

Relief is available for sales tax on bad debts if the debt is over six months old (measured from the date of the supply) and has been written off in the payable's accounts. Where a supplier of goods or services has accounted for sales tax on the supply and the customer does not pay, the supplier may claim a refund of sales tax on the amount unpaid.

Where payments on account have been received, they are attributed to debts in date order. The consideration must be money and ownership of goods must have passed.

If the customer later pays all or part of the amount owed, a corresponding part of the sales tax repaid must be paid back to the tax authorities.

In order to claim the relief, the supplier must have a copy of the tax invoice and records to show that the sales tax has been accounted for and the debt has been written off. The sales tax is reclaimed on the payable's sales tax return.

2 Accounting for sales tax

Registered businesses charge output sales tax on sales and suffer input sales tax on purchases. Sales tax does not affect the income statement, but is simply being collected on behalf of the tax authorities to whom a quarterly payment is made.

2.1 Income statement

A business does not make any profit out of the sales tax it charges. It therefore follows that its income statement figures should not include sales tax. For example, if a business sells goods for $600 + sales tax $105, ie for $705 total price, the sales account should only record the $600 excluding sales tax. The accounting entries to record the sale would be as follows.

DEBIT	Cash or trade receivables	$705	
CREDIT	Sales		$600
CREDIT	Sales tax payable (output sales tax)		$105

(a)   If input sales tax is recoverable, the cost of purchases should exclude the sales tax and be recorded net of tax. For example, if a business purchases goods on credit for $400 + sales tax $70, the transaction would be recorded as follows.

DEBIT	Purchases	$400	
DEBIT	Sales tax payables (input sales tax recoverable)	$70	
CREDIT	Trade payables		$470

(b)   If the input sales tax is not recoverable, the cost of purchases must include the tax, because it is the business itself which must bear the cost of the tax.

	Purchases	Sales
Income statement	Irrecoverable input sales tax: include	Exclude sales tax
	Recoverable input sales tax: exclude	

2.2 Sales tax in the cash book, sales day book and purchase day book

When a business makes a credit sale the total amount invoiced, including sales tax, will be recorded in the sales day book. The analysis columns will then separate the sales tax from the sales income of the business as follows.

		Sales	
Date	Total	income	Sales tax
	$	$	$
A Detter and Sons	235	200	35

When a business is invoiced by a supplier the total amount payable, including sales tax, will be recorded in the purchase day book. The analysis columns will then separate the recoverable input sales tax from the net purchase cost to the business as follows.

Date	Total	Purchase	Sales tax
	$	$	$
A Splier (Merchants)	188	160	28

When receivables pay what they owe, or payables are paid, there is **no need to show** the sales tax in an analysis column of the cash book, because input and output sales tax arise when the sale is made, not when the debt is settled.

However, sales tax charged on **cash sales** or sales tax paid on **cash purchases** will be analysed in a separate column of the cash book. This is because output sales tax has just arisen from the cash sale and must be credited to the sales tax payables in the ledger accounts. Similarly input sales tax paid on cash purchases, having just arisen, must be debited to the sales tax payable.

For example, the receipts side of a cash book might be written up as follows.

					Output sales tax
Date	Narrative	Total	Sales ledger	Cash sales	on cash sales
		$	$	$	$
	A Detter & Sons	235	235		
	Owen	660	660		
	Cash sales	329		280	49
	Newgate Merchants	184	184		
	Cash sales	94		80	14
		1,502	1,079	360	63

The payments side of a cash book might be written up as follows.

Date	Narrative	Total	Purchase ledger	Analysis columns Cash purchases and sun- dry items	Input sales tax on cash purchases
		$	$	$	$
	A Splier (Merchants)	188	188		
	Telephone bill paid	141		120	21
	Cash purchase of stationery	47		40	7
	Sales tax paid to tax authorities	1,400		1,400	
		1,776	188	1,560	28

Question

Sales tax

Are trade receivables and trade payables shown in the accounts inclusive of sales tax or exclusive of sales tax?

Answer

They are shown **inclusive** of sales tax, as the balance sheet must reflect the total amount due from receivables and due to payables.

Assessment focus point

A small element of sales tax is quite likely in questions. It is worth spending a bit of time ensuring that you understand the logic behind the way sales tax is accounted for, rather than trying to learn the rules by rote. This will ensure that even if you forget the rules, you will be able to work out what should be done.

2.3 Payable for sales tax

FAST FORWARD

An outstanding payable for sales tax will appear as a current liability in the balance sheet.

The sales tax paid to the authorities each quarter is the difference between recoverable input sales tax on purchases and output sales tax on sales. For example, if a business is invoiced for input sales tax of $8,000 and charges sale tax of $15,000 on its credit sales and sales tax of $2,000 on its cash sales, the sales tax payable account would be as follows.

SALES TAX PAYABLE

	$		$
Payables (input sales tax)	8,000	Receivables (output sales tax invoiced)	15,000
Cash (payment to authorities)	9,000	Cash (output sales tax on cash sales)	2,000
	17,000		17,000

Payments to the authorities do not coincide with the end of the accounting period of a business, and so at the balance sheet date there will be a balance on the sales tax payable account. If this balance is for an amount payable to the authorities, the outstanding payable for sales tax will appear as a current liability in the balance sheet.

Occasionally, a business will be owed money back by the authorities, and in such a situation, the sales tax refund owed by the authorities would be a current asset in the balance sheet.

Question

A business in its first period of trading charges $4,000 of sales tax on its sales and suffers $3,500 of sales tax on its purchases which include $250 sales tax on business entertaining. Prepare the sales tax payable account.

Answer

SALES TAX PAYABLE ACCOUNT

	$		$
Payables	3,250	Receivables	4,000
Balance c/d (owed to tax authorities)	750		
	4,000		4,000
		Balance b/d	750

The main points

(a) Credit sales

(i) Include sales tax in sales day book; show it

(ii) Include gross receipts from receivables in cashbook; no need to show sales tax separately

(iii) Exclude sales tax element from income statement

(iv) Credit sales tax payable with output sales tax element of receivables invoiced

(b) Credit purchases

(i) Include sales tax in purchases day book; show it separately

(ii) Include gross payments in cashbook; no need to show sales tax separately

(iii) Exclude recoverable sales tax from income statement

(iv) Include irrecoverable sales tax in income statement

(v) Debit sales tax payable with recoverable input sales tax element of credit purchases

(c) Cash sales

(i) Include gross receipts in cashbook; show sales tax separately

(ii) Exclude sales tax element from income statement

(iii) Credit sales tax payable with output sales tax element of cash sales

(d) Cash purchases

(i) Include gross payments in cashbook: show sales tax separately

(ii) Exclude recoverable sales tax from income statement

(iii) Include irrecoverable sales tax in income statement

(iv) Debit sales tax payable with recoverable input sales tax element of cash purchases

Chapter roundup

- **Sales tax** is an indirect tax levied on the sale of goods and services. It is administered by the tax authorities.

- If output sales tax exceeds input sales tax, the business pays the difference in tax to the authorities. If output sales tax is less than input sales tax in a period, the tax authorities will refund the difference to the business.

- Where sales tax is not recoverable, for any of the reasons described above, it must be regarded as part of the cost of the items purchased and included in the I/S charge or in the balance sheet as appropriate.

- Registered businesses charge output sales tax on sales and suffer input sales tax on purchases. Sales tax does not affect the profit and loss account, but is simply being collected on behalf of the tax authorities to whom a quarterly payment is made.

- An outstanding payable for sales tax will appear as a current liability in the balance sheet.

Quick quiz   o

1   Sales tax is:

    A   A direct tax levied on sales of goods and services
    B   An indirect tax levied on the sales of goods and services
    C   Administered by the Treasury
    D   Charged by businesses on taxable supplies

2   What are the two rates of sales tax which may be applicable to taxable outputs?

    (1)   _____

    (2)   _____

3   When sales tax is not recoverable on the cost of a motor car, it should be treated in which of the following ways?

    A   Deducted from the cost of the asset capitalised
    B   Included in the cost of the asset capitalised
    C   Deducted from output tax for the period
    D   Written off to I/S as an expense

4   Purchases of goods costing $500 subject to sales tax at 17.5% occur. Which of the following correctly records the **credit purchase**?

A	Dr	Purchases	$500.00	
	Dr	Sales tax	$87.50	
	Cr	Payables		$587.50
B	Dr	Purchases	$587.50	
	Cr	Payables		$587.50
C	Dr	Purchases	$412.50	
	Dr	Sales tax	$87.50	
	Cr	Payables		$500.00
D	Dr	Purchases	$500.00	
	Cr	Sales tax		$87.50
	Cr	Payables		$412.50

5   A business purchases goods valued at $400. Sales tax is charged at 17.5%. The double entry to record the purchase is:

DEBIT   _____ $_____

DEBIT   _____ $_____

CREDIT   _____ $_____

6   Fill in the blanks.

Input sales tax is _____, output sales tax
is _____.

7   When a cash sale is made for $117.50 (including sales tax) the entries made are:

DEBIT   _____ account $_____

CREDIT   _____ account $_____

CREDIT   _____ account $_____

8   When a cash purchase of $117.50 is made (including sales tax) the entries are:

DEBIT   _____ account $_____

DEBIT   _____ account $_____

CREDIT   _____ account $_____

9   The sales tax paid to the tax authorities each quarter is the difference between _____
_____ and _____
_____.

Answers to quick quiz

1   B   Correct

     A   Incorrect, the consumer has a choice as to whether or not to consume so sales tax is only chargeable when this choice is exercised.

     C   Incorrect, sales tax is administrated by the tax authorities.

     D   Only sales tax registered traders can charge sales tax.

2   Zero-rate and standard-rate (17.5%).

3   B   Correct the balance sheet value will therefore include sales tax and the depreciation charge will rise accordingly

     A   Incorrect, it must be added.

     C   Incorrect.

     D   Incorrect, the motor car is a non-current asset not an expense, sales tax will form part of the depreciable amount of the asset.

4   A   Correct, recoverable input tax is debited to the sales tax a/c and the purchases account is debited net of sales tax.
     B   Incorrect, the sales tax has not been reclaimed.
     C   Incorrect, the $500 is subject to sales tax.
     D   Incorrect, reversal of the sales tax transaction has occurred.

5   DEBIT: PURCHASES $400
                   Sales tax $70
     CREDIT: CASH or PAYABLES $470

6   Input sales tax is sales tax suffered on goods and services brought by a business, output sales tax is the sales tax collected on sales.

7   DEBIT   Cash account $117.50
     CREDIT   Sales account $100.00
     CREDIT   Sales tax account $17.50

8   DEBIT   Purchases account $100.00
     DEBIT   Sales tax account $17.50
     CREDIT   Cash account $117.50

9   The sales tax paid to the tax authorities each quarter is the difference between output sales tax collected on sales and input sales tax suffered on purchases and expenses.

Now try the questions below from the Question Bank

Question numbers	Page
60–63	405

Accounting for payroll

Introduction

The salary paid to the bank or the jangle of coins in the wages packet is the final result of a long process of recording and calculation. This is often referred to as payroll processing and payroll accounting, a payroll being simply a list of employees and what they are to be paid. Being on the payroll of an organisation means that you are selling your labour to it for an agreed price.

From an employer's point of view, too, the wages and salaries bill is of great importance. It is often one of the largest items of expenditure an employer has to incur.

Most people have to pay some of what they earn to the government as taxation (Income Tax) which pays for general social benefits, eg the Health Service. In addition, people pay National Insurance Contributions (NIC), which, in practice, is similar to a tax. The tax and NIC is collected by the employer when the employee is paid. The system is called PAYE (Pay As You Earn). This system is the subject of Section 1.

While you might think that the employer is doing the government a favour by acting as a tax collector, the legal apparatus surrounding PAYE is quite strict. It is vital therefore, that proper accounting records are kept. This is covered in Section 2 of the chapter.

Topic list	Syllabus references
1 Gross pay and deductions	B (9)
2 Accounting for wages and salaries	B (9)

1 Gross pay and deductions

Key terms

> **Gross pay** is the full amount that an employee earns.
>
> **Deductions** are the amounts taken from gross pay for income tax, National Insurance contributions and any other reasons agreed by employer and employee such as pension contributions.
>
> **Net pay** is gross pay less deductions, ie the amount actually received by the employee.

FAST FORWARD

A business must deduct PAYE income tax and employees' NIC from employees' gross pay. Only the net amount is then paid to employees. The amounts deducted are paid over every month by the employer to HM Revenue and Customs (HMRC).

1.1 How are deductions collected?

The government requires that businesses should act as collecting agents on behalf of HMRC. When a business makes a wages or salary payment to an employee, it calculates the amount of tax and NIC due. These amounts are deducted from the employee's gross remuneration and paid by the business to HMRC. The employee receives only the net amount remaining after these deductions.

An employee effectively pays his income tax liability in instalments each time he receives a wages payment. This system of income tax collection is called PAYE or pay-as-you-earn.

Apart from these compulsory deductions, which all businesses must operate, there may be other voluntary deductions from an employee's pay.

(a)   **Savings schemes**. An employee agrees to save $5 a week. Each week the $5 is deducted from his gross pay and held for him by his employer until he decides to withdraw it.

(b)   **Contributions to charity**. An employee might agree to a weekly deduction of 50c as a contribution to Oxfam. The employer deducts the agreed amount each week and at suitable intervals hands over the money collected to the charity.

(c)   **Pension schemes**.

1.2 Example: accounting for deductions from gross pay

Mr Little's gross pay for the week ending 31 October 20X6 is $140. His employer, Mr Big, calculates that income tax of $20 and NIC of $13 are due on that level of earnings. In addition, Little received a loan from the business in June 20X6 which he is repaying by weekly deductions of $5. He also voluntarily contributes 20p per week to a local charity, again by deduction from his gross wages.

How should these amounts be accounted for?

Solution

The cost to Mr Big is the gross pay of $140 and this is charged in his income statement. The amount actually paid to Little is only $101.80 ($140 – $20 – $13 – $5 – 20c).

The deductions should be accounted for as follows.

(a)   PAYE of $20 and NIC of $13 are paid over to HMRC. In practice, this payment would not be made every week. Mr Big would accumulate the amounts due in respect of all his employees and would make a single payment to HMRC once a month.

(b)   The $5 deduction is applied to reduce the amount of the loan outstanding from Little.

(c)   The 20p deduction is handed over to the local charity. Again, it would probably be convenient to accumulate these amounts for a number of weeks before payment.

1.3 Employer's National Insurance contributions and pension contributions

ST FORWARD

The cost to a business of employing its workforce is gross pay plus employer's NIC and any employer's pension contributions.

Employees are normally obliged to pay NIC which is deducted from their gross pay and paid over by their employer on their behalf. But employers also have to make a contribution themselves in respect of each of their employees. This is **not** a deduction from the employee's gross pay, it is an **extra** cost borne by the employer. Also, the employer is likely to make contributions to pension schemes. The employer's income statement must show the total cost of employing staff and this includes not only the gross pay, but also the employer's NIC and any employer's pension contributions.

An employer's monthly payment to HMRC therefore includes the following.

- **PAYE** income tax for each employee (deducted from the employees' gross pay)
- **Employees'** NIC (deducted from the employees' gross pay)
- **Employer's** NIC, paid from the employer's own funds

Question

Gross pay

An employee earns $10 an hour gross and has worked 48 hours this week. His income tax liability is $58 and his NIC is $12. Voluntary deductions are $5 sports club subscription and pension contributions of $40. The employer's NIC is $25 and pension contribution is $20.

The employee's net pay is $_____.

The gross payroll cost to the employer is $_____.

Answer

The employee's net pay is $365. (($10 × 48) = $480 − $58 − $12 − $5 − $40 = $365)

The gross payroll cost to the employer is $525. ($480 + $25 + $20 = $525)

**ssessment
ocus point**

> Amounts owed to HMRC and pension funds are current payables in the balance sheet.

1.4 National Insurance contributions

Calculating NIC is easy. An employee pays a fixed percentage of his gross income, the percentage depending on the level of his income. For the employer's contribution, again a fixed percentage is applied to the employee's gross pay, but the percentage may differ from that used in calculating the employee's contribution.

Employees' NIC is subject to a maximum amount. There is no limit on the amount of an employer's contributions.

The government publishes tables detailing the amount of NIC payable at all levels of income. Therefore employers simply extract the amounts due from the tables.

1.5 Calculating PAYE deductions

PAYE contributions are more complicated, but again the use of HMRC tables simplifies matters in practice.

First add the amount of the employee's gross pay for the current period to the previous total of gross pay. This gives his gross pay for the tax year to date. (Tax years run from 6 April to 5 April.) Next calculate the amount of tax due for the year to date. This will depend on the employee's tax code, which reflects the amount of tax free pay he can earn.

The tax due for the year to date is then compared with the tax actually paid by the employee up to and including the previous week/month. The difference is the amount of tax due from the employee in the current week/month, and is the amount deducted from his gross pay.

Sometimes the tax due for the year to date is less than the tax already paid by the employee. In that case the employee will be entitled to a tax refund as an **addition** to his gross pay.

2 Accounting for wages and salaries

FAST FORWARD

At any time, a business may have on hand tax and insurance amounts which have not yet been paid over to HMRC. These will appear in the accounts under payables.

2.1 Ledger entries

Three accounts are needed.

- Wages control account
- PAYE control account
- NIC control account

First calculate the total costs of employment to be borne by the business. These consist of employees' gross pay plus employer's NIC. The following accounting entries are made.

DEBIT	I/S account – wages/salaries (gross pay + employer's NIC)
CREDIT	Wages control account (gross pay)
CREDIT	NIC control account (employer's NIC)

Then the amount of deductions are calculated for PAYE and employee's NIC.

DEBIT	Wages control account (total deductions)
CREDIT	PAYE control account (PAYE)
CREDIT	NIC control account (employee's NIC)

Then pay employees their net pay.

DEBIT	Wages control account
CREDIT	Cash account

In due course, the credit balances on PAYE control and NIC control are eliminated by making payments to HMRC.

Any voluntary deductions permitted by employees must be debited to wages control account and credited to a liability account until they are eventually paid over by the employer as appropriate.

2.2 Example: ledger accounts for wages and salaries

At 1 November 20X5 Netpay had the following credit balances on ledger accounts.

	$
PAYE control account	4,782
NIC control account	2,594
Employee savings account	1,373

The company's wages records for the month of November 20X5 showed the following.

	$
Total gross pay	27,294
PAYE	6,101
Employer's NIC	2,612
Employees' NIC	2,240
Employees' savings deductions	875
Net amounts paid to employees	18,078

The company paid $9,340 to HMRC during the month, being $4,750 PAYE and $4,590 NIC.

Show the ledger accounts recording these transactions.

Solution

WAGES CONTROL ACCOUNT

	$		$
PAYE control	6,101	Wages expense a/c – gross pay	27,294
NIC control – employees' contributions	2,240		
Employee savings a/c	875		
Bank – net pay	18,078		
	27,294		27,294

PAYE CONTROL ACCOUNT

	$		$
Bank	4,750	Balance b/f	4,782
Balance c/d	6,133	Wages control	6,101
	10,883		10,883
		Balance b/d	6,133

NIC CONTROL ACCOUNT

	$		$
Bank	4,590	Balance b/f	2,594
Balance c/d	2,856	Wages control – employees' NIC	2,240
		Wages expense a/c – employer's NIC	2,612
	7,446		7,446
		Balance b/d	2,856

EMPLOYEE SAVINGS ACCOUNT

	$		$
Balance c/d	2,248	Balance b/f	1,373
		Wages control	875
	2,248		2,248
		Balance	2,248

Note. This account shows the company's liability to employees, who may wish to withdraw their savings at any time.

Question   **Accounting for salaries**

At 1 March 20X3 Brubeck had the following credit balances on ledger accounts.

	$
PAYE control account	23,000
NIC control account	12,500
Employee savings account	26,250

The company's wages records for the month of March 20X3 showed the following.

	$
PAYE	30,505
Employer's NIC	13,060
Employees' NIC	11,200
Employees' savings deductions	4,375
Net amounts paid to employees	90,390

The company paid $46,700 to the HMRC during the month, being $23,750 PAYE and $22,950 NIC.

(a) How much was gross pay for the month?
(b) What is the balance c/d on the PAYE control account, if any?
(c) What is the balance c/d on the NIC control account, if any?
(d) What is the balance c/d on the Employee Savings account, if any?

Answer

(a) $136,470 ($90,390 + $30,505 + $11,200 + $4,375)
(b) $29,755   credit ($23,000 + $30,505 − $23,750)
(c) $13,810   credit ($12,500 + $13,060 + $11,200 − $22,950)
(d) $30,625   credit ($26,250 + $4,375)

Assessment focus point

As long as you understand the principles of control accounts and logically follow through the double entry, you should not experience too many difficulties. Do not be put off by the 'tax' content. PAYE is just another payable.

Chapter roundup

- A business must deduct PAYE income tax and employees' NIC from employees' gross pay. Only the net amount is then paid to employees. The amounts deducted are paid over every month by the employer to HM Revenue and Customs (HMRC).

- The cost to a business of employing its workforce is gross pay plus employer's NIC and any employer's pension contributions.

- At any time, a business may have on hand tax and insurance amounts which have not yet been paid over to HMRC. These will appear in the accounts under payables.

Quick quiz

1   PAYE stands for? (In relation to income tax issues.)

   A   Payroll and your earnings
   B   Pay as you earn
   C   Pay after you earn
   D   Payroll accounting year end

2   Three voluntary deductions that an employee might permit from his gross pay are:

   (1) _____   (2) _____

   (3) _____

3   The total cost of employing staff shown in an employer's income statement is _____
   _____.

4   At 31.12.20X0 a company had the following balance in its records: PAYE control a/c $15,800. NIC control a/c $7,600. Deductions from pay in January 20X1 were: income tax $8,600, NIC $3,400. Employer's NIC were $2,800. PAYE payments were $6,800. NI payments were $3,400. Calculate the PAYE and NI control account balances as at 31.1.20X1.

   A   PAYE $19,400 (cr)   NIC $13,200 (cr)
   B   PAYE $17,600 (cr)   NIC $7,600 (cr)
   C   PAYE $17,600 (dr)   NIC $10,400 (dr)
   D   PAYE $17,600 (cr)   NIC $10,400 (cr)

5   An employee has a gross pay of $150, a bonus of $25, income tax and NIC amount to $30 and pension contributions are made totalling $15. The employers NIC and pension contributions amount to $55. The gross payroll cost to the employer is?

   A $230
   B $175
   C $130
   D $185

6   What ledger accounting entries are made in respect of voluntary deductions permitted by employees?

   DEBIT   _____

   CREDIT   _____

Answers to quick quiz

1   B   The employer is responsible for deducting income tax from employees and accounting for these deductions to the HMRC.

2   • Savings scheme
     • Charity contributions
     • Pension scheme

3   The gross salary, plus employer's NIC and employer's pension contribution

4   D   Correct.

PAYE Control A/C

Bank	6,800	Balance b/d	15,800
Balance c/d	17,600	Wages control	8,600
	24,400		24,400

NIC Control A/C

Bank	3,400	Balance b/d	7,600
Balance c/d	10,400	Wages control	3,400
		Wages control	2,800
	13,800		13,800

A   Incorrect, you have reversed the opening and closing balances.

B   Incorrect, you have omitted the employers NI contribution.

C   Incorrect, these are liabilities not assets.

5   A   Correct, employees wage plus bonus plus employers contributions.
     B   Incorrect, this is the total gross pay.
     C   Incorrect, this is the employees net pay.
     D   Incorrect, this is net pay plus employers contributions.

6   DEBIT   Wages control

     CREDIT   Deduction liability account

Now try the questions below from the Question Bank

Question numbers	Page
64–67	406

Correction of errors

Introduction

We have nearly reached our goal of preparing of the final accounts of a sole trader.

This chapter continues the subject of errors in accounts. You have already learned about errors which arise in the context of the cash book or the sales and purchase ledgers and receivables and payables control account. Here we deal with errors that may be corrected by means of the journal or a suspense account.

Topic list	Syllabus references
1 Types of error in accounting	C (4)
2 The correction of errors	C (4)
3 Suspense accounts	C (4)

1 Types of error in accounting

FAST FORWARD

It is not possible to draw up a complete list of all the errors which might be made by bookkeepers and accountants. However, it is possible to describe five **types** of error which cover most of the errors as:

- Errors of **transposition**
- Errors of **omission**
- Errors of **principle**
- Errors of **commission**
- **Compensating** errors

1.1 Dealing with errors

Once an error has been detected, it needs to be put right.

(a)   If the correction involves a double entry in the ledger accounts, then it is done by using a journal entry.

(b)   When the error breaks the rule of double entry and prevents the trial balance balancing, it is corrected by the use of a suspense account as well as a journal entry.

Key term

> An **error of transposition** is when **a number of digits** in an amount are accidentally recorded the **wrong way round**.

For example, suppose that a sale is recorded in the sales account as $6,843, but it is incorrectly recorded in the total receivables account as $6,483. The error is the transposition of the 4 and the 8. The consequence is that total debits will not be equal to total credits. You can often detect a transposition error by checking whether the difference between debits and credits can be divided exactly by 9. For example, $6,843 − $6,483 = $360; $360 ÷ 9 = 40. Such an error will stop the trial balance balancing, but if the sale of $6,843 had been recorded in both the sales and the receivables account as $6,483, the trial balance should balance.

Key term

> An **error of omission** means **failing to record** a transaction at all, or making one entry but not the corresponding double entry.

For example:

(a)   A business receives an invoice from a supplier for $250. The transaction might be omitted from the books entirely. As a result, both the total debits and the total credits of the business will be out by $250, and the trial balance still balances.

(b)   A business receives an invoice from a supplier for $300. The payables control account is credited, but the debit entry in the purchases account is omitted. In this case, the total credits would not equal total debits (total debits are $300 less than they ought to be), so the trial balance will not balance.

Key term

> An **error of principle** involves making a double entry in the belief that the transaction is being entered in the correct accounts, but subsequently finding out that the accounting entry **breaks the 'rules'** of an accounting principle or concept. A typical example of such an error is to treat revenue expenditure incorrectly as capital expenditure.

For example, $100 spent repairing a car is recorded as debit non-current assets (cars), credit cash; when it should be debit motor expenses, credit cash. This error does not stop the trial balance balancing.

Key term

> **Errors of commission** are where the bookkeeper makes a mistake in recording transactions in the accounts.

For example:

(a) **Putting a debit entry or a credit entry in the wrong account** eg telephone expenses of $540 are debited to the electricity expenses account.

(b) **Errors of casting (adding up)** eg the total of the sales day book should add up to $28,425, but is incorrectly added up as $28,825.

These two types of errors will not stop the trial balance balancing.

(c) **Casting errors when balancing nominal ledger accounts** eg adding up the sales account incorrectly will cause an imbalance in the trial balance.

Key term

> **Compensating errors** are errors which are, coincidentally, **equal and opposite** to one another.

For example, two transposition errors of $540 occur in extracting ledger balances, one on each side of the double entry. In the administration expenses account, $2,282 is written instead of $2,822. While in the sundry income account, $8,391 is written instead of $8,931. Both the debits and the credits are $540 too low and the mistake is not apparent when the trial balance is cast.

Question   Errors

Which of the following errors would stop the trial balance balancing? And by how much?

(i) A cheque is written out for $96, but is incorrectly recorded in the cash book as $69.

(ii) The sales day book is correctly totalled as $324 but is recorded in the nominal ledger as $342 in both the sales account and the receivables control account.

(iii) The sale day book is correctly totalled as $324 and correctly posted to the receivables control account, but is recorded as $234 in the sales account.

(iv) An invoice from a supplier for $200 is not entered in the purchases day book.

(v) The only posting made from the purchases day book to the nominal ledger is to debit purchases account with the total of $3,000.

(vi) Goods costing $100 bought for a proprietor's private use are recorded in the purchases day book, which is then correctly posted to the nominal ledger.

Answer

(i) The trial balance will balance.

(ii) The trial balance will balance.

(iii) The trial balance will not balance. Receivables control account has been debited with $324. Sales has been debited with $234. So the trial balance debits will exceed credits by $90.

(iv) The trial balance will balance.

(v) The trial balance will not balance. Purchases has been debited $3,000. No credit entry has been made. So in the trial balance debits will exceed credits by $3,000.

(vi) The trial balance will balance.

2 The correction of errors

FAST FORWARD   Errors which leave total debits and total credits in balance can be corrected by using journal entries.

2.1 Journal entries

Errors are corrected by journal entries. The format of a journal entry is:

Date		Folio	Debit	Credit
			$	$
Account to be debited			X	
Account to be credited				X
(Narrative to explain the transaction)				

2.2 Example

Suppose a bookkeeper accidentally posts a bill for $40 to the rates account instead of to the electricity account. A trial balance is drawn up, and total debits are $40,000 and total credits are $40,000.

Show the journal entry made to correct the misposting error.

Solution

1.7.20X7

DEBIT	Electricity account	$40	
CREDIT	Rent account		$40

To correct a misposting of $40 from the rent account to electricity account.

After the journal has been posted, total debits will still be $40,000 and total credits will be $40,000. Total debits and totals credits are still equal.

 Question   **Journal entries**

Write out the journal entries which would correct the following errors.

(a)   A business receives an invoice for $250 from a supplier which was omitted from the books entirely.

(b)   Repairs worth $150 were incorrectly debited to the non-current asset (machinery) account instead of the repairs account.

(c)   Telephone expenses of $540 are incorrectly debited to the electricity account.

(d)   A page in the sales day book has been added up to $28,425 when it should be $28,825.

Answer

(a) DEBIT   Purchases $250
    CREDIT   Payables $250

   A transaction previously omitted.

(b) DEBIT   Repairs account $150
    CREDIT   Non-current asset (machinery) a/c $150

   The correction of an error of principle. Repairs costs incorrectly added to non-current asset costs.

(c) DEBIT   Telephone expenses $540
    CREDIT   Electricity expenses $540

   Correction of an error of commission. Telephone expenses wrongly charged to the electricity account.

(d) DEBIT   Receivables $400
    CREDIT   Sales $400

   The correction of a casting error in the sales day book.

   ($28,825 – $28,425 = $400)

3 Suspense accounts

Errors which create an imbalance between debits and credits will need to be corrected by a suspense account entry. When the error has been located it can be corrected by journal and the suspense account balance cleared. A suspense account posting is always **temporary**.

Key term

A **suspense account** is a **temporary** account which is opened because either:

- A trial balance does not balance

- The bookkeeper does not know where to post one side of a transaction (eg a cash payment is credited to cash, but the bookkeeper does not know what the payment is for and so will not know which account to debit).

3.1 Use of suspense account: when the trial balance does not balance

When an error has occurred which results in an imbalance between total debits and total credits in the ledger accounts, the first step is to open a suspense account.

3.2 Example

Suppose an accountant draws up a trial balance and finds that, for some as yet unknown reason, total debits exceed total credits by $162. There is an error somewhere, and for the time being, open a suspense account and enter a credit of $162 in it. This serves two purposes.

- A reminder of an outstanding error
- The suspense account balances the trial balance

Solution

When the cause of the $162 discrepancy is tracked down, it is corrected by means of a journal entry. For example, suppose it turned out that the accountant had accidentally failed to record a credit of $162 to payables control. The journal entry would be:

DEBIT	Suspense a/c	$162	
CREDIT	Payables control a/c		$162

To close off suspense a/c and correct error.

Assessment focus point	Whenever an error occurs which results in total debits not being equal to total credits, the first step an accountant makes is to open up a suspense account.

3.3 Example: transposition error

The bookkeeper of Mixem Gladly made a transposition error when entering an amount for sales in the sales account. Instead of entering the correct amount of $37,453.60 he entered $37,543.60, transposing the 4 and 5. The receivables were posted correctly, and so when total debits and credits on the ledger accounts were compared, it was found that credits exceeded debits by $(37,543.60 – 37,453.60) = $90.

Solution

The initial step is to equalise the total debits and credits by posting a debit of $90 to a suspense account.

When the cause of the error is discovered, the double entry to correct it should be logged in the journal as:

DEBIT	Sales	$90	
CREDIT	Suspense a/c		$90

To close off suspense a/c and correct transposition error.

3.4 Example: error of omission

When Guttersnipe Builders paid the monthly salary cheques to its office staff, the payment of $5,250 was correctly entered in the cash account, but the bookkeeper omitted to debit the office salaries account. As a consequence, the total debit and credit balances on the ledger accounts were not equal, and credits exceeded debits by $5,250.

Solution

The initial step in correcting the situation is to debit $5,250 to a suspense account.

When the cause of the error is discovered, the double entry to correct it should be logged in the journal.

DEBIT	Office salaries account	$5,250	
CREDIT	Suspense account		$5,250

To close off suspense account and correct error of omission.

3.5 Example: error of commission

A bookkeeper makes a mistake by entering what should be a debit entry as a credit, or vice versa. For example, a credit customer pays $460 of the $660 he owes, but the bookkeeper has debited $460 on the debtors account in the nominal ledger by mistake.

The total debit balances in Ashdown's ledger accounts would now exceed the total credits by 2 × $460 = $920.

Solution

The initial step in correcting the error would be to make a credit entry of $920 in a suspense account. When the cause of the error is discovered, it should be corrected as follows.

DEBIT	Suspense account	$920
CREDIT	Receivables	$920

To close off suspense account and correct error of commission.

In the receivables account in the nominal ledger, the correction would appear therefore as follows.

RECEIVABLES ACCOUNT

	$		$
Balance b/f	660	Suspense account: error corrected	920
Payment incorrectly debited	460	Balance c/f	200
	1,120		1,120

3.6 Use of suspense account: not knowing where to post a transaction

Suspense accounts are also used when a bookkeeper does not know in which account to post one side of a transaction. Until the mystery is sorted out, the entry is recorded in a suspense account. A typical example is when the business receives cash through the post from a source which cannot be determined. The double entry in the accounts would be a debit in the cash book, and a credit to a suspense account.

3.7 Example: not knowing where to post a transaction

Windfall Garments received a cheque in the post for $620. The name on the cheque is R J Beasley Esq, but Windfall Garments have no idea who this person is, nor why he should be sending $620. The bookkeeper decides to open a suspense account.

DEBIT	Cash	$620
CREDIT	Suspense account	$620

Eventually, it transpires that the cheque was in payment for a debt owed by the Haute Couture Corner Shop and paid out of the proprietor's personal bank account.

DEBIT	Suspense account	$620
CREDIT	Receivables	$620

3.8 Suspense accounts might contain several items

If more than one error or unidentifiable posting to a ledger account arises during an accounting period, they will all be merged together in the same suspense account. Indeed, until the causes of the errors are discovered, the bookkeepers are unlikely to know exactly how many errors there are.

Assessment focus point

A question might give you a balance on a suspense account, together with enough information to make the necessary corrections, leaving a nil balance on the suspense account and correct balances on various other accounts. In practice, of course, finding these errors is far from easy!

Remember!

Not all corrections will affect the suspense account. If the original error did not stop the trial balance balancing, its correction will not involve the suspense account.

3.9 Example: suspense account with several items

Chi Knitwear is an old fashioned firm with a hand-written set of books. A trial balance is extracted at the end of each month, and an income statement and balance sheet are computed. This month however the trial balance will not balance, the credits exceeding debits by $1,536.

You are asked to help and after inspection of the ledgers discover the following errors.

(a) A balance of $87 on a receivables account has been omitted from the schedule of debtors, the total of which was entered as receivables in the trial balance.

(b) A small piece of machinery purchased for $1,200 had been written off to repairs.

(c) The receipts side of the cash book had been undercast by $720.

(d) The total of one page of the sales day book had been carried forward as $8,154, whereas the correct amount was $8,514.

(e) A credit note for $179 received from a supplier had been posted to the wrong side of his account; the schedule of payables balances was used as the payables figure in the trial balance.

(f) An electricity bill in the sum of $152, not yet accrued for, is discovered in a filing tray.

(g) Mr Smith whose past debts to the company had been the subject of a provision, at last paid $731 to clear his account. His personal account has been credited but the cheques has not yet been entered in the cash account.

Required

(a) Write up the suspense account to clear the trial balance difference.
(b) State the effect on the accounts of correcting each error.

Solution

(a)

SUSPENSE ACCOUNT

	$		$
Opening balance	1,536	Receivables – balance omitted	87
Sales – under-recorded	360	Cash book – receipts undercast	720
		Payables: credit note posted to wrong side	358
		Cash: Mr Smith's debt paid but cash receipt not recorded	731
	1,896		1,896

BPP
LEARNING MEDIA

Notes

(i) Error (b) is an error of principle, whereby a non-current asset item (capital expenditure) has been accounted for as revenue expenditure. The correction will be logged in the journal, but since the error did not result in an inequality between debits and credits, the suspense account would not have been used.

(ii) The electricity bill has been omitted from the accounts entirely. The error of omission means that both debits and credits will be logged in the journal, but the suspense account will not be involved, since there is equality between debits and credits in the error.

(b) (i) The error means that receivables are understated. The correction of the error will increase the total amount for receivables to be shown in the balance sheet.

(ii) The correction of this error will add $1,200 to non-current assets at cost (balance sheet item) and reduce repair costs by $1,200. The income statement will therefore show an increased profit of $1,200, less any depreciation now charged on the non-current asset.

(iii) The undercasting (ie under-adding) of $720 on the receipts side of the cash book means that debits of cash will be $720 less than they should have been. The correction of the error will add $720 to the cash balance in the balance sheet.

(iv) This transposition error means that total sales would be under-recorded by $8,514 – $8,154 = $360 in the sales account. The correction of the error will add $360 to total sales, and thus add $360 to the profits in the income statement.

(v) The credit note must have been issued for a purchase return to the supplier by the business. It should have been debited to the payable's account, but instead has been credited. Assuming that the purchase returns account was credited correctly, the effect of the error has been to overstate total creditors by 2 × $179 = $358, and this amount should be credited from the suspense account and debited to the payables account. The effect will be to reduce the total for payables in the balance sheet by $358.

(vi) The electricity bill, when entered in the accounts, will increase payables by $152, and reduce profits (by adding to electricity expenses) by $152, assuming that none of this cost is a prepayment of electricity charges.

(vii) Since the cheque has not yet been recorded in the cash book, the correction of the error will add $731 to the cash balance in the balance sheet. At the same time, the allowance for receivables can be reduced, which will increase the net amount for receivables in the balance sheet by $731 (ie receivables less allowance for receivables, although the reduction in gross receivables by $731 has already been accounted for, due to the cash received) and increase profits by $731.

3.10 Suspense accounts are temporary

It must be stressed that a suspense account can only be temporary. Postings to a suspense account are only made when the bookkeeper doesn't know yet what to do or when an error has occurred. Mysteries must be solved, and errors must be corrected. Under no circumstances should there still be a suspense account when it comes to preparing the balance sheet of a business. The suspense account must be cleared and all the correcting entries made before the final accounts are drawn up.

ssessment
cus point

In the assessment, you may be asked to calculate the original balance on a suspense account given a number of corrections that have been made. Try the next question to get a feel for this.

Question

When the trial balance was prepared a suspense account was opened. These errors were discovered:

(i) Opening inventory of $2,000 was omitted from the trial balance.

(ii) $400 was received from a customer whose debt had been written off and the bookkeeper credited the bad debts expense account and the receivables control account and debited cash.

What was the balance on the suspense account?

A $1,600 debit
B $2,400 debit
C $1,600 credit
D $2,400 credit

Answer

B is correct.

Opening inventory is a debit, so omitting it puts $2,000 debit into suspense. Then, when cash was received from the written off receivable the entries made were debits of $400 and credits of $800, putting another $400 debit into suspense.

Chapter roundup

- It is not possible to draw up a complete list of all the errors which might be made by bookkeepers and accountants. However, it is possible to describe five types of error which cover most of the errors as:

  - Errors of transposition
  - Errors of omission
  - Errors of principle
  - Errors of commission
  - Compensating errors

- Errors which leave total debits and total credits in balance can be corrected by using journal entries.

- Errors which create an imbalance between debits and credits will need to be corrected by a suspense account entry. When the error has been located it can be corrected by journal and the suspense account balance cleared. A suspense account posting is always **temporary**.

- Suspense accounts are also used when a bookkeeper does not know in which account to post one side of a transaction. Until the mystery is sorted out, the entry is recorded in a suspense account. A typical example is when the business receives cash through the post from a source which cannot be determined. The double entry in the accounts would be a debit in the cash book, and a credit to a suspense account.

Quick quiz

1   Which of the following is an error of principle?

    A   Recording the income from selling a non-current asset as a miscellaneous receipt in the income statement

    B   Petty cash expense $50 credited to expense and debited to petty cash

    C   Failing to record an invoice in the sales ledger

    D   Recording an inventory purchase invoice for $500 as

        Dr purchases $500
        Cr payables control a/c

2   A business incurred an expense costing $600. The expense was only entered in the cash account as a debit. Which of the following journal entries is required to correct the error? (Assume a suspense account has been used to clear the imbalance.)

A	Dr Expense	600		Cr Bank	600
B	Dr Suspense	600		Cr Bank	1,200
	Dr Expense	600			
C	Dr Suspense	600		Cr Bank	600
D	Dr Bank	1,200		Cr Suspense	600
				Cr Expense	600

3   What is the function of a suspense account?

    A   A device used to enable the production of the financial statements, when required, despite the presence of errors.

    B   A method of ensuring the trial balance will agree.

    C   A way of focusing attention upon the corrective action required to ensure the trial balance does agree and the integrity of the accounting system is maintained.

    D   A way of recording transactions when the ultimate accounting treatment required in unclear.

4   Correction of an error will only involve an entry to a suspense account if the original error _____
_____. (Complete the sentence.)

Answers to quick quiz

1   A   Correct, the sale of a non-current asset must not be confused with a revenue item – gross profit will be overstated.

     B   This is a reversal error.

     C   This is an error of omission.

     D   This entry has been correctly recorded, there is no error.

2   B   Correct, it is necessary to correct the error and record the transactions hence the duplication of the $600 posting to bank.

     A   Incorrect, you have not cleared the suspense account balance which will arise as a result of the incomplete but incorrect entry.

     C   Incorrect, this will clear the suspense account but will not record the transaction.

     D   Incorrect, the entry is reversed.

3   C   This is the correct answer.

     A   A suspense account can be used, expediently, to allow the production of accounts provided it is acknowledged the accounts may be flawed.

     B   Opening a suspense account will ensure the trial balance agrees, but the function of a trial balance is to reveal errors. The suspense account focuses attention upon those errors.

     D   Whilst suspense accounts are often used for this purpose, the transactions 'in suspense' must be journalised out when the treatment has been clarified.

4   Correction of an error will only involve an entry to a suspense account if the original error prevented the trial balance from balancing.

Now try the questions below from the Question Bank

Question numbers	Page
68–74	406

Part C
Final accounts and audit

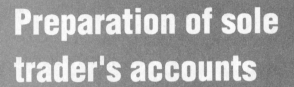

Preparation of sole trader's accounts

Introduction

We have now reached our goal of preparing of the final accounts of a sole trader!

We will deal with the case of a trial balance and then making adjustments to produce final accounts.

This chapter also acts as a review of what we have covered to date.

Topic list	Syllabus references
1 Preparation of final accounts	D (1)

1 Preparation of final accounts

FAST FORWARD

> You should now be able to prepare a set of final accounts for a sole trader from a trial balance after incorporating period end adjustments for depreciation, inventory, prepayments, accruals, bad debts, and allowances for receivables.

1.1 Adjustments to accounts

Assessment focus point

This chapter acts as a consolidation of all the work you have done to date and is useful revision.

You should now use what you have learned to produce a solution to the following exercise, which involves preparing an income statement and balance sheet.

Question	Adjustment to accounts

The financial affairs of Newbegin Tools prior to the commencement of trading were as follows.

NEWBEGIN TOOLS
BALANCE SHEET AS AT 1 AUGUST 20X5

	$	$
Non-current assets		
Motor vehicle		2,000
Shop fittings		3,000
		5,000
Current assets		
Inventories		12,000
Cash		1,000
		18,000
Capital		12,000
Current liabilities		
Bank overdraft	2,000	
Trade payables	4,000	
		6,000
		18,000

At the end of six months the business had made the following transactions.

(a) Goods were purchased on credit at a list price of $10,000.

(b) Trade discount received was 2% on list price and there was a settlement discount received of 5% on settling debts to suppliers of $8,000. These were the only payments to suppliers in the period.

(c) Closing inventories of goods were valued at $5,450.

(d) All sales were on credit and amounted to $27,250.

(e) Outstanding receivables balances at 31 January 20X6 amounted to $3,250 of which $250 were to be written off. An allowance for receivables is to be made amounting to 2% of the remaining outstanding receivables.

(f) Cash payments were made in respect of the following expenses.

		$
(i)	Stationery, postage and wrapping	500
(ii)	Telephone charges	200
(iii)	Electricity	600
(iv)	Cleaning and refreshments	150

(g)   Cash drawings by the proprietor, Alf Newbegin, amounted to $6,000.

(h)   The outstanding overdraft balance as at 1 August 20X5 was paid off. Interest charges and bank charges on the overdraft amounted to $40.

Prepare the income statement of Newbegin Tools for the six months to 31 January 20X6 and a balance sheet as at that date. Ignore depreciation.

Answer

INCOME STATEMENT
FOR THE SIX MONTHS ENDED 31 JANUARY 20X6

	$	$
Sales		27,250
Opening inventories	12,000	
Purchases (note (a))	9,800	
	21,800	
Less closing inventories	5,450	
Cost of goods sold		16,350
Gross profit		10,900
Discounts received (note (b))		400
		11,300
Electricity (note (c))	600	
Stationery, postage and wrapping	500	
Bad debts written off	250	
Allowance for receivables (note (d))	60	
Telephone charges	200	
Cleaning and refreshments	150	
Interest and bank charges	40	
		1,800
Net profit		9,500

Notes

(a)   Purchases at cost $10,000 less 2% trade discount.

(b)   5% of $8,000 = $400.

(c)   Expenses are grouped into sales and distribution expenses (here assumed to be electricity, stationery and postage, bad debts and allowance for receivables) administration expenses (here assumed to be telephone charges and cleaning) and finance charges.

(d)   2% of $3,000 = $60.

The preparation of a balance sheet is not so easy, because we must calculate the value of payables and cash in hand.

(a)   Payables as at 31 January 20X6

The amount owing to payables is the sum of the amount owing at the beginning of the period, plus the cost of purchases during the period (net of all discounts), less the payments already made for purchases.

	$
Payables as at 1 August 20X5	4,000
Add purchases during the period, net of trade discount	9,800
	13,800
Less settlement discounts received	(400)
	13,400
Less payments to payables during the period*	(7,600)
	5,800

* $8,000 less cash discount of $400.

(b) Cash at bank and in hand at 31 January 20X6

You need to identify cash payments received and cash payments made.

		$
(i)	*Cash received from sales*	
	Total sales in the period	27,250
	Add receivables as at 1 August 20X5	0
		27,250
	Less unpaid debts as at 31 January 20X6	3,250
	Cash received	24,000

		$
(ii)	*Cash paid*	
	Trade payables (see (a))	7,600
	Stationery, postage and wrapping	500
	Telephone charges	200
	Electricity	600
	Cleaning and refreshments	150
	Bank charges and interest	40
	Bank overdraft repaid	2,000
	Drawings by proprietor	6,000
		17,090

Note. It is easy to forget some of these payments, especially drawings.

		$
(iii)	Cash in hand at 1 August 20X5	1,000
	Cash received in the period	24,000
		25,000
	Cash paid in the period	(17,090)
	Cash at bank and in hand as at 31 January 20X6	7,910

(c) When bad debts are written off, the value of outstanding receivables must be reduced by the amount written off. Receivables in the balance sheet will be valued at $3,250 less bad debts $250 and the allowance for receivables of $60 – ie at $2,940.

(d) Non-current assets should be depreciated. However, in this exercise depreciation has been ignored.

NEWBEGIN TOOLS
BALANCE SHEET AS AT 31 JANUARY 20X6

	$	$
Non-current assets		
Motor vehicles	2,000	
Shop fittings	3,000	
		5,000
Current assets		
Inventories	5,450	
Receivables, less allowance for receivables	2,940	
Cash	7,910	
		16,300
		21,300

	$	$
Capital		
Capital at 1 August 20X5		12,000
Net profit for the period		9,500
		21,500
Less drawings		6,000
Capital at 31 January 20X6		15,500
Current liabilities		
Trade payables		5,800
		21,300

The bank overdraft has now been repaid and is therefore not shown.

1.2 Example: accounts preparation from a trial balance

The following trial balance was extracted from the ledger of Stephen Chee, a sole trader, as at 31 May 20X1 – the end of his financial year.

STEPHEN CHEE
TRIAL BALANCE AS AT 31 MAY 20X1

	Dr	Cr
	$	$
Property, at cost	120,000	
Equipment, at cost	80,000	
Provisions for depreciation (as at 1 June 20X0)		
– on property		20,000
– on equipment		38,000
Purchases	250,000	
Sales		402,200
Stock, as at 1 June 20X0	50,000	
Discounts allowed	18,000	
Discounts received		4,800
Returns out		15,000
Wages and salaries	58,800	
Bad debts	4,600	
Loan interest	5,100	
Other operating expenses	17,700	
Trade payables		36,000
Trade receivables	38,000	
Cash in hand	300	
Bank	1,300	
Drawings	24,000	
Allowance for receivables		500
17% long term loan		30,000
Capital, as at 1 June 20X0		121,300
	667,800	667,800

The following additional information as at 31 May 20X1 is available.

(a) Inventory as at the close of business has been valued at cost at $42,000.

(b) Wages and salaries need to be accrued by $800.

(c)   Other operating expenses are prepaid by $300.

(d)   The allowance for receivables is to be adjusted so that it is 2% of trade receivables.

(e)   Depreciation for the year ended 31 May 20X1 has still to be provided for as follows.

Property: 1.5% per annum using the straight line method; and
Equipment: 25% per annum using the reducing balance method.

Required

Prepare Stephen Chee's income statement for the year ended 31 May 20X1 and his balance sheet as at that date.

Solution

STEPHEN CHEE
INCOME STATEMENT
FOR THE YEAR ENDED 31 MAY 20X1

	$	$
Sales		402,200
Cost of sales		
Opening inventory	50,000	
Purchases	250,000	
Purchases returns	(15,000)	
	285,000	
Closing inventory	42,000	
		243,000
Gross profit		159,200
Other income – discounts received		4,800
		164,000
Expenses		
Operating expenses		
Wages and salaries ($58,800 + $800)	59,600	
Discounts allowed	18,000	
Bad debts (W1)	4,860	
Loan interest	5,100	
Depreciation (W2)	12,300	
Other operating expenses ($17,700 – $300)	17,400	
		117,260
Net profit for the year		46,740

STEPHEN CHEE
BALANCE SHEET AS AT 31 MAY 20X0

	Cost $	Accumulated depn. $	Net book value $
Non-current assets			
Property	120,000	21,800	98,200
Equipment	80,000	48,500	31,500
	200,000	70,300	129,700
Current assets			
Stock		42,000	
Trade receivables net of allowance for receivables ($38,000 – 760 (W1))		37,240	
Prepayments		300	
Bank		1,300	
Cash in hand		300	
			81,140
			210,840
Capital			
Balance at 1 June 20X0			121,300
Net profit for the year			46,740
			168,040
Drawings			24,000
			144,040
Non-current liabilities			
17% loan			30,000
Current liabilities			
Trade payables		36,000	
Accruals		800	
			36,800
			210,840

Workings

		$
1	Bad debts	
	Previous allowance	500
	New allowance (2% × 38,000)	760
	Increase	260
	Per trial balance	4,600
	Income statement	4,860
2	Depreciation	
	Property	
	Opening provision	20,000
	Provision for the year (1.5% × 120,000)	1,800
	Closing provision	21,800
	Equipment	
	Opening provision	38,000
	Provision for the year (25% × 42,000)	10,500
	Closing provision	48,500
	Total charge in I/S	12,300

Question

Donald Brown, a sole trader, extracted the following trial balance on 31 December 20X0.

TRIAL BALANCE AS AT 31 DECEMBER 20X0

	Debit $	Credit $
Capital at 1 January 20X0		26,094
Receivables	42,737	
Cash in hand	1,411	
Payables		35,404
Fixtures and fittings at cost	42,200	
Discounts allowed	1,304	
Discounts received		1,175
Inventory at 1 January 20X0	18,460	
Sales		491,620
Purchases	387,936	
Motor vehicles at cost	45,730	
Lighting and heating	6,184	
Motor expenses	2,862	
Rent	8,841	
General expenses	7,413	
Bank overdraft		19,861
Provision for depreciation		
Fixtures and fittings		2,200
Motor vehicles		15,292
Drawings	26,568	
	591,646	591,646

The following information as at 31 December is also available.

(a) $218 is owing for motor expenses.

(b) $680 has been prepaid for rent.

(c) Depreciation is to be provided of the year as follows.

Motor vehicles: 20% on cost
Fixtures and fittings: 10% reducing balance method

(d) Inventory at the close of business was valued at $19,926.

Required

Prepare Donald Brown's income statement for the year ended 31 December 20X0 and his balance sheet at that date.

Answer

Tutorial note. You should note these points.

(a) Discounts allowed are an expense of the business and should be shown as a deduction from gross profit. Similarly, discounts received is a revenue item and should be added to gross profit.

(b) The figure for depreciation in the trial balance represents accumulated depreciation up to and including 20W9. You have to calculate the charge for the year 20X0 for the income statement and add this to the trial balance figure to arrive at the accumulated depreciation figure to be included in the balance sheet.

DONALD BROWN
INCOME STATMENT
FOR THE YEAR ENDED 31 DECEMBER 20X0

	$	$
Sales		491,620
Less cost of sales		
Opening inventory	18,460	
Purchases	387,936	
	406,396	
Closing inventory	19,926	
		386,470
Gross profit		105,150
Discounts received		1,175
		106,325
Less expenses:		
discounts allowed	1,304	
lighting and heating	6,184	
motor expenses (2,862 + 218)	3,080	
rent (8,841 – 680)	8,161	
general expenses	7,413	
depreciation (W)	13,146	
		39,288
Net profit		67,037

Working: depreciation charge

Motor vehicles: $45,730 \times 20\% = \$9,146$
Fixtures and fittings: $10\% \times \$(42,200 - 2,200) = \$4,000$
Total: $\$4,000 + \$9,146 = \$13,146$.

DONALD BROWN
BALANCE SHEET AS AT 31 DECEMBER 20X0

	Cost	Depreciation	Net
	$	$	$
Non-current assets			
Fixtures and fittings	42,200	6,200	36,000
Motor vehicles	45,730	24,438	21,292
	87,930	30,638	57,292
Current assets			
Inventory		19,926	
Receivables		42,737	
Prepayments		680	
Cash in hand		1,411	
			64,754
			122,046

Capital

Balance b/f	26,094
Net profit for year	67,037
	93,131
Less drawings	26,568
	66,563

Current liabilities

Payables	35,404	
Accruals	218	
Bank overdraft	19,861	
		55,483
		122,046

Chapter roundup

- You should now be able to prepare a set of final accounts for a sole trader from a trial balance after incorporating period end adjustments for depreciation, inventory, prepayments, accruals, bad debts, and allowances for receivables.

Quick quiz

1   Which of the following is the correct formula for cost of sales?

    A   Opening inventory – purchases + closing inventory.

    B   Purchases – closing inventory + sales.

    C   Opening inventory – closing inventory + purchases.

    D   Opening inventory + closing inventory – purchases.

2   The trial balance is the final phase prior to preparation of the accounts. True or false?

3   Which is the correct order of current assets in the balance sheet?

    A   Bank, prepayments, receivables, inventory

    B   Inventory, receivables, prepayments, bank

    C   Inventory, prepayments, receivables, bank

    D   Inventory, bank, receivables, prepayments

Answers to quick quiz

1   C   Correct, this is a version of the more normal formula: opening inventory + purchases − closing inventory.

     A   Incorrect.

     B   Incorrect. Sales should never form part of cost of sales.

     C   Incorrect.

2   False. The trial balance checks that the double entry has been done correctly. After the trial balance has been struck, there are usually adjustments (eg for accruals, prepayments, depreciation) before the financial statements are prepared.

3   B   Remember that current assets are listed in order of increasing liquidity (inventory being the least easy to turn into cash).

Now try the questions below from the Question Bank

Question numbers	Page
75–76	407

Limited liability companies

Introduction

In this chapter we study the accounts of **limited liability companies**. The accounting rules and conventions for recording the business transactions of limited liability companies and then preparing their final accounts, are much the same as for sole traders. For example, companies will have a cash book, sales day book, purchase day book, journal, sales ledger, purchase ledger and nominal ledger etc. They also prepare an income statement annually, and a balance sheet at the end of the accounting year.

We shall see that, in the balance sheet, the treatment of assets and liabilities is basically the same but the particular nature of limited liability companies calls for changes in the owners' equity section. Similarly, in the income statement, the principal differences are found in the statement of changes in equity, a statement which shows how the profit or loss for the period has been divided.

One important difference is the legal requirement that limited liability companies must publish their accounts. The relevant legislation specifies certain information which must be included in the published financial statements of a limited liability company.

It should be stressed that, while you do not have to learn the published accounts formats by heart at this stage, it is important for you to have an overall awareness of the form of company accounts. In Chapter 25 you will learn about interpretation of accounts and this will include items in company accounts formats.

Topic list	Syllabus references
1 Limited liability companies	A (6), D (6)
2 Share capital and reserves	D (6)
3 Bonus and rights issues	D (6)
4 The final accounts of limited liability companies	A (6), D (6)
5 Loan stock	D (6)
6 Statement of changes in equity	D (6)
7 Taxation	D (6)
8 The ledger accounts of limited liability companies	D (6)

1 Limited liability companies

Company accounts preparation in the UK is governed by the Companies Act.

Companies issue shares to shareholders who enjoy limited liability.

Key terms

There are two classes of limited liability company in the UK.

(a) **Private companies**. These have the word 'limited' at the end of their name. Being private, they cannot invite members of the public to invest in their equity (shares).

(b) **Public companies.** These are much fewer in number than private companies, but are generally much larger in size. They have the words 'public limited company' – shortened to PLC or plc (or the Welsh language equivalent) at the end of their name. Public limited companies can invite members of the general public to invest in their equity, and the 'shares' of these companies are traded on a Stock Exchange.

Assessment focus point

Under IFRS, public companies are usually 'Inc' and private companies 'Co'.

1.1 Limited liability

Key term

Limited liability companies offer **limited liability** to their owners. This means that the liability of an owner is limited to any amounts not yet paid up for shares bought from the company. So, unlike sole traders, the owners (shareholders) of a company do not have to use their own, private, finances to pay payables if there are insufficient funds in the business.

2 Share capital and reserves

2.1 Share capital

The proprietors' capital in a limited liability company consists of **share capital**. A company issues **shares**, which are paid for by investors, who then become shareholders of the company.

When a company is set up with a **share capital** of, say, $100,000, it may be decided to issue

- 100,000 shares of $1 each nominal value
- 200,000 shares of 50c each
- 400,000 shares of 25c each
- 250,000 shares of 40c each

$1, 50c, 25c or 40c is the nominal value of the share. The nominal value is not the same as the market value, which is the price someone is prepared to pay for the share.

Key term

The authorised share capital is the maximum amount of share capital that the company is empowered to issue. Issued share capital is the nominal amount of share capital that has been issued to shareholders. This cannot exceed the authorised share capital. Called up share capital is the total amount of issued share capital for which the shareholders are required to pay. Paid up share capital is the amount of share capital paid by the shareholders.

2.2 Dividends

Profits paid out to shareholders are called **dividends**.

- An **interim** dividend is a dividend paid part-way through the year
- At the end of the year, the company might pay a further **final** dividend.

The **total dividend** for the year is the sum of the interim and final dividends. (Not all companies pay an interim dividend. Interim dividends are commonly paid by public limited companies.)

Usually, at the end of an accounting year, a company's directors will propose a final dividend payment, but this will not yet have been paid. This means that the final dividend will be shown as a note to the financial statements. It is not a liability until the dividend is approved at the AGM.

2.3 The terminology of dividend

The terminology of dividend payments can be confusing, since they may be expressed either in the form, as 'x cents per share' or as 'y per cent'. In the latter case, the meaning is always 'y per cent of the **nominal** value of the shares in issue'. For example, suppose a company's issued share capital consists of 100,000 50c ordinary shares. The company's balance sheet would include the following.

Called up share capital: 100,000 50c ordinary shares $50,000

If the directors wish to pay a dividend of $5,000, they may propose any of the following.

- A dividend of 5c per share (100,000 × 5c = $5,000)
- A dividend of 10% (10% × $50,000 = $5,000)
- A dividend of 10c in the pound ($50,000 × 10c = $5,000)

Any profits not paid out as dividends are put in reserves (see below).

2.4 Ordinary shares and preference shares

The two types of shares most often encountered are preference shares and ordinary shares.

T FORWARD

Preference shares carry the right to a fixed dividend which is expressed as a percentage of their nominal value: eg a 6% $1 preference share carries a right to an annual dividend of 6c.

Preference dividends have priority over ordinary dividends. If the directors of a company wish to pay a dividend (which they are not obliged to do) they must pay any preference dividend first. Otherwise, no ordinary dividend may be paid.

T FORWARD

Ordinary shares are by far the most common. They carry no right to a fixed dividend but are entitled to all profits left after payment of any preference dividend. In most companies only ordinary shares carry voting rights.

Should the company be wound up, any surplus is shared between the ordinary shareholders.

Question

Dividends 1

At the year-end, the trial balance for KT shows a debit balance of $20,000 in respect of dividends. The Share Capital account of $1m comprises 200,000 5% preference shares of $1 with the balance made up of 50c ordinary shares. The dividends account represents a half-year's preference dividend and an interim ordinary dividend. A final dividend of 5c per ordinary share was proposed before the trial balance was prepared.

Calculate the interim and final dividends for each category of share.

Answer

A full year's dividend on the preference shares is 200,000 @ 5% = $10,000, therefore a half-year's dividend was $5,000, with a final dividend of the same amount.

The interim ordinary dividend was therefore $15,000 ($20,000 – $5,000).

As the share capital account amounts to $1m, $800,000 ($1m – $200k) must relate to ordinary shares. However, the ordinary shares are only 50c each, meaning that there are 1.6 million of them. The final dividend is therefore $80,000 (1.6m × 5c)

Assessment focus point

It is worth spending a few minutes getting to grips with dividend calculations, as they are a likely assessment topic. You are unlikely to get a calculation more difficult than that involved in the exercise above.

Question

Dividends 2

A company's share capital is:

50c	Ordinary shares	$2m
$1	6% preference shares	$1m

Dividends to ordinary shareholders have been:

		Amount	*Date declared*
20X2	Final dividend	4c per share	31 Jan 20X3
20X3	Interim dividend	3c per share	13 July 20X3
20X3	Final dividend	5c per share	20 Jan 20X4

What is the figure for dividends in the financial statements to 31 December 20X3?

A $160,000
B $220,000
C $320,000
D $340,000

Answer

D is correct.

	$
1m 6% preference shares	60,000
20X2 final (4c × 4m shares)	160,000
20X3 interim (3c × 4m shares)	120,000
Total	340,000

The 20X3 final dividend was declared after the year end and so will be disclosed in a note to the financial statements.

2.5 Reserves

Reserves are profits that have not been distributed (paid out) to shareholders.

The ordinary shareholders' total investment in a company is called the **equity** and consists of ordinary share capital plus **reserves**.

Shareholders' funds is the total of all share capital, both ordinary and preference, and the reserves.

The important point to note is that all reserves are **owned** by the ordinary shareholders.

A distinction should be made between the two types of reserves.

Key terms

Statutory reserves are reserves which a company is required to set up by law and which are not available for the distribution of dividends.

Non-statutory reserves are reserves consisting of profits which are distributable as dividends, if the company so wishes.

2.5.1 Retained profits

Key term

These are profits earned by the company and **not appropriated** by dividends, taxation or transfer to another reserve account. This reserve generally increases from year to year, as most companies do not distribute all their profits as dividends. If a loss is made in one particular year, a dividend can still be paid from previous years' retained profits.

For example, if a company makes a loss of $100,000 in one year, yet has unappropriated profits from previous years totalling $250,000, it can pay a dividend not exceeding $150,000.

Very occasionally, you come across a debit balance on the retained profits account. This indicates that the company has accumulated losses.

This is the most significant non-statutory reserve, and it is described in many different ways.

- Revenue reserve
- Retained profits
- Retained earnings
- Undistributed profits
- Unappropriated profits

2.5.2 Other non-statutory reserves

The company directors may choose to set up other reserves. These may have a specific purpose (for example plant and machinery replacement reserve) or not (for example general reserve). The creation of these reserves usually indicates a general intention not to distribute the profits involved at any future date, although legally any such reserves, being non-statutory, remain available for the payment of dividends.

Profits are transferred to these reserves by making an appropriation out of profits, usually profits for the year. Typically, you might come across the following.

	$	$
Profit after taxation		100,000
Appropriations of profit		
Dividend	60,000	
Transfer to general reserve	10,000	
		70,000
Retained profits for the year		30,000
Retained profits b/f		250,000
Retained profits c/f		280,000

There is no real significance about the creation of separate non-statutory reserves. After all, there is little difference between the following two balance sheet extracts.

			$	$
(a)	Total assets			3,500
	Financed by			
	Share capital			2,000
	Reserves:	general (distributable as dividend)	1,000	
		retained profits (distributable)	500	
				1,500
				3,500

		$
(b)	Total assets	3,500
	Financed by	
	Share capital	2,000
	Reserves: retained profit (distributable)	1,500
		3,500

The establishment of a 'plant and machinery replacement reserve' (or something similar) indicates an intention by a company to keep funds in the business to replace its plant and machinery. However, the reserve would still (legally) represent distributable profits. The existence of such a reserve no more guarantees the company's ability to replace its non-current assets in the future, than the accumulated provision for depreciation in the balance sheet.

2.6 The share premium account

FAST FORWARD

The **share premium account** is a statutory reserve created if shares are issued for more than their nominal value. The excess received over nominal value is credited to the share premium account.

When a company is first incorporated (set up) the issue price of its shares will probably be the same as their nominal value and so there would be no share premium. If the company does well the market value of its shares will increase, but not the nominal value. The price of any new shares issued will be approximately their market value. The difference between cash received by the company and the nominal value of the new shares issued is transferred to the share premium account.

2.7 Example

X Co issues 1,000 $1 ordinary shares at $2.60. What entries record this issue?

Solution

		$	$
DEBIT	Cash	2,600	
CREDIT	Ordinary share capital		1,000
CREDIT	Share premium account		1,600

A share premium account only comes into being when a company issues shares at a price in excess of their nominal value. The market price of the shares, once they have been issued, has no bearing at all on the company's accounts, and so if their market price goes up or down, the share premium account would remain unaltered.

2.8 Revaluation reserve

 A **revaluation reserve** is a statutory reserve which must be created when a company revalues its non-current assets.

Revaluations frequently occur with freehold property, as the market value of property rises. The directors might wish to show a more 'reasonable' value of the asset in their balance sheet to avoid giving a misleading impression about the financial position of the company.

When an asset is revalued the revaluation reserve is credited with the difference between the revalued amount of the asset, and its net book value before the revaluation took place. Depreciation is subsequently charged on the revalued amount.

2.9 Example: revaluation reserve

X Co bought freehold land and buildings for $20,000 ten years ago; their net book value (after depreciation of the buildings) is now $19,300. A professional valuation of $390,000 has been given, and the directors wish to reflect this in the accounts. Show the entries to record this revaluation.

Solution

The revaluation surplus is $390,000 – $19,300 = $370,700. The entry to be made is thus.

		$	$
DEBIT	Freehold property	370,700	
CREDIT	Revaluation reserve		370,700

The balance sheet will then include the following.

	$
Reserves	
Revaluation reserve	370,700
Non-current assets	
Freehold property (at valuation)	390,000

An unrealised capital profit (such as the $370,700 above) is generally not distributable, whereas a realised capital profit (ie if the property is actually sold for $390,000) usually is distributable.

2.10 Distinction between reserves and provisions

Key term

A **reserve** is an appropriation of distributable profits for a specific purpose (eg plant replacement) while a **provision** is an amount charged against revenue as an expense.

A provision relates either to a diminution in the value of an asset (eg allowance for receivables) or a known liability (eg audit fees), the amount of which cannot be established with any accuracy. Provisions (for depreciation, allowance for receivables etc) are dealt with in company accounts in the same way as in the accounts of other types of business.

Question

(a) A public company has 10,000,000 25c shares in issue and their current value on the stock market is $4.97 per share. What is the value of share capital in the company's nominal ledger?

(b) The retained profits of a limited liability company the same thing as the trading account of a sole trader. True or false?

(c) A freehold property is revalued from $180,000 to $500,000. What is the balance on the revaluation reserve after this revaluation?

Answer

(a) $2.5m.
(b) False. The reserve is for *retained* profits, not profits of the current year only.
(c) $320,000 (ie $500,000 – $180,000).

3 Bonus and rights issues

FAST FORWARD

A company may choose to expand its capital base by issuing further shares to existing shareholders. It can do this by means of a bonus issues or a rights issue.

3.1 Bonus issues

A company may wish to increase its share capital without needing to raise additional finance by issuing new shares. For example, a profitable company might expand from modest beginnings over a number of years. Its profitability would be reflected in large balances on its reserves, while its original share capital might look like that of a much smaller business.

It is open to such a company to **re-classify some of its reserves as share capital**. This is purely a paper exercise which **raises no funds**. Any reserve may be re-classified in this way, including a share premium account or other statutory reserve. Such a re-classification **increases the capital base** of the company and gives **creditors greater protection**.

3.2 Example: bonus issue

BUBBLES CO
BALANCE SHEET (EXTRACT)

	$'000	$'000
Equity		
Share capital		
$1 ordinary shares (fully paid)		1,000
Reserves		
Share premium	500	
Undistributed profit (retained profit)	2,000	
		2,500
Shareholders' funds		3,500

Bubbles decided to make a '3 for 2' bonus issue (ie 3 new shares for every 2 already held). So shares with a nominal value of $1,500,000 need to be issued.

The double entry is

		$'000	$'000
DEBIT	Share premium	500	
	Undistributed profit	1,000	
CREDIT	Ordinary share capital		1,500

After the issue the balance sheet is as follows

	$'000
Share capital	
$1 ordinary shares (fully paid)	2,500
Reserves	
Undistributed profit	1,000
Shareholders' funds	3,500

1,500,000 new ('bonus') shares are issued to existing shareholders, so that if Mr X previously held 20,000 shares he will now hold 50,000. The total value of his holding should theoretically remain the same however, since the net assets of the company remain unchanged and his share of those net assets remains at 2% (ie 50,000/2,500,000; previously 20,000/1,000,000).

3.3 Rights issues

A rights issue (unlike a bonus issue) is an issue of shares for cash. The 'rights' are offered to existing shareholders, who can sell them if they wish.

3.4 Example: rights issue

Bubbles Co (above) decides to make a rights issue, shortly after the bonus issue. The terms are '1 for 5 @ $1.20' (ie one new share for every five already held, at a price of $1.20). Assuming that all shareholders take up their rights (which they are not obliged to) the double entry is:

		$'000	$'000
DEBIT	Cash	600	
CREDIT	Ordinary share capital		500
	Share premium		100

Mr X who previously held 50,000 shares will now hold 60,000, and the value of his holding should increase (all other things being equal) because the net assets of the company will increase. The new balance sheet will show:

	$'000	$'000
Share capital		
$1 ordinary shares		3,000
Reserves		
Share premium	100	
Undistributed profit	1,000	
		1,100
Shareholders' funds		4,100

The increase in funds of $600,000 represents the cash raised from the issue of 500,000 new shares at a price of $1.20 each.

Rights issues are a popular way of **raising cash** by issuing shares and they are **cheap to administer**. In addition, **shareholders retain control** of the business as their holding is not diluted.

The disadvantages of a rights issue is that shareholders are **not obliged** to take up their rights and so the issue could fail to raise the money required. For this reason companies usually try to find a broker to 'underwrite' the issue, ie who will buy any rights not taken up by the shareholders.

4 The final accounts of limited liability companies

FAST FORWARD

> The preparation and publication of the final accounts of limited liability companies in the UK are governed by the CA 2006. This permits the use of financial statements under IAS 1.

4.1 IAS 1 format

At this stage in your studies, you do not have to learn the detailed regulations laid down by IAS 1. However, the general format of the balance sheet and income statement of a limited liability company is important.

ABC CO
BALANCE SHEET AS AT 31 DECEMBER 20X2

	20X2 $'000	20X2 $'000	20X1 $'000	20X1 $'000
Assets				
Non-current assets				
Property, plant and equipment	X		X	
Goodwill	X		X	
Other intangible assets	X		X	
		X		X
Current assets				
Inventories	X		X	
Trade and other receivables	X		X	
Other current assets	X		X	
Cash and cash equivalents	X		X	
		X		X
Total assets		X		X
Equity and liabilities				
Equity				
Issued capital	X		X	
Reserves	X		X	
Retained profits/(losses)	X		X	
		X		X
Non-current liabilities				
Long-term borrowings	X		X	
Long-term provisions	X		X	
		X		X
Current liabilities				
Trade and other payables	X		X	
Short-term borrowings	X		X	
Current portion of long-term borrowings	X		X	
Current tax payable	X		X	
		X		X
Total equity and liabilities		X		X

ABC CO
INCOME STATEMENT FOR THE YEAR ENDED 31 DECEMBER 20X2
Illustrating the classification of expenses by function

	20X2	20X1
	$'000	$'000
Revenue	X	X
Cost of sales	(X)	(X)
Gross profit	X	X
Other income	X	X
Distribution costs	(X)	(X)
Administrative expenses	(X)	(X)
Other expenses	(X)	(X)
Finance cost	(X)	(X)
Profit before tax	X	X
Income tax expense	(X)	(X)
Net profit for the period	X	X

Important!

Investments are non-current assets if the company intends to hold on to them for a long time, and current assets if they are only likely to be held for a short time before being sold.

Year end dividends proposed will not appear in the accounts unless they are proposed before the balance sheet date.

5 Loan stock

FAST FORWARD

If a company wants to raise funds without issuing shares, it can do so by means of a loan stock issue.

Key term

Loan stock are long-term liabilities described on the balance sheet as loan capital. They are different from share capital for the following reasons.

(a) Shareholders are members of a company, while providers of loan capital are payables.

(b) Shareholders receive dividends (appropriations of profit) whereas the holders of loan capital are entitled to a fixed rate of interest (an expense charged against revenue).

(c) Loan capital holders can take legal action against a company if their interest is not paid when due, whereas shareholders cannot enforce the payment of dividends.

(d) Loan stock are often secured on company assets, whereas shares are not.

5.1 Loan interest

Interest is calculated on the nominal value of loan capital, regardless of its market value. If a company has $700,000 (nominal value) 12% loan stock in issue, interest of $84,000 will be charged in the income statement per year. Interest is usually paid half-yearly and examination questions often require an accrual to be made for interest due at the year end. Accrued interest is shown as a current liability in the year-end balance sheet.

For example, if a company has $700,000 of 12% loan stock in issue, pays interest on 30 June and 31 December each year, and ends its accounting year on 30 September, there would be an accrual of three months' unpaid interest ($3/12 \times$ $84,000) = $21,000 at the end of each accounting year that the debentures are still in issue.

6 Statement of changes in equity

Key term

The **statement of changes in equity** shows those items which reduce profits but which are not expenses incurred in the day to day running of the business. In other words, it shows how profits are set aside for particular purposes.

6.1 Purpose of the statement

Essentially, profits are set aside (appropriated) for three purposes.

- Pay tax
- Pay dividends to shareholders (ordinary and preferred dividends)
- Reinvest in the business

The amount reinvested in the business is the amount left after the tax and dividends have been paid. This amount is called retained profit for the year.

The retained profit at the beginning of the year is the reserve as described in paragraph 2.5.1. The retained profit for the current year is added to this opening balance to give the retained profit balance at the end of the year.

6.2 Statement of changes in equity (SOCIE)

ABC CO
STATEMENT OF CHANGES IN EQUITY

	Equity $	Share premium a/c $	Revaluation surplus $	Reserves $	Retained earnings $
Bal b/f	X	X	X	X	X
Changes in shareholders' equity resulting from capital contributions and dividend payments					
Capital contributions	X	X			
Dividend payments					(X)
Other changes in shareholders' equity not recognised in income					
Exchange differences					(X)
Other differences					X
Changes in shareholders' equity recognised in income					
Allocation to retained earnings				(X)	X
Income after taxes for the period					X
	X̲	X̲	X̲	X̲	X̲

Further details are needed of any additions to reserves or utilisations of reserves during the period.

Assessment focus point

Statements of changes in equity are a very likely topic. Common errors include putting dividends in the main income statement and putting loan interest into the statement of changes in equity.

6.3 Example of published financial statements

The accountant of Wislon Co has prepared the following list of nominal ledger balances as at 31 December 20X7.

	$'000
50c ordinary shares (fully paid)	350
7% $1 preference shares (fully paid)	100
10% loans (secured)	200
Retained earnings 1 January 20X7	242
General reserve 1 January 20X7	171
Freehold land and buildings 1 January 20X7 (cost)	430
Plant and machinery 1 January 20X7 (cost)	830
Provision for depreciation	
Freehold buildings 1 January 20X7	20
Plant and machinery 1 January 20X7	222
Inventory 1 January 20X7	190
Sales	2,695
Purchases	2,152
Preference dividend	7
Ordinary dividend (interim)	8
Loan interest	10
Wages and salaries	254
Light and heat	31
Sundry expenses	113
Suspense account	135
Receivables	179
Payables	195
Cash	126

Notes

(a) Sundry expenses include $9,000 paid in respect of insurance for the year ending 1 September 20X8. Light and heat does not include an invoice of $3,000 for electricity for the three months ending 2 January 20X8, which was paid in February 20X8. Light and heat also includes $20,000 relating to salesmen's commission.

(b) The suspense account is in respect of the following items.

	$'000
Proceeds from the issue of 100,000 ordinary shares	120
Proceeds from the sale of plant	300
	420
Less paid to acquire Mary & Co	285
	135

(c) The net assets of Mary & Co were purchased on 3 March 20X7. Assets were valued as follows.

	$'000
Investments	230
Inventory	34
	264

All the inventory acquired was sold during 20X7. The investments were still held by Wislon at 31 December 20X7.

(d) The freehold property was acquired some years ago. The buildings element of the cost was estimated at $100,000 and the estimated useful life of the assets was fifty years. As at 31 December 20X7 the property is to be revalued at $800,000.

(e)   The plant which was sold had cost $350,000 and had a net book value of $274,000 as on 1 January 20X7. $36,000 depreciation is to be charged on plant and machinery for 20X7.

(f)   The loans have been in issue for some years. The 50c ordinary shares all rank for dividends at the end of the year.

(g)   The directors wish to provide for

   (i)   loan interest due
   (ii)   a final ordinary dividend of 2c per share – proposed on 27 December 20X7
   (iii)   a transfer to general reserve of $16,000
   (iv)   audit fees of $4,000

(h)   Inventory as at 31 December 20X7 was valued at $220,000 (cost).

(i)   Taxation is to be ignored.

Required

Prepare the final accounts of Wislon Co.

Approach and suggested solution

(a)   The usual adjustments are needed for accruals and prepayments (insurance, light and heat, debenture interest and audit fees). The loan interest accrued is calculated as follows.

	$'000
Charge needed in I/S (10% × $200,000)	20
Amount paid so far, as shown in trial balance	10
Accrual – presumably six months' interest now payable	10

The accrued expenses shown in the balance sheet comprise

	$'000
Loan interest	10
Light and heat	3
Audit fee	4
	17

(b)   The misposting of $20,000 to light and heat is also adjusted, by reducing the light and heat expense, but charging $20,000 to salesmen's commission.

(c)   Depreciation on the freehold building is calculated as $\dfrac{\$100,000}{50} = \$2,000$.

The net book value of the freehold property is then $430,000 – $20,000 – $2,000 = $408,000 at the end of the year. When the property is revalued a reserve of $800,000 – $408,000 = $392,000 is then created.

(d)   The profit on disposal of plant is calculated as proceeds $300,000 (per suspense account) less NBV $274,000 ie $26,000. The cost of the remaining plant is calculated at $830,000 – $350,000 = $480,000. The depreciation provision at the year end is made up of the following.

	$'000
Balance 1 January 20X7	222
Charge for 20X7	36
Less depreciation on disposals (350 – 274)	(76)
	182

(e)   Goodwill arising on the purchase of Mary & Co is calculated as follows.

	$'000
Paid (per suspense account)	285
Assets at valuation	264
Goodwill	21

In the absence of other instructions, this is shown as an asset on the balance sheet. The investments, being owned by Wislon at the year end, are also shown on the balance sheet, whereas Mary's inventory, acquired and then sold, is added to the purchases figure for the year.

(f) The other item in the suspense account is dealt with as follows.

	$'000
Proceeds of issue of 100,000 ordinary shares	120
Less nominal value 100,000 × 50c	50
Excess of consideration over nominal value (= share premium)	70

(g) Appropriations of profit must be considered. The final ordinary dividend was proposed before the year end and so is shown as a current liability in the balance sheet. It is calculated as follows.

(700,000 + 100,000 ordinary shares) × 2c = $16,000

(h) The transfer to general reserve increases that reserve to $171,000 + $16,000 = $187,000.

WISLON CO
INCOME STATEMENT FOR THE YEAR ENDING 31 DECEMBER 20X7

	$'000	$'000	$'000
Sales			2,695
Less cost of sales			
Opening inventory		190	
Purchases (2,152 + 34)		2,186	
		2,376	
Less closing inventory		220	
			2,156
Gross profit			539
Profit on disposal of plant			26
			565
Less expenses			
Wages, salaries and commission (254 + 20)		274	
Sundry expenses [113 − (2/3 × 9)]		107	
Light and heat (31 + 3 − 20)		14	
Depreciation: freehold buildings		2	
plant		36	
Audit fees		4	
Loan interest		20	
			457
Net profit for the period			108

WISLON CO
STATEMENT OF CHANGES IN EQUITY FOR THE YEAR ENDING 31 DECEMBER 20X7

	Equity	Share Premium	Revaluation reserve	General reserve	Retained Earnings
	$'000	$'000	$'000	$'000	$'000
Bal b/f	350	–	–	171	242
Share issue	50	70	–	–	–
Dividend payments	–	–	–	–	(31)
Revaluation of property	–	–	392	–	–
Transfer to general reserve	–	–	–	16	(16)
Net profit for the period	–	–	–	–	108
	400	70	392	187	303

WISLON LIMITED
BALANCE SHEET AS AT 31 DECEMBER 20X7

	Cost/ val'n	Dep'n	$'000
	$'000	$'000	
Non-current assets			
Intangible assets			
Goodwill			21
Tangible assets			
Freehold property	800	–	800
Plant and machinery	480	182	298
	1,280	182	
Investments			230
			1,349
Current assets			
Inventory		220	
Receivables		179	
Prepayment		6	
Cash		126	
			531
Total assets			1,880
Equity and liabilities			
Equity			
Called up share capital			
50c ordinary shares (350 + 50)		400	
7% $1 preference shares		100	
			500
Reserves			
Share premium		70	
Revaluation reserve		392	
General reserve		187	
Retained earnings		303	
			952
			1,452
Non-current liabilities			
10% loan stock (secured)			200
Current liabilities			
Payables		195	
Accrual expenses		17	
Proposed dividends		16	
			228
			1,880

7 Taxation

7.1 Corporation tax

Companies pay **corporation tax** on the profits they earn. The charge for corporation tax on profits for the year is shown as a deduction from net profit before appropriations. In the balance sheet, tax payable to the government is generally shown as a current liability (ie it has not yet been paid out at the year end).

When corporation tax on profits is calculated for the profit and loss account the calculation is only an estimate of what the company thinks its tax liability will be. In subsequent dealings with the Inland Revenue, a different corporation tax charge might eventually be agreed. Any difference is adjusted in the estimated taxation charge for the following year.

7.2 Example: taxation

Urals Co made a profit before tax of $150,000 in the year to 30 September 20X3 and of $180,000 in the following year (to 30 September 20X4).

The estimated corporation tax for the first year was $60,000 and in the second year was $75,000. The actual tax charge in the year to 30 September 20X3 was finally agreed with HMRC at $55,000.

Required

Compute the charge for taxation in the year to 30 September 20X4.

Solution

	To 30 September	
	20X3	*20X4*
	$	$
Estimate of tax on profits	60,000	75,000
Actual tax charge	55,000	
Overestimate of tax in 20X3	5,000	
		(5,000)
Tax charge in year to 30 September 20X4		70,000

The effect will be to increase profits in 20X4 by $5,000, to correct the 'error' in 20X3 when profits were reduced by $5,000 due to the overestimate of the tax charge.

8 The ledger accounts of limited liability companies

8.1 Additional accounts

Limited liability companies keep ledger accounts and the only difference from the ledger accounts of sole traders is that some additional accounts need to be kept.

There will be an account for each of the following items.

(a)   Taxation

   (i)   Tax charged against profits will be accounted for as follows.

      DEBIT   I/S account
      CREDIT   Taxation account

   (ii)   The outstanding balance on the taxation account will be a liability in the balance sheet, until eventually paid, when the accounting entry would be as follows.

      DEBIT   Taxation account
      CREDIT   Cash

(b)   *Dividends*

   A separate account will be kept for the dividends for each different class of shares (eg preference, ordinary).

   (i)   Dividends declared out of profits will be accounted for as follows.

      DEBIT   Statement of design in equity
      CREDIT   Dividends payable account

   Dividends payable (but not yet paid) are a current liability.

   (ii)   When dividends are paid the following entries would be made.

      DEBIT   Dividends payable account
      CREDIT   Cash

(c)   *Loan stocks*

   Loan stocks are a long term liability and will be shown as a credit balance in a loan stock account. Interest payable on such loans is not credited to the loan account, but is credited to a separate payables account for interest until it is eventually paid.

   DEBIT   Interest account (an expense, chargeable against profits)
   CREDIT   Interest payable (a current liability until eventually paid).

(d)   *Share capital and reserves*

   There will be a separate account for each different class of share capital and for each different type of reserve. The balance on the share capital account will always be a credit and the balance on the reserve account will nearly always be a credit.

Chapter roundup

- Company accounts preparation in the UK is governed by the Companies Act.

- Companies issue shares to shareholders who enjoy limited liability.

- The proprietors' capital in a limited liability company consists of **share capital**. A company issues **shares**, which are paid for by investors, who then become shareholders of the company.

- **Preference shares** carry the right to a fixed dividend which is expressed as a percentage of their nominal value: eg a 6% $1 preference share carries a right to an annual dividend of 6c.

- **Ordinary shares** are by far the most common. They carry no right to a fixed dividend but are entitled to all profits left after payment of any preference dividend. In most companies only ordinary shares carry voting rights.

- **Reserves** are profits that have not been distributed (paid out) to shareholders.

- The ordinary shareholders' total investment in a company is called the **equity** and consists of ordinary share capital plus **reserves**.

- **Shareholders' funds** is the total of all share capital, both ordinary and preference, and the reserves.

- The important point to note is that all reserves are **owned** by the ordinary shareholders.

- The **share premium account** is a statutory reserve created if shares are issued for more than their nominal value. The excess received over nominal value is credited to the share premium account.

- A **revaluation reserve** is a statutory reserve which must be created when a company revalues its non-current assets.

- A company may choose to expand its capital base by issuing further shares to existing shareholders. It can do this by means of a bonus issues or a rights issue.

- The preparation and publication of the final accounts of limited liability companies in the UK are governed by the CA 1985 as amended by the CA 1989. This permits the use of financial statements under IAS 1.

- If a company wants to raise funds without issuing shares, it can do so by means of a loan stock issue.

Quick quiz

1   The nominal value of a share is?

    A   Its market price
    B   The price at which it was issued
    C   The price which it can be purchased for
    D   The 'face value' of a share

2   What does the phrase 'called up share capital' mean?

    A   The total amount of issued share capital which the shareholders are required to pay for
    B   The share capital actually issued
    C   The amount of share capital paid by the shareholders
    D   The amount of capital which is company has decided to issue

3   A provision is an amount charged as an expense, while a reserve is an appropriation of profit for a specific purpose. True or false?

4   At the year end a proposed dividend may be declared. Which of the following statements is correct regarding the proposed dividend?

        A   Treated as an expense in the I/S account

        B   Shown in the balance sheet as a long term liability

        C   If declared after the balance sheet date, it is merely disclosed by note

        D   It is always the total profit which the company has agreed to distribute for the year

Answers to quick quiz

1   D   This is correct, the nominal value can be any value.

      A   Incorrect, the quoted price bears no relationship to the nominal value.

      B   This will be nominal value plus a premium on issue which in total equals the issue price.

      C   This is the market price.

2   A   Correct. Called up share capital means the capital which has been paid for plus current 'calls' outstanding.

      B   This is issued capital.

      C   This is paid up capital.

      D   This capital has not yet been issued and must be less than authorised capital.

3   True. A provision is an amount charged as an expense, while a reserve is an appropriation of profit for a specific purpose.

4   C   Correct.

      A   Dividends are appropriations of profit not expenses and are shown in the SOCIE.

      B   Proposed dividends are current liabilities, but only if declared before the balance sheet date.

      D   There may be an interim dividend as well, so the total distribution equals interim dividend paid plus proposed final dividend.

Now try the questions below from the Question Bank

Question numbers	Page
77–80	408

Incomplete records

Introduction

So far in your work on preparing the final accounts for a sole trader we have assumed that a full set of records is kept. In practice many sole traders do not keep a full set of records and you must apply certain techniques to arrive at the necessary figures.

Incomplete records questions are a very good test of your understanding of the way in which a set of accounts is built up.

Limited liability companies are obliged by law to keep proper accounting records. However a small company may still lose records eg in a fire.

Topic list	Syllabus references
1 Incomplete records questions	D (9)
2 The opening balance sheet	D (9)
3 Credit sales and receivables	D (9)
4 Purchases and trade payables	D (9)
5 Establishing purchases, inventories, or cost of sales	D (9)
6 Using gross profit margin and mark-up to find figures in the trading account	D (9)
7 Stolen goods or goods destroyed	D (9)
8 The cash book	D (9)
9 Accruals and prepayments	D (9)
10 Drawings	D (9)
11 The business equation	D (9)
12 Dealing with incomplete records problems	D (9)
13 Using a receivables account to calculate both cash sales and credit sales	D (9)

1 Incomplete records questions

Incomplete records occur when a business does not have a full set of accounting records because:

(a)   The proprietor of the business does not keep a full set of accounts.
(b)   Some of the business accounts are accidentally lost or destroyed.

1.1 Preparing accounts from incomplete records

The accountant must prepare a set of year-end accounts for the business ie an income statement, and a balance sheet. Since the business does not have a full set of accounts, it is not a simple matter of closing off accounts and transferring balances to the income statement, or showing outstanding balances in the balance sheet. The task of preparing the final accounts involves establishing the following.

- Cost of purchases and other expenses
- Total amount of sales
- Amount of payables, accruals, receivables and prepayments at the end of the year

Key term

The final accounts you are asked to prepare a may include a **statement of affairs**. This simply means a balance sheet in summary form because there is insufficient data for a full one, or one which is not in a standard format.

To understand what incomplete records are about, it will obviously be useful now to look at what exactly might be incomplete. The items we shall consider in turn are:

(a)   The opening balance sheet.
(b)   Credit sales and receivables.
(c)   Purchases and trade payables.
(d)   Purchases, inventories and the cost of sales.
(e)   Stolen goods or goods destroyed.
(f)   The cash book.
(g)   Accruals and prepayments.
(h)   Drawings.

2 The opening balance sheet

Where accounts for the previous period are not available, the accountant will have to reconstruct an opening balance sheet.

2.1 Example: opening balance sheet

A business has the following assets and liabilities as at 1 January 20X3.

	$
Fixtures and fittings at cost	7,000
Provision for depreciation, fixtures and fittings	4,000
Motor vehicles at cost	12,000
Provision for depreciation, motor vehicles	6,800
Inventory	4,500
Trade receivables	5,200
Cash at bank and in hand	1,230
Trade payables	3,700
Prepayment	450
Accrued rent	2,000

You are required to prepare a balance sheet for the business, inserting a balancing figure for proprietor's capital.

Solution

Balance sheet as at 1 January 20X3

	$	$
Non-current assets		
Fixtures and fittings at cost	7,000	
Less accumulated depreciation	4,000	
		3,000
Motor vehicles at cost	12,000	
Less accumulated depreciation	6,800	
		5,200
		8,200
Current assets		
Inventory	4,500	
Trade receivables	5,200	
Prepayment	450	
Cash	1,230	
		11,380
		19,580
Proprietor's capital as at 1 January 20X3 (balancing figure)		13,880
Current liabilities		
Trade payables	3,700	
Accrual	2,000	
		5,700
		19,580

3 Credit sales and receivables

ST FORWARD

If a business does not keep a record of its sales on credit, the value of these sales can be derived from the opening balance of trade receivables, the closing balance of trade receivables, and the payments received from trade receivables during the period.

Formula to learn

	$
Credit sales are:	
Payments received from trade receivables	X
Plus closing balance of trade receivables (since these represent sales in the current period for which cash payment has not yet been received)	X
Less opening balance of trade receivables (these will represent sales made in a **previous** period)	(X)
	X

Assessment focus point

Throughout this chapter, we will give you a number of formulae to learn. You must learn these formats as they will not be given in the assessment.

3.1 Example: sales and receivables

A business had trade receivables of $1,750 on 1 April 20X4 and $3,140 on 31 March 20X5. If payments received from trade receivables during the year to 31 March 20X5 were $28,490, and there were no bad debts, calculate credit sales for the period.

Solution

	$
Cash received from receivables	28,490
Plus closing receivables	3,140
Less opening receivables	(1,750)
Credit sales	29,880

The same calculation could be made in a T account, with credit sales being the balancing figure to complete the account.

RECEIVABLES

	$		$
Opening balance b/f	1,750	Cash received	28,490
Credit sales (balancing fig)	29,880	Closing balance c/f	3,140
	31,630		31,630

The same interrelationship between balances can be used to derive a missing figure for cash from receivables (or opening or closing receivables), given the values for the three other items.

3.2 Example: to find cash received

Opening receivables are $6,700, closing receivables are $3,200 and credit sales for the period are $69,400. What was cash received from receivables during the period?

Solution

RECEIVABLES

	$		$
Opening balance	6,700	Cash received (balancing figure)	72,900
Sales (on credit)	69,400	Closing balance c/f	3,200
	76,100		76,100

If there are bad debts during the period, the value of sales will be increased by the amount of bad debts written off, no matter whether they relate to opening receivables or credit sales during the current period.

Question	Credit sales

Opening receivables are $1,500, closing receivables are $1,800. During the year $45,800 was received from receivables including $800 in respect of debts written off in an earlier period. $3,200 of debts were written off and the allowance for receivables increased by $700. What are the credit sales for the year?

Answer

$48,500.

RECEIVABLES ACCOUNT

	$		$
B/d	1,500	Cash	45,000
Credit sales (balance)	48,500	Bad debts expense	3,200
		C/d	1,800
	50,000		50,000

Remember that cash received from debts written off in an earlier period is not credited to receivables, and that the movement in the allowance for receivables does not go through receivables.

4 Purchases and trade payables

 ST FORWARD

A similar relationship exists between purchases of inventory during a period, the opening and closing balances for trade payables, and amounts paid to trade payables during the period.

Formula to learn

	$
Payments to trade payables during the period	X
Plus closing balance of trade payables	X
(since these represent purchases in the current period for which payment has not yet been made)	
Less opening balance of trade payables	(X)
(these debts, paid in the current period, relate to purchases in a previous period)	
Purchases during the period	X

4.1 Example: purchases and trade payables

A business had trade payables of $3,728 on 1 October 20X5 and $2,645 on 30 September 20X6. If payments to trade payables during the year to 30 September 20X6 were $31,479, what was purchases during the year?

Solution

	$
Payments to trade payables	31,479
Plus closing balance of trade payables	2,645
Less opening balance of trade payables	(3,728)
Purchases	30,396

The same calculation could be made in a T account, with purchases being the balancing figure to complete the account.

PAYABLES

	$		$
Cash payments	31,479	Opening balance b/f	3,728
Closing balance c/f	2,645	Purchases (balancing figure)	30,396
	34,124		34,124

5 Establishing purchases, inventories, or cost of sales

FAST FORWARD

In some questions you must use the information in the trading account rather than the trade payables account to find the cost of purchases. This information could also be used to find inventories or cost of sales.

Formula to learn

		$
Since	opening inventories	X
	plus purchases	X
	less closing inventories	(X)
	equals the cost of goods sold	X
then	the cost of goods sold	X
	plus closing inventories	X
	less opening inventories	(X)
	equals purchases	X

5.1 Example: using a trading account

The inventory of a business on 1 July 20X6 was $8,400, and an inventory count at 30 June 20X7 showed inventory to be valued at $9,350. Sales for the year to 30 June 20X7 are $80,000, and the cost of goods sold was $60,000. What were the purchases during the year?

Solution

	$
Cost of goods sold	60,000
Plus closing inventory	9,350
Less opening inventory	(8,400)
Purchases	60,950

6 Using gross profit margin and mark-up to find figures in the trading account

A question may ask you to use profit percentages to calculate sales or cost of sales.

FAST FORWARD

Where inventory, sales or purchases is the unknown figure, it will be necessary to use information on gross profit percentages in order to construct a trading account in which the unknown figure can be inserted as a balance.

Formula to learn

Gross margin is: $\dfrac{\text{Gross profit}}{\text{Sales}}$ Mark-up is: $\dfrac{\text{Gross profit}}{\text{Cost of goods sold}}$ (also described as gross profit on cost)

6.1 Example

Sales are $1,000 and cost of goods sold are $600. What are the profit margin and mark-up?

Solution

	$
Sales	1,000
Cost of goods sold	600
Gross profit	400

Profit margin is: $\dfrac{\$400}{\$1,000} = 40\%$ Mark-up is: $\dfrac{\$400}{\$600} = 66^2/_3\%$

Question   **Purchases**

At 1 May 20X3 inventory was $4,000, at 30 April 20X4 it was $3,000. Sales for the year were $80,000 and the business always has a mark up of $33^1/_3\%$. What were purchases for the year?

Answer

Working backwards:

	$	%
Purchases	59,000	
Opening inventory	4,000	
	63,000	
Less: Closing inventory	3,000	
Cost of sales	60,000	100
Gross profit or mark up	20,000	$33^1/_3$
Sales	80,000	$133^1/_3$

Take care that you correctly interpret whether you are dealing with gross profit on sales or gross profit on cost of sales.

7 Stolen goods or goods destroyed

ST FORWARD ▶ A similar type of calculation can derive the value of goods stolen or destroyed.

7.1 Example: cost of goods destroyed

Orlean Flames is a shop which sells fashion clothes. On 1 January 20X5, it had inventory which cost $7,345. During the 9 months to 30 September 20X5, the business purchased goods from suppliers costing $106,420. Sales during the same period were $154,000. The shop makes a gross profit of 40% on **cost** (mark-up) for everything it sells. On 30 September 20X5, there was a fire in the shop which destroyed most of the inventory in it. Only a small amount of inventory, known to have cost $350, was undamaged and still fit for sale.

How much inventory was lost in the fire?

Solution

(a)

	$
Sales (140%)	154,000
Gross profit (40%)	44,000
Cost of goods sold (100%)	110,000

(b)

	$
Opening inventory, at cost	7,345
Plus purchases	106,420
	113,765
Less closing inventory, at cost	350
Equals cost of goods sold and goods lost	113,415

(c)

	$
Cost of goods sold and lost	113,415
Cost of goods sold	110,000
Cost of goods lost	3,415

7.2 Accounting for inventory destroyed, stolen or otherwise lost

When inventory is stolen, destroyed or otherwise lost, the loss must be accounted for somehow.

The account that is to be debited is one of two possibilities, depending on whether or not the lost goods were insured.

(a)   If the lost goods were not insured, the business must bear the loss, and the loss is shown in the income statement.

DEBIT   I/S expense
CREDIT   Trading account

(b)   If the lost goods were insured, the business will not suffer a loss, because the insurance will pay back the cost of the lost goods.

DEBIT   Insurance claim account (receivable account)
CREDIT   Trading account

with the cost of the loss. The insurance claim will then be a current asset, and shown in the balance sheet of the business as such. When the claim is paid, the account is then closed by

DEBIT   Cash
CREDIT   Insurance claim account

> ## Question
>
> **Stolen inventory**
>
> Beau Gullard runs a jewellery shop in the High Street. On 1 January 20X9, his inventory, at cost, amounted to $4,700 and his trade payables were $3,950.
>
> During the six months to 30 June 20X9, sales were $42,000. Beau Gullard makes a gross profit of $33^{1}/_{3}\%$ on the **sales value** (margin) of everything he sells.
>
> On 30 June, there was a burglary at the shop, and all the inventory was stolen.
>
> In trying to establish how much inventory had been taken, Beau Gullard was only able to say that
>
> (a)   he knew from his bank statements that he had paid $28,400 to payables in the 6 month period to 30 June 20X9.
> (b)   he currently owed payables $5,550.
>
> *Required*
>
> (a)   Calculate the amount of inventory stolen.
> (b)   Prepare a trading account for the 6 months to 30 June 20X9.

Answer

(a)   The first 'unknown' is the amount of purchases during the period. This is established by writing up a payables account.

PAYABLES

	$		$
Payments to payables	28,400	Opening balance b/f	3,950
Closing balance c/f	5,550	Purchases (balancing figure)	30,000
	33,950		33,950

(b)   The cost of goods sold is also unknown, but this can be established from the **gross profit margin** and the sales for the period.

		$
Sales	(100%)	42,000
Gross profit	(33⅓%)	14,000
Cost of goods sold	(66⅔%)	28,000

(c)   The cost of the goods stolen is

	$
Opening inventory at cost	4,700
Purchases	30,000
	34,700
Less closing inventory (after burglary)	0
Cost of goods sold and goods stolen	34,700
Cost of goods sold (see (b) above)	28,000
Cost of goods stolen	6,700

(d)   The cost of the goods stolen is a charge in the income statement, and so the trading account for the period is as follows.

BEAU GULLARD
TRADING ACCOUNT FOR THE SIX MONTHS TO 30 JUNE 20X9

	$	$
Sales		42,000
Less cost of goods sold		
Opening inventory	4,700	
Purchases	30,000	
	34,700	
Less inventory stolen	(6,700)	
		28,000
Gross profit		14,000

8 The cash book

ST FORWARD

If no cash book has been kept it may need to be written up from available information. This is sometimes done as a two-column bank/cash book.

8.1 Writing up the cash book

We have already seen in this chapter that information about cash receipts or payments might be needed to establish:

- Purchases during a period
- Credit sales during a period

Other items of receipts or payments might be relevant to establishing

- Cash sales
- Certain expenses in the I/S account
- Drawings by the business proprietor

Often, to answer a question, we need to write up a cash book. Where there appears to be a sizeable volume of receipts and payments in cash (ie notes and coins), then it is helpful to construct a two column cash book. This is a cash book with one column for cash receipts and payments, and one column for money paid into and out of the business bank account.

8.2 Example: two column cash book

Jonathan Slugg owns and runs a shop selling fishing tackle, making a gross profit of 25% on the cost of everything he sells. He does not keep a cash book.

On 1 January 20X7 the balance sheet of his business was as follows.

	$	$
Net non-current assets		20,000
Inventory	10,000	
Cash in the bank	3,000	
Cash in the till	200	
	13,200	
Trade payables	1,200	
		12,000
		32,000
Proprietor's capital		32,000

In the year to 31 December 20X7

(a) there were no sales on credit.

(b) $41,750 in receipts were banked.

(c) the bank statements of the period show the following payments.

		$
(i)	to trade payables	36,000
(ii)	sundry expenses	5,600
(iii)	in drawings	4,400

(d) payments were also made in cash out of the till.

		$
(i)	to trade payables	800
(ii)	sundry expenses	1,500
(iii)	in drawings	3,700

At 31 December 20X7, the business had cash in the till of $450 and trade payables of $1,400. The cash balance in the bank was not known and the value of closing inventory has not yet been calculated. There were no accruals or prepayments. No further non-current assets were purchased during the year. The depreciation charge for the year is $900.

Required

(a) Prepare a two column cash book for the period.

(b) Prepare the income statement for the year to 31 December 20X7 and the balance sheet as at 31 December 20X7.

Discussion and solution

A two column cash book is completed as follows.

(a) Enter the opening cash balances.

(b) Enter the information given about cash payments (and any cash receipts, if there had been any such items given in the problem).

(c) The cash receipts banked are a 'contra' entry, being both a debit (bank column) and a credit (cash in hand column) in the same account.

(d) Enter the closing cash in hand (cash in the bank at the end of the period is not known).

CASH BOOK

	Cash in hand $	Bank $		Cash in hand $	Bank $
Balance b/f	200	3,000	Trade payables	800	36,000
Cash receipts banked			Sundry expenses		
(contra)		41,750		1,500	5,600
Sales*	48,000		Drawings	3,700	4,400
			Cash receipts banked		
			(contra)	41,750	
Balance c/f		*1,250	Balance c/f	450	
	48,200	46,000		48,200	46,000

* Balancing figure

(e) The closing balance of money in the bank is a balancing figure.

(f) Since all sales are for cash, a balancing figure that can be entered in the cash book is sales, in the cash in hand (debit) column.

It is important to notice that since not all receipts from cash sales are banked, the value of cash sales during the period is the balance on the cash account or it could be calculated as:

	$
Receipts banked	41,750
Plus expenses and drawings paid out of the till in cash	
$(800 + 1,500 + 3,700)$	6,000
Plus any cash stolen (here there is none)	0
Plus the closing balance of cash in hand	450
	48,200
Less the opening balance of cash in hand	(200)
Equals cash sales	48,000

The cash book has enabled us to establish both the closing balance for cash in the bank and also the volume of cash sales. Now calculate purchases.

PAYABLES

	$		$
Cash book:		Balance b/f	1,200
Payments from bank	36,000	Purchases (balancing figure)	37,000
Cash book:			
Payments in cash	800		
Balance c/f	1,400		
	38,200		38,200

The gross profit margin of 25% on cost indicates that the cost of the goods sold is $38,400.

	$
Sales (125%)	48,000
Gross profit (25%)	9,600
Cost of goods sold (100%)	38,400

The closing inventory amount is now a balancing figure in the trading account.

JONATHAN SLUGG
INCOME STATEMENT
FOR THE YEAR ENDED 31 DECEMBER 20X7

	$	$
Sales		48,000
Less cost of goods sold		
Opening inventory	10,000	
Purchases	37,000	
	47,000	
Less closing inventory (balancing figure)	8,600	
		38,400
Gross profit (25/125 × $48,000)		9,600
Expenses		
Sundry $(1,500 + 5,600)	7,100	
Depreciation	900	
		8,000
Net profit		1,600

JONATHAN SLUGG
BALANCE SHEET AS AT 31 DECEMBER 20X7

	$	$
Net non-current assets $(20,000 – 900)		19,100
Inventory	8,600	
Cash in the till	450	
		9,050
		28,150
Proprietor's capital		
Balance b/f		32,000
Net profit for the year		1,600
		33,600
Drawings $(3,700 + 4,400)		(8,100)
Balance c/f		25,500
Current liabilities		
Bank overdraft	1,250	
Trade payables	1,400	
		2,650
		28,150

8.3 Theft of cash from the till

When cash is stolen from the till, the amount stolen will be a credit entry in the cash book, and a debit in either the I/S account or insurance claim account, depending on whether the business is insured.

9 Accruals and prepayments

9.1 Working out the charge

> Where there is an accrued expense or a prepayment, the charge to be made in the I/S account for the item concerned should be found from the opening balance b/f, the closing balance c/f, and cash payments for the item during the period.

The charge in the I/S account is perhaps most easily found as the balancing figure in a T account.

9.2 Example: prepayments

On 1 April 20X6 a business had prepaid rent of $700. During the year to 31 March 20X7 it pays $9,300 in rent and at 31 March 20X7 the prepayment of rent is $1,000.

Calculate the I/S figure for rent expense.

Solution

The cost of rent in the I/S account for the year to 31 March 20X7 is the balancing figure in the following T account. (Remember that a prepayment is a current asset, and so is a debit balance b/f.)

RENT EXPENSE

	$		$
Prepayment: balance b/f	700	I/S (balancing figure)	9,000
Cash	9,300	Prepayment: balance c/f	1,000
	10,000		10,000
Balance b/f	1,000		

9.3 Example: Accrual

Similarly, if a business has accrued telephone expenses as at 1 July 20X6 of $850, pays $6,720 in telephone bills during the year to 30 June 20X7, and has accrued telephone expenses of $1,140 as at 30 June 20X7.

Calculate the I/S figure for telephone expense.

Solution

The telephone expense to be shown in the I/S account for the year to 30 June 20X7 is the balancing figure in the following T account. (Remember that an accrual is a current liability, and so is a credit balance b/f.)

TELEPHONE EXPENSES

	$		$
Cash	6,720	Balance b/f (accrual)	850
Balance c/f (accrual)	1,140	I/S (balancing figure)	7,010
	7,860		7,860
		Balance b/f	1,140

10 Drawings

Drawings are cash withdrawals made by the proprietor for his personal use. He may also pay personal funds into the business bank account.

Assessment focus point

Drawings would normally represent no particular problem at all in preparing a set of final accounts from incomplete records, but it is not unusual for questions to introduce a situation in which:

(a)   the business owner pays income into his bank account which has nothing whatever to do with the business operations. For example, the owner might pay dividend income, or other income from personal investments into the bank.

(b)   the business owner pays money out of the business bank account for items which are not business expenses, eg life insurance premiums or holidays.

10.1 Accounting for drawings

Where such personal items of receipts or payments are made.

(a)   Receipts should be set off against drawings. For example, if a business owner receives $600 in personal dividend income and pays it into his business bank account then the accounting entry is

DEBIT   Cash
CREDIT   Drawings

(b)   Payments should be charged to drawings.

DEBIT   Drawings
CREDIT   Cash

10.2 Drawings: beware of the wording in a question

You should note the following.

(a)   If a question states that a proprietor's drawings during the year are 'approximately $40 per week', you should assume that drawings for the year are $40 × 52 weeks = $2,080.

(b)   If a question states that drawings in the year are 'between $35 and $45 per week', do **not** assume that the drawings average $40 per week and so amount to $2,080 for the year. You could not be certain that the actual drawings did average $40, and so you should treat the drawings figure as a missing item that needs to be calculated.

11 The business equation

The business equation is:

Profit(loss) = movement in net assets − capital introduced + drawings

11.1 Computing net profit

The most obvious incomplete records situation is that of a sole trader who has kept no trading records. It may not be possible to reconstruct his whole income statement, but it will be possible to compute his profit for the year using the **business equation**.

BPP
LEARNING MEDIA

Here is the basic balance sheet format:

Assets		XX
Capital	X	
Liabilities	X	XX

This can be rearranged as:

Assets	XX	
Liabilities	(X)	X
Capital		X

So this gives us a figure for capital – assets less liabilities, or **net assets**.

What will increase or decrease capital?

Capital is changed by:

(a) Money paid in by the trader
(b) Drawings by the trader
(c) Profits or losses

So, if we are able to establish the traders net assets at the beginnings and end of the period, we can compute profits as follows:

Profit (loss) = movement in net assets – capital introduced + drawings

We want to eliminate any movement caused by money paid in or taken out for personal use by the trader. So we take out capital introduced and add back in drawings.

The formula can be written as $P = I + D - Ci$, where I is increase in net assets.

11.2 Example: business equation

Joe starts up his camera shop on 1 January 20X1, from rented premises, with $5,000 inventory and $3,000 in the bank. All of his sales are for cash. He keeps no record of his takings.

At the end of the year he has stock worth $6,600 and $15,000 in the bank. He owes $3,000 to suppliers. He had paid in $5,000 he won on the lottery and drawn out $2,000 to buy himself a motorbike. The motorbike is not used in the business. He has been taking drawings of $100 per week. What is his profit at 31 December 20X1?

Solution

Opening net assets

Inventory	5,000
Cash	3,000
	8,000

Closing net assets

Inventory	6,600
Cash	15,000
Payables	(3,000)
	18,600

Movement in capital	10,600
Less capital paid in	(5,000)
Plus drawings ((100 × 52) + 2000)	7,200
Profit	12,800

12 Dealing with incomplete records problems

12.1 Suggested approach

A suggested approach to dealing with incomplete records problems brings together the various points described so far in this chapter. The nature of the 'incompleteness' in the records will vary from problem to problem, but the approach should be successful in arriving at the final accounts whatever the particular characteristics of the problem.

The approach is as follows.

Step 1   If it is not already known, establish the opening balance sheet and the proprietor's interest.

Step 2   Open up four accounts.

         (i)   Trading account (if you wish, leave space underneath for entering the rest of the income statement later)

         (ii)   A cash book, with two columns if cash sales are significant and there are payments in cash out of the till

         (iii)   A receivables account

         (iv)   A payables account

Step 3   Enter the opening balances in these accounts.

Step 4   Work through the information you are given line by line. Each item should be entered into the relevant account, as appropriate.

         You should also try to recognise each item as a 'I/S income or expense item' or a 'closing balance sheet item'.

         It may be necessary to calculate an amount for drawings and an amount for non-current asset depreciation.

Step 5   Look for the balancing figures in your accounts. In particular you might be looking for a value for credit sales, cash sales, purchases, the cost of goods sold, the cost of goods stolen or destroyed, or the closing bank balance. Calculate these missing figures, and make any necessary double entry (eg to the trading account from the payables account for purchases).

Step 6   Now complete the income statement and balance sheet. Working T accounts might be needed where there are accruals or prepayments.

13 Using a receivables account to calculate both cash sales and credit sales

FAST FORWARD

A final point which needs to be considered is how a missing value can be found for cash sales and credit sales, when a business has both, but takings banked by the business are not divided between takings from cash sales and takings from credit sales.

13.1 Example: using a receivables account to find total sales

A business had, on 1 January 20X8, trade receivables of $2,000, cash in the bank of $3,000, and cash in hand of $300.

During the year to 31 December 20X8 the business banked $95,000 in takings.

It also paid out the following expenses in cash from the till.

Drawings	$1,200
Sundry expenses	$800

On 29 August 20X8 a thief broke into the shop and stole $400 from the till.

At 31 December 20X8 trade receivables amounted to $3,500, cash in the bank $2,500 and cash in the till $150.

What was the value of sales during the year?

Solution

If we tried to prepare a receivables account and a two column cash book, we would have insufficient information, in particular about whether the takings which were banked related to cash sales or credit sales. All we do know is that the combined sums from receivables and cash takings banked is $95,000.

The value of sales can be found instead by using the receivables account, which should be used to record cash takings banked as well as payments by receivables. The balancing figure in the receivables account will then be a combination of credit sales and some cash sales. The cash book only needs to be a single column.

RECEIVABLES

	$		$
Balance b/f	2,000	Cash banked	95,000
Sales – to trading account	96,500	Balance c/f	3,500
	98,500		98,500

CASH (EXTRACT)

	$		$
Balance in hand b/f	300	Payments in cash:	
Balance in bank b/f	3,000	Drawings	1,200
Receivables a/c	95,000	Expenses	800
		Other payments	?
		Cash stolen	400
		Balance in hand c/f	150
		Balance in bank c/f	2,500

The remaining 'undiscovered' amount of cash sales is now found as follows.

	$	$
Payments in cash out of the till		
Drawings	1,200	
Expenses	800	
		2,000
Cash stolen		400
Closing balance of cash in hand		150
		2,550
Less opening balance of cash in hand		(300)
Further cash sales		2,250

(This calculation is similar to the one described above for calculating cash sales.)

Total sales for the year are

	$
From receivables account	96,500
From cash book	2,250
Total sales	98,750

A similar technique can be used to find cash and credit purchases using a payables account.

Chapter roundup

- Incomplete records occur when a business does not have a full set of accounting records because:
    - The proprietor of the business does not keep a full set of accounts.
    - Some of the business accounts are accidentally lost or destroyed.

- Where accounts for the previous period are not available, the accountant will have to reconstruct an opening balance sheet.

- If a business does not keep a record of its sales on credit, the value of these sales can be derived from the opening balance of trade receivables, the closing balance of trade receivables, and the payments received from trade receivables during the period.

- A similar relationship exists between purchases of inventory during a period, the opening and closing balances for trade payables, and amounts paid to trade payables during the period.

- In some questions you must use the information in the trading account rather than the trade payables account to find the cost of purchases. This information could also be used to find inventories or cost of sales.

- Where inventory, sales or purchases is the unknown figure, it will be necessary to use information on gross profit percentages in order to construct a trading account in which the unknown figure can be inserted as a balance.

- A similar type of calculation can derive the value of goods stolen or destroyed.

- If no cash book has been kept it may need to be written up from available information. This is sometimes done as a two-column bank/cash book.

- Where there is an accrued expense or a prepayment, the charge to be made in the I/S account for the item concerned should be found from the opening balance b/f, the closing balance c/f, and cash payments for the item during the period.

- Drawings are cash withdrawals made by the proprietor for his personal use. He may also pay personal funds into the business bank account.

- The business equation is:

    Profit(loss) = movement in net assets − capital introduced + drawings

- A final point which needs to be considered is how a missing value can be found for cash sales and credit sales, when a business has both, but takings banked by the business are not divided between takings from cash sales and takings from credit sales.

Quick quiz

1   Given cash sales $15,000, receipts from credit customers $23,000, opening receivables (at 1.1.X1) $7,500 and closing receivables (at 31.12.X1) $9,500, calculate the total sales for a business, which does not keep full records, for 20X1.

   A $36,000
   B $38,000
   C $40,000
   D $25,000

2   A business has opening payables (1.7.20X1) $5,000, closing payables (30.6.20X2) $7,000, cash purchases $1,500, cash payments to credit suppliers $28,000. Calculate the total purchases figure for inclusion in the trading account.

   A $27,500
   B $29,500
   C $31,500
   D $30,000

3   The term 'incomplete records' means that?

   A   The business has not kept a full set of accounting records
   B   The records have been lost
   C   Small limited liability companies are not under an obligation to keep full accounts
   D   The business is unable to complete its financial statements

4   A business has the following assets and liabilities at 1.1.X1, calculate the owners capital at 1.1.X1. Premises $15,000, van $5,000, inventory $2,000, payables $8,000, receivables $6,000, accruals $1,000, bank loan $10,000, bank overdraft $1,200.

   A $10,200
   B $9,800
   C $7,800
   D $23,800

Answers to quick quiz

1   C   Correct: $23,000 + $9,500 − $7,500 + $15,000.

     A   Incorrect, you have reversed opening and closing receivables balances.

     B   Incorrect, this is cash sales plus receipts from receivables which must be adjusted for opening and closing receivables.

     D   Incorrect, this is credit sales, you were asked for total sales.

2   C   Correct, 28,000 + 7,000 − 5,000 = $30,000 credit purchases + $1,500 cash purchases.
     A   Incorrect, you have transposed opening and closing payables.
     B   Incorrect, payments to credit suppliers must be adjusted for payables changes.
     D   This is the credit, not total, purchases figure.

3   A   Correct.

     B   If records have been lost, it will be necessary to create financial statements from the data which remains.

     C   Small limited liability companies must keep 'proper accounting records'.

     D   This is a consequence of not keeping proper records, the business accountant will work from incomplete data which will make the task more difficult and expensive.

4   C   Correct: 15,000 + 5,000 + 2,000 − 8,000 + 6,000 − 1,000 − 10,000 − 1,200 = 7,800 = net assets = capital.

     A   Incorrect, you have treated the bank overdraft as an asset.

     B   Incorrect, you have treated both receivables and payables incorrectly.

     D   Incorrect, you have included payables as an asset – be careful how you extract data from lists of items given in questions.

Now try the questions below from the Question Bank

Question numbers	Page
81–91	409

The accounts of unincorporated organisations
(income and expenditure accounts)

Introduction

So far you have dealt with the accounts of businesses. This chapter considers non-trading organisations, that is organisations which are not incorporated under the Companies Act and whose objectives are to provide services to their members or the pursuit of one or a number of activities rather than the earning of profit.

If subscriptions are charged, there will be a need for some financial records, the minimum possible being a cash book and petty cash book. Clubs, which rely on this minimum package, often confine their annual accounts to a **receipts and payments account**. This is simply a summary of cash received and paid for a period, and is discussed in Section 1 of this chapter.

A receipts and payments account may be adequate for some clubs but has important deficiencies when used by clubs which have substantial assets (in addition to cash) and liabilities. The arguments in favour of accruals-based accounting apply to clubs as well as profit-making entities. Most large clubs do produce financial statements based on accruals accounting. In particular many clubs produce what is basically an income statement but they call it an **income and expenditure account.** This is the subject of Section 2 and 3 of this chapter.

Topic list	Syllabus references
1 The receipts and payments account	D (8)
2 Income and expenditure account	D (8)
3 Preparing income and expenditure accounts	D (8)

1 The receipts and payments account

The **receipts and payments** account is effectively a summary of an organisation's cash book. For small clubs with a few straightforward transactions, this statement may be sufficient. For larger concerns it will be used to prepare an income and expenditure account and balance sheet.

Assessment focus point This chapter deals with the financial statements for **non-profit making organisations**.

1.1 Use of the receipts and payments account

Many charities and clubs keep records only of cash paid and received. To facilitate production of the financial statement, an analysed cash book may be used. No balance sheet is produced with a receipts and payments account.

1.2 Example: receipts and payments account

HIGH LEE STRONG TENNIS CLUB
RECEIPTS AND PAYMENTS ACCOUNT
FOR THE YEAR ENDED 30 APRIL 20X0

Receipts	$	Payments	$
Balance b/f	16	Bar expenses	106
Bar takings	160	Rent	50
Subscriptions	328	Wages	140
		Postage	10
		Printing	12
		Affiliation fees to LTS	18
		Lawn mower*	50
		Heat and light	60
		Balance c/f	58
	504		504

*Item of capital expenditure

The table lists **advantages** and **disadvantages** of this type of financial statement.

Advantages		Disadvantages	
(a)	Very easy to produce and understand.	(a)	Takes no account of any amounts owing or prepaid.
(b)	Serves as a basis for the preparation of the income and expenditure account and balance sheet.	(b)	Includes items of capital expenditure and makes no distinction between capital and revenue items.
		(c)	Takes no account of depreciation of fixed assets.

2 Income and expenditure account

An **income and expenditure account** is the name given to what is effectively the income statement of a non-trading organisation, eg sports clubs, social clubs, societies, charities and so on. The principles of 'accruals' accounting (the matching concept) are applied to income and expenditure accounts in the same way as for income statements.

2.1 Non-trading entities

In a non-trading organisation the result for the year is described as a surplus or deficit, not a profit or loss, and the capital of the organisation is known as the accumulated fund.

There are a few differences between the final accounts of a non-trading organisation and those of a business.

(a) Since non-trading organisations do not exist to make profits, the difference between income and matching expenditure in the **income and expenditure account** is referred to as a **surplus** or a **deficit** rather than a profit or loss.

(b) The capital or proprietorship of the organisation is referred to as the **accumulated fund**, rather than the capital account. In addition, other separate funds might be kept by the organisation.

(c) There is usually no separate trading account. Instead, it is usual to net off expenditure against income for like items.

2.2 Sources of income for non-trading organisations

Non-trading organisations differ in purpose and character, but we shall concentrate here on sports clubs, social clubs or societies. These will obtain their income from various sources which include the following.

- Membership subscriptions
- Payments for life membership
- 'Profits' from bar sales
- 'Profits' from the sale of food in the club restaurant or cafeteria
- 'Profits' from social events, such as dinner-dances
- Interest received on investments

Netting off expenditure against income for like items means that where some sources of income have associated costs, the net surplus or deficit should be shown in the income and expenditure account.

For example:

(a) If a club holds an annual dinner-dance the income and expenditure account will net off the costs of the event against the revenue to show the surplus or deficit.

(b) If a club has a bar, the income and expenditure account will show the surplus or deficit on its trading. Although the organisation itself does not trade, the bar does and so it is correct to refer to 'profits' from the bar.

Where there is trading activity within a non-trading organisation (eg bar sales, cafeteria sales etc) so that the organisation must hold inventories of drink or food etc it is usual to prepare a trading account for that particular activity, and then to record the surplus or deficit from trading in the income and expenditure account. An example is shown below.

FOOLSMATE CHESS CLUB
BAR TRADING ACCOUNT FOR THE YEAR TO 31 DECEMBER 20X5

	$	$
Sales		18,000
Less cost of goods sold		
Bar inventories 1 January 20X5	1,200	
Purchases	15,400	
	16,600	
Less bar inventories at 31 December 20X5	1,600	
		15,000
Bar profit (taken to income and expenditure account)		3,000

2.3 Funds of non-trading organisations

Although the capital of a non-trading organisation is generally accounted for as the accumulated fund, some separate funds might be set up for particular purposes.

(a) A life membership fund is a fund for the money subscribed for life membership by various members of the organisation. The money paid for life membership is commonly invested outside the organisation (for example in a building society account). The investment then earns interest for the organisation.

(b) A building fund might be set up whereby the organisation sets aside money to save for the cost of a new building extension. The money put into the fund will be invested outside the organisation, earning interest, until it is needed for the building work. It might take several years to create a large enough fund.

2.4 Accounting for special funds

The double entry is:

(a) When money is put into the fund

DEBIT   Cash
CREDIT   Special-purpose fund

(b) When the cash is invested

DEBIT   Investments (eg building society account)
CREDIT   Cash

(c) When the investments earn interest

DEBIT   Cash
CREDIT   Interest received (special-purpose fund) account

3 Preparing income and expenditure accounts

3.1 Sources of income

FAST FORWARD

Before looking at an example of an income and expenditure account we need to look at each of the following items in some detail.

- Membership subscriptions
- Bar trading account
- Life membership

These are items which we have not come across previously because they are not found in the accounts of businesses. Remember, however, that in many respects the accounts of non-trading organisations are similar to those of businesses with non-current assets, depreciation, current assets and current liabilities, expense accounts, accruals and prepayments.

3.2 Membership subscriptions

T FORWARD

Subscriptions received in advance are treated as a current liability.

Subscriptions in arrears are treated as a current asset.

Annual membership subscriptions of clubs and societies are usually payable one year in advance.

A club or society therefore receives payments from members for benefits which the members have yet to enjoy. They are receipts in advance and are shown in the balance sheet of the society as a current liability.

3.3 Example: subscriptions in advance

The Mudflannels Cricket Club charges an annual membership of $50 payable in advance on 1 October each year. All 40 members pay their subscriptions promptly on 1 October 20X4. The club's accounting year ends on 31 December

Solution

Total subscriptions of $40 \times \$50 = \$2,000$ would be treated as follows.

(a) $\dfrac{9\,\text{months}}{12\,\text{months}} \times \$2,000 = \$1,500$ appears in the balance sheet of the club as a current liability 'subscriptions in advance' (1 January to 30 September 20X5).

(b) $\dfrac{3\,\text{months}}{12\,\text{months}} \times \$2,000 = \$500$ appears as income in the income and expenditure account for the period 1 October to 31 December 20X4.

When members are in arrears with subscriptions and owe money to the club or society, they are 'debtors' of the organisation and so appear as current assets under the heading 'subscriptions in arrears'. These should be shown as a separate item and should not be netted off against subscriptions in advance.

3.4 Example: when subscriptions are in arrears

Bluespot Squash Club has 100 members, each of whom pays an annual membership of $60 on 1 November. Of those 100 members, 90 pay their subscriptions before 31 December 20X5 (for the 20X5/X6 year) but 10 have still not paid.

Solution

As at 31 December 20X5 the balance sheet of the club would include the following items.

(a) Subscriptions in advance (current liability)

$90\,\text{members} \times \dfrac{10\,\text{months}}{12\,\text{months}} \times \$60 = \$4,500$

(b) Subscriptions in arrears (current asset)

$10\,\text{members} \times \dfrac{2\,\text{months}}{12\,\text{months}} \times \$60 = \$100$

It is common for clubs to take no credit for subscription income until the money is received. In such a case, subscriptions in arrears are **not** credited to income and **not** shown as a current asset. It is essential to read the question carefully.

3.5 Example: subscriptions account

At 1 January 20X8, the Little Blithering Debating Society had membership subscriptions paid in advance of $1,600, and subscriptions in arrears of $250. During the year to 31 December 20X8 receipts of subscription payments amounted to $18,400. At 31 December 20X8 subscriptions in advance amounted to $1,750 and subscriptions in arrears to $240.

What is the income from subscriptions to be shown in the income and expenditure account for the year to 31 December 20X8?

Solution

The question does not say that subscriptions are only accounted for when received. You may therefore assume that the society takes credit for subscriptions as they become due.

The income for the income and expenditure account would be calculated as follows.

	$	$
Payments received in the year		18,400
Add: subscriptions due but not yet received (ie subscriptions in arrears 31 Dec 20X8)	240	
subscriptions received last year relating to current year (ie subscriptions in advance 1 Jan 20X8)	1,600	
		1,840
		20,240
Less: subscriptions received in current year relating to last year (ie subscriptions in arrears 1 Jan 20X8)	250	
subscriptions received in current year relating to next year (ie subscriptions in advance 31 Dec 20X8)	1,750	
		2,000
Income from subscriptions for the year		18,240

You may find it simpler to do this calculation as a ledger account.

SUBSCRIPTIONS ACCOUNT

	$		$
Subscriptions in arrears b/f	250	Subscriptions in advance b/f	1,600
I & E a/c (balancing figure)	18,240	Cash	18,400
Subscriptions in advance c/d	1,750	Subscriptions in arrears c/d	240
	20,240		20,240
Subscriptions in arrears b/d	240	Subscriptions in advance b/d	1,750

 | Question | **Subscriptions**

The following information relates to a sports club.

	$
20X4 subscriptions unpaid at beginning of 20X5	410
20X4 subscriptions received during 20X5	370
20X5 subscriptions received during 20X5	6,730
20X6 subscriptions received during 20X5	1,180
20X5 subscriptions unpaid at end of 20X5	470

The club takes credit for subscription income when it becomes due, but takes a prudent view of overdue subscriptions. What amount is credited to the income and expenditure account for 20X5?

Answer

SUBSCRIPTIONS

	$		$
Balance b/f	410	Bank: 20X4	370
		20X5	6,730
∴ I & E account	7,200	20X6	1,180
		20X4 subs written off	40
Balance c/f	1,180	Balance c/f	470
	8,790		8,790

Note that the net figure taken to the income and expenditure account will be $7,160 ($7,200 – $40) as the 20X4 subs write off will be netted off against the income and expenditure figure.

3.6 Bar trading account

If a club has a bar or cafeteria a separate trading account will be prepared for its trading activities. A bar trading account will contain the following items.

- Bar takings
- Opening inventories of goods, purchases and closing inventories of goods (cost of bar sales)
- Gross profit (takings less cost of bar takings)
- Other expenses directly related to the running of the bar (if any)
- Net profit (gross profit less any expenses)

The net bar profit is then included under income in the income and expenditure account. A loss on the bar would be included under expenditure.

3.7 Life membership

Some clubs offer membership for life in return for a given lump sum subscription. Life members, having paid this lump sum, do not pay any further annual subscriptions. The club receives a sum of money, which it can then invest, with the annual interest from these investments being accounted for as income in the income and expenditure account.

The payments from life members are not income relating to the year in which they are received by the club, because the payment is for the life of the members, which can be a very long time to come. As they are long-term payments, they are recorded in the club accounts as an addition to a life membership fund as follows.

DEBIT   Cash
CREDIT   Life membership fund

The life membership fund is shown in the balance sheet of the club or society immediately after the accumulated fund.

Life members enjoy the benefits of membership over their life, and so their payment to the club is 'rewarded' as time goes by. Accounting for life membership over time can be explained with an example.

Suppose that Annette Cord pays a life membership fee of $300 to the Tumbledown Tennis Club. The $300 will initially be put into the club's life membership fund. We will suppose that this money is invested by the club, and earns interest of $30 per annum.

There are two ways of accounting for the life membership fee.

(a)   **To keep the $300 in the life membership fund until Annette Cord dies.** (Since the $300 earns interest of $30 pa this interest can be said to represent income for the club in lieu of an annual subscription.) When Annette eventually dies, the $300 she contributed can then be transferred out of the life membership fund and directly into the accumulated fund.

(b)   **To write off subscriptions to the life membership fund by transferring a 'fair' amount from the fund into the income and expenditure account.** A 'fair' amount will represent the proportion of the total life membership payment which relates to the current year. We do not know how long any life member will live, but use an estimated average life say 20 years. In each year, one-twentieth of life membership fees would be deducted from the fund and added as income in the income and expenditure account.

In the case of Annette Cord, the annual transfer under (b) is $15 and, after 20 years, her contribution to the fund has been written off in full and transferred to the income and expenditure accounts of those 20 years. This transfer of $15 is in addition to the annual interest of $30 earned by the club each year from investing the fee of $300.

If method (b) is selected in preference to method (a), the life membership fund can be written down by either a straight line method or a reducing balance method, in much the same way as non-current assets are depreciated. However it is a capital fund being written off and the amount of the annual write-off is **income** to the club, and not an expense.

A further feature of method (b) is that there is no need to record the death of individual members (unlike method (a)). The annual write off is based on an average expected life of members and it does not matter when any individual member dies.

A possible reason for preferring method (b) to method (a) is that life membership subscriptions regularly pass through the income and expenditure account as income of the club.

In spite of the logical reasons why method (b) should perhaps be preferable, method (a) is still commonly used.

Assessment focus point	Unless you are told about a rate for 'writing off' the life membership fund annually, you should assume that method (a) should be used, where the question gives you information about the death of club life members.

3.8 Example: life membership fund

The Coxless Rowing Club has a scheme where members can opt to pay a lump sum which gives them membership for life. Lump sum payments received for life membership are held in a life membership fund but then credited to the income and expenditure account in equal instalments over a ten year period, beginning in the year when the lump sum payment is made and life membership is acquired.

The treasurer of the club, Beau Trace, establishes the following information.

(a)   At 31 December 20X4, the balance on the life membership fund was $8,250.
(b)   Of this opening balance, $1,220 should be credited as income for the year to 31 December 20X5.
(c)   During the year to 31 December 20X5, new life members made lump sum payments totalling $1,500.

Required

Show the movements in the life membership fund for the year to 31 December 20X5, and in doing so, calculate how much should be transferred as income from life membership fund to the income and expenditure account.

Solution

LIFE MEMBERSHIP FUND

	$	$
As at 31 December 20X4		8,250
New life membership payments received in 20X5		1,500
		9,750
Less transfer to income and expenditure account:		
out of balance as at 31 December 20X4	1,220	
out of new payments in 20X5 (10% of $1,500)	150	
		1,370
Fund as at 31 December 20X5		8,380
The income and expenditure account for the year would show:		
Income from life membership		1,370

3.9 Accounting for the sale of investments and non-current assets

In accounting for clubs and societies, the income and expenditure account is used to record the surplus or deficit in the transactions for the year. Occasionally a club or society might sell off some of its investments or fixed assets, and in doing so might make a profit or loss on the sale.

(a)   The profit/loss on the sale of an investment is simply the difference between the sale price and the balance sheet value (usually cost) of the investment.

(b)   The profit/loss on the sale of a non-current asset is the difference between the sale price and the net book value of the asset at the date of sale.

There is nothing different or unusual about the accounts of non-trading organisations in computing the amount of such profits or losses. What is different, however, is how the profit or losses should be recorded in the accounts.

(a)   The profit or loss on the sale of investments is not shown in the income and expenditure account. Instead, the profit is directly added to (or loss subtracted from) the accumulated fund.

(b)   The profit or loss on the sale of a non-current asset which is not subject to depreciation charges in the income and expenditure account, is also taken directly to the accumulated fund.

(c)   The profit or loss on the sale of non-current assets which have been subject to depreciation charges is recorded in the income and expenditure account.

The point of difference in (c) compared with (a) and (b) is that since depreciation on the asset has been charged in the income and expenditure account in the past, it is appropriate that a profit or loss on sale should also be reported through the account.

3.10 Example: income and expenditure accounts

The assets and liabilities of the Berley Sports Club at 31 December 20X4 were as follows.

	$
Pavilion at cost less depreciation	13,098
Bank and cash	1,067
Bar inventory	291
Bar receivables	231
Rates prepaid	68
Contributions owing to sports club by users of sports club facilities	778
Bar payables	427
Loans to sports club	1,080
Accruals: water	13
electricity	130
miscellaneous	75
loan interest	33
Contributions paid in advance by users of sports club facilities	398

A receipts and payments account for the year ended 31 December 20X5 was produced as follows.

	$		$
Opening balance	1,067	Bar purchases	2,937
Bar sales	4,030	Repayment of loan capital	170
Telephone	34	Rent of ground	79
Contributions from users of club		Rates	320
facilities	1,780	Water	38
Socials	177	Electricity	506
Miscellaneous	56	Insurance	221
		Repairs to equipment	326
		Expenses of socials	67
		Maintenance of ground	133
		Wages of groundsman	140
		Telephone	103
		Bar sundries	144
		Loan interest	97
		Miscellaneous	163
		Closing balance	1,700
	7,144		7,144

The following information as at 31 December 20X5 was also provided.

	$
Bar inventory	394
Bar receivables	50
Bar payables	901
Rent prepaid	16
Water charges owing	23
Electricity owing	35
Payables for bar sundries	65
Contributions by users of sports club facilities:	
owing to sports club	425
paid in advance to sports club	657
Rates prepaid	76

Depreciation on the pavilion for the year was $498.

You are asked to prepare a statement showing the gross and net profits earned by the bar, an income and expenditure account for the year ended 31 December 20X5 and a balance sheet as at that date.

Solution

We are not given the size of the accumulated fund as at the beginning of the year, but it can be calculated as the balancing figure to make total liabilities plus capital equal to total assets (as at 31 December 20X4).

Calculation of accumulated fund at 1 January 20X5

	$	$
Assets		
Pavilion at cost less depreciation		13,098
Bank and cash		1,067
Bar inventory		291
Bar receivables		231
Rates prepaid		68
Contributions in arrears		778
		15,533
Liabilities		
Bar payables	427	
Loans	1,080	
Accrued charges $(13 + 130 + 75 + 33)$	251	
Contributions received in advance	398	
		2,156
∴ Accumulated fund at 1 January 20X5		13,377

The next step is to analyse the various items of income and expenditure.

(a) There is a bar, and so a bar trading account can be prepared.
(b) Income from the telephone can be netted off against telephone expenditure.
(c) The revenue from socials has associated expenses to net off against it.
(d) There is also miscellaneous income and contributions from club members.

The bar trading account can only be put together after we have calculated bar sales and purchases.

(a) We are given bar receivables as at 1 January 20X5 and 31 December 20X5 and also cash received from bar sales. The bar sales for the year can therefore be calculated.

BAR RECEIVABLES

		$			$
1.1.20X5	Balance b/f	231	31.12.20X5	Cash	4,030
31.12.20X5	∴ Bar sales	3,849	31.12.20X5	Balance c/f	50
		4,080			4,080

(b) Similarly, purchases for the bar are calculated from opening and closing amounts for bar payables, and payments for bar purchases.

BAR PAYABLES

		$			$
31.12.20X5	Cash	2,937	1.1.20X5	Balance b/f	427
31.12.20X5	Balance c/f	901	31.12.20X5	∴ Bar purchases	3,411
		3,838			3,838

(c)   Understand that cash receipts from bar sales and cash payments for bar supplies are not the bar sales and cost of bar sales that we want. Cash receipts and payments in the year are not for matching quantities of goods, nor do they relate to the actual goods sold in the year.

(d)   Other bar trading expenses are bar sundries.

	$
Cash payments for bar sundries	144
Add payables for bar sundries as at 31.12.20X5	65
	209
Less payables for bar sundries as at 1.1.20X5	0
Expenses for bar sundries for the year	209

BAR TRADING ACCOUNT
FOR THE YEAR ENDED 31 DECEMBER 20X5

	$	$
Sales		3,849
Cost of sales		
Opening inventory	291	
Purchases	3,411	
	3,702	
Less closing inventory	394	
		3,308
Gross profit		541
Sundry expenses		209
Net profit		332

Contributions to the sports club for the year should be calculated in the same way as membership subscriptions. Using a T account format below, the income from contributions (for the income and expenditure account) is the balancing figure. Contributions in advance brought forward are liabilities (credit balance b/f) and contributions in arrears brought forward are assets (debit balance b/f).

CONTRIBUTIONS

		$			$
1.1.20X5	Balance in arrears b/f	778	1.1.20X5	Balance in advance b/f	398
31.12.20X5	∴ Income and expenditure	1,168	31.12.20X5	Cash	1,780
31.12.20X5	Balance in advance c/f	657	31.12.20X5	Balance in arrears c/f	425
		2,603			2,603

BERLEY SPORTS CLUB – INCOME AND EXPENDITURE ACCOUNT
FOR THE YEAR ENDED 31 DECEMBER 20X5

	$	$
Income		
Contributions		1,168
Net income from bar trading		332
Income from socials: receipts	177	
less expenses	67	
		110
Miscellaneous		56
		1,666
Expenses		
Ground rent (79 – 16)	63	
Rates (320 + 68 – 76)	312	
Water (38 – 13 + 23)	48	
Electricity (506 – 130 + 35)	411	
Insurance	221	
Equipment repairs	326	
Ground maintenance	133	
Wages	140	
Telephone (103 – 34)	69	
Loan interest (97 –33)	64	
Miscellaneous expenses (163 – 75)	88	
Depreciation	498	
		2,373
Deficit for the year		(707)

BERLEY SPORTS CLUB
BALANCE SHEET AS AT 31 DECEMBER 20X5

	$	$
Non-current assets		
Pavilion at NBV $(13,098 – 498)		12,600
Current assets		
Bar inventory	394	
Bar receivables	50	
Contributions in arrears	425	
Prepayments $(16+76)	92	
Cash at bank	1,700	
	2,661	
Current liabilities		
Bar payables $(901+65)	966	
Accrued charges $(23 + 35)	58	
Contributions in advance	657	
	1,681	
Net current assets		980
		13,580
Long-term liability		
Loan $(1,080-170)		910
		12,670
Accumulated fund		
Balance at 1 January 20X5		13,377
Less deficit for year		(707)
		12,670

Chapter roundup

- The receipts and payments account is effectively a summary of an organisation's cash book. For small clubs with a few straightforward transactions, this statement may be sufficient. For larger concerns it will be used to prepare an income and expenditure account and balance sheet.

- An income and expenditure account is the name given to what is effectively the income statement of a non-trading organisation, eg sports clubs, social clubs, societies, charities and so on. The principles of 'accruals' accounting (the matching concept) are applied to income and expenditure accounts in the same way as for income statements.

- In a non-trading organisation the result for the year is described as a surplus or deficit, not a profit or loss, and the capital of the organisation is known as the accumulated fund.

- Netting off expenditure against income for like items means that where some sources of income have associated costs, the net surplus or deficit should be shown in the income and expenditure account.

- Before looking at an example of an income and expenditure account we need to look at each of the following items in some detail.

    - Membership subscriptions
    - Bar trading account
    - Life membership

- Subscriptions received in advance are treated as a current liability.

- Subscriptions in arrears are treated as a current asset.

Quick quiz

1   Three differences between the accounts of a non-trading organisation and those of a business are:

(1)   _____

(2)   _____

(3)   _____

2   If a 'not for profit' organisation does make a surplus it will be?

A   Credit to capital
B   Credit to the accumulated fund
C   Repaid to the contributions or members
D   Added to the bank account balance

3   A club has 150 members who pay $10 each for membership. The opening subscription receivable was $70 and 5 members had paid subscriptions in advance at the year end. How much money was collected from members?

A $1,500
B $1,740
C $1,620
D $1,520

4   The assets and liabilities of a social club were (at 31.12.20X1) equipment $1,500, premises $16,000, bar inventory $1,300, bar payables $1,100, managers wage owing $250, subscriptions in arrears $500, prepaid subscriptions $350, cash $1,900. The accumulated fund is:

A $21,200
B $19,650
C $19,500
D $200,000

Answers to quick quiz

1   (1)   A non-trading organisation does not make profits, so the income statement is replaced by an income and expenditure account.

    (2)   The 'capital' account is the accumulated fund.

    (3)   There is no separate trading account.

2   B   Correct.
    A   Non trading organisations such as clubs and societies refer to their capital as 'accumulated funds'.
    C   Incorrect, unless in the unlikely event of the club or society specifying this is to happen.
    D   Incorrect.

3   C   Correct.

Subscriptions A/C

Balance b/f	70	Bank	1,620
I&E (subscriptions)			
150 × $10	1,500		
Bal c/f 5 × $10	50		
	1,620		1,620

    A   Incorrect, you have not adjusted for opening subscriptions in arrears or closing prepaid subscriptions.

    B   Incorrect, you have posted subscription income to the credit of the subscription a/c incorrectly.

    D   Incorrect, the closing prepayment of subscriptions must be treated as a payable.

4   C   Correct, $1,500 + $16,000 + $1,300 − $1,100 − $250 + $500 − $350 + $1,900 = 19,500.
    A   Incorrect, this is the amount of the total assets of the club.
    B   Incorrect, you have treated the subscriptions incorrectly.
    D   Incorrect, you have treated the outstanding wages as an asset.

Now try the questions below from the Question Bank

Question numbers	Page
92–93	411

Manufacturing accounts

Introduction

So far in our studies of accounts preparation we have confined ourselves to the accounts of trading organisations. Britain has been called a nation of shopkeepers, but we would be a very hungry nation if no one actually made things. In Section 1 of this chapter we consider the problems of preparing accounting statements for manufacturing firms.

The most obvious difference between a manufacturing and a trading firm is that the former has many more different types of expense. The **purchases** of the trading firm are replaced by the myriad expenses that arise when, for example, a willow tree is converted into a cricket bat. The traditional way of showing the cost of goods produced is the **manufacturing account**.

Topic list	Syllabus references
1 Manufacturing accounts	D (7)

1 Manufacturing accounts

A **manufacturing account** is an account in which the costs of producing finished goods are calculated. It is prepared for internal use.

Direct factory costs are factory costs which change every time an extra unit is made. For example, direct factory wages are wages paid to production workers who are paid per unit made.

Production overheads or **indirect factory costs** are factory costs which do not change every time an extra unit is made. For example, indirect factory wages are wages paid to production managers who are paid the same each month regardless of how many units are made.

Prime cost is raw material costs plus direct factory costs.

1.1 Cost of goods sold

A company's trading account will usually include a cost of goods sold derived as the total of opening inventory plus purchases, less closing inventory. This is particularly suitable for a retail business which buys in goods and sells them on to customers without altering their condition. But for a manufacturing company it would be truer to say that the cost of goods sold is as follows.

	$
Opening inventory of finished goods	X
Plus cost of finished goods produced in the period	X
	X
Less closing inventory of finished goods	(X)
Cost of finished goods sold	X

Assessment focus point

A pro-forma manufacturing account is set out below with illustrative figures. Make sure you learn the format.

MANUFACTURING ACCOUNT
FOR THE YEAR ENDED 31 DECEMBER 20X6

	$	$
Raw materials		
Opening inventory	4,000	
Purchases (net of returns)	207,000	
	211,000	
Less closing inventory	23,000	
		188,000
Direct factory wages		21,000
Prime cost		209,000
Production overhead		
Factory power	4,000	
Plant depreciation	3,000	
Plant maintenance	1,500	
Rent and insurance	2,500	
Light and heat	3,000	
Sundry expenses	5,000	
Factory manager's salary	9,000	
Building depreciation	1,000	
		29,000
Production cost of resources consumed		238,000

	$	$
Work in progress		
Opening inventory	8,000	
Closing inventory	(17,000)	
Increase in work in progress inventory		(9,000)
Production cost of finished goods produced		229,000

1.2 Work in progress

At the balance sheet date, there will be work in progress in the production departments, ie work which has been partly converted but which has not yet reached the stage of being finished goods.

The value of this work in progress is the cost of the raw materials, the wages of employees who have worked on it plus a share of overheads. To arrive at the cost of finished goods produced, an increase in work in progress must be deducted from the total production costs. Of course, if the value of work in progress had **fallen** during the period, this fall would be an **increase** in the cost of finished goods produced.

1.3 Example: manufacturing account and income statement

> The manufacturing account is needed to calculate the cost of finished goods. This figure is then carried forward into the income statement to replace purchases in the cost of sales calculation.

A manufacturing company has its factory and offices at the same site. Its results for the year to 31 December 20X5 were:

	$
Sales	179,000
Purchases of raw materials	60,000
Direct labour	70,000
Depreciation of equipment	10,000
Rent	5,000
Depreciation of building	2,000
Heating and lighting	3,000
Telephone	2,000
Other manufacturing overheads	2,300
Other administration expenses	2,550
Other selling expenses	1,150

Shared overhead costs are to be apportioned as follows.

	Manufacturing	*Administration*	*Selling*
Depreciation of equipment	80%	5%	15%
Rent	50%	30%	20%
Depreciation of building	50%	30%	20%
Heating and lighting	40%	35%	25%
Telephone	–	40%	60%

The values of inventories are as follows.

	At 1 January 20X5 $	At 31 December 20X5 $
Raw materials	5,000	3,000
Work in progress	4,000	3,000
Finished goods	16,000	18,000

Required

Prepare the manufacturing account and income statement of the company for the period to 31 December 20X5.

Solution

MANUFACTURING ACCOUNT FOR THE YEAR ENDED 31 DECEMBER 20X5

	$	$
Opening inventory of raw materials		5,000
Purchases		60,000
		65,000
Closing inventory of raw materials		3,000
Raw materials used in production		62,000
Direct labour		70,000
Prime cost		132,000
Manufacturing overheads		
Depreciation of equipment (80% of $10,000)	8,000	
Rent (50% of $5,000)	2,500	
Depreciation of building (50% of $2,000)	1,000	
Heating and lighting (40% of $3,000)	1,200	
Other expenses	2,300	
		15,000
Manufacturing costs during the year		147,000
Add opening inventory of work in progress	4,000	
Less closing inventory of work in progress	(3,000)	
Reduction in inventory of work in progress		1,000
Cost of finished goods fully produced, transferred to income statement		148,000

INCOME STATEMENT
FOR THE YEAR ENDED 31 DECEMBER 20X5

	$	$	$
Sales			179,000
Opening inventory of finished goods		16,000	
Cost of finished goods produced		148,000	
		164,000	
Closing inventory of finished goods		18,000	
Cost of goods sold			146,000
Gross profit			33,000
Selling expenses			
Depreciation of equipment (15% of $10,000)	1,500		
Rent (20% of $5,000)	1,000		
Depreciation of building (20% of $2,000)	400		
Heating and lighting (25% of $3,000)	750		
Telephone (60% of $2,000)	1,200		
Other expenses	1,150		
		6,000	
Administration expenses			
Depreciation of equipment (5% of $10,000)	500		
Rent (30% of $5,000)	1,500		
Depreciation of building (30% of $2,000)	600		
Heating and lighting (35% of $3,000)	1,050		
Telephone (40% of $2,000)	800		
Other expenses	2,550		
		7,000	
			13,000
Net profit			20,000

Question	Manufacturing account and income statement

The following information has been extracted from the books of account of the Marsden Manufacturing Company for the year to 30 September 20X4.

	$
Advertising	2,000
Depreciation for the year to 30 September 20X4	
Factory equipment	7,000
Office equipment	4,000
Direct wages	40,000
Factory: insurance	1,000
heat	15,000
indirect materials	5,000
power	20,000
salaries	25,000
Finished goods (at 1 October 20X3)	24,000
Office: electricity	15,000
general expenses	9,000
postage and telephones	2,900
salaries	70,000
Raw material purchases	202,000
Raw material inventory (at 1 October 20X3)	8,000
Sales	512,400
Work in progress (at 1 October 20X3)	12,000

Notes

(a)   At 30 September 20X4 the following inventories were on hand.

	$
Raw materials	10,000
Work in progress	9,000
Finished goods	30,000

(b)   At 30 September 20X4 there was an accrual for advertising of $1,000, and it was estimated that $1,500 had been paid in advance for electricity. These items had not been included in the books of account for the year to 30 September 20X4.

Required

Prepare Marsden's manufacturing account and income statement for the year to 30 September 20X4.

Answer

MANUFACTURING ACCOUNT AND INCOME STATEMENT
FOR THE YEAR ENDED 30 SEPTEMBER 20X4

	$	$
Raw materials		
Opening inventory	8,000	
Purchases	202,000	
	210,000	
Less closing inventory	10,000	
		200,000
Factory wages		40,000
Prime cost		240,000
Indirect production expenses		
Insurance	1,000	
Heat	15,000	
Indirect materials	5,000	
Power	20,000	
Salaries	25,000	
Depreciation of factory equipment	7,000	
		73,000
		313,000
Work in progress		
Opening inventory	12,000	
Less closing inventory	9,000	
		3,000
Factory cost of goods produced		316,000

	$	$
Sales		512,400
Less cost of goods sold		
Opening inventory of finished goods	24,000	
Factory cost of goods produced	316,000	
	340,000	
Less closing inventory of finished goods	30,000	
		310,000
Gross profit		202,400
Expenses		
Advertising $(2,000 + 1,000)$	3,000	
Depreciation of office equipment	4,000	
Electricity $(15,000 - 1,500)$	13,500	
General expenses	9,000	
Postage and telephones	2,900	
Salaries	70,000	
		102,400
Net profit		100,000

Chapter roundup

- A **manufacturing account** is an account in which the costs of producing finished goods are calculated. It is prepared for internal use.

- **Direct factory costs** are factory costs which change every time an extra unit is made. For example, direct factory wages are wages paid to production workers who are paid per unit made.

- **Production overheads** or **indirect factory costs** are factory costs which do not change every time an extra unit is made. For example, indirect factory wages are wages paid to production managers who are paid the same each month regardless of how many units are made.

- **Prime cost** is raw material costs plus direct factory costs.

Quick quiz

1   The production cost of finished goods is?

   A   Prime cost plus production overheads plus opening WIP less closing WIP
   B   Prime cost plus production overheads
   C   Prime cost plus opening WIP less closing WIP
   D   Prime cost plus opening inventory of materials less closing inventory of materials plus production overheads

2   Prime cost comprises several elements of costs, excluding which of the following?

   A   Purchases of raw materials
   B   Direct wages
   C   Opening and closing inventories of raw materials
   D   Factory overheads

Answers to quick quiz

1   A   Correct.

    B   Incorrect, no adjustment for work in progress has been made.

    C   This excludes production overheads.

    D   Prime cost has already been adjusted for changes in raw material inventory levels.

2   D   Not part of prime cost.

Now try the questions below from the Question Bank

Question numbers	Page
94–95	411

BPP LEARNING MEDIA

The regulatory system

Introduction

This chapter looks at the regulatory framework within which accounts, particularly those of limited liability companies, are prepared. The purpose of this section is to impress upon you the **importance** of this framework, which is to be studied in much more detail in the later stages of your qualification.

Topic list	Syllabus references
1 The regulatory framework of accounts	A (6)

1 The regulatory framework of accounts

There is a wide range of accounting concepts in use. There are also different conventions under which accounts can be prepared. It may seem as though almost anything goes. What rules are there?

For an **unincorporated** business, any form of accounting information is adequate if it gives the owner(s) of the business a basis for planning and control, and satisfies the requirements of external users such as the tax authorities.

The activities of **limited liability companies**, including the way they prepare their accounts, are closely regulated.

FAST FORWARD

The regulations on accounts come from four main sources.

- Company law enacted by Parliament
- Financial Reporting Standards issued by the Accounting Standards Board
- International Accounting Standards and International Financial Reporting Standards issued by the International Accounting Standards Board
- For quoted companies, the requirements of the Stock Exchange

1.1 Company law

Limited liability companies are required by law to prepare accounts annually for distribution to their shareholders. In the UK, a copy of these accounts must be lodged with the Registrar of Companies and is available for inspection by any member of the public. For this reason a company's statutory annual accounts are often referred to as its published accounts.

In 2006, all existing companies legislation was brought together in a consolidating Act, the Companies Act 2006 (CA 2006).

There are many differences between accounting systems found in the various European Union (EU) member states. For example, in the UK a 'true and fair view' is sought, whereas in West Germany a 'legal and correct view' is observed. Taxation and accounting principles differ and consolidation practices vary.

Since the United Kingdom became a member of the EU it has been obliged to comply with legal requirements decided on by the EU. It does this by enacting UK laws to implement EU directives. For example, the CA 1989 was enacted in part to implement the provisions of the seventh and eighth EU directives, which deal with consolidated accounts (for groups of companies) and auditors.

As far as the preparation of accounts is concerned, the overriding requirement of companies legislation is that accounts should show a 'true and fair view'. This phrase is not defined in the Companies Acts. What it certainly does **not** mean is that company accounts are to be exact to the penny. For one thing, many of the figures appearing in a set of accounts are arrived at partly by the exercise of judgement. For another, the amount of time and effort that such a requirement would cost would be out of all proportion to the advantages derived from it (see the discussion earlier in this chapter of the materiality concept).

The legislation also requires that the accounts of a limited liability company (except certain small companies) must be **audited**. An audit, for this purpose, may be defined as an 'independent examination of, and expression of opinion on, the financial statements of an enterprise'.

This means that a limited liability company must engage a firm of chartered or certified accountants to conduct an examination of its accounting records and its financial statements in order to form an opinion as to whether the accounts present a 'true and fair view'. At the conclusion of their audit, the auditors issue a report (addressed to the owners of the company, ie its **members** or **shareholders**) which is published as part of the accounts.

Audit is discussed in more detail in Chapter 23 of this Study Text. Note that under International Financial Reporting Standards, a 'true and fair view' is called **'fair presentation'.**

Do not neglect the role of auditors in the regulatory system.

1.2 Non-statutory regulation

Apart from company law, the main regulations affecting accounts in the UK derive from pronouncements issued by the accounting profession. Six accountancy bodies in the UK are represented on the Consultative Committee of Accountancy Bodies (CCAB). They are as follows.

- The Chartered Institute of Management Accountants (CIMA)
- The Institute of Chartered Accountants in England and Wales (ICAEW)
- The Institute of Chartered Accountants of Scotland (ICAS)
- The Institute of Chartered Accountants in Ireland (ICAI)
- The Association of Chartered Certified Accountants (ACCA)
- The Chartered Institute of Public Finance and Accountancy (CIPFA)

The CCAB is a major influence on the way in which accounts are prepared. Our main interest will be in the accounting standards published to lay down accounting treatments in areas where a variety of approaches might be taken. The value of accounts would be reduced if users were not able to count on a measure of comparability between them. The aim of accounting standards is to ensure that such comparability exists.

To understand how standards are set there are four bodies you need to know about.

- The Financial Reporting Council (FRC)
- The Accounting Standards Board (ASB)
- The Financial Reporting Review Panel (FRRP)
- The Urgent Issues Task Force (UITF)

The **Financial Reporting Council**. The FRC draws its membership from a wide spectrum of accounts preparers and users. Its chairman is appointed by the Government. The FRC operates through two arms: the FRRP and the ASB.

The **Accounting Standards Board**. The ASB is responsible for the issue of accounting standards. Accounting standards issued by the ASB are called **Financial Reporting Standard** (FRSs), of which nineteen have so far been published. Prior to August 1990 standards were issued by the Accounting Standards Committee (ASC, now abolished. These were known as Statements of Standard Accounting Practice (SSAPs).

Prior to publication, the ASB circulates its proposals in the form of a financial reporting exposure draft (inevitably referred to as a FRED) and invites comments. To avoid chaos, the ASB has 'adopted' those SSAPs still extant and they therefore remain in force.

The **Financial Reporting Review Panel**. The FRRP is the second operating arm of the FRC. Its task is to examine accounts published by companies if it appears that Companies Act requirements have been breached – in particular, the requirement that accounts should show a true and fair view. The panel has legal backing: if a public company departs from an accounting standard, the panel may apply to the courts, which may in turn instruct the company to prepare revised accounts.

The **Urgent Issues Task Force**. The UITF is an offshoot of the ASB. Its role is to assist the ASB in areas where an accounting standard or Companies Act provision already exists, but where unsatisfactory or conflicting interpretations have developed. As its name suggests, the UITF is designed to act quickly (more quickly than the full standard-setting process is capable of) when an authoritative ruling is urgently needed.

Question

Which body is responsible for issuing UK Financial Reporting Standards?

A   FRC

B   ASB

C   FRRP

D   UITF

Answer

B   The Accounting Standards Board is responsible for issuing UK standards.

1.3 International Financial Reporting Standards

FAST FORWARD

From 1 January 2005 all listed EU companies have to report under IFRS for their consolidated accounts.

The International Accounting Standards Committee (IASC) was set up in June 1973 in an attempt to co-ordinate the development of international accounting standards (IASs). It included representatives from many countries throughout the world, including the USA and the UK. The IASC has since been superseded by the International Accounting Standards Board (IASB) which issues International Financial Reporting Standards (IFRSs).

From 2005 UK listed companies have to report under IFRS for the preparation of their group accounts. During 2005 and 2006 most UK companies are expected to move over to complying with International Financial Reporting Standards rather than UK Financial Reporting Standards. There is a glossary of international terms on page (xxiii).

1.4 IFRS 1: First-time adoption of International Financial Reporting Standards

The IASB would like to make the transition to international standards as smooth as possible and has recently issued its first entirely new standard, IFRS 1 *First-time adoption of International Financial Reporting Standards,* which provides guidance on how companies should implement IFRS.

Companies reporting under IFRS for the first time in 2005 should begin by preparing an opening balance sheet for 1 January 2004 (if their year end is 31 December) which is correct under IFRS. This may involve adjustments for assets and liabilities which were recognised under the previous system (eg UK FRSs) but are not recognised under IFRS, or vice versa.

They will then be able to prepare IFRS accounts for 2004 which will provide comparatives for their first full set of IFRS accounts in 2005.

1.5 The Stock Exchange regulations

The Stock Exchange is a market for stocks and shares, and a company whose securities are traded in this market is known as a 'quoted' or 'listed' company.

When a share is granted a quotation on The Stock Exchange, it appears on the 'Official List' which is published in London each business day. The Official List shows the 'official quotation' or price for the share for that day. It is drawn up by the Quotations Department of The Stock Exchange, which derives its prices from those actually ruling in the market.

In order to receive a quotation for its securities, a company must conform with Stock Exchange Listing Rules issued by the Council of The Stock Exchange. The company commits itself to certain procedures and standards, including matters concerning the disclosure of accounting information, which are more extensive than the disclosure requirements of the Companies Acts. These include issuing the annual report within six months of the year end and publishing an interim report giving profit and loss information.

Question   **The regulatory framework**

To ensure you understand which regulations apply to which type of business, fill in the table below with a 'yes' where compliance is required and 'no' where it is not.

Type of Business	Companies Act	FRSs/SSAPs	IFRSs/IASs	Stock Exchange Listing Rules
Public Listed Company				
Public Listed Company – group accounts				
Private Limited Company				
Sole Proprietorship				

Answer

Type Of Business	Companies Act	FRSs/SSAPs	IFRSs/IASs	Stock Exchange Listing Rules
Public Listed Company	YES	YES	NO	YES
Public Listed Company – group accounts	YES	NO	YES	YES
Private Limited Company	YES	YES	NO	NO
Sole Proprietorship	NO	NO	NO	NO

Assessment focus point | Make sure you learn the answers above

Chapter roundup

- The regulations on accounts come from four main sources.
  - Company law enacted by Parliament
  - Financial Reporting Standards issued by the Accounting Standards Board
  - International Accounting Standards and International Financial Reporting Standards issued by the International Accounting Standards Board
  - For quoted companies, the requirements of the Stock Exchange
- From 1 January 2005 all listed EU companies have to report under IFRS for their consolidated accounts.

Quick quiz

1   Fill in the blanks.

The main statute governing the content of limited liability company accounts in the UK is _____
_____.

2   What major change to UK financial reporting took place from 1 January 2005?

A   All limited companies to use UK FRS in their accounts.
B   All listed companies to use IFRS in their accounts.
C   All listed companies to use UK FRS in their accounts.
D   All listed companies to use IFRS in group accounts.

Answers to quick quiz

1   The main statute governing the content of limited liability company accounts in the UK is **CA 2006**.

2   D   Since January 2005 listed companies have been required to prepare their group accounts to comply with IFRSs.

Now try the questions below from the Question Bank

Question numbers	Page
96–101	411

Internal and external audit

Introduction

So far you have been concerned with the preparation of accounts. The syllabus also includes an appreciation of the purpose of external and internal audit.

It is a requirement of the Companies Act that all companies must appoint **external auditors** who will report to the **members** of the company on whether in their opinion, the annual statutory accounts give a true and fair view (or 'fair presentation'). The duties of the external auditor are imposed by statute and cannot be limited, either by the directors or by the members of the company. External auditors are not employees of the company.

Internal auditors are employees of the company whose duties are fixed by management, and who report ultimately to **management**. In recent years it has become increasingly common for large companies to set up internal audit departments and for the external auditors to alter their audit approach to take account of the work done by the internal auditors.

Topic list	Syllabus references
1 Ownership v stewardship	A (1)
2 External audit	C (1)
3 Internal audit	C (2)
4 Internal control	C (3)
5 Controls over sales and receivables	C (3)
6 Controls over purchases and payables	C (3)
7 Evaluation of internal controls	C (3)
8 Audit trail	C (3)
9 The detection and prevention of fraud	C (4)

1 Ownership v stewardship

FAST FORWARD

It is important to distinguish between ownership and stewardship.

Key terms

Stewardship is the primary function of managers who are responsible for the running of the business on a day to day basis; it means the safeguarding of the business' assets.

An **audit** assures proprietors that the stewardship of the organisation was effectively carried out.

The stewardship concept is wider than ensuring that the assets of an organisation are properly recorded, valued and insured. It also includes the control of costs, the improvement of efficiency and the optimisation of profits. Additionally whilst management's stewardship responsibilities extend primarily to the owners of the business it also includes all other users of the accounts.

2 External audit

FAST FORWARD

External auditors report to the members of the company on whether, in their opinion, the annual statutory accounts give a true and fair view. Their duties are imposed by statute and they are not employees of the company. Under International Financial Reporting Standards, auditors report on 'fair presentation'.

Key term

An **external audit** is an independent examination of, and expression of opinion on the financial statements of an enterprise.

2.1 The audit

If the 'enterprise' is a limited company, 'external audit' means statutory audit, that is, under the Companies Act 2006. The statutory audit requirement, arose as discussed in Section 1, because of the separation of owners (shareholders) and managers (directors).

External auditors are generally firms of chartered or certified accountants. They summarise their conclusions on the company's financial statements by issuing an audit report, addressed to the shareholders. The report must state whether in the auditors opinion.

(a)   The balance sheet gives a true and fair view of the state of affairs of the company at the end of the financial year.

(b)   The profit and loss account (income statement) gives a true and fair view of the profit or loss of the company for the financial year.

(c)   The financial statements have been properly prepared in accordance with the Companies Act.

FAST FORWARD

'True and fair' is not defined in company law or accounting standards. The words are used together rather than separately and the term is generally taken to mean 'reasonably accurate and free from bias or distortion'. Under IFRS, the term is 'fair presentation'.

Although there is no official definition of 'true and fair', the Companies Act states that the directors may depart from any provisions of company law or accounting standards if these are inconsistent with the requirement to give a true and fair view. This 'true and fair override' has been treated as an important loophole in the law and has been the cause of much argument and dissatisfaction within the accounting profession.

Remember that a statutory audit is limited to the above aims. Auditors may also be asked to do other work.

2.2 Non-statutory audits

Non-statutory audits are performed by independent auditors because the owners, members, trustees, governing bodies or other interested parties desire them, not because the law requires them. Auditing may therefore extend to any kind of undertaking which produces accounts (eg clubs, sole traders, charities, partnerships), and may extend to forms of financial statements other than the annual report and accounts. Examples include an audit of a statement of expenditure in support of an application for a regional development grant, and a value for money audit to ensure that managers are spending money wisely.

3 Internal audit

FORWARD

Internal auditors are employees of the company whose duties are fixed by management and who report to management.

Key term

'**Internal auditing** is an independent appraisal function established within an organisation to examine and evaluate its activities as a service to the organisation. The objective of internal auditing is to assist members of the organisation in the effective discharge of their responsibilities. To this end internal auditing furnishes them with analysis, appraisals, recommendations, counsel and information concerning the activities reviewed.'(*Institute of Internal Auditors*)

3.1 Scope of internal audit

FORWARD

The scope of an internal audit varies widely and may range from systems review to implementation of corporate policies, plans and processes.

The CIMA's Official Terminology defines an audit as a systematic examination of the activities and status of an entity based primarily on investigation and analysis of its systems, controls and records. Internal audit is now defined as per the Institute of Internal Auditors, and the CIMA's own definition is currently:

'an independent appraisal function established within a organisation to examine and evaluate its activities as a service to the organisation'.

Internal audit has a much wider scope than external audit. External auditors need **only** consider whether a company's accounts give a true and fair view of its financial position. They need not comment in their audit reports on ways in which the company's results or controls could be improved.

From the definitions of the internal audit the two main features of internal audit emerge.

(a) **Independence**. Although an internal audit department is part of an organisation, it should be independent of the line management whose sphere of authority it may audit. The department should therefore report to the board or to a special internal audit committee and not to the finance director. The reason for this is best seen by thinking about what could happen if the internal audit department reported some kind of irregularity to a finance director without realising that the finance director was actually involved. The director would take the report and decide that it was all very interesting, but not worth pursuing. A very different line might be taken by another, independent director!

It is also important that internal auditors should have appropriate scope in carrying out their responsibilities, and unrestricted access to records, assets and personnel.

'In the ideal situation, the internal audit function reports to the highest level of management but also has a direct line of communication to the entity's main board or audit committee and is free of any other operating responsibility.'

(b)   **Appraisal**. Internal audit is concerned with the appraisal of work done by other people in the organisation, and internal auditors should not themselves carry out any of the work being audited. The appraisal of operations provides a service to management, providing information on strengths and weaknesses throughout the organisation. Such information is invaluable to management when it comes to taking action to improve performance, or planning future activities of the company.

3.2 Objectives of internal audit

After giving its broad definition, the Institute of Internal Auditors goes on to state the following.

'The objective of internal auditing is to assist members of the organisation in the effective discharge of their responsibilities. To this end internal auditing furnishes them with analyses, appraisals, recommendations, counsel and information concerning the activities reviewed.'

Internal audit is an important element of management control, as it is a tool used to ensure that all financial and any other internal controls are working satisfactorily. Internal auditors will investigate systems within the organisation, identify any weaknesses or scope for improvement, and make recommendations to the 'line' managers responsible for the system that they have audited.

3.3 Differences between internal and external audit

FAST FORWARD

Contrary to popular belief, it is not the responsibility of external auditors to detect fraud; they are merely obliged to plan their audit tests so that they have a reasonable expectation of detecting fraud. It is the responsibility of the **directors** to set up an adequate system of internal control to deter and expose fraud. Internal audit is one type of internal control.

There are three main differences between internal and external audit.

(a)   **Appointment**. External auditors are appointed by the shareholders (although they are usually only ratifying the directors' choice) and must be independent of the company, whereas internal auditors are employees of the organisation.

(b)   **Responsibility**. External auditors are responsible to the owners (ie shareholders, the public or Parliament), whereas internal auditors are responsible to senior management.

(c)   **Objectives**. The objectives for external auditors are defined by statute, whereas those for internal auditors are set by management. In other words, management – perhaps the internal auditors themselves – decide what parts of the organisation or what systems they are going to look at, and what type of audit should be carried out for example a systems audit, or a value for money audit.

3.4 Essential elements of internal audit

As well as *independence*, other essential elements of internal audit can be identified.

(a) **Staffing and training**

    (i)   The internal audit department should possess or have access to all the necessary skills for performing its function. It must be adequately staffed, and staff are likely to be drawn from a variety of disciplines.

    (ii)   Internal audit staff should be trained to carry out their work competently.

(b) **Relationships**

Without surrendering their objectivity, internal auditors should try to establish good working relationships and mutual understanding with:

- Management
- External auditors
- If there is one, the organisation's auditing committee

Internal audit plans should be discussed with senior management, individual audits should be arranged in consultation with the management concerned, and audit reports should be discussed with the management when they are being prepared.

Internal auditors should have regular meetings with the external auditors (who may be able to place reliance on some of the work done by the internal auditors). They should discuss their audit plans, so as to avoid unnecessary overlaps in their work.

(c) **Due care**

Internal auditors should exercise due care in fulfilling their responsibilities. The chief internal auditor should ensure that his staff maintain standards of integrity and of adequate quality in their work.

(d) **Planning, controlling and recording**

Internal auditors should plan, control and record their work.

(e) **Evidence**

Internal auditors should obtain sufficient, relevant and reliable evidence on which to base reasonable conclusions and recommendations.

Deciding just what evidence will be needed for any particular audit work calls for judgement by the auditors.

- The scope of the audit assignment
- The significance of the matters under review
- Just what evidence is available and obtainable
- What it would cost and how long it would take to obtain

(f) **Reporting**

Internal auditors should report their findings, conclusions and recommendations promptly to management.

'The chief internal auditor should ensure that reports are sent to managers who have a direct responsibility for the unit or function being audited and who have the authority to take corrective action.'

If the internal auditors find evidence of a serious weakness or malpractice, this should be reported, orally or in writing, as soon as it is discovered, in an 'interim report'.

The internal auditors, having made recommendations in their report, should subsequently follow up their work by checking to see whether their recommendations have been implemented by management.

Assessment focus point	As you will see later in this chapter, internal checks and controls should show up any discrepancies in the system. This is called **exception reporting** in that the manager's attention is brought to things that have gone wrong. In the same way, an internal auditors report should include exception reporting.

3.5 Auditing standards and guidelines

Key term	**Auditing standards** and guidelines have been issued by the Auditing Practices Board (APB) and its forerunner the Auditing Practices Committee (APC), largely for the benefit of external auditors. However, many can be applied to internal audit and used to define 'best practice'. For example, a guideline on internal control will tell a business what type of internal control they should have, and external auditors what type of internal control they should expect to find.

4 Internal control

 FAST FORWARD The eight types of internal control can be remembered by using the mnemonic SPAMSOAP.

4.1 Internal control systems

One of the main tasks of the internal auditors is to check the operational 'systems' within their organisation, to find out whether the system's **internal controls** are sufficient and are working properly. If they are not, it is the auditors' task to recommend improvements.

An **internal control system** is defined by guidance of the Committee on the Financial Aspects of Corporate Governance (Cadbury Committee) as:

Key term	'The whole system of **controls**, financial and otherwise, established in order to provide reasonable assurance of: (a) effective and efficient operations; (b) internal financial control; and (c) compliance with laws and regulations.'

The Cadbury Code is concerned with the financial aspects of corporate governance and thus principally with 'internal financial control'. This is defined as:

'the internal controls established in order to provide reasonable assurance of:

(a) the safeguarding of assets against unauthorised use or disposition; and

(b) the maintenance of proper accounting records and the reliability of financial information used within the business or for publication.'

These definitions are fairly broad, and a more comprehensive list of the range of internal controls which may exist in an organisation is given in the appendix to the old guideline of the Auditing Practices Committee *Internal Controls*. There are eight types of control listed (one way of remembering them is to use the mnemonic SPAM SOAP).

S egregation of duties

P hysical

A uthorisation and approval

M anagement

S upervision

O rganisation

A rithmetical and accounting

P ersonnel

4.2 Segregation of duties

The APC stated: 'one of the prime means of control is the separation of those responsibilities or duties which would, if combined, enable one individual to record and process a complete transaction. Segregation of duties reduces the risk of intentional manipulation or error and increases the element of checking. Functions which should be separated include those of authorisation, execution, custody, recording and, in the case of a computer-based accounting system, systems development and daily operations.'

A classic example of segregation of duties, which both internal and external auditors look for, concerns the receipt, recording and banking of cash. It is not a good idea for the person who opens the post (and 'receives' the cash) to be the person responsible for recording that the cash has arrived – and even poorer practice for him to be the person responsible for taking the cash to the bank. If these duties are not segregated, there is always the chance that he will simply pocket the cash, and nobody would be any the wiser. Dividing the duties so that no one person carries all these responsibilities is therefore a form of internal control, in this case helping to safeguard cash receipts.

4.3 Physical

These internal controls were defined by the APC as being 'concerned mainly with the custody of assets and involve procedures and security measures designed to ensure that access to assets is limited to authorised personnel. This includes both direct access and indirect access via documentation. These controls assume importance in the case of valuable, portable, exchangeable or desirable assets.' An example of a physical control is locking the cash box.

4.4 Authorisation and approval

The APC stated: 'all transactions should require authorisation or approval by an appropriate responsible person. The limits for these authorisations should be specified.'

For example, a company might set the rule that the head of a particular department may authorise revenue expenditure up to $500, but that for anything more expensive he must seek the approval of a director. Such authorisation limits will vary from company to company: $500 could be quite a large amount for a small company, but seem insignificant to a big one.

4.5 Management

The APC stated: 'these are the controls exercised by management outside the day-to-day routine of the system. They include the overall supervisory controls exercised by management, the review of management accounts and comparison thereof with budgets, the internal audit function and any other special review procedures.'

4.6 Supervision

The APC stated: 'any system of internal control should include the supervision by responsible officials of day-to-day transactions and the recording thereof.' For example, the chief accountant may review and sign a bank reconciliation each month.

4.7 Organisation

As stated by the APC: 'enterprises should have a plan of their organisation, defining and allocating responsibilities and identifying lines of reporting for all aspects of the enterprise's operations, including the controls. The delegation of authority and responsibility should be clearly specified.'

For example, it could happen that an employee in a company finds himself working for two masters, say a product manager (who is responsible for the production, marketing and profitability of one particular product) and a sales manager (who supervises the company sales policy for all products). A company which is organised in this overlapping fashion is said to have a matrix organisation. The point here is that the employee might be confused. He might not know who he is supposed to be working for at any one time; he might not know his priorities; he might work harder for one manager at the expense of the other. Such a state of affairs would be detrimental to the company, so it is sensible to set clear lines of authority and responsibility – in short, the company should utilise organisational controls.

4.8 Arithmetical and accounting

The APC stated: 'these are the controls within the recording function which check that the transactions to be recorded and processed have been authorised, that they are all included and that they are correctly recorded and accurately processed. Such controls include checking the arithmetical accuracy of the records, the maintenance and checking of totals, reconciliations, control accounts and trial balances, and accounting for documents.'

4.9 Personnel

This last type of internal control was defined by APC as:

'procedures to ensure that personnel have capabilities commensurate with their responsibilities. Inevitably, the proper functioning of any system depends on the competence and integrity of those operating it. The qualifications, selection and training as well as the innate personal characteristics of the personnel involved are important features to be considered in setting up any control system.'

As an example, a company accountant should be suitably qualified. It is no good asking somebody to produce a set of financial statements if he does not know a profit and loss account from a balance sheet. Nowadays, 'qualified' tends to mean someone who possesses a professional qualification of some sort, but it is important to remember that others are still able to do a job because of work experience – they are 'qualified' through that experience.

Question

Internal controls

The chief accountant reviewing and signing a bank reconciliation is what type of internal control?

A   Authorisation and approval
B   Management
C   Segregation of duties
D   Supervision

Answer

D is correct.

4.10 Internal control system

A company's operational systems (eg its purchasing system, its stock control system, its sales system, its capital expenditure planning system, its computerised management information systems etc) will incorporate some internal controls from the SPAM SOAP list above. The controls that there are will depend on the particular circumstances of the company, but the range of internal controls it ends up with is called the company's or the system's **internal control system**.

An operational system need not possess **all** of the SPAM SOAP internal controls – or indeed the organisation may not be able to implement all of them, perhaps because they would be too expensive and so not worth having. For example, a very small organisation may have insufficient staff to be able to organise a desirable level of segregation of duties.

Management has the responsibility for deciding what internal controls there should be. The internal auditors contribute to internal controls by measuring and evaluating the other internal controls installed by management and reporting to management on their effectiveness.

4.11 Administrative controls and accounting controls

It is useful to distinguish between administrative controls and accounting controls.

Key terms

(a)   **Administrative controls** are concerned with achieving the objectives of the organisation and with implementing policies. The controls relate to the following.

- Establishing a suitable organisation structure
- The division of managerial authority
- Reporting responsibilities
- Channels of communication

(b)   **Accounting controls** aim to provide accurate accounting records and to achieve accountability.

- The recording of transactions
- Establishing responsibilities for records, transactions and assets

Accounting controls are applied to procedures/assets and liabilities such as cash and cheques, inventories, sales and receivables, purchases and payables, non-current assets, investments, capital expenditure, and debt capital and equity.

4.12 Detect controls and prevent controls

Yet another way of analysing internal controls is to distinguish between detect controls and prevent controls.

Key terms

(a)   **Detect controls** are controls that are designed to detect errors once they have happened.

(b)   **Prevent controls** are controls that are designed to prevent errors from happening in the first place.

Examples of detect controls in an accounting system are bank reconciliations and regular checks of physical inventories against book records of inventories.

Examples of prevent controls are:

(a) Checking invoices from suppliers against goods received notes before paying the invoices.

(b) Regular checking of delivery notes against invoices, to ensure that all deliveries have been invoiced.

(c) Signing of goods received notes, credit notes, overtime records etc, to confirm that goods have actually been received, credit notes properly issued, overtime actually authorised and worked etc.

<table>
<tr><td>**Assessment focus point**</td><td>You might need to specify the types of controls you would expect to find in certain areas of operations, for example:

(a)   cash and cheques
(b)   wages and salaries
(c)   purchases and payables
(d)   sales and receivables
(e)   non-current assets
(f)   investments

These are all financial systems, but internal audit can apply to any other system, eg management information systems or decision-making systems. Controls over sales/receivables and purchases/payables will be considered below.</td></tr>
</table>

5 Controls over sales and receivables

FAST FORWARD

There are three separate elements into which sales accounting controls may be divided. They are selling (authorisation), goods outwards (custody) and accounting (recording).

5.1 Selling

(a) What arrangements are to be made to ensure that goods are sold at their correct price and to deal with and check exchanges, discounts and special reductions including those in connection with cash sales.

(b) Who is to be responsible for, and how control is to be maintained over, the granting of credit terms to customers.

(c) Who is to be responsible for accepting customers' orders and what procedure is to be adopted for issuing production orders and despatch notes.

(d) Who is to be responsible for the preparation of invoices and credit notes and what controls are to be instituted to prevent errors and irregularities (for instance, how selling prices are to be ascertained and authorised, how the issue of credit notes is to be controlled and checked, what checks there should be on prices, quantities, extensions and totals shown on invoices and credit notes, and how such documents in blank or completed form are to be protected against loss or misuse).

(e) What special controls are to be exercised over the despatch of goods free of charge or on special terms.

5.2 Goods outwards

(a) Who may authorise the despatch of goods and how is such authority evidenced.

(b) What arrangements are to be made to examine and record goods outwards (preferably this should be done by a person who has no access to inventories and has no accounting or invoicing duties).

(c) The procedure to be instituted for agreeing goods outwards records with customers' orders, despatch notes and invoices.

5.3 Accounting

So far as possible sales ledger staff should have no access to cash, cash books or stocks, and should not be responsible for invoicing and other duties normally assigned to sales staff. The following are amongst matters which should be considered.

(a) The appointment of persons as far as possible separately responsible for the following.

    (i) Recording sales and sales returns
    (ii) Maintaining customers' accounts
    (iii) Preparing receivables' statements

(b) The establishment of appropriate control procedures in connection with sales returns, price adjustments and similar matters.

(c) Arrangements to ensure that goods dispatched but not invoiced (or vice versa) during an accounting period are properly dealt with in the accounts of the periods concerned (cut-off procedures).

(d) The establishment of arrangements to deal with sales to companies or branches forming part of the same group.

(e) What procedures are to be adopted for the preparation, checking and despatch of debtors' statements and for ensuring that they are not subject to interference before despatch.

(f) How discounts granted and special terms are to be authorised and evidenced.

(g) Who is to deal with customers' queries arising in connection with statements.

(h) What procedure is to be adopted for reviewing and following up overdue accounts.

(i) Who is to authorise the writing off of bad debts, and how such authority is to be evidenced.

(j) The institution of a receivables control account and its regular checking preferably by an independent official against customers' balances on the sales ledger.

6 Controls over purchases and payables

T FORWARD

There are also three separate elements into which accounting controls may be divided in the consideration of purchase procedures. They are buying (authorisation), receipt of goods (custody) and accounting (recording).

6.1 Buying

Factors to be considered include the following.

(a) The procedure to be followed when issuing requisitions for additions to and replacement of stocks, and the persons to be responsible for such requisitions.

(b) The preparation and authorisation of purchase orders (including procedures for authorising acceptance where tenders have been submitted or prices quoted).

(c) The institution of checks for the safe-keeping of order forms and safeguarding their use.

(d) As regards capital items, any special arrangements as to authorisations required.

6.2 Goods inwards

Factors to be considered include the following.

    (a)   Arrangements for examining goods inwards as to quantity, quality and condition; and for evidencing such examination.

    (b)   The appointment of a person responsible for accepting goods, and the procedure for recording and evidencing their arrival and acceptance.

    (c)   The procedure to be instituted for checking goods inwards records against authorised purchase orders.

6.3 Accounting

Factors to be considered include the following.

    (a)   The appointment of persons so far as possible separately responsible for

        (i)   Checking suppliers' invoices.
        (ii)   Recording purchases and purchase returns.
        (iii)   Maintaining suppliers' ledger accounts or similar records.
        (iv)   Checking suppliers' statements.
        (v)   Authorising payment.

    (b)   Arrangements to ensure that before accounts are paid.

        (i)   The goods concerned have been received, accord with the purchase order, are properly priced and correctly invoiced.

        (ii)   The expenditure has been properly allocated.

        (iii)   Payment has been duly authorised by the official responsible.

 Question   **Accounting systems**

You should get into the habit of thinking about the accounting and other systems you have come across at work (or which your friends and colleagues have worked with) and trying to spot the internal controls. Ask yourself two questions.

    (a)   What could go wrong?
    (b)   How could these problems be prevented and, if not prevented, detected (cost-effectively)?

7 Evaluation of internal controls

FAST FORWARD

Internal controls need to be evaluated for adequacy and risk.

7.1 Doing the evaluation

The evaluation of internal controls within a system comes from the following sources.

    (a)   **System documentation**: ie deciding how the system works, and describing this 'on paper'.

(b) **Identification of potential errors**: ie recognising what can go wrong in this system. Potential errors can arise whenever there is a chance that one of the following objectives might not be achieved or satisfied.

(i) Existence or occurrence – ie proof that something exists or has happened.

(ii) Completeness – ie that an account balance contains every item that it should.

(iii) Valuation or measurement – ie that a proper system of valuation has been used.

(iv) Ownership – ie proof of ownership of assets.

(v) Disclosure – ie that items are disclosed whenever disclosure is appropriate.

(c) **Identification of controls:** ie recognising the controls within the system that are designed to detect or prevent errors in the system.

Having identified potential errors and the controls to detect or prevent them, the auditors can assess whether the controls appear to be good enough to do their job sufficiently well.

When a control is evaluated, the auditors must assess the level of 'risk' that the control is inadequate or might not be properly applied. Factors to consider include the following.

(a) The nature of the control itself.

(b) The timing and frequency of the control check.

(c) Who performs the control, taking into consideration the competence, experience and integrity of staff, and the degree of supervision.

(d) What errors the control has succeeded in identifying and eliminating in the past.

(e) Whether there have been changes in the system or in staff, bearing in mind that control procedures might weaken and become slack in the early period of a new system or just after a change of staff.

8 Audit trail

T FORWARD

In general terms an **audit trail** is a means by which an auditor can follow through a transaction from its origin to its ultimate location or vice versa.

8.1 Following the audit trail

In a manual accounting system an audit trail is created by preserving hard copy evidence of transactions with the hard copy of various documents being preserved and stored for future checking or evidence if required.

An example of an audit trail for purchases would be the purchase order, the goods received note, the purchase invoice, the purchase day book and the purchases account.

An audit trail can be used by both internal and external auditors 'in both directions', depending on the auditors' objective. Thus the auditors can start with a sales order and trace it through to 'sales' in the profit and loss account or can trace a sale from the income statement back through the sales account, the sales day book, the sales invoice and the despatch note to the sales order.

Special considerations apply to computerised accounting systems which are, of course, the majority. For the purposes of computerised systems an audit trail may be defined slightly differently as:

'…a record of the file updating which takes place during a specific transaction. It enables a trace to be kept of all operations on files'

(Glossary of Computing Terms of the British Computer Society)

An audit trail should ideally be provided so that every transaction on a file contains a unique reference back to the original source of the input, for example, a sales system transaction record should hold a reference to the customer order, delivery note and invoice.

Where master file records are updated several times, or from several sources, the provision of a satisfactory audit trail is more difficult but some attempt should nevertheless be made to provide one.

Question

Why is it important that all transactions should leave an audit trail?

A   So every transaction is posted

B   So every transaction can be traced through the system

C   So every transaction is authorised

D   So every transaction can be summarised

Answer

B. So every transaction can be traced from source documents and day books through to final postings to the ledgers.

9 The detection and prevention of fraud

Key term

In *Derry v Peek*, **fraud** was defined as: 'a false representation of fact made with the knowledge of its falsity, or without belief in its truth, or recklessly careless, whether it be true or false'.

The auditing guideline concerns financial fraud, and the definition runs as follows:

'The word 'irregularities' is used to refer to intentional distortions of financial statements, for whatever purpose, and to misappropriations of assets, whether or not accompanied by distortions of financial statements. Fraud is one type of irregularity. The word 'fraud' is used to refer to irregularities involving the use of criminal deception to obtain an unjust or illegal advantage.'

FAST FORWARD

In internal auditing, detection of fraud is an important objective. Auditors should be aware of the common types of fraud and should be particularly watchful when internal controls are poor.

9.1 Types of fraud

Give an employee responsibility, and he may manage the resources under his control dishonestly. The incidence of financial fraud, particularly in a computer environment, is increasing fast. This trend, together with the increasing sophistication of fraudsters, creates difficult problems for management and for internal auditors.

The mere presence of internal auditors will serve to discourage fraudsters for fear of being discovered, but the public's expectations go much further.

The profession has responded in a number of ways, not least the issue of the Auditing Practices Board's Statement of Auditing Standards SAS 110 *Fraud and error* (January 1995).

The auditors will best be able to detect frauds if they are knowledgeable (not experienced!) in the most common methods of fraud. These are as follows.

- Ghost employees on the payroll
- Miscasting of the payroll
- Stealing unclaimed wages
- Collusion with external parties
- Teeming and lading
- Altering cheques after signature
- Inflating expense claims
- Using the company's assets for personal gain
- Stealing fully depreciated assets
- Issuing false credit notes or fraudulently writing off debts
- Failing to record all sales

Ghost employees. These are imaginary employees for whom the wages department prepare wage packets which are distributed amongst the fraudsters. This type of fraud arises when there is extensive reliance on casual workers, and minimal record keeping for such workers. Inflated overtime claims can also result from poor time recording systems. Such frauds can be detected from a review of the numbers of employees required to achieve a standard amount of work. If at some times of the year a larger number appear to be required, there may be something amiss. Scrutiny of signatures given as proof of receipt of wages should also be made.

Miscasting of the payroll. This fraud often succeeds due to its simplicity. If there are twenty employees, each to be paid $100, then the computer program for the payroll could be adjusted so that an extra $50 is added to the total added up for the amounts to be paid. Thus management approve a payment of $2,050 for the period's wages, each employee gets his $100 and the fraudster collects his extra $50. Manual payroll systems can be manipulated in a similar way. When employees are paid in cash, this type of fraud can be hard to trace and all too easy to perpetrate.

Stealing **unclaimed wages** is also common. This is effectively confined to wages paid in cash and can occur when an employee leaves without notice or is away sick. In the case of a subsequent claim for unpaid wages, it could be claimed that the cash in the original pay packet was paid back into the bank.

Collusion with external parties could involve suppliers, customers or their staff. Possible frauds are overcharging on purchase invoices, undercharging on sales invoices or the sale of confidential information (eg customer lists, expansion plans) to a competitor. Management should watch out for unusual discounts or commissions being given or taken, or for an excessive zeal on the part of an employee to handle all business with a particular company.

Teeming and lading is a 'rolling' fraud rather than a 'one-off' fraud. It occurs when a clerk has the chance to misappropriate payments from receivables or to payables. Cash received by the company is borrowed by the cashier rather than being kept as petty cash or banked. (It is also possible, although riskier and more difficult to organise, to misappropriate cheques made payable to the company.) When the cashier knows that a reconciliation is to be performed, or audit visit planned, he pays the money back so that everything appears satisfactory at that point, but after the audit the teeming and lading starts again. Surprise visits by auditors and independent checking of cash balances should discourage this fraud.

A common fraud arising when one employee has sole control of the sales ledger and recording debtors' cheques is to pay cheques into a separate bank account, either by forged endorsement or by opening an account in a name similar to the employer's.

The clerk has to allocate cheques or cash received from other receivables against the account of the receivable whose payment was misappropriated. This prevents other staff from asking why the account is still overdue or from sending statements etc to the receivables. However, the misallocation has to continue as long as the money is missing. This fraud, therefore, never really stops. It can be detected by independent verification of receivables balances (eg by writing to them) and by looking at unallocated payments, if the sales ledger is organised to show this. In addition, sending out itemised monthly statements to receivables should act as a deterrent, although in a really elaborate fraud the clerk may be keeping two sets of books, so that the statements show the receivable's own analysis of amounts due and paid off in the month, but do not agree with the books.

Altering cheques and **inflating expense claims** are self-explanatory.

Using the company's assets for personal gain and stealing fully depreciated assets are both encountered in practice. Whether or not the private use of company telephones and photocopiers is a serious matter is up to the company to judge, but it may still be fraudulent. More serious examples include the sale by employees of unused time on the computer, which is a growing fraud.

Another way of avoiding detection when cash and cheques received from debtors have been misappropriated is to **issue a credit note** which is not sent to the customer (who has paid his account) but is recorded in the books. Again, the issue of itemised statements monthly should show this up, as the customer would query the credit note. However, any company with sufficiently lax controls to allow one clerk both to receive and record cash and additionally to authorise and issue credit notes is unlikely to ensure that someone else issues and follows up statements. A similar tactic is to **write a debt off** as bad to cover up the disappearance of the payment.

A very elaborate fraud may be perpetrated in a business with extremely poor controls over sales recording and minimal segregation of duties. In such circumstances, a dishonest bookkeeper may invoice customers but fail to record the invoices so that the customer's payments never have to be recorded and the misappropriation is not missed.

This type of fraud can occur where a customer is receiving large numbers of invoices from the business every month and so the bookkeeper's failure to record one or two invoices (if detected by auditors or his superiors) is simply put down to incompetence rather than fraud.

A warning sign here is the perception by customers that 'your accounts department is a mess ... always getting things wrong ... we've given up trying to get our account right...'.

9.2 The role of the internal auditors

The internal auditors should start their work by identifying the areas of the business most susceptible to fraud. These will include areas where cash is involved, and the other areas where the auditors' judgement is that the internal controls are insufficient to safeguard the assets.

The existence of a properly functioning system of internal controls will diminish the incidence of frauds, so the auditors' opinion on the internal control system is of fundamental importance.

Whenever a fraud is discovered, they should judge whether a weakness in internal controls has been highlighted, and if so what changes are needed.

9.3 Prevention of fraud

Fraud will only be prevented successfully if potential fraudsters perceive the risk of detection as being high, and if personnel are adequately screened before employment and given no incentive to turn against the company once employed. The following safeguards should therefore be implemented.

(a)   A good internal control system.
(b)   Continuous supervision of all employees.
(c)   Surprise audit visits.
(d)   Thorough personnel procedures.

The work of employees must be monitored as this will increase the perceived risk of being discovered. Actual results must regularly be compared against budgeted results, and employees should be asked to explain significant variances.

Surprise audit visits are a valuable contribution to preventing fraud. If a cashier is carrying out a teeming and lading fraud and is told that an audit visit is due the following week, he may be able to square up the books before the visit so that the auditors will find nothing wrong. But if the threat of a surprise visit is constantly present, the cashier will not be able to carry out a teeming and lading fraud without the risk of being discovered, and this risk is usually sufficient to prevent the fraud.

The auditors do not need to carry out any sophisticated audit tests during their surprise visit. There are stories of internal auditors arriving without warning, and taking all the books into a room of their own to read the newspaper for an hour – but the fraud deterrent effect on the employee is highly significant, because the employee thinks that every figure is being checked.

Finally, personnel procedures must be adequate to prevent the occurrence of frauds.

(a) Whenever a fraud is discovered, the fraudster should be dismissed and the police should be informed. Too often an employee is 'asked to resign' and then moves on to a similar job where the fraud is repeated, often because management fear loss of face or investor confidence. This is a self-defeating policy.

(b) All new employees should be required to produce adequate references from their previous employers.

(c) If an employee's lifestyle changes dramatically, explanations should be sought.

(d) Every employee must be made to take his annual holiday entitlement. Sometimes in practice the employee who is 'so dedicated that he never takes a holiday' is in fact not taking his leave for fear of his fraud being discovered by his replacement worker while he is away.

(e) Pay levels should be adequate and working conditions of a reasonable standard. If employees feel that they are being paid an unfairly low amount or 'exploited', they may look for ways to supplement their pay dishonestly.

9.4 Management fraud

So far, this chapter has concentrated on employee fraud. However, arguably more serious (and very much more difficult to prevent and detect) is the growing problem of management fraud.

While employee fraud is usually undertaken purely for the employee's financial gain, management fraud is often undertaken to improve the company's apparent performance, to reduce tax liabilities or to improve manager's promotion prospects.

Managers are often in a position to override internal controls and to intimidate their subordinates into collusion or turning a blind eye. This makes it difficult to detect such frauds. In addition, where the company is benefiting financially rather than the manager, it can be difficult to persuade staff that any dishonesty is involved.

This clash of interest between loyalty to an employer and professional integrity can be difficult to resolve and can compromise an internal auditor's independence.

Management fraud often comes to light after a take-over or on a change of audit staff or practices. Its consequences can be far reaching for the employing company in damaging its reputation or because it results in legal action. Because management usually have access to much larger sums of money than more lowly employees, the financial loss to the company can be immense.

Chapter roundup

- It is important to distinguish between ownership and stewardship.

- External auditors report to the members of the company on whether, in their opinion, the annual statutory accounts give a true and fair view. Their duties are imposed by statute and they are not employees of the company. Under International Accounting Standards, auditors report on 'fair presentation'.

- 'True and fair' is not defined in company law or accounting standards. The words are used together rather than separately and the term is generally taken to mean 'reasonably accurate and free from bias or distortion'. Under IAS, the term is 'fair presentation'.

- Internal auditors are employees of the company whose duties are fixed by management and who report to management.

- The scope of an internal audit varies widely and may range from systems review to implementation of corporate policies, plans and processes.

- Contrary to popular belief, it is not the responsibility of external auditors to detect fraud; they are merely obliged to plan their audit tests so that they have a reasonable expectation of detecting fraud. It is the responsibility of the directors to set up an adequate system of internal control to deter and expose fraud. Internal audit is one type of internal control.

- The eight types of internal control can be remembered by using the mnemonic SPAMSOAP.

- There are three separate elements into which sales accounting controls may be divided. They are selling (authorisation), goods outwards (custody) and accounting (recording).

- There are also three separate elements into which accounting controls may be divided in the consideration of purchase procedures. They are buying (authorisation), receipt of goods (custody) and accounting (recording).

- Internal controls need to be evaluated for adequacy and risk.

- In general terms an audit trail is a means by which an auditor can follow through a transaction from its origin to its ultimate location or vice versa.

- In internal auditing, detection of fraud is an important objective. Auditors should be aware of the common types of fraud and should be particularly watchful when internal controls are poor.

Quick quiz

1   The auditor's report states whether the financial statements give a 'true and fair' view. True and fair has never been statutorily defined. True or false?

2   To whom should the head of internal audit report in a large company?

    A   The finance director

    B   The chief accountant

    C   The chairman of the board of directors

    D   The external auditors

3   Which of the following statements concerning the status of an external auditor is incorrect?

    A   All companies must appoint external auditors

    B   The duties of an auditor are defined by the Companies Act 1985

    C   The auditor gives an opinion on the financial statements

    D   The auditor reports to the members of the company

4   Which of the following procedures is unlikely to be encountered in following through an 'audit trail' in a computerised accounting system?

    A   The authorisation of input documents

    B   One for one checking of master file amendments

    C   Output being completely checked against input data in a system producing budgetary control reports

    D   Authorisation of changes to a computer program

5   What is a 'teeming and lading fraud'?

    A   Stealing cash

    B   Colluding with external partners to submit false invoices

    C   Stealing cash, concealing the theft by delaying bankings or making good the shortage by transfers from other sources

    D   Altering cheques and cash receipt records to record lesser amounts and pocketing the difference

Answers to quick quiz

1   True

2   C   Correct. This is ideal, an alternative would be to report to the board or an audit committee.

     A   Independence will be compromised and recommendations possibly diluted.

     B   The chief accountant may lack authority to implement the needed changes following an internal audit review and independence may be compromised.

     D   The external auditors must not be involved in executive decisions within a client, otherwise their independence could be compromised.

3   A   Correct. Small limited companies and unincorporated businesses or partnerships need not have an external audit.

4   C   Correct. It is more usual to find output on a exceptions basis, such as the investigation of significant variances in the example given.

     A   A key element of control over input, difficult to achieve in on-line or real-time systems.

     B   An important procedure to preserve the integrity of master file data.

     D   This would be present in the systems documentation.

5   C   Correct. The characteristics of this type of fraud are theft (or 'borrowing') coupled with a scheme to conceal typically involving delayed bankings.

     A   The objective of a teeming and lading fraud is to misappropriate cash, it is how it is concealed which is unique.

     B   This is not a teeming and fraud, although it is a common type of fraud.

     D   This is a straightforward receipts fraud.

Now try the questions below from the Question Bank

Question numbers	Page
102–114	412

Part D
Interpretation of accounts

Cash flow statements

Introduction

In the long run, a profit will result in an increase in the company's cash balance but, as Keynes observed, 'in the long run we are all dead'. In the short run, **the making of a profit will not necessarily result in an increased cash balance.** The observation leads us to two questions. The first relates to the importance of the distinction between cash and profit. The second is concerned with the usefulness of the information provided by the balance sheet and income statement in the problem of deciding whether the company has, or will be able to generate, sufficient cash to finance its operations.

The importance of the **distinction between cash and profit** and the scant attention paid to this by the income statement has resulted in the development of cash flow statements.

This chapter adopts a systematic approach to the preparation of cash flow statements in examinations; you should learn this method and you will then be equipped for any problems in the exam itself.

Topic list	Syllabus references
1 IAS 7 *Cash flow statements*	D (11)
2 Preparing a cash flow statement	D (11)

1 IAS 7 Cash flow statements

Cash flow statements are a useful addition to the financial statements of a company because accounting profit is not the only indicator of performance. Cash flow statements concentrate on the sources and uses of cash and are a useful indicator of a company's liquidity and solvency.

It has been argued that 'profit' does not always give a useful or meaningful picture of a company's operations. Readers of a company's financial statements might even be **misled by a reported profit figure**.

(a) Shareholders might believe that if a company makes a profit after tax, of say, $100,000 then this is the amount which it could afford to **pay as a dividend**. Unless the company has **sufficient cash** available to stay in business and also to pay a dividend, the shareholders' expectations would be wrong.

(b) Employees might believe that if a company makes profits, it can afford to **pay higher wages** next year. This opinion may not be correct: the ability to pay wages depends on the **availability of cash**.

(c) Survival of a business entity depends not so much on profits as on its **ability to pay its debts when they fall due**. Such payments might include income statement items such as material purchases, wages, interest and taxation etc, but also capital payments for new non-current assets and the repayment of loan capital when this falls due (for example on the redemption of loan stock).

From these examples, it may be apparent that a company's performance and prospects depend not so much on the 'profits' earned in a period, but more realistically on liquidity or **cash flows**.

1.1 Funds flow and cash flow

Some countries, either currently or in the past, have required the disclosure of additional statements based on **funds flow** rather than cash flow. However, the definition of 'funds' can be very vague and such statements often simply require a rearrangement of figures already provided in the balance sheet and income statement. By contrast, a statement of cash flows is unambiguous and provides information which is additional to that provided in the rest of the accounts. It also lends itself to organisation by activity and not by balance sheet classification.

Cash flow statements are frequently given as an **additional statement**, supplementing the balance sheet, income statement and related notes. The group aspects of cash flow statements (and certain complex matters) have been excluded as they are beyond the scope of your syllabus.

1.2 Objective of IAS 7

The aim of IAS 7 is to provide information to users of financial statements about an entity's **ability to generate cash and cash equivalents**, as well as indicating the cash needs of the entity. The cash flow statement provides *historical* information about cash and cash equivalents, classifying cash flows between operating, investing and financing activities.

1.3 Scope

A cash flow statement should be presented as an **integral part** of an entity's financial statements. All types of entity can provide useful information about cash flows as the need for cash is universal, whatever the nature of their revenue-producing activities. Therefore **all entities are required by the standard to produce a cash flow statement.**

1.4 Benefits of cash flow information

The use of cash flow statements is very much **in conjunction** with the rest of the financial statements.

Users can gain further appreciation of the change in net assets, of the entity's financial position (liquidity and solvency) and the entity's ability to adapt to changing circumstances by adjusting the amount and timing of cash flows. Cash flow statements

enhance comparability as they are not affected by differing accounting policies used for the same type of transactions or events.

Cash flow information of a historical nature can be used as an indicator of the amount, timing and certainty of future cash flows. Past forecast cash flow information can be **checked for accuracy** as actual figures emerge. The relationship between profit and cash flows can be analysed as can changes in prices over time. All this information helps management to control costs by controlling cash flow.

1.5 Definitions

The standard gives the following definitions, the most important of which are **cash** and **cash equivalents**.

Key terms

- **Cash** comprises cash on hand and demand deposits.
- **Cash equivalents** are short-term, highly liquid investments that are readily convertible to known amounts of cash and which are subject to an insignificant risk of changes in value.
- **Cash flows** are inflows and outflows of cash and cash equivalents.
- **Operating activities** are the principal revenue-producing activities of the enterprise and other activities that are not investing or financing activities.
- **Investing activities** are the acquisition and disposal of non-current assets and other investments not included in cash equivalents.
- **Financing activities** are activities that result in changes in the size and composition of the equity capital and borrowings of the entity.

(IAS 7)

1.6 Cash and cash equivalents

The standard expands on the definition of cash equivalents: they are not held for investment or other long-term purposes, but rather to meet short-term cash commitments. To fulfil the above definition, an investment's **maturity date should normally be three months from its acquisition date**. It would usually be the case then that equity investments (ie shares in other companies) are *not* cash equivalents. An exception would be where redeemable preference shares were acquired with a very close redemption date.

Loans and other borrowings from banks are classified as investing activities. In some countries, however, **bank overdrafts** are repayable on demand and are treated as part of an enterprise's total cash management system. In these circumstances an overdrawn balance will be included in cash and cash equivalents. Such banking arrangements are characterised by a balance which fluctuates between overdrawn and credit.

Movements between different types of cash and cash equivalent are not included in cash flows. The investment of surplus cash in cash equivalents is part of cash management, not part of operating, investing or financing activities.

1.7 Presentation of a cash flow statement

IAS 7 requires cash flow statements to report cash flows during the period classified by **operating, investing and financing activities**.

1.8 Example: Simple cash flow statement

Flail Co commenced trading on 1 January 20X1 with a medium-term loan of $21,000 and a share issue which raised $35,000. The company purchased non-current assets for $21,000 cash, and during the year to 31 December 20X1 entered into the following transactions.

(a)   Purchases from suppliers were $19,500, of which $2,550 was unpaid at the year end.

(b)   Wages and salaries amounted to $10,500, of which $750 was unpaid at the year end.

(c)   Interest on the loan of $2,100 was fully paid in the year and a repayment of $5,250 was made.

(d)   Sales turnover was $29,400, including $900 receivables at the year end.

(e)   Interest on cash deposits at the bank amounted to $75.

(f)   A dividend of $4,000 was proposed as at 31 December 20X1.

You are required to prepare a historical cash flow statement for the year ended 31 December 20X1.

Solution

FLAIL CO
CASH FLOW STATEMENT FOR
THE YEAR ENDED 31 DECEMBER 20X1

	$	$
Cash flows from operating activities		
Cash received from customers ($29,400 – $900)	28,500	
Cash paid to suppliers ($19,500 – $2,550)	(16,950)	
Cash paid to and on behalf of employees ($10,500 – $750)	(9,750)	
Interest paid	(2,100)	
Interest received	75	
Net cash flows from operating activities		(225)
Investing activities		
Purchase of non-current assets		(21,000)

	$	$
Financing activities		
Issue of shares	35,000	
Proceeds from medium-term loan	21,000	
Repayment of medium-term loan	(5,250)	
Net cash flows from financing activities		50,750
Net increase in cash and cash equivalents		29,525
Cash and cash equivalents at 1 January 20X1		–
Cash and cash equivalents at 31 December 20X1		29,525

Note that the dividend is only proposed and so there is no related cash flow in 20X1.

Question	**Cash flow statement 1**

The managers of Flail Co have the following information in respect of projected cash flows for the year to 31 December 20X2.

(a)   Non-current asset purchases for cash will be $3,000.

(b)   Further expenses will be:

   (i)   purchases from suppliers – $18,750 ($4,125 owed at the year end).
   (ii)   wages and salaries – $11,250 ($600 owed at the year end).
   (iii) loan interest – $1,575.

(c)   Turnover will be $36,000 ($450 debtors at the year end).

(d)   Interest on bank deposits will be $150.

(e)   A further capital repayment of $5,250 will be made on the loan.

(f)   A dividend of $5,000 will be proposed and last year's final dividend paid.

(g)   Income taxes of $2,300 will be paid in respect of 20X1.

Prepare the cash flow forecast for the year to 31 December 20X2.

Answer

FLAIL CO
STATEMENT OF FORECAST CASH FLOWS FOR
THE YEAR ENDING 31 DECEMBER 20X2

	$	$
Cash flows from operating activities		
Cash received from customers	36,450	
($36,000 + $900 − $450)		
Cash paid to suppliers ($18,750 + $2,550 − $4,125)	(17,175)	
Cash paid to and on behalf of employees		
($11,250 + $750 − $600)	(11,400)	
Interest paid	(1,575)	
Interest received	150	
Taxation	(2,300)	
Net cash flows from operating activities		4,150
Investing activities		
Purchase of non-current assets		(3,000)
Financing activities		
Repayment of medium-term loan	(5,250)	
Dividend payment	(4,000)	
Cash flows from financing activities		(9,250)
Forecast net decrease in cash and cash		
equivalents at 31 December 20X2		(8,100)
Cash and cash equivalents as at 31 December 20X1		29,525
Forecast cash and cash equivalents as at 31 December 20X2		21,425

The manner of presentation of cash flows from operating, investing and financing activities **depends on the nature of the enterprise**. By classifying cash flows between different activities in this way users can see the impact on cash and cash equivalents of each one, and their relationships with each other. We can look at each in more detail.

1.8.1 Operating activities

This is perhaps the key part of the cash flow statement because it shows whether, and to what extent, companies can **generate cash from their operations**. It is these operating cash flows which must, in the end pay for all cash outflows relating to other activities, ie paying loan interest, dividends and so on.

Most of the components of cash flows from operating activities will be those items which **determine the net profit or loss of the enterprise**, ie they relate to the main revenue-producing activities of the enterprise. The standard gives the following as examples of cash flows from operating activities.

(a) Cash receipts from the sale of goods and the rendering of services
(b) Cash receipts from royalties, fees, commissions and other revenue
(c) Cash payments to suppliers for goods and services
(d) Cash payments to and on behalf of employees

Certain items may be included in the net profit or loss for the period which do *not* relate to operational cash flows, for example the profit or loss on the sale of a piece of plant will be included in net profit or loss, but the cash flows will be classed as **financing**.

1.8.2 Investing activities

The cash flows classified under this heading show the extent of new investment in **assets which will generate future profit and cash flows**. The standard gives the following examples of cash flows arising from investing activities.

(a)   Cash payments to acquire property, plant and equipment, intangibles and other non-current assets, including those relating to capitalised development costs and self-constructed property, plant and equipment

(b)   Cash receipts from sales of property, plant and equipment, intangibles and other non-current assets

(c)   Cash payments to acquire shares or debentures of other enterprises

(d)   Cash receipts from sales of shares or debentures of other enterprises

(e)   Cash advances and loans made to other parties

(f)   Cash receipts from the repayment of advances and loans made to other parties

1.8.3 Financing activities

This section of the cash flow statement shows the share of cash which the enterprise's capital providers have claimed during the period. This is an indicator of **likely future interest and dividend payments**. The standard gives the following examples of cash flows which might arise under these headings.

(a)   Cash proceeds from issuing shares

(b)   Cash payments to owners to acquire or redeem the enterprise's shares

(c)   Cash proceeds from issuing debentures, loans, notes, bonds, mortgages and other short or long-term borrowings

(d)   Cash repayments of amounts borrowed

1.9 Reporting cash flows from operating activities

The standard offers a choice of method for this part of the cash flow statement.

(a)   **Direct method:** disclose major classes of gross cash receipts and gross cash payments

(b)   **Indirect method**: net profit or loss is adjusted for the effects of transactions of a non-cash nature, any deferrals or accruals of past or future operating cash receipts or payments, and items of income or expense associated with investing or financing cash flows

The **direct method is the preferred method** because it discloses information, not available elsewhere in the financial statements, which could be of use in estimating future cash flows. The example below shows both methods.

1.9.1 Using the direct method

There are different ways in which the **information about gross cash receipts and payments** can be obtained. The most obvious way is simply to extract the information from the accounting records. This may be a laborious task, however, and the indirect method below may be easier. The example and question above used the direct method.

1.9.2 Using the indirect method

This method is undoubtedly **easier** from the point of view of the preparer of the cash flow statement. The net profit or loss for the period is adjusted for the following.

(a)   Changes during the period in inventories, operating receivables and payables

(b)   Non-cash items, eg depreciation, provisions, profits/losses on the sales of assets

(c)   Other items, the cash flows from which should be classified under investing or financing activities.

A **proforma** of such a calculation is as follows and this method may be more common in the exam.

	$
Profit before interest and tax (income statement)*	X
Add depreciation	X
Loss (profit) on sale of non-current assets	X
(Increase)/decrease in inventories	(X)/X
(Increase)/decrease in receivables	(X)/X
Increase/(decrease) in payables	X/(X)
Cash generated from operations	X
Interest (paid)/received	(X)
Income taxes paid	(X)
Net cash flows from operating activities	X

* Take profit before tax and add back any interest expense

It is important to understand why **certain items are added and others subtracted**. Note the following points.

(a) Depreciation is not a cash expense, but is deducted in arriving at the profit figure in the income statement. It makes sense, therefore, to eliminate it by adding it back.

(b) By the same logic, a loss on a disposal of a non-current asset (arising through underprovision of depreciation) needs to be added back and a profit deducted.

(c) An increase in inventories means less cash – you have spent cash on buying inventory.

(d) An increase in receivables means the company's receivables have not paid as much, and therefore there is less cash.

(e) If we pay off payables, causing the figure to decrease, again we have less cash.

1.9.3 Indirect versus direct

The direct method is encouraged where the necessary information is not too costly to obtain, but IAS 7 does not demand it. In practice, therefore, the direct method is rarely used. It could be argued that companies ought to monitor their cash flows carefully enough on an ongoing basis to be able to use the direct method at minimal extra cost.

1.10 Interest and dividends

Cash flows from interest and dividends received and paid should each be **disclosed separately**. Each should be classified in a consistent manner from period to period as either operating, investing or financing activities.

Dividends paid by the enterprise can be classified in **one of two ways**.

(a) As a **financing cash flow**, showing the cost of obtaining financial resources.

(b) As a component of **cash flows from operating activities** so that users can assess the enterprise's ability to pay dividends out of operating cash flows.

1.11 Taxes on income

Cash flows arising from taxes on income should be **separately disclosed** and should be classified as cash flows from operating activities *unless* they can be specifically identified with financing and investing activities.

Taxation cash flows are often **difficult to match** to the originating underlying transaction, so most of the time all tax cash flows are classified as arising from operating activities.

1.12 Components of cash and cash equivalents

The components of cash and cash equivalents should be disclosed and a **reconciliation** should be presented, showing the amounts in the cash flow statement reconciled with the equivalent items reported in the balance sheet.

It is also necessary to disclose the **accounting policy** used in deciding the items included in cash and cash equivalents, in accordance with IAS 1 *Presentation of financial statements*, but also because of the wide range of cash management practices worldwide.

1.13 Other disclosures

All enterprises should disclose, together with a **commentary by management**, any other information likely to be of importance, for example:

(a)   restrictions on the use of or access to any part of cash equivalents;

(b)   the amount of undrawn borrowing facilities which are available; and

(c)   Cash flows which increased operating capacity compared to cash flows which merely maintained operating capacity.

1.14 Example of a cash flow statement

In the next section we will look at the procedures for preparing a cash flow statement. First, look at this **example**, adapted from the example given in the standard (which is based on a group and therefore beyond the scope of your syllabus).

1.14.1 Direct method

CASH FLOW STATEMENT (DIRECT METHOD)
YEAR ENDED 20X7

	$m	$m
Cash flows from operating activities		
Cash receipts from customers	30,330	
Cash paid to suppliers and employees	(27,600)	
Cash generated from operations	2,730	
Interest paid	(270)	
Income taxes paid	(900)	
Net cash from operating activities		1,560
Cash flows from investing activities		
Purchase of property, plant and equipment	(900)	
Proceeds from sale of equipment	20	
Interest received	200	
Dividends received	200	
Net cash used in investing activities		(480)
Cash flows from financing activities		
Proceeds from issuance of share capital	250	
Proceeds from long-term borrowings	250	
Dividends paid*	(1,290)	
Net cash used in financing activities		(790)
Net increase in cash and cash equivalents		290
Cash and cash equivalents at beginning of period (Note)		120
Cash and cash equivalents at end of period (Note)		410

* This could also be shown as an operating cash flow

1.14.2 Indirect method

CASH FLOW STATEMENT (INDIRECT METHOD)
YEAR ENDED 20X7

	$m	$m
Cash flows from operating activities		
Net profit before taxation	3,570	
Adjustments for:		
Depreciation	450	
Investment income	(500)	
Interest expense	400	
Operating profit before working capital changes	3,920	
Increase in trade and other receivables	(500)	
Decrease in inventories	1,050	
Decrease in trade payables	(1,740)	
Cash generated from operations	2,730	
Interest paid	(270)	
Income taxes paid	(900)	
Net cash from operating activities		1,560

	$m	$m
Cash flows from investing activities		
Purchase of property, plant and equipment	(900)	
Proceeds from sale of equipment	20	
Interest received	200	
Dividends received	200	
Net cash used in investing activities		(480)
Cash flows from financing activities		
Proceeds from issuance of share capital	250	
Proceeds from long-term borrowings	250	
Dividends paid*	(1,290)	
Net cash used in financing activities		(790)
Net increase in cash and cash equivalents		290
Cash and cash equivalents at beginning of period (Note)		120
Cash and cash equivalents at end of period (Note)		410

* This could also be shown as an operating cash flow

The following note is required to both versions of the statement.

Note: Cash and cash equivalents

Cash and cash equivalents consist of cash on hand and balances with banks, and investments in money market instruments. Cash and cash equivalents included in the cash flow statement comprise the following balance sheet amounts.

	20X7	20X6
	$m	$m
Cash on hand and balances with banks	40	25
Short-term investments	370	95
Cash and cash equivalents	410	120

The company has undrawn borrowing facilities of $2,000 of which only $700 may be used for future expansion.

Assessment focus point	In practice, cash flow statements are usually prepared using the indirect method.

2 Preparing a cash flow statement

FAST FORWARD You need to be aware of the **format** of the statement as laid out in IAS 7. Setting out the format is the first step. Then follow the **step-by-step preparation procedure**.

In essence, preparing a cash flow statement is very straightforward. You should therefore simply learn the format and apply the steps noted in the example below. Note that the following items are treated in a way that might seem confusing, but the treatment is logical if you **think in terms of cash**.

(a) **Increase in inventory** is treated as **negative** (in brackets). This is because it represents a cash **outflow**; cash is being spent on inventory.

(b) An **increase in receivables** would be treated as **negative** for the same reasons; more receivables means less cash.

(c) By contrast an **increase in payables is positive** because cash is being retained and not used to settle accounts payable. There is therefore more of it.

2.1 Example: Preparation of a cash flow statement

Colby Co's income statement for the year ended 31 December 20X2 and balance sheets at 31 December 20X1 and 31 December 20X2 were as follows.

COLBY CO
INCOME STATEMENT FOR THE YEAR ENDED 31 DECEMBER 20X2

	$'000	$'000
Sales		720
Raw materials consumed	70	
Staff costs	94	
Depreciation	118	
Loss on disposal of non-current asset	18	
		(300)
		420
Interest payable		(28)
Profit before tax		392
Taxation		(124)
Profit for the period		268

COLBY CO
BALANCE SHEETS AS AT 31 DECEMBER

	20X2		20X1	
	$'000	$'000	$'000	$'000
Assets				
Property, plant and equipment				
Cost	1,596		1,560	
Depreciation	318		224	
		1,278		1,336
Current assets				
Inventory	24		20	
Trade receivables	76		58	
Bank	48		56	
		148		134
Total assets		1,426		1,470
Equity and liabilities				
Capital and reserves				
Share capital	360		340	
Share premium	36		24	
Retained earnings	686		490	
		1,082		854
Non-current liabilities				
Non-current loans		200		500
Current liabilities				
Trade payables	12		6	
Taxation	102		86	
Proposed dividend	30		24	
		144		116
		1,426		1,470

During the year, the company paid $90,000 for a new piece of machinery.

Dividends paid and proposed for the year (before the balance sheet date) totalled $72,000.

Required

Prepare a cash flow statement for Colby Co for the year ended 31 December 20X2 in accordance with the requirements of IAS 7, using the indirect method.

Solution

Step 1   **Set out the proforma cash flow statement** with the headings required by IAS 7. You should leave plenty of space. Ideally, use three or more sheets of paper, one for the main statement, one for the notes and one for your workings. It is obviously essential to know the formats very well.

Step 2   Begin with the **reconciliation of profit before tax to net cash from operating activities** as far as possible. When preparing the statement from balance sheets, you will usually have to calculate such items as depreciation, loss on sale of non-current assets, profit for the year and tax paid (see Step 4). Note that you may not be given the tax charge in the income statement. You will then have to assume that the tax paid in the year is last year's year-end provision and calculate the charge as the balancing figure.

Step 3   Calculate the cash flow figures for **dividends paid, purchase or sale of non-current assets, issue of shares and repayment of loans** if these are not already given to you (as they may be).

Step 4   If you are not given the profit figure, open up a **working for the trading, income and expense account**. Using the opening and closing balances, the taxation charge and dividends paid and proposed, you will be able to calculate profit for the year as the balancing figure to put in the net profit to net cash flow from operating activities section.

Step 5   You will now be able to **complete the statement** by slotting in the figures given or calculated.

COLBY CO
CASH FLOW STATEMENT FOR THE YEAR ENDED 31 DECEMBER 20X2

	$'000	$'000
Net cash flow from operating activities		
Profit before tax	392	
Depreciation charges	118	
Loss on sale of property, plant and equipment	18	
Interest expense	28	
Increase in inventories	(4)	
Increase in receivables	(18)	
Increase in payables	6	
Cash generated from operations	540	
Interest paid	(28)	
Dividends paid (72 – 30 + 24)	(66)	
Tax paid (86 + 124 – 102)	(108)	
Net cash flow from operating activities		338
Cash flows from investing activities		
Payments to acquire property, plant and equipment	(90)	
Receipts from sales property, plant and equipment	12	
Net cash outflow from investing activities		(78)
Cash flows from financing activities		
Issues of share capital (360 + 36 – 340 – 24)	32	
Long-term loans repaid (500 – 200)	(300)	
Net cash flows from financing		(268)
Decrease in cash and cash equivalents		(8)
Cash and cash equivalents at 1.1.X2		56
Cash and cash equivalents at 31.12.X2		48

Working: property, plant and equipment

COST

	$'000		$'000
At 1.1.X2	1,560	At 31.12.X2	1,596
Purchases	90	Disposals (balance)	54
	1,650		1,650

ACCUMULATED DEPRECIATION

	$'000		$'000
At 31.1.X2	318	At 1.1.X2	224
Depreciation on disposals		Charge for year	118
(balance)	24		
	342		342

NBV of disposals	30
Net loss reported	(18)
Proceeds of disposals	12

Cash flow statement 2

Set out below are the financial statements of Shabnum Co. You are the financial controller, faced with the task of implementing IAS 7 *Cash flow statements*.

SHABNUM CO
INCOME STATEMENT FOR THE YEAR ENDED 31 DECEMBER 20X2

	$'000
Revenue	2,553
Cost of sales	(1,814)
Gross profit	739
Distribution costs	(125)
Administrative expenses	(264)
	350
Interest received	25
Interest paid	(75)
Profit before taxation	300
Taxation	(140)
Profit for the period	160

SHABNUM CO
BALANCE SHEETS AS AT 31 DECEMBER

	20X2	20X1
Assets	$'000	$'000
Non-current assets		
Property, plant and equipment	380	305
Intangible assets	250	200
Investments	–	25
Current assets		
Inventories	150	102
Receivables	390	315
Short-term investments	50	–
Cash in hand	2	1
Total assets	1,222	948

	$'000	$'000
Equity and liabilities		
Equity		
Share capital ($1 ordinary shares)	200	150
Share premium account	160	150
Revaluation reserve	100	91
Retained earnings	160	100
Non-current liabilities		
Loan	170	50
Current liabilities		
Trade payables	127	119
Bank overdraft	85	98
Taxation	120	110
Dividends proposed	100	80
Total equity and liabilities	1,222	948

The following information is available.

(a)   The proceeds of the sale of non-current asset investments amounted to $30,000.

(b)   Fixtures and fittings, with an original cost of $85,000 and a net book value of $45,000, were sold for $32,000 during the year.

(c)   The following information relates to property, plant and equipment

	31.12.20X2	31.12.20X1
	$'000	$'000
Cost	720	595
Accumulated depreciation	340	290
Net book value	380	305

(d)   50,000 $1 ordinary shares were issued during the year at a premium of 20c per share.

(e)   Dividends for 20X2 were declared before the balance sheet date. No payment has yet been made.

Required

Prepare a cash flow statement for the year to 31 December 20X2 using the format laid out in IAS 7.

Answer

SHABNUM CO
CASH FLOW STATEMENT FOR THE YEAR ENDED 31 DECEMBER 20X2

	$'000	$'000
Net cash flows from operating activities		
Profit before tax	300	
Depreciation charge (W1)	90	
Interest expense	50	
Loss on sale of property, plant and equipment (45 – 32)	13	
Profit on sale of non-current asset investments	(5)	
(Increase)/decrease in inventories	(48)	
(Increase)/decrease in receivables	(75)	
Increase/(decrease) in payables	8	
Cash generated from operating activities	333	
Interest received	25	
Interest paid	(75)	
Dividends paid	(80)	
Tax paid (110 + 140 – 120)	(130)	
Net cash flow from operating activities		73

	$'000	$'000
Cash flows from investing activities		
Payments to acquire property, plant and equipment (W2)	(201)	
Payments to acquire intangible non-current assets	(50)	
Receipts from sales of property, plant and equipment	32	
Receipts from sale of non-current asset investments	30	
Net cash flows from investing activities		(189)
Cash flows from financing activities		
Issue of share capital	60	
Long-term loan	120	
Net cash flows from financing		180
Increase in cash and cash equivalents (Note)		64
Cash and cash equivalents at 1.1 X2 (Note)		(97)
Cash and cash equivalents at 31.12.X2 (Note)		(33)

NOTES TO THE CASH FLOW STATEMENT

Note: analysis of the balances of cash and cash equivalents as shown in the balance sheet

	20X2 $'000	20X1 $'000	Change in year $'000
Cash in hand	2	1	1
Short term investments	50		50
Bank overdraft	(85)	(98)	13
	(33)	(97)	64

Workings

1   *Depreciation charge*

	$'000	$'000
Depreciation at 31 December 20X2		340
Depreciation 31 December 20X1	290	
Depreciation on assets sold (85 – 45)	40	
		250
Charge for the year		90

2   *Purchase of property, plant and equipment*

PROPERTY, PLANT AND EQUIPMENT

	$'000		$'000
1.1.X2 Balance b/d	595	Disposals	85
Revaluation (100 – 91)	9		
Purchases (bal fig)	201	31.12.X2 Balance c/d	720
	805		805

2.2 The advantages of cash flow accounting

The advantages of cash flow accounting are as follows.

(a)   Survival in business depends on the **ability to generate** cash. Cash flow accounting directs attention towards this critical issue.

(b)   Cash flow is **more comprehensive** than 'profit' which is dependent on accounting conventions and concepts.

(c)   **Lenders** (long and short-term) are more interested in an enterprise's ability to repay them than in its profitability. Whereas 'profits' might indicate that cash is likely to be available, cash flow accounting is more direct with its message.

(d)   Cash flow reporting provides a better means of **comparing the results** of different companies than traditional profit reporting.

(e)   Cash flow reporting **satisfies the needs of all users** better.

   (i)   For **management**, it provides the sort of information on which decisions should be taken: (in management accounting, 'relevant costs' to a decision are future cash flows); traditional profit accounting does not help with decision-making.

   (ii)   For **shareholders and auditors**, cash flow accounting can provide a satisfactory basis for stewardship accounting.

(iii)   As described previously, the information needs of **lenders and employees** will be better served by cash flow accounting.

(f)   Cash flow forecasts are **easier to prepare**, as well as more useful, than profit forecasts.

(g)   They can in some respects be **audited more easily** than accounts based on the accruals concept.

(h)   The accruals concept is confusing, and cash flows are **more easily understood**.

(i)   Cash flow accounting should be both retrospective, and also include a forecast for the future. This is of **great information value** to all users of accounting information.

(j)   **Forecasts** can subsequently be **monitored** by the publication of variance statements which compare actual cash flows against the forecast.

Question   Cash flow accounting

Can you think of some possible disadvantages of cash flow accounting?

Answer

The main disadvantages of cash accounting are essentially the advantages of accruals accounting (proper matching of related items). There is also the practical problem that few businesses keep historical cash flow information in the form needed to prepare a historical cash flow statement and so extra record keeping is likely to be necessary.

2.3 Criticisms of IAS 7

The inclusion of **cash equivalents** has been criticised because it does not reflect the way in which businesses are managed: in particular, the requirement that to be a cash equivalent an investment has to be within three months of maturity is considered **unrealistic**.

The management of assets similar to cash (ie 'cash equivalents') is not distinguished from other investment decisions.

Assessment focus point | You could be asked to calculate the cash flow from any section.

Question   Operating cash flow

What is the cash flow from operating activities?

A   Profit adjusted for non-cash items.
B   Cash from selling non-current assets
C   Cash from issuing long-term loans
D   Cash from the issue of share capital

Answer

A. Cash flow from operating activities is the profit adjusted to remove non-cash items such as depreciation.

Chapter roundup

- **Cash flow statements** are a useful addition to the financial statements of companies because it is recognised that accounting profit is not the only indicator of a company's performance.

- Cash flow statements concentrate on the sources and uses of cash and are a useful indicator of a company's **liquidity and solvency**.

- You need to be aware of the **format** of the statement as laid out in **IAS 7.** Setting out the format is the first step. then follow the **step-by-step preparation procedure**.

Quick quiz

1   What is the objective of IAS 7?

2   What are the benefits of cash flow information according to IAS 7?

3   Define cash and cash equivalents according to IAS 7.

4   Which of the following headings is not a classification of cash flows in IAS 7?

  A   Operating
  B   Investing
  C   Administration
  D   Financing

5   What is the 'indirect method' of preparing a cash flow statement?

6   Set out the five steps required in preparing a cash flow statement.

7   What are the advantages of cash flow accounting?

Answers to quick quiz

1   To provide information to users about the company's ability to generate cash and cash equivalents.

2   Further information is available about liquidation and solvency, of the change in net assets, the ability to adapt to changing circumstances and comparability between enterprises.

3   See Para 1.5, Key Terms.

4   C. Administration costs are a classification in the income statement, not the cash flow statement.

5   The operating cash flow is arrived at by adjusting net profits (or loss) for non-cash items and changes in inventories, operating receivables and operating payables.

6   See Paragraph 2.1.

7   See Paragraph 2.2.

Now try the questions below from the Question Bank

Question numbers	Page
115–119	414

BPP
LEARNING MEDIA

Interpreting company accounts

Introduction

So far your studies have concentrated on the **preparation** of accounts. This chapter focuses on **interpretation** primarily by means of ratio analysis.

The purpose of financial statement analysis is to aid decision-making. The financial statements help interested persons decide on questions such as whether to lend a business money or invest in its shares.

It has already been mentioned (in Chapter 1) that the users of financial statements extend beyond present and potential shareholders and payables and include such groups as employees, government bodies and society at large. We will not attempt to deal with the possible decision needs of each class of user - such a discussion would require a book of its own. Instead we will concentrate on three aspects relevant to all groups of users, namely its profitability, liquidity and gearing. The topics will be discussed in terms of limited companies, but it should be realised that most of the points will be relevant when examining the accounts of other business entities.

Topic list	Syllabus references
1 Ratio analysis	D (10)
2 Profit margin, asset turnover and return on capita employed	D (10)
3 Working capital	D (10)
4 Liquidity	D (10)
5 Gearing	D (10)
6 Items in company accounts formats	D (10)

1 Ratio analysis

> Ratio analysis is the calculation of ratios (eg profit margin) from a set of financial statements which is used for comparison with either earlier years or similar businesses to provide information for decision-making.

1.1 Comparing different businesses

When ratio analysis is used to assess the relative strength of a particular business, by comparing its profitability and financial stability with another business, the two businesses should be largely similar.

- In size
- In their line of activities

If the businesses are not broadly similar in size or in what they do, then differences revealed by ratio analysis might merely arise as a natural consequence of the size difference, or the varying lines of business they operate in. We do not need ratios to tell us that one business is larger, or that two businesses operate in entirely different industries!

2 Profit margin, asset turnover and return on capital employed

2.1 Profit margin

Key term

> **Profit margin.** This is the ratio of profit to sales, and may also be called 'profit percentage' or 'profit to turnover ratio'. It is calculated as $\dfrac{\text{Net or gross profit}}{\text{Sales}} \times 100\%$

For example, if a company makes a profit of $20,000 on sales of $100,000 its profit percentage or profit margin is 20%. This also means that its costs are 80% of sales. A high profit margin indicates.

(a) **Either** costs are being kept well under control because if the ratio of costs:sales goes down, the profit margin will automatically go up. For example, if the costs:sales ratio changes from 80% to 75%, the profit margin will go up from 20% to 25%.

(b) **Or** sales prices are high. For example, if a company sells goods for $100,000 and makes a profit of $16,000 costs would be $84,000 and the profit margin is 16%. Now if the company can raise selling prices by 20% to $120,000 without affecting the volume of goods sold or their costs, profits would rise by the amount of revenue increase ($20,000) to $36,000 and the profit margin would also rise (from 16% to 30%).

2.2 Asset turnover

Key term

> **Asset turnover.** This is the ratio of sales in a year to the amount of net assets (capital) employed. It is calculated as $\dfrac{\text{Sales}}{\text{Net assets or capital employed}}$

For example, if a company has sales in 20X4 of $720,000 and has assets of $360,000, the asset turnover will be

$$\frac{\$720,000}{\$360,000} = 2 \text{ times.}$$

This means that for every $1 of assets employed, the company can generate sales turnover of $2 per annum. To utilise assets more efficiently, managers should try to create a higher volume of sales and so a higher asset turnover ratio. For example, suppose that our firm with assets of $360,000 can increase its sales turnover from $720,000 to $900,000 per annum. The asset turnover would improve to

$$\frac{\$900,000}{\$360,000} = 2.5 \text{ times.}$$

The significance of this improvement is that if a business can create more sales turnover from the same amount of assets it should make larger profits (because of the increase in sales) without having to increase the size of its investment.

2.3 Return on Capital Employed

Key term

> **Return on capital employed (ROCE)** is the amount of profit as a percentage of capital employed. It is calculated as
>
> $$\frac{\text{Profit}}{\text{Capital employed or net assets}} \times 100\%$$

Return in an investing sense means a reward for investing in a business.

If a company makes a profit of $30,000, we do not know how good or bad this profit is until we look at the amount of capital which has been invested to achieve the profit. $30,000 might be a good-sized profit for a small firm, but it would not be good enough for a 'giant' firm such as Marks and Spencer.

For this reason, it is helpful to measure performance by relating profits to the amount of capital employed, and because this seems to be the **only** satisfactory ratio or percentage which judges profits in relation to the size of the business, it is sometimes called the **primary ratio** in financial analysis.

Question

Ratios

A business has the following results

Sales	$450,000
Profit	$100,000
Net assets	$400,000

Calculate:

(a)   The profit margin
(b)   Asset turnover
(c)   Return on capital employed

Answer

(a) $\dfrac{\$100,000}{\$450,000} \times 100\% = 22.22\%$

(b) $\dfrac{\$450,000}{\$400,000} = 1.125 \text{ times}$

(c) $\dfrac{100,000}{400,000} \times 100\% = 25\%$

2.4 Relationship between ratios

You may already have realised that there is a mathematical connection between return on capital employed, profit margin and asset turnover, since sales in the right-hand side of the equation below cancel out.

Formula to learn

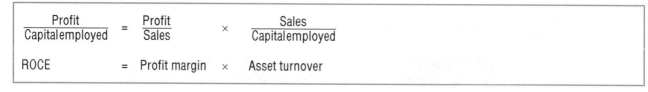

$$\frac{\text{Profit}}{\text{Capital employed}} = \frac{\text{Profit}}{\text{Sales}} \times \frac{\text{Sales}}{\text{Capital employed}}$$

ROCE = Profit margin × Asset turnover

Assessment focus point

You **must** learn these formulae, as they will not be given in the assessment.

This is important. If we accept that ROCE is the most important single measure of business performance, comparing profit with the amount of capital invested, we can go on to say that business performance is dependent on two separate 'subsidiary' factors, each of which contributes to ROCE.

(a)   Profit margin.

(b)   Asset turnover.

For this reason, just as ROCE is sometimes called the **primary ratio**, the profit margin and asset turnover ratios are sometimes called the **secondary ratios**.

The implications of this relationship must be understood. Suppose that a return on capital employed of 20% is thought to be a good level of business performance in the retail trade for electrical goods.

(a)   Company A might decide to sell its products at a fairly high price and make a profit margin on sales of 10%. It would then need only an asset turnover of 2.0 times to achieve a ROCE of 20%:

   20% = 10% × 2

(b)   Company B might decide to cut its prices so that its profit margin is only 2½%. Provided that it can achieve an asset turnover of 8 times a year, attracting more customers with its lower prices, it will still make the desired ROCE:

   20% = 2½% × 8

Company A might be a department store and company B a discount warehouse. Each will have a different selling price policy, but each, in its own way, can be effective in achieving a target ROCE. In this example, if we supposed that both companies had capital employed of $100,000 and a target return of 20% or $20,000.

(a)   Company A would need annual sales of $200,000 to give a profit margin of 10% and an asset turnover of 2 times

   $$\frac{\$20,000}{\$100,000} = \frac{\$20,000}{\$200,000} \times 2$$

(b)   Company B would need annual sales of $800,000 to give a profit margin of only 2½% but an asset turnover of 8 times.

   $$\frac{\$20,000}{\$100,000} = \frac{\$20,000}{\$800,000} \times 8$$

FAST FORWARD   The interpretation of financial statements requires a large measure of common sense.

Clearly, a higher return on capital employed can be obtained by increasing the profit margin or the asset turnover ratio. The profit margin can be increased by reducing costs or by raising selling prices.

However, if selling prices are raised, it is likely that sales demand will fall, with the possible consequence that the asset turnover will also decline. If higher prices mean lower sales turnover, the increase in profit margin might be offset by the fall in asset turnover, so that total return on capital employed might not improve.

2.5 Example: profit margin and asset turnover

Suppose that Swings and Roundabouts Ltd achieved the following results in 20X6.

Sales	$100,000
Profit	$5,000
Capital employed	$20,000

The company's management wish to decide whether to raise its selling prices. They think that if they do so, they can raise the profit margin to 10% and by introducing extra capital of $55,000, sales turnover would be $150,000.

Evaluate the decision in terms of the effect on ROCE, profit margin and asset turnover.

Solution

Currently the ratios are

Profit margin (5/100)	5%
Asset turnover (100/20)	5 times
ROCE (5/20)	25%

With the proposed changes, the profit would be 10% × $150,000 = $15,000, and the asset turnover would be:

$$\frac{\$150,000}{\$(20,000+55,000)} = \text{2 times, so that the ratios would be}$$

$$\text{Profit margin} \times \text{Asset turnover} = \text{ROCE}$$

$$0\% \times \text{2 times} = 20\% \left(\frac{\$15,000}{\$75,000}\right)$$

In spite of increasing the profit margin and raising the total volume of sales, the extra assets required ($55,000) only raise total profits by $(15,000 − 5,000) = $10,000.

The return on capital employed falls from 25% to 20% because of the sharp fall in asset turnover from 5 times to 2 times.

Question	Ratios

A trader has the following results.

	$
Sales	200,000
Profit	36,000
Capital employed	120,000

Fill in the blanks.

Profit margin = _____

Asset turnover = _____

ROCE = _____

Answer

Profit margin $= \dfrac{\$36,000}{\$200,000} = 18\%$

Asset turnover $= \dfrac{200,000}{120,000} = 1^2/_3$ times

ROCE $= \dfrac{36,000}{120,000} = 30\%$

2.6 Different definitions of 'profit' and 'capital employed'

FAST FORWARD

ROCE can be calculated in a number of ways. Unless told otherwise in the exam, use:

$$\dfrac{\text{Net profit before tax and interest}}{\text{Average capital employed}}$$

where capital employed includes long-term finance.

We have calculated Return on Capital Employed as a measure of how well a company is performing. What do we mean by 'return' and by capital employed?

Key terms

Return is a reward for investing in a business.

Capital employed means the funds that finance a business.

The providers of finance to a business expect some return on their investment.

(a) Trade payables and most other current liabilities merely expect to be paid what they are owed.

(b) A bank charges interest on overdrafts.

(c) Interest must be paid to the holders of loan stock.

(d) Preference shareholders expect a dividend at a fixed percentage rate of the nominal value of their shares.

(e) Ordinary shareholders also expect a dividend, and, any retained profits kept in the business also represent funds 'owned' or 'provided' by them.

So, when calculating return on capital employed, what measure of 'return' and what measure of 'capital employed' should be used?

For a company, ROCE $= \dfrac{\text{Net profit before interest and tax}}{\text{Share capital} + \text{reserves} + \text{long term debt}}$

which is the same as, ROCE $= \dfrac{\text{Net profit before interest and tax}}{\text{Non} - \text{current assets plus net current assets}}$

2.7 Example: ROCE

For example, suppose that Draught reports the following income statement and balance sheet.

INCOME STATEMENT FOR 20X4 (EXTRACT)

	$
Profit before interest and tax	120,000
Interest	(20,000)
Profit before tax	100,000
Taxation	(40,000)
Profit after tax (earnings)	60,000

Note. An ordinary dividend of $50,000 was paid during the period.

BALANCE SHEET AT 31 DECEMBER 20X4

	$
Non-current assets: tangible assets	350,000
Current assets	400,000
	750,000
Capital and reserves	
Called up share capital (ordinary shares of $1)	100,000
Retained profits	300,000
	400,000
Non-current liabilities	
10% debenture loans	200,000
Current liabilities	150,000
	750,000

Solution

ROCE $= \dfrac{\text{Profits before interest and tax}}{\text{Total assets less current liabilities}} \times 100\%$

Where, total assets less current liabilities is equal to share capital plus reserves plus long term finance (ie the 10% debenture loan).

If assets financed by debt capital are included below the line, it is more appropriate to show profits before interest above the line because interest is the return on debt capital.

$\dfrac{\$120,000}{\$600,000} \times 100\% = 20\%$

Average capital employed = (capital employed at beginning of the accounting period + capital employed at the end of the accounting period) ÷ 2

Question

Using the information in the last example for Draught Co, calculate ROCE.

Relevant figures as at 31 December 20X3 are as follows.

	$
10% loans	200,000
Ordinary share capital	100,000
Retained earnings	290,000
	590,000

Answer

Average capital employed = (590 + 600) ÷ 2 = $595,000

$$\text{ROCE} = \frac{120,000}{595,000} = 20.2\%$$

3 Working capital

FAST FORWARD

Working capital is the difference between current assets (mainly inventory, receivables and cash) and current liabilities (such as trade payables and a bank overdraft).

3.1 Current assets and liabilities

Current assets are items which are either cash already, or which will soon lead to the receipt of cash. Inventories will be sold to customers and create receivables; and receivables will soon pay in cash for their purchases.

Current liabilities are items which will soon have to be paid for with cash. Trade payables will have to be paid and bank overdraft is usually regarded as a short-term borrowing which may need to be repaid fairly quickly (or on demand, ie immediately).

In balance sheets, the word 'current' is applied to inventories, receivables, short-term investments and cash (current assets) and amounts due for payment within one year's time (current liabilities).

3.2 Working capital and trading operations

Current assets and current liabilities are a necessary feature of a firm's trading operations. There is a repeated cycle of buying and selling which is carried on all the time. For example, suppose that on 1 April a firm has the following items.

	$
Inventories	3,000
Receivables	0
Cash	2,000
	5,000
Payables	0
Working capital	5,000

It might sell all the inventories for $4,500, and at the same time obtain more inventories from suppliers at a cost of $3,500. The balance sheet items would now be

	$
Inventories	3,500
Receivables	4,500
Cash	2,000
	10,000
Payables	(3,500)
Working capital	6,500

(The increase in working capital to $6,500 from $5,000 is caused by the profit of $1,500 on the sale of the inventories.)

The receivables for $4,500 will eventually pay in cash and the payables for $3,500 must also be paid. This would give us

	$
Inventories	3,500
Receivables	0
Cash (2,000 + 4,500 − 3,500)	3,000
	6,500
Payables	0
Working capital	6,500

However, if the inventories are sold on credit for $5,500 and further purchases of inventories costing $6,000 are made, the cycle of trading will continue as follows.

	$
Inventories	6,000
Receivables	5,500
Cash	3,000
	14,500
Payables	(6,000)
Working capital (boosted by further profit of $2,000)	8,500

From this basic example you might be able to see that working capital items are part of a continuous flow of trading operations. Purchases add to inventories and payables at the same time, payables must be paid and receivables will pay for their goods. The cycle of operations always eventually comes back to cash receipts and cash payments.

3.3 The operating cycle or cash cycle

Key term

> The **operating cycle** (or cash cycle) is a term used to describe the time taken from the purchase of raw materials to the sale of finished goods.

A firm buys raw materials, probably on credit. The raw materials might be held for some time in stores before being issued to the production department and turned into an item of finished goods. The finished goods might be kept in a warehouse for some time before they are eventually sold to customers. By this time, the firm will probably have paid for the raw materials purchased. If customers buy the goods on credit, it will be some time before the cash from the sales is eventually received.

The cash cycle, or operating cycle, measures the period of time between the time cash is paid out for raw materials and the time cash is received in from receivables.

This cycle of repeating events is shown diagrammatically below.

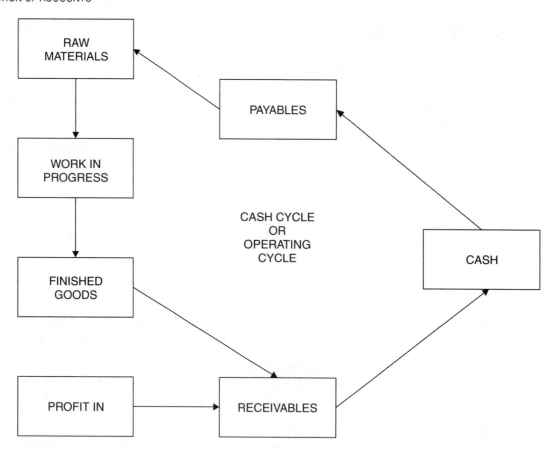

Suppose that a firm buys raw materials on 1½ months' credit, holds them in store for 1 month and then issues them to the production department. The production cycle is very short, but finished goods are held for 1 month before they are sold. Receivables take two months' credit. The cash cycle would be

	Months
Raw material inventory turnover period	1.0
Less: credit taken from suppliers	(1.5)
Finished goods inventory turnover period	1.0
Receivable's payment period	2.0
Cash cycle	2.5

There would be a gap of 2½ months between paying cash for raw materials and receiving cash (including profits) from receivables. A few dates might clarify this point. Suppose the firm purchases its raw materials on 1 January. The sequence of events would then be as follows.

	Date
Purchase of raw materials	1 Jan
Issue of materials to production (one month after purchase)	1 Feb
Payment made to suppliers (1½ months after purchase)	15 Feb
Sale of finished goods (one month after production begins)	1 Mar
Receipt of cash from receivables (two months after sale)	1 May

The cash cycle is the period of 2½ months from 15 February, when payment is made to suppliers, until 1 May, when cash is received from customers.

3.4 Turnover periods

Key term

> A **'turnover'** period is an (average) length of time.

(a) In the case of inventory turnover, it is the length of time an item of inventory is held in stores before it is used.

    (i) A raw materials inventory turnover period is the length of time raw materials are held before being issued to the production department.

    (ii) A work in progress turnover period is the length of time it takes to turn raw materials into finished goods in the factory.

    (iii) A finished goods inventory turnover period is the length of time that finished goods are held in a warehouse before they are sold.

    (iv) When a firm buys goods and re-sells them at a profit, the inventory turnover period is the time between their purchase and their resale.

(b) The receivables' turnover period, or debt collection period, is the length of the credit period taken by customers – it is the time between the sale of an item and the receipt of cash for the sale from the customer.

(c) Similarly, the payables' turnover period, or period of credit taken from suppliers, is the length of time between the purchase of materials and the payment to suppliers.

Turnover periods can be calculated from information in a firm's income statement and balance sheet.

Formula to learn

> Inventory turnover periods are calculated as follows.
>
> (a) Raw materials: $\dfrac{(\text{Average})\text{ raw material inventories held}}{\text{Total raw material consumed in one year}} \times 12 \text{ months}$
>
> (b) Work in progress (the length of the production period):
>
> $\dfrac{(\text{Average})\text{ WIP}}{\text{Total cost of production in the year}} \times 12 \text{ months}$
>
> (c) Finished goods: $\dfrac{(\text{Average})\text{ inventories}}{\text{Total cost of goods sold in one year}} \times 12 \text{ months}$
>
> (d) Inventories of items bought for re-sale: $\dfrac{(\text{Average})\text{ inventories}}{\substack{\text{Total (materials) cost of goods} \\ \text{bought and sold in one year}}} \times 12 \text{ months}$

The word 'average' is put in brackets because although it is strictly correct to use average values, it is more common to use the value of inventories shown in a single balance sheet – at one point in time – to estimate the turnover periods. But if available use opening and closing balances divided by two.

3.5 Example

A company buys goods costing $620,000 in one year and uses goods costing $600,000 in production (in regular monthly quantities) and the cost of material in inventory at 1 January is $100,000.

Solution

The inventory turnover period could be calculated as:

$$\frac{\$100,000}{\$600,000} \times 12 \text{ months} = 2 \text{ months}$$

In other words, inventories are bought two months before they are used or sold.

3.6 Trade receivables collection period

Formula to learn

The debt collection period is calculated as:

$$\frac{\text{Average receivables}}{\text{Annual credit sales}} \times 12 \text{ months}$$

3.7 Example

If a company sells goods for $1,200,000 per annum in regular monthly quantities, and if receivables in the balance sheet are $150,000.

Solution

The trade receivables collection period is

$$\frac{\$150,000}{\$1,200,000} \times 12 \text{ months} = 1.5 \text{ months}$$

In other words, receivables will pay for goods 1¹/₂ months on average after the time of sale.

3.8 Trade payables payment period

Formula to learn

The period of credit taken from suppliers is calculated as:

$$\frac{\text{Average trade payables}}{\text{Total purchases in one year}} \times 12 \text{ months}$$

Notice that the payables are compared with materials bought whereas for raw material inventory turnover, raw material inventories are compared with materials used in production. This is a small, but very significant difference.

3.9 Example

For example, if a company sells goods for $600,000 and makes a gross profit of 40% on sales, and if the amount of trade payables in the balance sheet is $30,000.

Solution

The period of credit taken from the suppliers is:

$$\frac{£30,000}{(60\% \text{ of } £600,000)} \times 12 \text{ months} = 1 \text{ month}$$

In other words, suppliers are paid in the month following the purchase of goods.

Question
                                                                    Cash cycle

Legion's 20X4 accounts show the following.

	$
Sales	360,000
Cost of goods sold	180,000
Inventories	30,000
Receivables	75,000
Trade payables	45,000

Calculate the length of the cash cycle.

Answer

Inventory turnover	Debt collection period	Credit taken from suppliers
$\dfrac{30,000}{180,000} \times 12$	$\dfrac{75,000}{360,000} \times 12$	$\dfrac{45,000}{180,000} \times 12$
= 2 months	= $2^1/2$ months	= 3 months

The cash cycle is

	Months
Inventory turnover period	2.0
Credit taken from suppliers	(3.0)
Debt collection period	2.5
Cash cycle	1.5

In this example, Legion pays its suppliers one month after the inventories have been sold, since the inventory turnover is two months but credit taken is three months.

3.10 Turnover periods and the total amount of working capital

If the inventory turnover period gets longer or if the debt collection period gets longer, the total amount of inventories or of receivables will increase. Similarly, if the period of credit taken from the suppliers gets shorter, the amount of payables will become smaller. The effect of these changes would be to increase the size of working capital (ignoring bank balances or overdrafts).

3.11 Example

Suppose that a company has annual sales of $480,000 (in regular monthly quantities, all on credit) and a materials cost of sales of $300,000. (*Note*. A 'materials cost of sales' is the cost of materials in the cost of sales.)

(a)   If the inventory turnover period is 2 months, the debt collection period 1 month and the period of credit taken from suppliers is 2 months, the company's working capital (ignoring cash) would be

		$
Inventories	(2/12 × $300,000)	50,000
Receivables	(1/12 × $480,000)	40,000
		90,000
Payables	(2/12 × $300,000)	(50,000)
		40,000

The cash cycle would be (2 + 1 − 2) = 1 month.

(b)   Now if the inventory turnover period is extended to 3 months and the debt collection period to 2 months, and if the payment period for purchases from suppliers is reduced to one month, the company's working capital (ignoring cash) would be

		$
Inventory	(3/12 × $300,000)	75,000
Receivables	(2/12 × $480,000)	80,000
		155,000
Payables	(1/12 × $300,000)	(25,000)
		130,000

and the cash cycle would be (3 + 2 − 1) = 4 months.

3.12 Working capital and the cash cycle

If we ignore the possible effects on the bank balance or bank overdraft, (which are themselves included in working capital) it should be seen that a lengthening of the cash cycle will result in a larger volume of working capital.

If the volume of working capital required by a business varies with the length of the cash cycle, it is worth asking the question: 'Is there an ideal length of cash cycle and an ideal volume of working capital?'

Obviously, inventories, receivables and payables should be managed efficiently.

(a)   Inventories should be sufficiently large to meet the demand for inventory items when they are needed, but they should not be allowed to become excessive.

(b)   Receivables should be allowed a reasonable credit period, but overdue payments should be 'chased up', to obviate the risk of bad debts.

(c)   Suppliers should be asked to allow a reasonable period of credit and the firm should make use of the credit periods offered by them.

4 Liquidity

Liquidity may be more important than profitability when looking at whether or not a business can continue to operate.

Key term

The word **'liquid'** means 'readily converted into cash' and a firm's **liquidity** is its ability to convert its assets into cash to meet all the demands for payments when they fall due.

4.1 Current assets and liabilities

The most liquid asset, of course, is cash itself (or a bank balance). The next most liquid assets are short-term investments (stocks and shares) because these can be sold quickly for cash should this be necessary.

Receivables are fairly liquid assets because they should be expected to pay their bills in the near future. Inventories are the least liquid current asset because they must first be sold (perhaps on credit) and the customers given a credit period in which to pay before they can be converted into cash.

Current liabilities are items which must be paid for in the near future. When payment becomes due, enough cash must be available. The managers of a business must therefore make sure that a regular supply of cash comes in (from current assets) at all times to meet the regular flow of payments it is necessary to provide for.

As the previous description of the cash cycle might suggest, the amount of current assets and current liabilities for any business will affect its liquidity. In other words, the volume of working capital helps us to judge the firm's ability to pay its bills.

4.2 The financing of working capital and business assets

Example

BALANCE SHEET AS AT 31 DECEMBER 20X6

	$'000	$'000
Non-current assets		
Goodwill		50
Premises		700
Plant and machinery		300
		1,050
Current costs		
Inventories	99	
Receivables	50	
Cash in hand	1	
		150
		1,200
Capital and reserves		
Share capital		400
Reserves		500
		900
Long-term liabilities		
Loan stock		200
Current liabilities		
Bank overdraft	20	
Trade payables	50	
Taxation due	30	
		100
		1,200

The **long-term funds** of the business are share capital and reserves of $900,000 and loan stock of $200,000, making $1,100,000 in total. These funds help to finance the business and we can calculate that these funds are being used as follows.

	$
To 'finance' goodwill	50,000
To finance premises	700,000
To finance plant and machinery	300,000
To finance working capital	50,000
	1,100,000

Working capital is therefore financed by the long-term funds of the business.

If a company has more current liabilities than current assets, it has **negative** working capital. This means that to some extent, current liabilities are helping to finance the non-current assets of the business. In the following balance sheet, working capital is negative (net current liabilities of $20,000).

BALANCE SHEET AS AT ....

	$
Non-current assets	220,000
Current assets	60,000
	280,000
Capital and reserves	200,000
Current liabilities	280,000
	280,000

The non-current assets of $220,000 are financed by share capital and reserves ($200,000), but also by net current liabilities ($20,000). Since current liabilities are debts which will soon have to be paid, the company is faced with more payments than it can find the cash from liquid assets to pay for. This means that the firm will have to

(a)   Sell off some non-current assets to get the cash.

(b)   Borrow money to overcome its cash flow problems, by offering any unmortgaged property as security for the borrowing.

(c)   Be forced into 'bankruptcy' or 'liquidation' by the payables who cannot be paid.

Clearly, a business must be able to pay its bills on time and this means that to have negative working capital would be financially unsound and dangerous. To be safe, a business should have current assets in excess of current liabilities, not just equality with current assets and current liabilities of exactly the same amount.

The next question to ask then is whether there is an 'ideal' amount of working capital which it is prudent to have. In other words, is there an ideal relationship between the amount of current assets and the amount of current liabilities? Should a minimum proportion of current assets be financed by the long-term funds of a business?

These questions cannot be answered without a hard-and-fast rule, but the relative size of current assets and current liabilities are measured by so-called **liquidity ratios**.

4.3 Liquidity ratios

There are two common liquidity ratios.

(a)   The current ratio or working capital ratio
(b)   The quick ratio or acid test ratio

Key term

> The **current ratio** or **working capital ratio** is the ratio of current assets to current liabilities.

A 'prudent' current ratio is sometimes said to be 2:1. In other words, current assets should be twice the size of current liabilities. This is a rather simplistic view though, and particular attention needs to be paid to certain matters.

(a)   Bank overdrafts: these are technically repayable on demand, and therefore must be classified as current liabilities. However, many companies have semi-permanent overdrafts in which case the likelihood of their having to be repaid in the near future is remote. It would also often be relevant to know a company's overdraft limit – this may give a truer indication of liquidity than a current or quick ratio.

(b)   Are the year-end figures typical of the year as a whole? This is particularly relevant in the case of seasonal businesses. For example, many large retail companies choose an accounting year end following soon after the January sales and their balance sheets show a higher level of cash and lower levels of inventory and payables than would be usual at any other time in the year.

In practice, many businesses operate with a much lower current ratio and in these cases, the best way to judge their liquidity would be to look at the current ratio at different dates over a period of time. If the trend is towards a lower current ratio, we would judge that the liquidity position is getting steadily worse.

For example, if the liquidity ratios of two firms A and B are as follows.

	1 Jan	1 Apr	1 July	1 Oct
Firm	A1.2 : 1	1.2 : 1	1.2 : 1	1.2 : 1
Firm	B1.3 : 1	1.2 : 1	1.1 : 1	1.0 : 1

we could say that firm A is maintaining a stable liquidity position, whereas firm B's liquidity is deteriorating. We would then begin to question firm B's continuing ability to pay its bills. A bank for instance, would need to think carefully before granting any request from firm B for an extended overdraft facility.

It is dangerous however to leap to conclusions when analysing ratios. As well as seasonal variations, it is possible that there is not so much overtrading as deliberately selling hard in order to build up business over time. What looks like a poor balance sheet in one year may develop later into a much bigger and better one.

The quick ratio is used when we take the view that inventories take a long time to get ready for sale, and then there may be some delay in getting them sold, so that inventories are not particularly liquid assets. If this is the case, a firm's liquidity depends more heavily on the amount of receivables, short-term investments and cash that it has to match its current liabilities.

Key term

> The **quick ratio** is the ratio of current assets **excluding inventories** to current liabilities.

A 'prudent' quick ratio is 1:1. In practice, many businesses have a lower quick ratio (eg 0.5:1), and the best way of judging a firm's liquidity would be to look at the trend in the quick ratio over a period of time. The quick ratio is also known as the **liquidity ratio** and as the **acid test ratio.**

4.4 Example: working capital ratios

The cash balance of Wing Co has declined significantly over the last 12 months. The following financial information is provided.

	Year to 31 December	
	20X2	20X3
	$	$
Sales	573,000	643,000
Purchases of raw materials	215,000	264,000
Raw materials consumed	210,000	256,400
Cost of goods manufactured	435,000	515,000
Cost of goods sold	420,000	460,000
Receivables	97,100	121,500
Payables	23,900	32,500
Inventories: raw materials	22,400	30,000
work in progress	29,000	34,300
finished goods	70,000	125,000

All purchases and sales were made on credit.

Required

Analyse the above information, which should include calculations of the cash operating cycle (the time lag between making payment to suppliers and collecting cash from customers) for 20X2 and 20X3.

Notes

(a)   Assume a 360 day year for the purpose of your calculations and that all transactions take place at an even rate.

(b)   All calculations are to be made to the nearest day.

Solution

The information should be analysed in as many ways as possible, and you should not omit any important items. The relevant calculations would seem to be as follows.

(i)

	20X2 $	20X3 $
Sales	573,000	643,000
Cost of goods sold	(420,000)	(460,000)
Gross profit	153,000	183,000
Gross profit percentage	26.7%	28.5%

(ii) Size of working capital and liquidity ratios, ignoring cash/bank overdrafts.

	$	$
Receivables	97,100	121,500
Inventories: raw materials	22,400	30,000
work in progress	29,000	34,300
finished goods	70,000	125,000
	218,500	310,800
Payables	(23,900)	(32,500)
Working capital (ignoring cash or overdraft)	194,600	278,300
Current ratio	$\dfrac{218,500}{23,900}$	$\dfrac{310,800}{32,500}$
	= 9.1:1	= 9.6:1

(iii) *Turnover periods*

	20X2	days	20X3	days
Raw materials in inventory	$\dfrac{22,400}{210,000} \times 360 =$	38.4	$\dfrac{30,000}{256,400} \times 360 =$	42.1
Work in progress	$\dfrac{29,000}{435,000} \times 360 =$	24.0	$\dfrac{34,300}{515,000} \times 360 =$	23.9
Finished goods inventory	$\dfrac{70,000}{420,000} \times 360 =$	60.0	$\dfrac{125,000}{460,000} \times 360 =$	97.8
Receivables' collection period	$\dfrac{97,100}{573,000} \times 360 =$	61.0	$\dfrac{121,500}{643,000} \times 360 =$	68.0
Payables' payment period	$\dfrac{23,900}{215,000} \times 360 =$	(40.0)	$\dfrac{32,500}{264,000} \times 360 =$	(44.3)
Cash cycle		143.4		187.5

5 Gearing

Companies are financed by different types of capital and each type expects a return in the form of interest or dividend. Gearing measures the degree to which the company is financed by non-equity investors.

Key term

Gearing is a method of comparing how much of the long-term capital of a business is provided by equity (ordinary shares and reserves) and how much is provided by 'prior charge capital' investors who are entitled to interest or dividend before ordinary shareholders can have a dividend themselves.

The two most usual methods of measuring gearing are

(a) $\dfrac{\text{Prior charge capital (long − term loans and preference shares)}}{\text{Equity (ordinary shares plus reserves)}} \times 100\%$

   (i)   A business is low-geared if the gearing is less than 100%.

   (ii)   It is neutrally-geared if the gearing is exactly 100%.

   (iii) It is high-geared if the gearing is more than 100%.

(b) $\dfrac{\text{Prior charge capital (long − term loans and preference shares)}}{\text{Total long − term capital}} \times 100\%$

5.1 High and low gearing

A business is now low-geared if gearing is less than 50% (calculated under method (b)), neutrally-geared if gearing is exactly 50% and high-geared if it exceeds 50%.

Low gearing means that there is more equity finance in the business than there is prior charge capital. High gearing means the opposite – prior charge capital exceeds the amount of equity.

5.2 Example

A numerical example might be helpful.

Draught Co, the company in paragraph 2.19, has a gearing of

$\dfrac{\$200,000}{\$400,000}$ (loan stock plus preference shares) (ordinary shares plus reserves) $\times 100\% = 50\%$

5.3 Why is gearing important?

Gearing can be important when a company wants to raise extra capital, because if its gearing is already too high, we might find that it is difficult to raise a loan. Would-be lenders might take the view that ordinary shareholders should provide a fair proportion of the total capital for the business and that at the moment they are not doing so, or they might be worried that profits are not sufficient to meet future interest payments.

5.4 When does gearing become excessive?

Unfortunately, there is no hard and fast answer to this question. The 'acceptable' level of gearing varies according to the country (eg average gearing is higher among companies in Japan than in Britain), the industry, and the size and status of the individual company within the industry. The more stable the company is, the 'safer' higher gearing should be.

5.5 Advantages of gearing

The advantages of gearing (ie of using debt capital) are:

   (a)   Debt capital is cheaper.

      (i)   The reward (interest or preference dividend) is fixed permanently, and therefore diminishes in real terms if there is inflation. Ordinary shareholders, on the other hand, usually expect dividend growth.

      (ii)   The reward required by debt-holders is usually lower than that required by equity holders, because debt capital is often secured on company assets, whereas ordinary share capital is a more risky investment.

(iii)   Payments of interest attract tax relief, whereas ordinary (or preference) dividends do not.

(b)   Debt capital does not normally carry voting rights, but ordinary shares usually do. The issue of debt capital therefore leaves pre-existing voting rights unchanged.

(c)   If profits are rising, and interest is fixed, ordinary shareholders will benefit from the growth in profits.

The main disadvantage of gearing is that if profits fall even slightly, the profit available to shareholders will fall at a greater rate.

6 Items in company accounts formats

Question	Ratios

You are given summarised results of an electrical engineering business, as follows.

INCOME STATEMENT

	Year ended	
	31.12.X7	31.12.X6
	$'000	$'000
Turnover	60,000	50,000
Cost of sales	42,000	34,000
Gross profit	18,000	16,000
Operating expenses	15,500	13,000
	2,500	3,000
Interest payable	2,200	1,300
Profit before taxation	300	1,700
Taxation	350	600
(Loss) profit after taxation	(50)	1,100
Dividends paid	600	600

BALANCE SHEET

	$'000	$'000
Non-current assets		
Intangible	850	–
Tangible	12,000	11,000
	12,850	11,000
Current assets		
Inventories	14,000	13,000
Receivables	16,000	15,000
Bank and cash	500	500
	43,350	39,500
Capital and reserves		
Share capital	1,300	1,300
Share premium	3,300	3,300
Revaluation reserve	2,000	2,000
Retained earnings	6,750	7,400
	13,350	14,000
Current liabilities	24,000	20,000
Non-current liabilities	6,000	5,500
	43,350	39,500

Required

Prepare a table of the following 12 ratios, calculated for both years, clearly showing the figures used in the calculations.

Current ratio
Quick assets ratio
Inventory turnover in days
Receivables turnover in days
Payables turnover in days
Gross profit %
Net profit % (before taxation)
ROCE
Gearing

Answer

	20X7	20X6
Current ratio	$\dfrac{30,500}{24,000} = 1.27$	$\dfrac{28,500}{20,000} = 1.43$
Quick assets ratio	$\dfrac{16,500}{24,000} = 0.69$	$\dfrac{15,500}{20,000} = 0.78$
Inventory (number of days held)	$\dfrac{14,000}{42,000} \times 365 = 122$ days	$\dfrac{13,000}{34,000} \times 365 = 140$ days
Receivables (number of days outstanding)	$\dfrac{16,000}{60,000} \times 365 = 97$ days	$\dfrac{15,000}{50,000} \times 365 = 109$ days
Payables (number of days outstanding)	$\dfrac{24,000}{42,000} \times 365 = 209$ days	$\dfrac{20,000}{34,000} \times 365 = 215$ days
Gross profit	$\dfrac{18,000}{60,000} = 30\%$	$\dfrac{16,000}{50,000} = 32\%$
Net profit % (before taxation)	$\dfrac{300}{60,000} = 0.5\%$	$\dfrac{1,700}{50,000} = 3.4\%$
ROCE	$\dfrac{2,500}{19,350} = 13\%$	$\dfrac{3,000}{19,500} = 15\%$
Gearing	$\dfrac{6,000}{19,350} = 31\%$	$\dfrac{5,500}{19,500} = 28\%$

Question   **Company accounts**

Try to get hold of as many sets of published accounts as possible. Study them carefully to familiarise yourself with the format. Try to form your own opinions on how well the companies are doing.

As a morale booster you should repeat this exercise at later stages in your studies. You may be pleasantly surprised at the progress you make!

Assessment focus point

You must learn these formulae (all mentioned in the syllabus), understand what they indicate and be able to explain what an increase or decrease means.

Current ratio

$$\frac{\text{Current assets}}{\text{Current liabilities}}$$

Quick (acid test) ratio

$$\frac{\text{Current assets} - \text{inventory}}{\text{Current liabilties}}$$

Return on capital employed (ROCE)

$$\frac{\text{Net profit before interest}}{\text{Total long} - \text{term capital}}$$

Gearing

$$\frac{\text{Prior charge capital}}{\text{Total long-term capital}}$$

Receivables turnover
(trade receivables collection period)

$$\frac{\text{Receivables}}{\text{Sales per day}}, \text{ ie } \frac{\text{Receivables}}{\text{Sales}} \times 365$$

Payables turnover
(trade payables payment period)

$$\frac{\text{Payables}}{\text{Purchases per day}}, \text{ ie } \frac{\text{Payables}}{\text{Purchases}} \times 365$$

Gross profit margin

$$\frac{\text{Gross profit}}{\text{Sales}}$$

Net profit margin

$$\frac{\text{Net profit}}{\text{Sales}}$$

Inventory turnover
(inventory days)

$$\frac{\text{Average (or year} - \text{end) inventory}}{\text{Cost of sales per day}}, \text{ ie } \frac{\text{Inventory}}{\text{Cost of sales}} \times 365$$

Asset turnover

$$\frac{\text{Sales}}{\text{Net assets (or capital employed)}}$$

Assessment focus point

It is also possible that the assessor may use alternatives to the inventory/payables/receivables turnover ratios.

Rate of receivables turnover

$$\frac{\text{Sales}}{\text{Receivables}} \text{ eg } \frac{120{,}000}{20{,}000} = 6 \text{ times}$$

Rate of payables turnover

$$\frac{\text{Purchases}}{\text{Payables}} \text{ eg } \frac{60{,}000}{45{,}000} = 4 \text{ times}$$

Rate of inventory turnover

$$\frac{\text{Cost of sales}}{\text{Inventory}} \text{ eg } \frac{60{,}000}{20{,}000} = 3 \text{ times}$$

These ratios represent the number of times closing inventory/payables/receivables are used in the course of the year.

Chapter roundup

- Ratio analysis is the calculation of ratios (eg profit margin) from a set of financial statements which is used for comparison with either earlier years or similar businesses to provide information for decision-making.

- The interpretation of financial statements requires a large measure of common sense.

- ROCE can be calculated in a number of ways. Unless told otherwise in the exam, use:

  $$\frac{\text{Net profit before tax and interest}}{\text{Average capital employed}}$$

  where capital employed includes long-term finance.

- **Working capital** is the difference between current assets (mainly inventory, receivables and cash) and current liabilities (such as trade payables and a bank overdraft).

- Liquidity may be more important than profitability when looking at whether or not a business can continue to operate.

- Companies are financed by different types of capital and each type expects a return in the form of interest or dividend. Gearing measures the degree to which the company is financed by non-equity investors.

Quick quiz

1   A high profit margin will indicate?

    A   Effective cost control measures
    B   Increases in sales volume
    C   The use of trade discounts to secure extra sales
    D   Increase in suppliers prices

2   Given opening inventory $58,000, closing inventory $62,000, opening payables $15,000, closing payables $25,000, payments to payables $160,000. Calculate the rate of inventory turnover.

    A   2.74 times
    B   2.58 times
    C   2.66 times
    D   2.76 times

3   A lengthening of the cash cycle will result in a smaller volume of working capital. True or false?

4   What does the 'quick ratio' measure?

    A   The rate of change of cash resources
    B   The speed with which receivables are collected
    C   The relationship between current assets (minus inventory) and current liabilities
    D   The relationship between current assets and current liabilities

5   Capital gearing refers to?

    A   The relationship between ordinary shares and reserves
    B   The relationship between equity and preference shares
    C   A method of showing the relationship between prior charge capital and all forms of capital
    D   A method of explaining the risk of non payment of a dividend to the equity shareholders

Answers to quick quiz

1   A   Correct.

     B   Sales volume increases do not necessarily mean high margins. High levels of sales of loss making products would have the opposite effect.

     C   Trade discounts reduce invoiced prices and would tend to have the opposite effect.

     D   This would erode margins.

2   D   Correct: purchases = $160,000 + $25,000 − $15,000 = $170,000

          Cost of goods sold = $58,000 + $170,000 − $62,000 = $166,000

          Average inventory = $60,000, inventory turnover = $\dfrac{\$166,000}{\$60,000}$ = 2.76 times

     A   If average inventory is unobtainable, the use of average inventory and purchases will give an acceptable answer.

     B   This is payments divided by closing inventory.

     C   This is payments dividend by average inventory.

3   False

4   C   Correct, inventory is excluded because it has to be sold to create a receivable balance.
     A   Incorrect.
     B   Incorrect, this is the receivable collection period.
     D   Incorrect, this is the current ratio.

5   C   Correct, there is no single accepted definition but the key point is to compare outside borrowings with internally provided finance.

     A   Incorrect.

     B   Incorrect.

     D   The ordinary shareholders are always at risk, gearing is useful for the providers of debt capital as a measure of risk.

Now try the questions below from the Question Bank

Question numbers	Page
120–124	415

Question and answer bank (computer-based assessment)

1   List 5 user groups who would be interested in financial information about a large public company.

(a)   _____

(b)   _____

(c)   _____

(d)   _____

(e)   _____   **2 Marks**

2   Which of the following statements is true?

A   Financial accountants provide historical information for internal use
B   Financial accountants provide historical information for external use
C   Financial accountants provide forward looking information for internal use
D   Financial accountants provide forward looking information for external use   **2 Marks**

3   Fill in the missing word.

Management accounting is the preparation of accounting reports for .... use.   **2 Marks**

4   Which of the following statements gives the best definition of the objective of accounting?

A   To provide useful information to users
B   To record, categorise and summarise financial transactions
C   To calculate the taxation due to the government
D   To control the assets, liabilities and profitability of an entity.   **2 Marks**

5   Peter Reid decides he is going to open a bookshop called Easyread, which he does by investing $5,000 on 1 January 20X7. During the first month of Easyread's existence, the following transactions occur.

(a)   Bookshelves are purchased for $1,800.
(b)   Books are purchased for $2,000.
(c)   Half of the books are sold for $1,500 cash.
(d)   Peter draws $200 out of the business for himself.
(e)   Peter's brother John loans $500 to the business.
(f)   Carpets are purchased for $1,000 on credit (to be paid in two months time).
(g)   A bulk order of books worth $400 is sold on credit (to be paid in one month's time) for $600.

Required

Write down the accounting equation after all of these transactions have taken place

Assets	**=**	**Capital**	**+**	**Liabilities**
_____		_____		_____

                                                                                    2 Marks

6   Which statement is wrong for a balance sheet to balance?

A   Net assets   =   Proprietor's fund
B   Net assets   =   Capital + profit + drawings
C   Net assets   =   Capital + profit − drawings
D   Non-current assets + net current assets = capital + profit − drawings   **2 Marks**

7   James starts his secondhand car business with $155,000. He spends $80,000 on vehicles. One of them is a $5,000 van which he decides to keep and use in the business. During the first month he pays rent of $500 and sells two cars for a total of $10,000. They had cost $5,000 and he spent $1,000 having them repaired. He has not yet paid the repair bills.

State the accounting equation at the end of the month.

Assets		**= Capital**		**+ Liabilities**	
$_____		= $_____		+ $_____	**2 Marks**

8   Which of the following transactions is capital expenditure and which revenue expenditure? Tick the correct box.

		Capital	*Revenue*
(a)	A bookseller buys a car for its director for $9,000.		
(b)	In the first year, the car is depreciated by $900.		
(c)	The business buys books for $1,500.		
(d)	The business builds an extension for $7,600.		
(e)	The original building is repainted, a job costing $1,200.		
(f)	A new sales assistant is taken on and his salary in the first year is $10,000.		

2 Marks

9   A business has spent $200 replacing worn out parts on a machine. How should this $200 be treated in the accounts and why?

A   As revenue expenditure because it is repairing a non-current asset
B   As capital expenditure because it is improving a non-current asset
C   As revenue expenditure because it is likely to reoccur
D   As capital expenditure because it is a small amount   **2 Marks**

10   Which of the following costs of Café Edmundo would be classified as capital expenditure?

A   Cost of printing a batch of new menu cards
B   Repainting the restaurant
C   An illuminated sign advertising the business name
D   Knives and forks for the restaurant   **2 Marks**

11   Fill in the two missing words.

Return is a …………………………….. for …………………………… in a business.   **2 Marks**

12   The sales day book lists _____.

The purchase day book lists _____.

The sales returns day book lists _____.

The purchases returns day book lists _____.   **2 Marks**

13   Cash received from customers will be posted as follows:

(a)   Debit receivables/Credit cash
(b)   Debit cash/Credit sales revenue
(c)   Debit cash/Credit receivables
(d)   Debit sales revenue/Credit receivables   **2 Marks**

14 _____ are recorded in day books. The totals of day books are posted by double entry to ledger accounts in the _____ _____.

Individual invoice details in the day books are posted by single entry to accounts in the

_____ _____.   **2 Marks**

15 A company uses the imprest system for its petty cash, keeping to a float of $100. Since cash was last drawn, $20 has been paid to the cleaner, $15 has been spent on stationery and $7.50 paid to the milkman. One of the directors has repaid a $12 travel advance given to him several weeks ago.

The amount needed to restore the imprest is _____   **2 Marks**

16 (a) A company has been overcharged by one of its suppliers. They receive a credit note. This is posted as follows:

	DR	CR	
Cash			*Tick the*
Creditor			*correct box*
Purchases			

2 Marks

(b) As they are not making any further purchases, the supplier then sends a refund. This is posted as follows:

	DR	CR	
Cash			*Tick the*
Creditor			*correct box*
Purchases			

2 Marks

17 The total of the sales day-book is recorded in the nominal ledger as:

	Debit	*Credit*
A	Sales Account	Receivables Control Account
B	Receivables Control Account	Receivables
C	Receivables	Receivables Control Account
D	Receivables Control Account	Sales Account

2 Marks

18 Fill in the missing word.

The sales and purchases ledgers are not part of the double entry system. They are .... accounts only.   **2 Marks**

19 Which of the following postings from the cashbook payments side is wrong?

A   The total of the cash paid column to the debit of the cash control account.
B   The total of the discounts column to the credit of the discounts received account.
C   The total of the discounts column to the debit of the payables control account.
D   The total of the cash paid column to the credit of the cash control account.   **2 Marks**

20 The sales day book total for March of $250 was recorded in the nominal ledger as:

Cr   Sales account
Cr   Receivables account

At 31 December a trial balance was prepared. Would the trial balance balance?

A   Yes
B   No   Credits would exceed debits by 250
C   No   Credits would exceed debits by $500
D   No   Debits would exceed credits by $250   **2 Marks**

21 When a trial balance is prepared the clerk treats purchases of $3,000 as a credit balance. Credits exceed/are smaller than debits in the trial balance by $_____.   **2 Marks**

22 Fred's trial balance included the following.

	$	$
Purchases	6,000	
Opening inventory	400	
Carriage inwards	200	
Carriage outwards	150	
Sales		12,500

Closing inventory cost $1,000, but it is slightly water damaged. Fred thinks that he can sell it for $1,100 but only if he spends $200 on repackaging it.

Gross profit is $_____.   **2 Marks**

23 Which accounting concept is being followed in each of these scenarios?

(a)   Including costs in the period in which they are incurred, regardless of when payment is made

_____

(b)   Not changing depreciation policy from one year to the next _____

(c)   Providing for liabilities which are expected to arise _____   **2 Marks**

24 Which basic accounting concept is being followed when an allowance is made for bad debts and receivables?

A   Accruals
B   Consistency
C   Going concern
D   Prudence   **2 Marks**

25 Fill in the four missing words.

The accruals basis of accounting requires that, in computing profit, amounts are included in the accounts in the period when they are .... or ...., not .... or ....   **2 Marks**

26 Where there is tension between the concepts of accruals and prudence

A   Accruals must prevail
B   Seek help from external auditors
C   A neutral approach must be adopted that ensures a fair presentation
D   Prudence must prevail   **2 Marks**

27 Fill in the missing word.

The double entry system of bookkeeping is based on the concept of ………………………….. . **2 Marks**

28 Making allowances for receivables and valuing inventory on the same basis in each accounting period are examples of which accounting concepts?

	Allowance for receivables	Inventory valuation
A	Accruals	Consistency
B	Accruals	Going concern
C	Prudence	Consistency
D	Prudence	Going concern

2 Marks

29 Fill in three missing words

Prudence is the concept whereby in situations of …………………………….., appropriate ………………….is exercised in ……………………………… transactions in financial records. **2 Marks**

30 From the information given below you are required:

(a) To calculate the charge to the income statement for the year ended 30 June 20X6 in respect of rent, rates and insurance.

(b) To state the amount of accrual or prepayment for rent, rates and insurance as at 30 June 20X6.

The accruals and prepayments as at 30 June 20X5 were as follows.

	$
Rent accrued	2,000
Rates prepaid	1,500
Insurance prepaid	1,800

Payments made during the year ended 30 June 20X6 were as follows.

20X5		$
10 August	Rent, three months to 31 July 20X5	3,000
26 October	Insurance, one year to 31 October 20X6	6,000
2 November	Rates, six months to 31 March 20X6	3,500
12 December	Rent, four months to 30 November 20X5	4,000
20X6		
17 April	Rent, four months to 31 March 20X6	4,000
9 May	Rates, six months to 30 September 20X6	3,500

	(a) Income statement charge	(b) Accrual	Prepayment	
Rent	_____	_____	_____	**2 Marks**
Rates	_____	_____	_____	**2 Marks**
Insurance	_____	_____	_____	**2 Marks**

31 During the year, $3,000 was paid to the electricity board. At the beginning of the year, $1,000 was owed, at the year end, $1,200 was owed.

What is the charge for electricity in the year's income statement?

A $3,000
B $3,200
C $4,000
D $5,200 **2 Marks**

32 A business received or issued the following invoices and paid or received the invoiced amounts on the following dates:

	Invoice date	Invoice amount	Date paid or received
Purchase	2.6.X4	$1,000	26.6.X4
	25.6.X4	$1,500	2.7.X4
Sales	8.6.X4	$2,000	26.6.X4
	29.6.X4	$3,000	7.7.X4

There is no inventory at the beginning or end of June.

What is the difference between the profit for June calculated on a cash basis, and calculated on an accruals basis?

A   Nil
B $1,000
C $1,500
D $2,500   **2 Marks**

33 On 30 April 20X1 an engineering company purchases hardware upgrades for all of its computers, at a cost of $24,000. This upgrade will speed up design work and reduce costs. Nobody explains this to the accounts department, and the cost gets written off to computer repairs. Computer equipment is written off over 4 years with a proportional charge in the year of acquisition.

Profit for the year to 30 June 20X1 has been understated by _____   **2 Marks**

34 During the year, a car was traded in for $3,000 against the cost ($10,000) of a new car. The old car had cost $8,000 and had a net book value at the time of trade in of $2,000.

The balance due on the new car was paid in cash and was debited to the cars account. No other entries were made.

What net adjustment is required to the cars account?

A   Dr $10,000
B   Dr $3,000
C   Cr $8,000
D   Cr $5,000   **2 Marks**

35 On 31 March 20X9 a machine was sold which cost $20,000 on 1 May 20X5. The profit on disposal was $1,500. The depreciation policy is 20% pa straight line, with a full year being charged in year of acquisition and none in the year of sale. The year end is 31 December.

The sale proceeds were $_____.   **2 Marks**

36 A business buys a machine for $30,000. The depreciation policy for machinery is 15% pa reducing balance. What is the net book value of the machine after two years of use?

$_____.   **2 Marks**

37 Complete the two missing words.

Depreciation is a measure of the cost or revalued amount of the economic .... that have been .... during the period.   **2 Marks**

38 Fill in the missing two words.

An intangible non-current asset is an asset that does not have .... existence. It cannot be ....   **2 Marks**

39 A car was purchased by a florist business in May 20W7 for:

	$
Cost	20,000
Road tax	300
Total	20,300

The business adopts a date of 31 December as its year end.

The car was traded in for a replacement vehicle in August 20X0 at an agreed value of $10,000.

It has been depreciated at 25% per annum on the reducing-balance method, charging a full year's depreciation in the year of purchase and none in the year of sale.

What was the profit or loss on disposal of the vehicle during the year ended December 20X0?

A   Profit: $1,436
B   Profit: $1,562
C   Profit: $3,576
D   Profit: $3,672   **2 Marks**

40 On 1 June 20X9 a machine was sold which cost $10,000 on 31 July 20X5. Sale proceeds were $2,750 and the profit on disposal was $750. The depreciation policy for machinery is straight line with a full year being charged in the year of acquisition and none in the year of sale.

What is the depreciation rate?   %   **2 Marks**

41 At 1 January 20X1, there was allowance for receivables of $2,000. During the year, $1,000 of debts was written off, and $800 of bad debts were recovered. At 31 December 20X1, it was decided to adjust the allowance for receivables to 10% of receivables which are $30,000.

What is the total bad debt expense for the year?

A $200
B $1,200
C $2,000
D $2,800   **2 Marks**

42 At the beginning of the year, the allowance for receivables was $3,400. At the year-end, the allowance required was $4,000. During the year $2,000 of debts were written off, which includes $400 previously provided for.

What is the charge to income statement for bad debts for the year?

A $6,000
B $4,000
C $2,600
D $2,200   **2 Marks**

43 Insert one of the following in each box: receivables, payables, income statement, trading account.

Carriage inward is posted to:

DR [   ]   CR [   ]

Carriage outward is posted to:

DR [   ]   CR [   ]   **2 Marks**

44 A business receives and issues the following invoices and cash receipts and payments. There was no inventory of goods for sale at either the beginning or end of the month.

	Invoice date	Amount $	Date paid or received
Purchases	8.9.X1	100	20.9.X1
	10.9.X1	200	2.10.X1
Sales	12.9.X1	200	25.9.X1
	30.9.X1	300	5.10.X1

Required

(a) The profit earned in September on a cash basis was:

Sales	$
Purchase	$
Profit	$

(b) The profit earned in September on an accruals basis was:

Sales	$
Purchase	$
Profit	$

5 Marks

45 A trial balance contains the following:

	$
Opening inventory	2,000
Closing inventory	4,000
Purchases	20,000
Purchases returned	400
Carriage inwards	3,000
Prompt payment discounts received	1,600

What is the cost of sales?

A $17,600
B $19,000
C $20,600
D $24,600

2 Marks

46 Following the inventory count, a total inventory valuation is reached of $120,357. The auditors find the following additional information:

(i) 370 units of inventory which cost $4.0 have been valued at $0.40 each.

(ii) The inventory count includes damaged goods at their original cost of $2,885. These goods could be repaired at a cost of $921 and sold for $3,600.

(iii) The count includes 440 items at their original cost of $8.50. These are normally sold at $15 but, due to shortages in the market and increased demand, they will now be sold for $18.50 each.

The correct year end inventory figure is:_____

2 Marks

47 Which two of the following statements are true?

(i) In times of inflation, FIFO will give you a higher profit than LIFO.
(ii) In times of inflation LIFO will give you a higher profit than FIFO.
(iii) FIFO matches revenue with up to date costs
(iv) LIFO matches revenue with up to date costs

A (i) and (iii)
B (i) and (iv)
C (ii) and (iii)
D (ii) and (iv)

2 Marks

48 These records were kept for a inventory item in May.

May	1	100 units in inventory at $10 each
	5	50 units bought at $10 each
	12	60 units sold
	20	20 units bought at $8 each
	29	80 units sold

The value of the inventory at May 31st:

(a) Using FIFO is $_____.
(b) Using LIFO is $_____.

2 Marks

49 Carriage inwards $75,000 has been recorded in the I/S account as an expense. As a result?

A Net profit is understated by $75,000
B Gross profit is overstated by $75,000, net profit is unchanged
C Gross profit is understated by $75,000
D Net profit is overstated by $75,000

2 Marks

50 What does the phrase 'proper cut-off procedures' mean in relation to the sale of goods?

A All orders are processed and invoiced to customers.

B Inventory records correctly record receipts and dispatches of goods for resale.

C Arrangements to ensure that all goods dispatched prior to the cut off point are either invoiced or accrued in the financial statements.

D Having in place arrangements to check invoices prior to dispatch to customers.

2 Marks

51 Net realisable value means? (In relation to the valuation of inventory.)

A The expected selling price of the inventory.

B The expected selling price less disposals costs less, in the case of incomplete items, the cost of completion.

C The replacement cost of the inventory.

D The market price as adjusted for the condition of the inventory item.

2 Marks

52 The cash book has a balance of $1622, while the bank statement shows that the account is overdrawn by $370.

The reconciling items are as follows:

(a) A bounced cheque from a customer for $125 not posted to the cash book
(b) Cash of $3500 paid into the bank but not yet credited
(c) An unposted direct debit of $75
(d) Unpresented cheques totalling $1721
(e) Bank charges of $13 not posted

The correct month end cash balance is: $_____ **2 Marks**

53 A debit entry in the cash book will have which effect on the level of a bank overdraft and a bank balance?

	Bank overdraft	Bank balance
A	Increase	Increase
B	Decrease	Decrease
C	Increase	Decrease
D	Decrease	Increase

2 Marks

54 When preparing a bank reconciliation, it is realised that:

(i) There are unpresented cheques of $3,000.
(ii) There are unrecorded lodgements of $2,500
(iii) Bank charges of $35 have not been recorded in the cash book.
(iv) A cheque written out to pay a supplier $39 was entered in the cash book as $93.

The necessary adjustment to the cash book is a debit/credit of $_____. **2 Marks**

55 When preparing a bank reconciliation, it is realised that:

(i) There are unpresented cheques of $16,000
(ii) There are unrecorded lodgements of $10,000
(iii) Bank charges of $134 have not been recorded in the cash book

What adjustment is required to the cash account?

A Debit $134
B Credit $134
C Debit $6,134
D Credit $6,134

2 Marks

56 At the year end the total of balances on the sales ledger is $17,251 and the balance on the receivables control account is $19,158.

The following discrepancies are discovered:

(a) A purchase ledger offset of $240 has not been posted to the receivables control account.

(b) The total of one sales ledger account has been overcast by $90

(c) The March daybook total of $7800 had been posted as $8700

(d) A bad debt of $325 had been removed from the sales ledger but no entry had been made in the receivables control account.

(e) A customer balance of $532 had been omitted from the list of balances

The correct sales ledger balance is: $_____ **2 Marks**

57 When reconciling the payables control account to the list of balances, it was discovered than an invoice received from a supplier for $72 had been recorded in the purchases day book as $27.

What adjustment is necessary to the control account and the list of balances?

	Control account	List of balances
A	Debit $45	Add $45
B	Credit $45	Add $45
C	Debit $45	Subtract $45
D	Credit $45	Subtract $45

2 Marks

58 Which of the following is *not* the purpose of a receivables control account?

A   A sales ledger control account provides a check on the arithmetical accuracy of the personal ledger
B   A sales ledger control account helps to improve separation of duties
C   A sales ledger control account ensures that there are no errors in the personal ledger
D   Control accounts deter fraud

2 Marks

59 When reconciling the receivables control account to the list of balances, it was discovered that the sales daybook has been overcast by $100.

What adjustment is necessary to the list of balances?

A   No adjustment
B   Add $100
C   Subtract $100
D   Subtract $200

2 Marks

60 The following transactions take place during a sales tax quarter:

	$
Sales on credit including sales tax at 17.5%	127,000
Purchases on credit including sales tax	58,000
Credit notes issued including sales tax	3,000
Sales tax incurred on deductible cash expenses	271.50

The amount payable to the tax authorities for the quarter will be $ _____

2 Marks

61 Which of the following is *not* a valid reason for not adding 17.5% sales tax on the goods sold by a business?

A   A business is not registered for sales tax.
B   The customer is not registered for sales tax.
C   The business made sales of exempt products.
D   The business made sales of zero-rated products.

2 Marks

62 In its first period of trading a business has charged sales tax of $12,000 on its credit sales and $2,000 on its cash sales. Sales tax suffered on credit purchases is $3,000 and on cash expenses and purchases is $1,500. The amount owed to the government is $_____.

2 Marks

63 Sales tax is administered by

A   Office of Value Added Taxes
B   The Treasury
C   The tax authorities
D   Commissioner of Indirect Taxes

2 Marks

64 A company has the following monthly payroll costs:

Net wages paid	13,330
PAYE deducted	4,070
Employee NI deducted	2,600
Employer NI contribution	2,900

The total income statement charge for wages for the month is $_____ **2 Marks**

65 Gross payroll cost recorded in the income statement is:

A   Gross pay paid to employees plus employers National Insurance contributions and any employers pension contributions.

B   Net pay paid to employees' plus employer's National Insurance contributions and any employer's pension contributions.

C   Gross pay paid to employees plus employer's and employees' National Insurance contributions.

D   Net pay paid to employees plus employer's and employees' National Insurance contributions.

2 Marks

66 The double entry to record PAYE and employees' National Insurance contributions is:

DEBIT   _____

CREDIT   _____

CREDIT   _____   **2 Marks**

67 An employee has a gross monthly salary of $2,000. In September the tax deducted was $400, the employee's national insurance was $120, and the employer's national insurance was $200. What was the charge for salaries in the income statement?

A $1,480
B $1,880
C $2,000
D $2,200   **2 Marks**

68 An invoice for $18 received from a supplier is recorded as $81 in the purchases day book. When this error is corrected, it will affect:

A   An account in the purchase ledger only
B   Accounts in the nominal ledger only
C   An account in the purchase ledger and accounts in the nominal ledger
D   No accounts   **2 Marks**

69 A business has prepared its draft income statement which shows gross profit of $5,500 and net profit of $3,000. It is then realised that an invoice for $250 relating to cost of sales has been treated as an administration expense by mistake.

The correction of this error will **increase/decrease** gross profit by $_____ and **increase/decrease** net profit by $_____.   **2 Marks**

70   When a trial balance was prepared, two ledger accounts were omitted.

Discounts received $1,500
Discounts allowed $1,000

The total of debit balances exceeds/falls below the total of credit balances by $_____.   **2 Marks**

71   The sales day book has been undercast by $50, and an invoice for $20 has been entered into the sales day book twice.

The necessary adjustment to the receivables control account is $_____ debit/credit.   **2 Marks**

72   When a trial balance was prepared, a suspense account was opened. It was discovered that the only error that had been made was to record $350 of discounts received on the wrong side of the trial balance.

What is the journal to correct this error?

A	Dr	Discounts received	$350
	Cr	Suspense	$350
B	Dr	Suspense	$350
	Cr	Discounts received	$350
C	Dr	Discounts received	$700
	Cr	Suspense	$700
D	Dr	Suspense	$700
	Cr	Discounts received	$700

2 Marks

73   Materials used to repair some machinery have been treated as purchases in the draft account. Correcting this error will have what effect on gross profit and net assets?

	Gross profit	Net assets
A	Increase	No change
B	Increase	Increase
C	Decrease	Decrease
D	No change	Increase

2 Marks

74   When a trial balance was prepared, two ledger accounts were omitted:

Discounts received $6,150
Discounts allowed $7,500

To make a trial balance balance, a suspense account was opened.

What was the balance on the suspense account?

A   Debit $1,350
B   Credit $1,350
C   Debit $13,650
D   Credit $13,650

2 Marks

75   A reduction in the cost of goods resulting from the nature of the trading transaction is a

A   Bad debt
B   Cash discount
C   Impairment
D   Trade discount

2 Marks

76   The following trial balance is extracted at 31 December 20X1:

	DR	CR
Sales		321,726
Purchases	202,419	
Carriage inwards	376	
Carriage outwards	729	
Wages and salaries	54,210	
Rent and rates	12,466	
Heat and light	4,757	
Inventory at 1 January 20X1	14,310	
Drawings	28,500	
Receivables	49,633	
Payables		32,792
Bank		3,295
Sundry expenses	18,526	
Cash	877	
Capital		28,990
	386,803	386,803

Closing inventory is 15,327

(a)   Gross profit for the year is $ _____   **2 Marks**

(b)   Net profit for the year is $ _____   **2 Marks**

(c)   Net assets are $ _____   **2 Marks**

77   Which of these transactions would *not* increase a company's retained profit for the year?

A   Revaluation of a freehold factory from $140,000 to $250,000.

B   Receipt of $5,000 from a receivable previously written off.

C   Receive discounts of $1,000 from a supplier.

D   Sell for $6,000 a car which cost $10,000 and has been depreciated by $4,500.   **2 Marks**

78   A company has profit before tax of $140,000. The tax charge for the year is $25,000 and $15,000 is to be transferred to a non-current asset reserve. A final dividend of 5c per ordinary share is proposed. In the year these dividends were paid:

	$
Last year's final dividend on 375,000 25c ordinary shares	15,000
This year's interim dividend on 375,000 25c ordinary shares	10,000
This year's interim dividend on 100,000 6% preference shares	3,000

The retained profit for the year is $_____.   **2 Marks**

79   When preparing financial statements in periods of inflation, directors

A   Must reduce asset values

B   Must increase asset values

C   Must reduce salaries

D   Need make no adjustments   **2 Marks**

80 A particular source of finance has the following characteristics: a fixed return, a fixed repayment date, it is secured and the return is classified as an expense.

Is the source of finance

A Ordinary share
B Hire purchase
C Loan stock
D Preference share   **2 Marks**

81 At 31 December 20X1, a business had net assets of $10,000. At 31 December 20X2 net assets had risen to $12,500. Profit for the year was $8,000 and no new capital was introduced. How much were drawings in the period.

A $2,500
B $3,000
C $5,500
D $10,500   **2 Marks**

82 At 1 January 20X4 a business had net assets of $13,000. By 31 December 20X4 it had:

	$
Buildings	4,000
Furniture	2,000
Bank overdraft	1,500
Receivables	3,500
Payables	2,000
Proprietors capital	6,000

During the year the proprietor had introduced $1,000 of new capital and had drawings of $800. The profit (loss) for the year is _____   **2 Marks**

83 On 30 April 20X1 part of a company's inventory was destroyed by fire.

The following information is available:

- Inventory at 1 April 20X1 $99,600
- Purchases for April 20X1 $177,200
- Sales for April 20X1 $260,000
- Inventory at 30 April 20X1 – undamaged items $64,000
- Standard gross profit percentage on sales 30%

Based on this information, the cost of the inventory destroyed is _____   **2 Marks**

84 Hamilton runs a bicycle repair shop and keeps no accounting records. All of his sales are for cash, which he says is all banked. He has a few unpaid bills and he shows you a copy of last year's balance sheet, which shows net assets of 8537. He withdraws $100 per week for living expenses.

You arrive at the following figures for the year ended 31.12.X1

Van:	
Cost	3,000
Depreciation	(1,800)
	1200
Inventory	125
Cash at bank	8,504
Cash on hand	127
Payables	1,035

His net profit for the year is $_____   **2 Marks**

85   At 1 January 20X1 payables were owed $10,000, by 31 December 20X1 they were owed $8,000. In the year, receivables and payables contras were $3,500, and $350 of debit balances were transferred to receivables, credit purchases were $60,000 and $2,500 of discounts were received.

What was paid to suppliers during the year?

A $55,650
B $56,000
C $56,350
D $58,000   **2 Marks**

86   During the year, all sales were made at a gross profit margin of 10%. Sales were $25,000, purchases were $22,000 and closing inventory was $5,000.

Opening inventory was $_____.   **2 Marks**

87   Sales for the year are 525,329 and the normal mark-up on cost is 25%. Opening inventory was 77,505 and closing inventory is 79,350.

Purchases are _____   **2 Marks**

88   At 31 March 20X8, a business had:

Motor cars	6,000
Inventory	1,500
Receivables	900
Accrued electricity expense	150
Rent prepaid	600

At 31 March 20X9, it had:

Motor cars	7,500
Inventory	300
Receivables	150
Payables	1,800
Accrued electricity expense	300
Rent prepaid	750

The owner has drawn $3,000 in cash over the year.

What is the profit or loss?

A   Loss $750
B   Profit $750
C   Loss $2,250
D   Profit $2,250   **2 Marks**

89   A business has opening inventory $30,000, achieves a mark up of 25% on sales, sales totalled $1,000,000, purchases were $840,000. Calculate closing inventory.

A $30,000
B $40,000
C $120,000
D $70,000   **2 Marks**

90 Opening inventory of raw materials was $29,000, closing inventory was $31,500, purchases were $128,000, purchase returns were $8,500. What was cost of sales?

    A $128,000
    B $117,000
    C $119,500
    D $122,000   **2 Marks**

91 A business achieves a margin of 25% on sales. Opening inventory was $36,000, closing inventory was $56,000 and purchases totalled $600,000. Calculate the sales for the period.

    A $773,333
    B $725,000
    C $826,666
    D $800,000   **2 Marks**

92 At 1 January 20X4 a club had $500 of subscriptions received in advance and 10 members still owed $20 each for their year's subscription. At 31 December $600 had been received in advance for next year and $180 was owed by members. During the year $1,200 was received from members.

The amount credited to the income and expenditure account for the year to 31.12.X4 was:

    A $480
    B $1,080
    C $1,200
    D $1,920   **2 Marks**

93 At the beginning of the year, a club had subscriptions in arrears of $50 and subscriptions received in advance of $80. At the end of the year, subscriptions in arrears were $100, and subscriptions received in advance were $60. Subscriptions received in the year were $2,060.

    (a)   The figure for subscriptions in an income and expenditure account would be $_____.

    (b)   The figure for subscriptions in a receipts and payments record would be $_____.   **2 Marks**

94 Which of the following costs would **not** be shown as a factory overhead in a manufacturing account?

    A   The cost of insurance on a factory
    B   The cost of extension to a factory
    C   The cost of depreciation on a factory
    D   The cost of rent on a factory   **2 Marks**

95 Which of the following costs would be included in the calculation of prime cost in a manufacturing account?

    A   Factory rent
    B   Office wages
    C   Direct production wages
    D   Depreciation and machinery   **2 Marks**

96 Write the full names of the following accounting bodies.

    (i)   FRC _____
    (ii)   FRRP _____
    (iii)   ASB _____   **2 Marks**

97   Who issues Financial Reporting Standards?

A   The Auditing Practices Board
B   The Stock Exchange
C   The Accounting Standards Board
D   CIMA   **2 Marks**

98   Which of the following is not a member of the Consultative Committee of Accounting Bodies (CCAB)?

A   The Chartered Institute of Management Accountants
B   The Chartered Association of Certified Accountants
C   The Institutes of Chartered Accountants in England, Wales, Scotland and Ireland
D   The Association of Accounting Technicians   **2 Marks**

99   Insert the missing two words

The International Accounting Standards Committee has been replaced by the ....
.... Accounting Standards ....   **2 Marks**

100   Auditing Standards and Guidelines are issued by

A   Audit Standards Board
B   The Audit Practices Board
C   The Audit Standards and Guidelines Committee
D   The Audit Practices Committee.   **2 Marks**

101   The role of the Financial Reporting Council is to?

A   Oversee the standard setting and regulatory process
B   Formulate accounting standards
C   Review defective accounts
D   Control the accountancy profession   **2 Marks**

102   Which two of the following are detect controls?

(i)   Bank reconciliations
(ii)   Reconciliation of asset register to physical assets
(iii)   Matching invoices to goods received notes prior to payment
(iv)   Matching wages calculations to clock cards prior to payment   **2 Marks**

103   Which is the single most important attribute of an auditor (external or internal)?

A   Professional skills and training
B   Computer literacy
C   Independence
D   Ability to work closely with management   **2 Marks**

104   An internal auditor identifies an internal control weakness in an accounting system. What action should now be taken?

A   Consider the effect of the weakness and identify counter controls
B   Report to management
C   Instruct the operators of the system to change the procedures in use
D   Report it to the police   **2 Marks**

105 The primary reason for an external audit is to:

A   Give an opinion on the financial statements
B   Detect any material errors or frauds
C   Supplement the work of internal audit
D   Confirm the financial viability and adaptability of the company   **2 Marks**

106 Fair presentation is determined by reference to:

A   Compliance with company law
B   Compliance with accounting standards
C   Compliance with generally accepted accounting practice
D   The meaning of the word 'fair'.   **2 Marks**

107 Who appoints external auditors?

A   Directors
B   Registrar of Companies
C   Finance director
D   Shareholders   **2 Marks**

108 Which of the following statements is correct?

A   External auditors report to the directors
B   External auditors are appointed by the directors
C   External auditors are required to give a report to shareholders
D   External auditors correct only material errors in financial statements   **2 Marks**

109 What is an audit trail in a computerised accounting system?

A   A list of all the transactions in a period
B   A list of all the transactions in a ledger account in a period
C   A list of all the items checked by the auditor
D   A list of special transactions printed for the auditor to examine   **2 Marks**

110 Which of the following is *not* an activity which internal auditors would normally carry out?

A   Fraud investigations
B   Value for money studies
C   Controls testing
D   The statutory audit   **2 Marks**

111 Internal control includes 'detect' controls and 'prevent' controls. Which of the following is a detect control?

A   Installation of security cameras
B   Matching purchase invoices with goods received notes
C   Preparing bank reconciliations
D   Matching sales invoices with delivery notes   **2 Marks**

112 What do you understand by the term 'management fraud'?

A   Abuse of company credit cards
B   Fraud designed to improve the company's position or performance
C   Using creative accounting
D   Theft by managers   **2 Marks**

113   What controls are concerned with achieving the objectives of the organisation and implementing policies?

A   Accounting controls
B   Financial controls
C   Administrative controls
D   Detect controls   **2 Marks**

114   Fill in the two missing words.

An external audit is an .... examination of, and expression of .... on the
financial statements of an enterprise.   **2 Marks**

115   The following information relates to transactions for the year ended 31 December 20X1.

	$'000
Depreciation	1,320
Increase in inventory	555
Cash paid to employees	4,230
Decease in receivables	420
Decrease in payables	585
Net profit before tax	3,555

Net cash flow from operating activities is $_____

116   A business had net cash flow from operating activities of $80,000, and these results:

	$
Operating profit	23,000
Depreciation	4,000
Loss on sale of non-current assets	22,000
Decrease in inventory	13,000
Increase in payables	10,000

What was the change in receivables?

A   No change
B   Decrease of $8,000
C   Increase of $18,000
D   Decrease of $5,000   **2 Marks**

117   Which two of the following would cause net cash flow from operating activities in the cash flow statement to be
bigger than operating profit in the income statement.

(i)   An increase in inventories of raw materials
(ii)   A decrease in inventories of finished goods
(iii)   A profit on the sale of a non-current asset
(iv)   A loss on the sale of a non-current asset   **2 Marks**

118   Barry Co has the following payments and receipts during its accounting period. Issue of shares $1,030,000,
debenture repaid $400,000, share premium received $460,000, proceeds of a rights issue $630,000, interest paid
$115,000. Calculate the 'financing' cash flow figure for its cash flow statement.

A $1,720,000
B $1,090,000
C $1,490,000
D $1,260,000   **2 Marks**

BPP
LEARNING MEDIA

119 When comparing two balance sheets you notice that:

(i) Last year the company had included in current assets investments of $5,000. This year there are no investments in current assets.

(ii) Last year the company had an overdraft of $4,000, this year the overdraft is $2,000.

In the cash flow statement, the change in cash would be:

A Increase $2,000
B Decrease $2,000
C Increase $3,000
D Decrease $3,000   **2 Marks**

120 A company has a gross profit margin of 10% and an asset turnover of 3 times a year.

What is the return on capital employed?

A 3.33%
B 7%
C 13%
D 30%   **2 Marks**

121 A company has sales of $420,000 spread evenly over the year. All sales are on credit with a trade receivables collection period of 2 months. Cost of sales are $240,000 and the inventory turnover period is 1 month. The company gets on average 45 days credit from its suppliers.

The company's working capital (excluding cash) is $_____.

The cash cycle is _____ months.   **2 Marks**

122 Working capital is?

A Current assets – inventory – current liabilities
B Current assets – current liabilities
C Total assets – total liabilities
D Liquid current assets – current liabilities   **2 Marks**

123 The annual sales of a company are $47,000 including sales tax at 17.5%. Half of the sales are on credit terms; half are cash sales. The receivables in the balance sheet are $4,700.

What is the trade receivables collection period (to the nearest day)?

A 37 days
B 43 days
C 73 days
D 86 days   **2 Marks**

124 If sales were $51,000, and cost of sales was $42,500, what was the gross profit percentage?

A 16.67%
B 20%
C 83.333%
D 120%   **2 Marks**

1   Shareholders
Potential investors
Employees
Providers of finance
Financial analysts
Government departments
Trade unions
Payables

2   B.

3   Management accounting is the preparation of accounting reports for internal use.

4   A   This is the actual objective of accounting.

5

Assets	=	**Capital**	+	**Liabilities**
7,000		5,500		1,500

6   B.

7   Assets = Capital + Liabilities

159,500 = 158,500 + 1,000

8   Capital expenditure: (a), (d)
Revenue expenditure: (b), (c), (e), (f) (Note that the value of the transactions is irrelevant.)

9   A   Correct.
B   Incorrect, this is repairs not improvement
C   Incorrect, reoccurrence is not important
D   Incorrect, the fact that it is such a small amount is more likely to justify its treatment as a revenue item

10   C   Correct, it is likely to be treated as capital expenditure.
A   This is printing and stationery, so it is revenue expenditure.
B   This is a repair and renewal expense so it would be likely to be treated as a revenue item.
D   Incorrect, these are unlikely to be sufficiently expensive to warrant treatment as capital expenditure.

11   Return is a reward for investment in a business.

12   The sales day book lists all invoices sent to customers.
The purchases day book lists all invoices received from suppliers.
The sales returns day book lists all credit notes sent to customers.
The purchases returns day book lists all credit notes received from suppliers.

13   C.

14   Source documents are recorded in day books. The totals of day books are posted by double entry to ledger accounts in the nominal ledger.

Individual invoice details in the day books are posted by single entry to accounts in the personal ledgers.

15 $30.50

16   (a)   DR   Payables   CR   Purchases
(b)   DR   Cash   CR   Payables

17   D

18   The sales and purchases ledgers are not part of the double entry system. They are memorandum accounts only.

19   A   The total of the cash paid column should be credited to the cash control account.

20   C is correct. The clerk has done two credits of $250, and no debit, so credits will exceed debits by $500.

21   Purchases should be a debit balance so credits will exceed debits by $6,000.

22   Gross profit is $6,800.

	$	$
Sales		12,500
Less cost of sales		
Opening inventory	400	
Purchases	6,000	
Carriage inwards	200	
	6,600	
Closing inventory $(1,100 – 200)$	(900)	
		(5,700)
Gross profit		6,800

23   Accruals
Consistency
Prudence

24   D   Making an allowance for receivables and bad debts follows the prudence concept, ie recognising a potential loss.

25   The accruals basis of accounting requires that, in computing profit, amounts are included in the accounts in the period when they are earned or incurred, not received or paid.

26   C   Where there is tension between the concepts of accruals and prudence a neutral approach must be adopted that ensures a fair presentation.

27   The double entry system of bookkeeping is based on the concept of duality.

28   C.

29   Prudence is the concept whereby in situations of uncertainty, appropriate caution is exercised in recognising transactions in financial records.

30   (a)   *Rent for the year ending 30 June 20X6*

	$
1 July 20X5 to 31 July 20X5 = $3,000/3	1,000
1 August 20X5 to 30 November 20X5	4,000
1 December 20X5 to 31 March 20X6	4,000
Accrued, 1 April 20X6 to 30 June 20X6 = 3/4 × $4,000	3,000
Charge to income statement for year ending 30 June 20X6	12,000

Rates for the year ending 30 June 20X6

	$	$
Rates prepaid last year, relating to this year		1,500
1 October 20X5 to 31 March 20X6		3,500
1 April 20X6 to 30 September 20X6	3,500	
Less prepaid July to September (3/6)	1,750	
April to June 20X6		1,750
Charge to income statement for year ending 30 June 20X6		6,750

Insurance for the year ending 30 June 20X6

	$	$
Insurance prepaid last year, relating to this year		1,800
1 November 20X5 to 31 October 20X6	6,000	
Less prepaid July to October (4/12)	2,000	
		4,000
Charge to income statement for year ending 30 June 20X6		5,800

(b) The accrual or prepayment for each expense can be summarised from the workings in part (a).

As at 30 June 20X6	$
Rent accrued	3,000
Rates prepaid	1,750
Insurance prepaid	2,000

31 B

ELECTRICITY EXPENSE ACCOUNT

	$		$
Cash	3,000	B/d	1,000
C/d	1,200	I/S	3,200
	4,200		4,200
		B/d	1,200

32 C On a cash basis

	$
Sales	2,000
Purchases	1,000
Profit	1,000

On an accruals basis

	$
Sales	5,000
Purchases	2,500
Profit	2,500

Thus, the difference is $1,500.

33 Profit has been understated by $23,000.

Charge put through accounts in error	24,000
Depreciation charge (24,000 × 25% × 2/12)	(1,000)
Total understated	23,000

34 D is correct.

	$	$
Existing debit in cars account (10,000 – 3,000)	7,000	
Transfer proceeds to disposals account	3,000	3,000
Cost of new car	10,000	
Transfer cost of car sold to disposal account		(8,000)
∴ Net adjustment		(5,000)

35 Sales proceeds were $5,500.

31.7.X5

	$
Cost	20,000
Depreciation y/e 31.12.X5 to y/e 31.12.X8	16,000
NBV at date of sale	4,000
Profit on disposal	1,500
⇒ Sale proceeds	5,500

36 $21,675

	$
Cost	30,000
1st year depreciation – 15%	(4,500)
Net book value	25,500
2nd year depreciation – 15%	3,825
Net book value	21,675

37 IAS 16 defines depreciation as a measure of the cost or revalued amount of the economic benefits that have been consumed during the period.

38 An intangible non-current asset is an asset that does not have physical existence. It cannot be touched.

39 B

	$
Cost	20,000
20W7 Depreciation	(5,000)
	15,000
20W8 Depreciation	(3,750)
	11,250
20W9 Depreciation	(2,812)
	8,438
20X0 Part exchange	10,000
Profit	(1,562)

40 20%

The asset has been depreciated for 4 years (X5, X6, X7 and X8).

	$
Sales proceeds	2,750
Profit on disposal	(750)
Net book value at disposal	2,000
Cost	10,000
Depreciation to date	8,000

ie $2,000 pa which is 20% of $10,000.

41 B

ALLOWANCE

	$		$
		B/d	2,000
C/d	3,000	Bad debts expense	1,000
	3,000		3,000

BAD DEBTS EXPENSE

	$		$
Receivables (write-off)	1,000	Cash (write-offs recovered)	800
Increase in allowance	1,000	I/S	1,200
	2,000		2,000

42 C

Allowance

		3,400	b/d
Write off	400		
C/d	4,000	1,000	Expense
	4,400	4,400	

Bad debts expense

Allowance increase	1,000		
Receivables W/O	1,600	2,600	I/S
	2,600	2,600	

43 DR Trading account   CR Payables
     DR Income statement   CR Payables

44 (a) The profit earned in September on a cash basis was:

	$
Sales	200
Purchases	(100)
Profit	100

(b) The profit earned in September on an accruals basis was:

	$
Sales	500
Purchases	(300)
Profit	200

45 C

	$
Purchases	20,000
Less purchase returns	(400)
	19,600
Add carriage inwards	3,000
Add opening inventory	2,000
Less closing inventory	(4,000)
Cost of sales	20,600

46 $121,483 (120,357 + (370 × $3.60) − 2,885 + 2,679)

47 B. (i) and (iv) are correct.

Under LIFO, inventory is the oldest receipts, so cost of sales is at current (higher) prices which reduces profit.

48   FIFO is $260, LIFO is $300.

Under FIFO

	Units		Value $
May 1	100	@ $10	1,000
May 5	50	@ $10	500
Balance	150	@ $10	1,500
May 12	(60)	@ $10	(600)
Balance	90	@ $10	900
May 20	20	@ $8	160
Balance	110	@ $8	1,060
May 29	(80)	@ $10	(800)
	30		260

Under LIFO

	Units		Value $
May 1	100	@ $10	1,000
May 5	50	@ $10	500
Balance	150	@ $10	1,500
May 12	(60)	@ $10	(600)
Balance	90	@ $10	900
May 20	20	@ $8	160
Balance	110	@ $8	1,060
May 29	(20)	@ $8	(160)
	(60)	@ $10	(600)
	30		300

49   B   Correct, carriage inwards should be treated as part of the cost of purchases in the trading account.

50   C   Correct. Under the accruals concept, all dispatches in a period must be invoiced or accrued so they can be matched with costs of sale. Goods dispatched must be deducted from inventory records.

    A   This is a completeness control.

    B   This is an accuracy control.

    D   Again, this is an accuracy control.

51   B   Correct.
    A   Incorrect.
    C   Incorrect.
    D   Incorrect.

52 $1,409

53   D is correct.

When cash is received by a business a debit entry is made in the cash book. A receipt of cash decreases an overdraft and increases a bank balance.

54 Debit $19.

Unpresented cheques and increased lodgements are timing differences so no adjustments is necessary.

The bank charges need a credit to cash of $35.

The transposition errors needs a debit to cash $54, ie a net debit of $19.

55 B   The only adjustment that should be made to the cash account is to record the bank charges. The cheques and lodgements will already have been recorded in the cash account.

56 $17,693

57 B.   This affects both the total which was posted to the control account and the individual posting to the purchase ledger.

58 C.

59 A   Remember, daybook totals are posted to the control account. Individual invoices are posted to the individual accounts, so an error in a total does not affect the list of balances.

60 $9,558.28

61 B is correct.

The others are all valid reasons for not adding sales tax on sales invoices.

62 $9,500

SALES TAX PAYABLE

	$		$
Payables	3,000	Receivables	12,000
Cash	1,500	Cash	2,000
C/d	9,500		
	14,000		14,000
		B/d	9,500

63 C   Sales tax is administered by the tax authorities.

64 $22,900

65 A.

66 Debit   Wages control account (total deductions)
Credit   PAYE control account (PAYE)
Credit   NIC control account (NIC)

67 D   The charge for the salary in the profit and loss account is the gross salary plus the employer's national insurance contribution. This is $2,000 plus $200 respectively, a total of $2,200.

68 C is correct. This error affects the total posted to the purchases account and the payables accounts in the nominal ledger, and it affects the amount posted to the suppliers account in the purchase ledger.

69 Decrease gross profit by $250

No effect on net profit.

This $250 must be 'moved up' to the trading account. This reduces gross profit and has no effect on net profit.

70 We have 'missed' income (and thus a credit balance) of $1,500 and an expense (and thus a debit balance) of $1,000. Thus debit balances will exceed credit balances by $500.

71 Debit $30.

For the undercast	debit $50
For the invoice entered invoice	credit $20
A net debit of	$30

72 D is correct.

Discounts received are income and thus, a credit balance. Recording them as a debit will have made debits in the trial balance exceed credits by $700, ie the suspense account balance is a credit of $700. So the correction is debit suspense $700, and credit discounts received $700.

73 A is correct.

The correction will increase expenses and reduce purchases. Thus gross profit will increase and net assets not change.

74 A

Suspense account

B/d	1,350		
Discounts received	6,150	7,500	Discounts allowed
	7,500	7,500	

75 D   A reduction in the cost of goods resulting from the nature of the trading transaction is a trade discount.

76 (a) $119,948
(b) $29,260
(c) $29,750

77 A.

'Profit' on revaluation must be credited to a revaluation reserve, not to retained profits for the year.

78 $115,000

	$
Profit before tax	140,000
Tax	(25,000)
Retained profit for the year	115,000

Remember that dividends and transfers to reserves are part of the SOCIE.

79 D.

80 C   Loan stock. The other items do not fit the criteria in the question.

81 C.

$P = I + D - C$

$8,000 = 2,500 + D - 0$

$\Rightarrow D = \$5,500$

82 (7,200)

Net assets at 31.12X4 = $4,000 + $2,000 − $1,500 + $3,500 − $2,000 = $6,000 (which is of course equal to capital)

So, the decrease in net assets is $7,000.

$P = I + D − C$

$P = −\$7,000 + \$800 − \$1,000$

$P = −\$7,200$

ie, a loss of $7,200

83

	$
Theoretical gross profit 30% x $260,000	78,000
Actual gross profit:	
$260,000 − $99600 − $177,200 + $64,000	47,200
Shortfall − missing inventory	30,800

84 This is very easy to work out using the business equation ($P = I + D − Ci$).

Net assets for the current year	8,921
Less net assets last year	(8,537)
Increase in net assets (capital)	384
Add drawings	5,200
Less capital introduced	–
Profit for the year	5,584

85 C is correct.

PAYABLES CONTROL ACCOUNT

	$		$
Contra	3,500	B/d	10,000
Discounts received	2,500	Transfers to receivables	350
Cash (balance)	56,350	Purchases	60,000
C/d	8,000		
	70,350		70,350

86 Opening inventory was $5,500.

	$	$
Sales (100%)		25,000
Opening inventory (balance)	5,500	
Purchases	22,000	
Less closing inventory	(5,000)	
Cost of sales (25,000 − 2,500) or 90%		(22,500)
Gross profit (10%)		2,500

87 Purchases are 422,108

Cost of sales = 525,329 × 4/5 =	420,263
Less opening inventory	(77,505)
Add closing inventory	79,350
	422,108

88   B

	$
Net assets 31/12/X1	
6,000 + 1,500 + 900 − 150 + 600	8,850
Net assets 31/12/X2	
7,500 + 300 + 150 − 1,800 − 300 + 750	6,600
Decrease in net assets	2,250

> From the business equation
> Change in net assets =   Capital + profit − drawings

$$-2,250 = \text{Profit} - \text{drawings (\$3,000)}$$
$$-2,250 + 3,000 = \text{Profit}$$
$$750 = \text{Profit}$$

89   D

	$	%
Opening inventory	30,000	
Purchases	840,000	
	870,000	
Closing inventory	(70,000)	
Cost of sales	800,000	100
Gross profit/mark up	200,000	25
Sales	1,000,000	125

Take care you correctly interpret whether you are dealing with gross profit on sales or gross profit on cost.

A   This is opening inventory.

B   This is the difference between cost of sales and purchases ignoring inventory changes.

C   You have incorrectly applied the mark up to sales.

90   B   Correct, $29,000 + $128,000 − $8,500 − $31,500 = $117,000.

A   Incorrect, returns and inventory changes must be allowed for.

C   Incorrect, changes in inventory levels must be allowed for.

D   Incorrect, you have transposed opening and closing inventories.

91   A

	$	%
Opening inventory	36,000	
Purchases	600,000	
	636,000	
Closing inventory	(56,000)	
Cost of sales	580,000	75
Gross profit	193,333	25
Sales	773,333	100

Take care you correctly interpret whether you are dealing with gross profit on sales or gross profit on cost.

B   Incorrect, you have applied the 25% margin to cost of sales.

C   Incorrect because you have transposed the inventory figures in the calculation of cost of sales.

D   Incorrect you have applied a mark up to purchases without the inventory adjustment, ie $600,000 ÷ 75%

92 B $1,080.

SUBSCRIPTIONS ACCOUNT

	$		$
Arrears b/f	200	Prepaids b/f	500
Income and expenditure a/c (balance)	1,080	Bank/cash	1,200
Prepaid c/f	600	Arrears c/f	180
	1,880		1,880

93

SUBSCRIPTIONS ACCOUNT

	$		$
Arrears b/f	50	Prepaid b/f	80
Income and expenditure a/c (bal)	2,130	Cash	2,060
Prepaid c/f	60	Arrears c/f	100
	2,240		2,240

The figure for subscriptions in an income and expenditure account would be $2,130.

The figure for subscriptions in a receipts and payments account would be $2,060.

94 B The cost of the extension is capital expenditure, which will be shown in non-current assets in the balance sheet.

95 C Prime cost includes only direct materials and direct production wages. Factory rent and machinery depreciation are factory overheads, so will be deducted before aiming at factory cost of finished goods. Office wages will go to the profit and loss account.

96 (i) Financial Reporting Council
(ii) Financial Reporting Review Panel
(iii) Accounting Standards Board

97 C The Accounting Standards Board
D CIMA – not really!

98 D Correct. Not a member, although the sponsoring bodies of AAT are.
A A member of CCAB.
B A member of CCAB.
C Members of CCAB.

99 The International Accounting Standards Committee has been replaced by the International Accounting Standards Board.

100 B Auditing Standards and Guidelines are issued by the Auditing Practice Board (APB).

101 A This is correct, the FRC also raises funds and controls the strategic direction of its subsidiary bodies such as the Accounting Standards Board.

B This is the role of the Accounting Standards Board.

C This is the role of the Financial Reporting Review Panel.

D Each professional body is essentially self regulatory. The only avenue for consultation is via the Consultative Committee of Accountancy Bodies.

102 (i) and (ii) are detect controls.
(iii) and (iv) are prevent controls.

103 C   Correct. Unless the auditor is independent from the company, the work or reports will lack credibility in the eyes of users.

      A   This is an important attribute.

      B   This is vital and is developed by adequate training and appropriate experience.

      D   Good relations with management help the audit go smoothly. But independence is key.

104 A   Correct. The impact of the weakness upon control risk should be evaluated, there may be an effective counter control which could mitigate the effects of the weakness.

      B   This should not be done until the facts are checked and cost effective solutions devised.

      C   The auditor should not enforce system changes, this is the role of management on receipt of recommendations from the auditors.

      D   Not valid, not a practical approach!

105 A.

106 B.

107 D   External auditors are appointed by the shareholders.

108 C   This is the Companies Act requirement.

109 D.

110 D   Correct, the responsibility rests with the external auditors (although they do rely on internal audit to carry out some of the work at times).

      A   Often in conjunction with the external auditors or a regulatory body.

      B   Studies of efficiency, economy and effectiveness of operations are commonly carried out.

      C   Verifying and suggesting improvements to controls is a key task for internal audit.

111 C.

112 B   Correct. Usually this is a characteristic, the fraud is often not performed for personal gain.

      A   This is an example of a type of fraud.

      C   Not all creative accounting devices are necessarily fraudulent.

      D   Management fraud can be simply the theft of assets, but usually it is more complex.

113 C   Administrative controls are concerned with achieving the objectives of the organisation and implementing policies.

114   An external audit is an independent examination of, and expression of, opinion on the financial statements of an enterprise.

115

	$'000	$'000
Net profit before taxation		3,555
Adjustment for depreciation		1,320
Changes in working capital:		
Increase in inventory	(555)	
Decrease in receivables	420	
Decrease in payables	(585)	(720)
Net cash flow from operating activities		4,155

116 B.

	$
Operating profit	23,000
Add depreciation	4,000
Add loss on sale of non-current assets	22,000
Add decrease in inventory	13,000
Add increase in payables	10,000
	72,000
Total cash inflow	80,000
Thus change in receivables produced cash inflow of	8,000

∴ a decrease in receivables

117 (ii) and (iv) are added to operating profit to get cash flow from operating activities.

118 A   Correct. $1,030,000 + $460,000 + $630,000 − $400,000 = $1,720,000

      B   Incorrect, you have not included the rights issue.

      C   Incorrect, you have included interest paid which is reported under 'returns on investment and servicing finance'.

      D   Incorrect, you have not included the share premium received.

119 A   The reduction in the overdraft is an increase in cash of $2,000.

      The reduction in short term investments (of $5,000) would be included in movement in liquid resources (not cash!)

120 D is correct.

ROCE = Profit margin × Asset turnover

30% = 10% × 3

121 The company's working capital (excluding cash) is $60,000.

The cash cycle is one and a half months.

	$
Inventories ($^1/_{12}$ × $240,000)	20,000
Receivables ($^2/_{12}$ × $420,000)	70,000
Less payables ($^{1.5}/_{12}$ × $240,000	(30,000)
Working capital	60,000

Cash cycle is 1 + 2 − 1.5 = 1.5 months.

122 B   Correct. Current assets are normally inventory, receivables, bank. Current liabilities are normally payables, overdraft.

123 C $\dfrac{\text{Receivables including Sales tax}}{\text{Credit sales including Sales tax}} = \dfrac{\$4,700}{\$23,500} \times 365 \text{ days} = 73 \text{ days}$

124 A   Gross profit is $51,000 − $42,500 = $8,500, which is 16.67% of $51,000.

Index

Note. **Key terms** and their page references are given in **bold**.